RAJANI PALME DUTT

A Study in British Stalinism

John Callaghan

AAKAR

RAJANI PALME DUTT: A Study in British Stalinism
John Callaghan

First Published in India 2015

ISBN 978-93-5002-364-8

Published in agreement with Lawrence and Wishart Limited, London for publication and sale only in the Indian Subcontinent (India, Pakistan, Bangladesh, Nepal, Maldives, Bhutan and Sri Lanka)

Published by

AAKAR BOOKS

28 E Pocket IV, Mayur Vihar Phase I, Delhi 110 091
Phone : 011 2279 5505 Telefax : 011 2279 5641
aakarbooks@gmail.com; www.aakarbooks.com

Printed at
Mudrak, 30-A, Patparganj, Delhi 110 091

CONTENTS

PREFACE

> The Goshes are high caste,
> The Boses are generous
> The Mitras are cunning
> But the Dutts are scoundrels' [1]

If that was all there was to it the anonymous Bengali soothsayer would have saved us the bother; R. Palme Dutt - Communist, apologist for Stalin's Russia, scoundrel. End of the story.

But it is more complex than that. The Communist movement was the most important political phenomenon of the twentieth century. It attracted millions upon millions of people, affected the lives of hundreds of millions more and reached out to every part of the globe. Communism cannot be explained as a personality disorder, unless the 'personality' be mass societies in periods of rapid transition and turbulence. And yet today the Communist movement is remembered for its monsters rather than the monsters it set out to slay. So it is with Dutt, memorable as Moscow's most trusted lieutenant in Britain - the scoundrel - not for the politics which took him down that path or the work which filled his days.

He was, arguably, the most important figure in the Communist Party of Great Britain. His political life was entirely consumed in the service of the Communist movement and spanned the whole period from its conception in world war and revolution to its ultimate dissolution and decay. From youthful Leninist, Dutt made the transition to faithful Stalinist, and survived the beginnings of de-Stalinisation to lead the Party into the 1960s. His life and the life of the Party ran concurrently and, given his prominence, it is to be doubted whether a history of British Communism could be written in which he was less than a central actor.

He was responsible for 'Bolshevising' the British Party in the 1920s and soon became the organisation's most prolific publicist. By 1930 Dutt was the most authoritative exponent of Party policy and ideology. For over forty years he not only belonged to the small group which led the Party in Britain but was also regarded as the most brilliant Marxist analyst in the English-speaking world - as likely to be read in the Middle East, South Asia or Africa as any Communist alive (Russians excepted of course). From the mid-1920s Dutt was one of the links - soon to become the principal link - between the Communist International, the CPGB and Communist politics in many parts of the British Empire - notably the Indian subcontinent, where the Communists were particularly dependent on his advice and guidance from a very early stage in their development.

In writing this book, then, I have grappled with the histories of the British and Indian Communist Parties within the larger context of the history of the Communist movement. Dutt was one of those revolutionaries with little or no personal life, few friends and strict habits of reserve and secrecy - the nature of his responsibilities demanded no less. But he also kept the thousands of documents on which this study is based; through this archive I have waded in search of an understanding of Communist commitment as well as Communist history. Whether I have succeeded or not is for the reader to judge, but I acknowledge sole responsibility for any errors I may have made along the way. With this proviso, then, I would like to thank the following individuals for their assistance; Monty Johnstone, Noreen Branson, Margot Heinemann, Brian Pollitt, George Matthews, John Saville, Angela Tuckett, Gabriel Carritt, Stanley Foreman, Douglas Hyde, Andrew Rothstein, Solly Kaye, Professor Zafar Imam, Raphael Samuel and M.I.Firsov.

The documentary sources for this research can be found in the British Museum CUP 1262 K1-K6 and the archive of the CPGB (references to this are normally indicated by a 'file no.')

NOTES

1 Quoted by M. Bose, *The Lost Hero*, Quartet 1982

1
TRUTH AND POWER

Rajani Palme Dutt was born in Cambridge in 1896, the youngest of three children, to Upendra Krishna Dutt, an Indian doctor who settled in England in 1875, and Anna Palme, a Swedish writer who dabbled in poetry. Dutt's parents came from sharply contrasting social backgrounds as well as different national cultures. His mother was the daughter of a county judge, reared in a solidly bourgeois milieu and from a family that could trace its line back to seventeenth century Holland; on this Scandinavian side of the family Dutt numbered bankers and lawyers among his relatives, and a future Prime Minister of Sweden, Olaf Palme. He never met this cousin - relations with this side of the family had been strained from the beginning of his parent's marriage, well before the next generation of young socialists embarked on their antagonistic political careers. For Anna Palme had married against 'the wishes and prejudices of her family', prejudices based on racism as well as the usual class snobbery; Upendra Krishna Dutt offended against both.

Dutt's father was one of nine children born into poor circumstances in Calcutta. His schooling had been entirely dependent on a succession of academic awards, culminating in the much coveted Gilchrist scholarship which provided funds sufficient for one Indian student each year to study in Britain. On this basis Upendra Dutt was able to study medicine at London University though the hardship apparently continued, and the children were told how their father had to borrow and laboriously copy all his essential textbooks in longhand. Upon graduation the doctor decided to set up practice in his adopted land, in spite of both the absence of any capital with which to buy a practice and the presence of the singular obstacle of 'colour prejudice'. Eventually he established himself in a working-class district of Cambridge in which railway workers predominated. Dutt maintained that 'life in the home was always financially difficult':

> but there were many testimonies of the deep affection in which he was held by the workers and all the poorer sections in Cambridge. At the same time we were always conscious of the prejudice in the upper class sections of the town against the coloured doctor. These early impressions of class and colour deeply affected our early childhood conceptions of life.[1]

There is perhaps more than a touch of Communist sentimentality in these memories of childhood. The Communists, were ideologically blind to many aspects of racism. They were inclined to regard it as a simple device of bourgeois rule, a substance poured, as it were, into the empty heads of 'backward' elements in the lower orders but not otherwise a working-class issue. But this is not the whole story.

Immigrants from the Indian subcontinent were negligible in number during Dutt's childhood but, more to the point, they were overwhelmingly from relatively privileged and educated backgrounds. They were just the sort of people, in short, to whom the Edwardian working-class habitually deferred, and it is unlikely that this did not affect their reception in such quarters. This would help to explain something about the pattern of racism remembered by Dutt, a pattern that seems to have been reproduced in the experience of Dutt's future comrade, also of Indian origin, Shapurji Saklatvala, the Member of Parliament for Battersea in the 1920s. Saklatvala also reported encountering more prejudice at the hands of respectable society than from among the working-class; when his Conservative opponent concluded one public debate with a racist remark, for instance, the largely working-class audience reacted with such anger that the unfortunate Tory was lucky to escape unharmed.[2]

There can be little doubt that his encounters with racism deeply wounded Dutt's pride and figured as a factor in his early political formation and sense of injustice. He confessed as much in later years.[3] When he came to write his autobiography (a project never completed, incidentally), he described the mixed national traditions of his family - and an exceptionally closely- knit, affectionate family it was - as having made him 'a typical Englishman - that is a mongrel'.[4] The wry note struck here itself testifies to Dutt's consciousness of outsider status. Within the family, by contrast, Dutt seems to have enjoyed the close support of both parents, emotionally and - even after he joined the Communist Party - politically. Their correspondence remained affectionate throughout the vicissitudes of his life of commitment, a commitment that was shared in equal measure by his older brother Clemens. When Dutt's father died in May 1938 the *Daily Worker* was able to describe him as one of its oldest supporters; and Dutt evidently believed that the shock of this loss contributed to his own serious illness, some months later. Though something of a cold fish in his relations with his closest colleagues, let alone the rest of the world, Dutt was nevertheless accustomed to a warm family intimacy in childhood, which endured into adulthood. Indeed one suspects a connection between the solidity of this supportive family and Dutt's capacity, as well as motivation, to take on the world.

But it would be quite wrong to attempt to hang the whole explanation of Dutt's subsequent career on this one flimsy peg. Much more important than his cosmopolitan background was the fact that it was also highly political. Thus he could honestly recall 'a strong current of hostility to the British Empire and to ruling class institutions in Britain' as part of the ordinary assumptions of family life. It was an important aspect of the intellectual legacy Dutt received from his father.

In fact the Dutts counted among their number a kinsman who had done more than most to undermine the positive attitude towards British rule to which most of political India subscribed in the first years of the twentieth century. Romesh Chandra Dutt was a retired officer of the Indian Civil Service, whose career had taken him as high as it was possible for an Indian public servant to get, when he turned to the contemplation of his country's economic history. His academic labours were subsequently responsible for providing the nascent Indian nationalist movement with an important and persuasive rationale for ridding the subcontinent of the British Raj. In his famous book *The Economic History of India in the Victorian Age* (1903), Romesh Dutt elaborated the theory that Britain had drained India of its wealth and thus retarded her economic development. By the time Rajani became conscious of Indian nationalism, this attempt to explain India's poverty as the result of foreign exploitation and conscious British destruction of Indian manufacturing had become one of its axioms. If India is poor today, went the argument, it is through the operation of economic causes and not because of nature, providence, or Eastern other-worldliness.

As it turned out Dutt had just entered his adolescence when the Indian National Congress (INC) became a rallying point for Indian Nationalism. Although the INC had existed since 1885 it had functioned as a loyalist debating society of the middle class for most of its life. But by 1907 the accustomed leadership of the Moderates, of whom G.K. Gokhale was the best known spokesman, was badly shaken by the crisis precipitated by Lord Curzon's partition of Bengal. Many nationalists perceived this as an imperialist manoeuvre designed to foster communalism and weaken the reformers. B.G. Tilak's so-called Extremist wing of the movement, which broke with tradition by actually demanding reforms, and used the language of Hindu revivalism to mobilise the people, now seemed to have the initiative. The Congress split in 1907 under the strain of these developments, and the new spirit among the politicised intellectuals seemed to be symbolised by the eruption of terrorism in Bengal in the same year. Nearly two hundred revolutionaries were killed or convicted of terrorism in the next ten years. These were also years of heated nationalist controversy - much of it inspired by the Indian Councils Act of 1909, popularly known as the Morley-Minto reforms, which introduced communalist constituencies and satisfied none of the radicals' aspirations.

The ferment in Indian nationalism reached as far as the Dutt household in Cambridge. Visiting nationalist leaders would call in and Dutt was witness to the arguments which ensued. Thus as a child he met such eminent nationalists as Surendranath Banerjea, Lala Lajpat Rai, Bepin Chandra Pal, and Balkrishna Gokhale and so was versed in the controversies of the movement before he was old enough to leave school.[5] When the first Asian Students' Society, or Majlis, was set up at Cambridge University, it met in Dutt's home; and it proved to be the medium through which Dutt first met Jawaharlal Nehru, his senior by six years. Dutt's identification with the cause of Indian nationalism was formed in these childhood years, but even at this early stage in his development it was not his only political allegiance. His father's appetite for politics embraced the advanced ideas of the British working-class movement as well as those of the Indian intelligentsia. Socialists such as H.M. Hyndman, the leader of the Marxist Social Democratic Federation, Philip Snowden of the Independent Labour Party and Tom Mann, the agitator and trade union organiser, also visited the Dutt household. Perhaps this traffic in socialists made Dutt aware, in his teenage years, of the divisions within the socialist movement - divisions enlarged by disillusionment with the Parliamentary Labour Party, and put on an exciting new footing by industrial unrest after 1910.

In later years when Dutt was represented as the personification of everything that was sinister and evil in the Communist movement - 'utterly unhuman', in the words of the renegade Douglas Hyde - it was said that he was 'one of the few who had reached Communism by the purely intellectual path, with neither emotions, idealism, nor even a real humanism playing any part in his evolution'.[6] But if his attachment to the cause of Indian emancipation can be regarded as a step in the formation of Dutt's later, more broadly based, anti-imperialist convictions, this judgement is obviously untrue. After all, filial loyalties were involved here and even his exposure to socialism was initially dependent on his parent's inclinations. Thus his own testimony may be judged as nearer to the truth when he said:

> I was a socialist before I knew what socialism was. My father had a practice in the working-class district in Cambridge. My mother would mix the medicines and the children would get a penny for taking them round, so one knew them. Then at the extreme other end of Cambridge would be the huge grounds of the professors and big people; mansions with slippery floors to walk on and cups you had to balance in your hands and high conversation about literature and art and all kinds of big questions. It was clear to me as a simple fact of life that these were the criminal classes living on the loot and the others were the ones that did the work.[7]

Dutt was an exceptionally gifted child academically, and one must suppose that he soon became aware of 'all kinds of big questions'. In many other countries his parents would have belonged to a broader alienated intelligentsia in which they might have found a niche. His mother was a writer who scorned the received prejudices of the time and defied her own family, while his father was such a rarity that he associated with socialists and Indian nationalists, taking his quest for enlightenment as far as a sustained correspondence with Tolstoy. Dutt must have perceived that the gulf that separated the high intellectual interests of this household and its radical views from those of the 'big people' in Cambridge, not to mention the rather dozy University, was as large as the status and income differences that divided them.

It is difficult to believe, notwithstanding an early empathy for the lower orders - as distant and abstract in some ways for Dutt as India was - that he could feel a sense of belonging in relation to any of the social groups he encountered. What was not separated by money, status, and 'race' was kept apart by unpopular views, culture and education. Together with his older brother Clemens and his sister Ellie, Rajani emulated his father's success in winning scholarships and thereby secured a decent formal education. Some financial sacrifice must nevertheless have been necessary for the boys to attend the Perse School in Cambridge and for Ellie to go to Roedean. By the time they left these schools all three children were avowed socialists. Ellie and Clemens subsequently obtained Firsts at Cambridge, in Mathematics and Botany respectively. Rajani went to Balliol College, Oxford - after coming first in a competition with 80 other candidates for one of three scholarships - and emerged as the leading Classics scholar of his year.

At Oxford he also learned to survive on bread, cheese, and biscuits - the scholarship only raising eighty pounds of the two hundred that were required for minimum subsistence. He later recalled the daily temptation to buy a hot meal and his capacity to resist. But when he won £10 for an essay on the partition of Africa he spent it on life membership of the Oxford Union.

THE GREAT WAR

It says a great deal about the nature of Dutt's political convictions at the age of eighteen that he joined the Independent Labour Party (ILP) as soon as he arrived at Oxford. The First World War had begun only weeks earlier and the first attempts to mobilise opposition to the conflagration had been swept away by a tide of chauvinism which affected the socialist organisations themselves. The trade union dominated Labour Party was of course committed to national defence, as was the German Social Democratic Party on the other side of the divide. The whole of the Second International seemed to be in ruins, and socialist opponents of the war were a persecuted, marginalised minority. Even two years later - after two years of bloody stalemate at the front - conscientious objectors of all persuasions in Britain amounted to less than twenty thousand people. Yet Dutt belonged to that even smaller minority - from which a generation of founder-members of the Communist movement were drawn - who denounced the war from the beginning as an imperialist abomination. He joined the ILP when it was losing members in 1914, because it was the biggest anti-war socialist group in the country; the Marxist British Socialist Party (BSP) was still divided on the issue, and the tiny Socialist Labour Party (SLP), though more consistently militant, had no presence in Oxford.

The University, needless to say, was virtually unanimous in supporting national defence and German-defiled Belgian neutrality. Even within the students' Socialist Society only half a dozen members could be found to come out immediately against the war. Meanwhile a phalanx of dons wrote learned tracts proving that Britain's participation in the war was necessary and righteous; German academics responded in kind. To swim against the pro-war tide required considerable courage and betokened an unpopular idealism. But to oppose the war, as Dutt did, as a socialist against imperialism, was to belong not only to an impotent, despised minority but also perhaps to feel betrayed by the great majority of fellow socialists, whose organisations had so dismally failed at the first serious test. Dutt described the collapse of the Second International as 'the blackest moment in modern history' and recalled a sense almost of bereavement, until the dramatic intervention of the Bolshevik Revolution apparently redeemed the situation at the end of 1917.[8]

As an opponent of the war who turned to Marxism from the beginning of 1915, Dutt's own sense of deliverance and vindication at the instant when the Bolshevik insurrection succeeded can only be imagined. The whole of this book is concerned one way or another with the impact of the revolution on Dutt and his generation of Communists, but there is no record of how he felt when the news of Lenin's triumph first became known in Britain. He was still only twenty-one and his socialism had taken a militant, uncompromising form from the beginning of his days at Oxford, exacting a personal cost into the bargain as we shall see. For now it will suffice to observe that the world war had already kindled Dutt's sense of the apocalyptic gallop of events and the Bolshevik Revolution initially only served to confirm his conviction that a new epoch was in the making.

We know that the war activated the already politicised young Dutt well before the overthrow of the Russian Tsar. Indeed 1914 was not yet out when Dutt was already to be found helping to arrange a debate on the origins of the conflict, with Bertrand Russell and A.D. Lindsay - Dutt's tutor in philosophy and a future Master of Balliol - as the principal speakers. Russell was of course imprisoned soon afterwards and deprived of his Fellowship at Trinity College, Cambridge while Lindsay became one of the prominent pro-war tractarians at Oxford. Dutt had only to wait a little longer for his own incarceration. In the meantime he was active in the Universities Socialist Federation and the Oxford Socialist Society. In December 1915 the *Morning Post* recorded his intervention in an Oxford Union debate on the war in which he predicted the demise of both Britain and Germany as Great Powers and dismissed the notion that Europe could enjoy a secure peace when the immediate conflict was over.[9] The students had been asked to consider the proposition that a secure peace demanded the destruction of German militarism; Dutt argued that it also required the destruction of British imperialism.

The Universities Socialist Federation had only existed for a couple of years before Dutt went to Balliol. In 1914 it was still operating on a small scale - linking the otherwise isolated groups of Fabians to be found in some of the universities. But among its founder members were socialists such as Clifford Allen, G.D.H. Cole, Robin Page Arnot, and Ellen Wilkinson. Dutt was able, through the USF, to keep in contact with a network of rising socialist intellectuals long after he had graduated from Balliol. He was also to meet such luminaries of the movement as the Webbs, Shaw, H.G. Wells, Ramsay MacDonald, Ben Tillet, Arthur Henderson, and Margaret Bondfield - all of whom gave lectures at USF conferences and Fabian summer schools held at Barrow House, Derwentwater and, after the war, at Cherwell Hall, Oxford. As a rising star in the USF and an intellectual match for any of those mentioned - certainly in the fields of social theory and politics - Dutt might have easily established himself in the labour movement's mainstream or on one of its more fashionable edges. But this seems never to have occured to him.

In 1916 he was imprisoned for refusing the draft. But his unorthodox background almost deprived him of the honour of conscientious objection when on grounds of race - he was classified as Anglo-Indian - his objection was initially dismissed as not subject to normal conscription rules. Only after successful appeal against this verdict was Dutt sentenced to six months detention and taken away to Aldershot Detention Barracks. Here he conducted a campaign against the 'scandalous conditions' in the military hospital and later claimed that a report which he compiled on the subject led to their exposure in the House of Commons.[10] The treatment he suffered almost broke his health and he was removed to the penal ward of the military hospital, which was mostly occupied by victims of venereal disease, with whom he had to share the same basic facilities. This was what he sought to expose. He was in any case soon removed to Winchester Gaol and then finally Wormwood Scrubs. If he was glad to leave Aldershot, the authorities were certainly delighted to see the back of him - after his release from the Scrubs he was presented with a certificate of absolute discharge from the army which declared, 'This man will be liable to £100 fine and two years imprisonment if he is caught trying to enter the Army again'.[11] Dutt returned to his studies at Oxford hardened by the experience and more determined than ever.

He shared a room in the town with Vere Gordon Childe, the Australian pre-historian who later became known for his unrivalled scholarship and knowledge of early Europe and Western Asia. Although Childe was attached to another college at the university, he was Dutt's closest friend during their Oxford days. They apparently planned to co-author a new introduction to Engels' *Origins of the Family, Private Property and the State*, with Childe providing the expert knowledge required to bring Engels up to date; but in the event they never found the time for this project. Childe's scholarly work in the 1920s and 1930s was to remain strongly informed by Marxism, however, and Dutt evidently retained fond memories of their student days - claiming that his friend had considered the life of the professional revolutionary and half regretted not taking it. When Childe committed suicide in Australia in 1957, Dutt recalled their arguments on Hegel, Marx and modern society which frequently ran on into the early hours, especially if some particularly knotty problem in Hegel's *Phenomenology* was the subject of discussion. Their early political views were mutually reinforcing on more mundane questions too; Childe's first book, *When Labour Governs*, was a scathing exposure of the fiasco of the first reformist government of Queensland, in which Childe served as private secretary to the Labour Prime Minister, Theodore. Although he subsequently steered clear of political activity, Childe's commitment to Marxism remained firm, according to Dutt, and his denunciations of fascist race theories in the 1930s were remembered with real warmth by his old friend.

There is no reason to believe, then, that Dutt's radical views condemned him to total isolation in the university - among his Oxford peers he could even count the son of a Bolshevik and fellow founder-member of the Communist Party, Andrew Rothstein. Indeed the Oxbridge of Dutt's generation produced a number of individuals who were to become prominent Communists, including Tom Wintringham, John Strachey, Ralph Fox, Montagu Slater, Raymond Postgate, M. Philips Price, W.N. Ewer, Emile Burns, James Klugmann, Maurice Dobb, and Claud Cockburn. But of course neither Oxford nor Cambridge were as congenial for Marxists during the world war as they became in the 1930s. Thus Rajani was as conspicuous in the one as his brother Clemens was in the other.

It has been suggested that 'the deeper disillusionment of the next generation of intellectuals ... owed far more to the political disenchantment of individual teachers in the public schools and universities with the arid complacency and hopelessness of Labour's efforts to save the nation by aping the values of the traditional ruling class than it owed to the propaganda of the struggling Communist Party'.[12] This is partly true - but it might be as well to remember that disillusionment with the Labour Party did not have to wait until the 1930s; it reached something of a crisis point in 1910 for many socialists and the party's war record hardly inspired the militants to unquestioning loyalty. It should also be recorded here that both Clemens and Rajani made every effort as Communists in later years to preserve their connections with the universities of Oxford and Cambridge and hardly trusted to the workings of 'individual teachers'. As early as 1924, for example, documents later confiscated by the British police show that the CPGB was already interested in, and knowledgeable of, the political composition of the Majlis at Oxford University. Rajani in fact lost no opportunity to address the Majlis, the Socialist Society, or the Union and normally had little difficulty in winning debates against apologists of empire or, indeed, of reformism. It has been suggested that Clemens was also instrumental in setting up the first Communist branch at Cambridge in 1931 - allegedly on instructions from the West European Bureau of the Comintern where, oddly enough, Rajani was then employed.[13] Whether this is true or not, the fact that it took until 1931 before the first Communist branch was established at Cambridge says something about the scarcity value of socialist students in Dutt's undergraduate days - as well as, perhaps, the low opinion the Communists had of them.

The Dutt brothers were by any standards singularly uncompromising and precocious in their socialist views. A contemporary recalled Rajani's lanky figure hiking miles through the countryside to give Workers' Education lectures in the Oxfordshire villages and Dutt later claimed that it was among such small groups of socialist workers that his own view of the war was reinforced.[14] Such educational activity was not an uncommon pursuit of radical intellectuals. But when, in March 1917, Rajani added calls for a second Russian revolution to his anti-war agitations he entered new territory and the patience of the university authorities finally snapped. This is how he recalled the circumstances of his expulsion from Oxford, on the occasion of a lecture which he gave at Moscow University in 1962:

> In the summer of 1917, at a joint meeting of the Socialist Students Society and the Majlis or Asiatic Students Society, I carried a resolution declaring the necessity of a second Socialist revolution in Russia if the counter-revolution were not to prevail, and pledging support in advance to that impending second Socialist Revolution, that is, the Bolshevik Revolution. In the last week of October I addressed a meeting of students

> on the subject of 'Socialism and the War'. There was the usual attempt of some hooligan jingo students to create a disturbance; but our stewards were well organised, and the rowdies did not succeed in entering or preventing the peaceful completion of the meeting; but only broke some windows and shouted jingo slogans outside. Next morning the wrath of the University authorities was visited, not on the rowdies who had created the disturbance, but on me for organising the meeting; and I was ordered to leave Oxford permanently within twenty-four hours. When a year later I was allowed to take the final examination of Literae Humaniores, it was only under explicit condition that I had to undertake to arrive only the night before the examination, to leave the day the examination ended, and to address no public meetings during the examination.[15]

In the event Dutt scored fourteen alphas in his examinations, won the Powell Prize and received honourable mention in the Ireland and Craven Scholarships. Whenever he was required to comment on his Oxford days Dutt was always insistent, however, that his political activities and expulsion should take pride of place since he would otherwise be 'sorry to see a mere tedious recital of commonplace examinations without reference to the highest honour which Oxford of the present era can bestow on an honest democrat'.[16] This dismal view of the place was no doubt reinforced by the backhanded compliment accorded to Dutt in the testimonial which the Master of Balliol provided for him in January 1919. For having referred to Dutt as being of the 'highest ability' in philosophy and 'pure scholarship', Arthur L. Smith considered that, 'whether the peculiar views in regard to the war, which he has expressed and acted upon consistently, affect his qualifications to be an instructor of young people in India is a matter which those who are responsible for making the appointment must be left to decide'.[17] Smith need not have worried; Dutt was banned from the countries of the British Empire from the day that he was first issued with a passport. This episode apparently reveals, however, that Dutt at least toyed with the idea of living and working in India at the beginning of 1919, only to be thwarted at the first hurdle.

He thus left Oxford believing that 'having taken the first place among students of my year in whatever examinations and honours were open, I discovered that every avenue of employment appeared closed'. To add insult to injury the recently created Oxford University Appointments Bureau suggested, with exquisite irony, that the young enemy of imperialism became a settler in Kenya. Dutt could not often have been so misunderstood, considering the pains he took to make himself the most conspicuous iconoclast at the university. He later professed that his

Oxford experiences had taught him that 'in existing class society any person can serve freedom and truth on one condition only, that he is prepared to pay for this freedom at any time with whatever consequences may follow. In that sense I chose freedom and have never regretted the choice'.[18] In fact, by his own account, Dutt had chosen Bolshevism, or at any rate some near approximation to it, and having declared war on society could hardly expect to receive its warm approbation. He was indeed in such open contempt of the authorities that no sooner had he left Oxford than he was to be found at Cambridge University helping his brother Clemens to stir up the students there. This brought the pair of them to the attention of the Vice Chancellor who was moved to write to no less a person than the Foreign Secretary, the die-hard imperialist Lord Curzon, complaining about some 'very sinister characters' of whom 'the worst elements are Mr. C.P. Dutt of Queens College ... and his brother Mr. R.P. Dutt'. They were described as 'men of extraordinary ability [who] have quite got control of the Socialist Club here,' and Lord Curzon was advised that 'they ought to be very closely watched'.[19] Dutt's audacity, persistent and rebellious as it was, does not suggest a man in search of a routine job.

Whatever Clemens' career ambitions - he lost a job at the Bristol Agricultural Research Institute because of his political activities in 1919 - Rajani would seem to have been determined on a political life by the time of his graduation. It is true that he worked as a schoolmaster at Leighton Park in Reading during the autumn term of 1918, and the headmaster expressed 'very real regret' at losing him. He also went to the trouble of passing the examination for the International Labour Organisation in 1919. But he turned down the chance to work for it (though his sister Ellie joined it in 1921) in order to become International Secretary of the Labour Research Department (LRD) - previously known as the Fabian Research Bureau. Here he joined forces with a number of other young men who would become founder members of the Communist Party of Great Britain - Robin Page Arnot, William Mellor, W.N. Ewer, Frank Horrabin and Emile Burns among them. The leading lights in the LRD were Guild Socialists to a man until the Bolshevik Revolution. Following the lead given by G.D.H. Cole in 1915 these young socialists had concluded that to avoid the state centralism which pervaded the philosophy of the Webbs it was necessary to construct a grassroots democracy upon the basis of workers' self-government in industry. It may seem ironic now - it is certainly instructive to note - that when the Bolshevik Revolution came, most of Cole's followers supported it precisely because the soviets seemed to establish a superior democracy to anything possible either in a liberal-parliamentary capitalist system or in the bureaucratic daydreams of the Webbs.

It would appear then that the conversion of these militants from Guild Socialism to Communism actually entailed the surrender of their former preoccupations with the nature of socialist democracy, in their zeal for Leninism and its preoccupation with the seizure of power. For now it is sufficient to observe that when Dutt joined the LRD it was already dominated by 'maximalists' and supporters of the Bolshevik revolution and there was no question of him wanting to align with Fabianism - or, for that matter, Guild Socialism. Nevertheless it has to be said that his contribution on *The Legal Regulation of Hours* (April 1919) was a typically Fabian tract - dryly statistical, historical and descriptive, without so much as a trace of Marxism.

In common with other officers of the LRD - enough, at any rate, for it to fall under Communist control in 1921 - Dutt was striving for bigger things than Fabian 'permeation' of an educated elite. Though only 23 years old, his work for the LRD had already brought him into close working contact with the Labour Party elite and a career in the leadership of the movement had opened before him. He served on the party's advisory committee on international questions together with Cole, Ramsay MacDonald, Sidney Webb, Arnold Toynbee, Leonard Woolf and C.R. Buxton. For almost two years after the war this committee allowed the pro-Communist element in the LRD - notably Emile Burns, W.N. Ewer and Robin Page Arnot, as well as Dutt - to help in the preparation of first drafts of policy statements for the National Executive Committee of the party. The influence of these militants shone through the committee's recommendations to the Parliamentary Labour Party (PLP) on the question of opposition to the Montford Reform Bill in May 1919, as the Government prepared constitutional reform in India. The advice proffered was that Labour should insist on responsible government at an all-India level, demand proper representation of urban workers in the proposed provincial legislatures and call for the extension of the franchise to women. These radical demands were actually adopted by the PLP in December 1919, but Dutt and his Marxist co- thinkers soon ran into conflict with the other members of the advisory committee, especially the trade unionists Ernest Bevin and William Gillies -

lifelong anti-Communists both of them. A clash was inevitable - Dutt was far too convinced of the approaching socialist revolution and collapse of capitalism to want to disguise his contempt for reformism.

He provides us with a useful insight into his state of mind in 1919 when, on the day the Treaty of Versailles was published, he was walking with George Bernard Shaw in Hyde Park and the older man gave his opinion of the peace settlement:

> 'The Germans', Shaw began, 'are prodigiously lucky; they are freed from the burden of armaments and will forge ahead commercially, while we shall be ruined with an intolerable arms expenditure.' With all the impetuous crudity of youth 'I set out to teach my grandfather the elements of politics and declared: 'That may be witty, but it is not true', and argued that the Versailles Treaty placed heavy burdens upon the German nation, against which they would sooner or later revolt. Shaw looked at me compassionately, as at a neophyte, and said: 'That may be true but it is not witty; and if you only speak the truth in England, however brilliantly, nobody will listen to you; you will be ignored'. He then proceeded to read me a long lecture of avuncular advice. He explained from his own experience that a young socialist writer must choose between two alternatives: either to write the truth to his own satisfaction in a few minute journals of infinitesimal circulation for a handful of an audience who would all violently disagree with you and abuse you for your pains; or to reach out to the millions by mixing up the truth with a fantastic amount of nonsense and conventional fictions, which would enable them to swallow the truth without knowing it. I remember that I obstinately answered back that there was in my opinion a third alternative: to tell the truth and also to reach the masses, that the Marxists in a certain number of countries had already solved this and that, although it was more difficult in England we should eventually solve it here also.[20]

The earnest young Dutt was obviously referring to the Bolsheviks in this conversation with Shaw; we shall see in later passages of this book that the claim that Leninism had 'solved' the problem of how the Marxist minority could direct the working-class masses was one of the strongest intoxicants it had to offer to those, like Dutt, dissatisfied with gradualism. Shaw was already committed to his own individualist brand of elitism when this conversation took place but there is no mistaking Dutt's tone of affectionate regard as he recorded the conversation over thirty years later. For, as he concluded in this memoir, 'even in the critical testing time of 1939-40, when all the rats ran to cover, Shaw stood by Stalin and the Soviet Union'. It is difficult not to see homage to the old Fabian's greater wisdom in this anecdote when we hear it today, because Dutt certainly became adept at 'mixing up the truth with a fantastic amount of nonsense'. But the story also imparts the strong idealism and optimism of the younger man who was already combining work for the Labour Party with a concerted effort to get the ILP to join the newly created Communist International (Comintern).

Sympathy for Bolshevism was strongest amongst socialist anti-war elements and by 1918 the ILP, with a membership of 16,000, contained the biggest concentration of such militants. On the eve of the ILP's Easter conference of 1920, Dutt was involved in the formation of a pro-Comintern faction inside the party which called itself the Left Wing Group. It was also around this time that he published his first book *The Two Internationals* (March 1920), in which he argued that the starting point of Communist theory was an analysis of liberal democracy, 'the typical form' of the modern state, as a mere cover for the class rule of the capitalist monopolies. His support for this position reveals that he already belonged to that activist minority inclined to regard bourgeois democracy as a mere sham. The Declaration of the Left Wing Group of 1920, which numbered Dutt among its 159 signatories, helps to explain why.

In the course of their exhortation for the affiliation of the ILP to the Comintern the authors referred to its 'proud war record' and the 'fear' they now felt. For 'it was not to line up with the militarist Socialists ... that our men and women faced the misunderstandings of their audiences, broke the ties of friendship and old associations, and, in hundreds of instances, elected to remain in gaol for years rather than obey the behests of their class enemies and oppressors'. This would only add to 'the shameless trickery of the last six years' and the secret diplomacy that preceded them. Socialists were now being asked 'to put their pathetic trust in the broken reed of American democracy' in order to 'rescue the world from chaos'. Yet those 'who have seen the League of Nations change from an idealist's vision to a bondholder's nightmare of blockade and intervention; who have before their eyes the pitiless murder of Central Europe by slow starvation of its helpless women and children, advise us to act and to organise as if the capitalists, when we knock upon the door, will be off and say no more. They advise us to think and act as if the propertied classes would acquiesce in their expropriation by parliamentary enactments'. According to the Left Wing group the violence unleashed by the war which continued to engulf much of Europe in its wake had rendered the hope of peaceful, parliamentary reform fantastic. Instead they believed that the 'whole structure of the state' would have to be 'dismantled' and democracy placed on a new foundation of 'Worker's Committees'.[21]

In the event the 1920 ILP conference, to which this statement was addressed, proved to be the climax of pro-Bolshevik sentiment in the party, although a resolution calling for immediate affiliation to the Comintern was defeated by 472 votes to 206. After the conference Dutt's co-thinkers began publication of *The International* with a view to further increasing their influence among the rank and file; but Dutt himself was so keen to take part in the Unity Conference which founded the British Communist Party in August of the same year that he joined one of the small groups involved in fusion, the National Guilds League. This was a mere device designed to overcome the fact that at this stage individuals were debarred from participating in the creation of the new party. Dutt's colleagues in the Left Wing Group - most prominently Shapurji Saklatvala, Emile Burns, Helen Crawfurd, J.T. Walton-Newbold, and J.R. Wilson - persisted in the ILP until Easter 1921 when they moved en bloc into the Communist Party with something between 500 and one thousand members. This was after the motion for ILP affiliation to the Comintern was finally defeated by 521 votes to 97.

THE NEW FAITH

In 1951 Nye Bevan claimed that 'the revolution of 1917 came to the working-class of Great Britain not as a social disaster but as one of the most emancipating events in the history of mankind'.[22] and there is no doubt that the Bolshevik Revolution was seen this way by most socialist activists. It is as well to remember, considering the millions upon millions of people throughout the world who came to identify with Communism during the next thirty years, that any serious analysis of this phenomenon would have to involve explanations of an objective kind, rather than those which invoke the psychological quirks of individuals. This point can be overlooked all too easily in the case of Britain, where the Communist Party was never very large, although even in this case hundreds of thousands passed through its ranks.

If we return to 1917 the first point to record is that the downfall of the Tsar in March was greeted with joy right across the political spectrum. For many it meant the end of the worst of all European tyrannies; in more cynical calculations the end of the autocracy promised a more efficient prosecution of the war against Germany and provided some credibility for the notion that the conflict could be characterised as a struggle of democracy against Prussian militarism.

The anti-war journals of the British Left, however - such as the *Labour Leader, The Call, The Socialist, The Women's Dreadnought,* and *The Herald* - hoped that the February Revolution would at the least bring a negotiated peace nearer; and they looked with interest at the activities of the Petrograd Soviet, which demanded a peace without annexations and indemnities, and had already abolished the old hierarchy in the armed forces. By May 1917 it was calling for an International Socialist Conference to be held in Stockholm to discuss the terms of peace. This was the context in June 1917 when the United Socialist Council - representing members of the ILP and the BSP - convened a conference in Leeds to discuss the events in Russia. The euphoria which swept the 1,200 delegates may be judged from the fact that the Leeds Convention resolved to set up Soviets in Britain, 'at once in every town, urban, and rural district council'. In fact the mood which momentarily united Marxists with confirmed gradualists such as Ramsay MacDonald and Philip Snowden produced no tangible results. Only the small Marxist groups such as the BSP, SLP, and Sylvia Pankhurst's Worker's Socialist Federation were wholly sympathetic to the 'Maximalists' in Russia. Their activities were blamed elsewhere in the labour movement for the collapse of the Russian front.

When news of the Bolshevik insurrection arrived, the Marxists of the BSP and SLP were jubilant; 'the expected has happened', announced *The Call*. 'Kerensky and the Provisional Council has been overthrown and the Soviet has taken control in Petrograd ... Maximalist opinion has rapidly spread throughout Russia'.[23] As we have seen only ten days earlier Dutt had been expelled from Oxford after making a speech in which he called for this second revolution. Before the end of the year the dream of a socialist breakthrough - always in contention, with confident prophecies concerning the imminent collapse of the new revolutionary state - was fed by reports that the Bolsheviks were championing a peace without annexations and indemnities. The revolutionaries had also declared the right of self-determination of nations, handed the land over to the peasants and exposed the machinations of the imperialist war-mongers. *The Call* was also able to celebrate social reforms such as the introduction of the eight-hour day and improvements in housing.[24] Even among Liberal intellectuals and leaders of the Labour Party there was admiration for the open diplomacy and social reforms carried out by the Bolsheviks. Few on the left could resist the sheer romance of the revolution which enabled the Bolsheviks, despite the war- ravaged condition of the country, to forge ahead with a range of enlightened reforms such as British socialists could only dream about.

Nevertheless there was also a fear in some circles, expressed for example in the chairman's address to the Labour Party conference in January 1918, that the Bolsheviks would withdraw Russia from the war and thereby weaken the Entente. When this actually happened with the Treaty of Brest-Litovsk in March 1918, only the ILP and the small Marxist groups began a determined 'Hands Off Russia' agitation, warning against military intervention to unseat the Bolsheviks. The formal creation of a national Hands off Russia Committee had to wait until January 1919, but the armed intervention against Bolshevism began in the Spring of 1918 and provoked an immediate anti-war agitation on the extreme Left. The Labour Party leadership, on the other hand, was inclined to accept British military intervention on the grounds that it was a necessary component of the struggle against Germany. The party's conference in the summer of 1918 heard Kerensky denounce the Bolsheviks as 'the vanguard of the triumphant German imperialism'.[25] His speech, though interrupted by a sprinkling of catcalls, ended with a chorus of 'For he's a jolly good fellow'.

This view of the Bolshevik revolution was upheld by the Labour delegation at the the Inter-Allied Conference of Labour and Socialist Parties held in London the following September, which resolved that 'if the Treaty of Brest-Litovsk stands it would confirm the collapse of the Russian Revolution and would most gravely compromise the future of the democracy of the world'.[26] Socialists within the Labour Party who urged immediate recognition of the Bolshevik state, even those of the stature of MacDonald and Snowden, were marginalised by the exigencies of war, and their own pacifist or quasi-pacifist records which were unrepresentative of both the party and the all-important unions affiliated to it. But it is instructive to note that such reformists were initially a good deal more charitable towards the Bolsheviks than they were to become only a few years later. On the eve of the armistice MacDonald, for example, told *Socialist Review* that:

> When the tale of [Lenin's] errors, his evil necessities and his tyrannies has been told to the full the balance will remain in his favour. He could not avoid unfortunate surrenders and deplorable tyranny as temporary

> troubles but he was saving Russia from a reign of terror. The terror comes with civil war, especially when outside powers take sides and with money, arms, and countenance support the parties to a counter- revolution.[27]

Snowden was even more positive and struck a characteristically ethical note in 1919 when reviewing the epoch-making events of the previous five years for the benefit of an ILP conference:

> The year last has been crowded with events of tremendous importance. We have seen the beginning of the end of the old order of class domination and economic slavery. Slowly and painfully humanity has climbed the hard road to the summit of Calvary, but the resurrection to the new life is at hand. Over two thirds of Europe the Red Flag of Socialism, red with the blood of our martyred dead, floats where but yesterday despotism held the people in vile subjection. The mighty reverberations of the Russian Revolution have sounded through the world ... With prophetic insight the Independent Labour Party in its manifesto issued on the outbreak of war in August 1914 said: 'In forcing this appalling crime upon the nations, it is the rulers and diplomatists, the militarists, who have sealed their doom. In tears and blood and bitterness the greater democracy will be born. With steadfast faith we greet the future; our cause is holy and imperishable, and the labour of our hands has not been in vain'. The state of the world today is a fulfillment of that prophesy.[28]

Snowden's remarks of 1919 were, of course, informed by the apparent advance of the socialist cause in Germany and Hungary as well as Russia. No doubt his and MacDonald's attitudes were at first influenced by the generally enthusiastic response of ordinary socialists to the new dawn heralded by the October revolution. But, as we shall see, they were soon made aware of the Bolshevik's enmity towards socialists such as themselves and had no stomach for the methods which the Bolsheviks employed in hanging on to state power. Thus when an attempt was made to reconstitute the Second International at Berne in January 1919, the majority view among the reformist socialists was already of the opinion that Bolshevism was more likely to discredit socialism than to achieve it, because 'a reorganised society permeated with Socialism cannot be realised ... unless it rests upon triumphs of Democracy and is rooted in principles of liberty'. This resolution, moved by Branting, was supported by MacDonald who observed that 'a revolution that does not establish liberty is not a revolution towards socialism and is not a revolution which socialists ought to make themselves responsible or allow the outside bourgeois reaction to impose responsibility for upon them'.[29] It was a view from which the Labour Party never wavered.

The terms of the debate between the Communists and the

socialists of the old Second International were defined at the outset, then, in relation to democracy. But for the militant pro- Bolshevik minority, of which Dutt was a typical instance, the democratic credentials of the reformists and the West European capitalist states had already been undermined by their involvement in the world war. Armed intervention to oust the Bolsheviks also made a nonsense of these democratic protestations. At a time when millions had only recently died for no good reason on the battlefields of Europe, when empires had crashed and revolution was in the air, the sense of apocalypse affected everyone. Beatrice Webb worried about 'a continent in rampant revolution over which there will be no government to which we can dictate our terms'; and saw Bolshevism like the plague of influenza 'spreading westwards from one country to another.'[30] Lloyd George, at the Paris Peace Conference, expressed himself in a similar vein:

> The whole of Europe is filled with the spirit of revolution. There is a deep sense not only of discontent, but of anger and revolt, amongst the workmen against pre-war conditions. The whole existing order in its political, social, and economic aspects is questioned by the masses of the population from one end of Europe to the other ... There is a danger that we may throw the masses of the population throughout Europe into the arms of the extremists ...
>
> The greatest danger that I see in the present situation is that Germany may throw in her lot with Bolshevism and place her resources, her brains, her vast organising power at the disposal of the revolutionary fanatics whose dream is to conquer the world for Bolshevism by force of arms. The danger is no mere chimera. The present Government in Germany is weak; it has no prestige; its authority is challenged; it lingers merely because there is no alternative but the Spartacists, and Germany is not yet ready for Spartacism, as yet. But the argument which the Spartacists are using with great effect at this very time is that they alone can save Germany from the intolerable conditions which have been bequeathed her by the war ....
>
> If Germany goes over to the Spartacists it is inevitable that she should throw in her lot with the Russian Bolshevists. Once that happens all Eastern Europe will be swept into the orbit of the Bolshevik revolution ...
>
> Bolshevik imperialism does not merely menace the States on Russia's borders. It threatens the whole of Asia and is as near to America as it is to France. It is idle to think that the Peace Conference can separate, however sound a peace it may have arranged with Germany, if it leaves Russia as it is today.[31]

Looking back on these years in 1937, the ex-Communist Arthur Rosenberg observed that 'in all countries after 1918 the radical and activist elements who were dissatisfied with existing conditions began to disregard democracy';[32] Lloyd George's comments help to explain why. The war had polarised opinion and, in taking a choice of sides, socialists like Dutt were moved by the consideration that it was possible and necessary to defend at all costs what had been achieved by the Bolshevik Revolution, and thereby simultaneously make the most of the crisis generated by the war. Appeals to democracy were redundant for such people convinced as they were of the approaching millenium.

Something of the nature of Dutt's beliefs can be gleaned from his public activities in 1921-2 which included a national lecturing tour on the theme of the impending collapse of capitalism. At the Universities Socialist Federation conference of April 1921, for example, Dutt reportedly lambasted Hugh Dalton's address on 'The Present World Crisis'. While Dalton, the Labour candidate for Cambridge and a lecturer at the London School of Economics, made no attempt to disguise the gravity of the situation in Europe, he invoked the allegedly anti-revolutionary psychology of the people to explain why Bolshevik techniques were inappropriate in Britain. Dutt's counterblast concluded with the declaration that 'in all countries the inherent tendencies of capitalism were working up to a collapse', especially in Central Europe, and the audience apparently found this intervention more persuasively argued than Dalton's.[33] Throughout the following year Dutt registered polemical victories on the 'Collapse of Capitalism' at public meetings across the country. It was a theme with resonance not simply because of the recent catastrophe of the world war and the actual chaos left in its wake but because - well beyond socialist circles - many people believed that 1914 had signalled the end of a more or less orderly epoch of capitalist progress and opened up a new era of disintegration. It is not too much to say that the empirical facts of breakdown were reinforced by a powerful metaphysical pessimism which, though provoked by August 1914 and its aftermath, acquired momentum as the war was progressively drained of its meaning and justification.

In referring to this pessimism I am not making claims about mass psychology but about the intellectual milieu inhabited by Dutt, to which many non-Communist socialists and liberal intellectuals contributed: for example, such people as J.A. Hobson, H.N. Brailsford, G.D.H. Cole, Harold Laski, Shaw and the Webbs, C.P. Trevelyan, J.F. Horrabin were also worried about 'the decay of capitalist civilisation'. The point is that, on this and many other issues, there was always an audience in sympathy with aspects of the Communist case which was much wider than the small group who unreservedly identified with the Party. Dutt and his colleagues were rarely voices crying in a wilderness; on the contrary, they could derive strength from the conviction that the only difference between themselves and those ideologically nearest to them was greater Communist consistency. Dutt himself was utterly convinced on this score and thus never ceased to display a withering intellectual arrogance. When Brailsford, for example, lectured a Labour Research Department summer school in September 1922 on the subjects of 'The Chaos in Europe' and (echoes of Dalton) 'Revolution and Working Class Capacity', Dutt replied for the Communists, in the words of the *Manchester Guardian*, with ripostes 'impressive in their effect, despite the lecturer's undisguised contempt for his audience and for all other points of view'.[34] Dutt was undoubtedly an extreme case of this superiority complex - an Oxford First is perhaps not entirely irrelevant here - but this sense of singular prescience affected most Communists and derived from both the substance and the style of Leninism, a point to which I will return later.

The character of British Marxism before 1917 also contributed to this arrogance, if only because it came to be seen as a model of incompetence and therefore as a convenient point of contrast with Leninism. After Lenin it seemed that the British Marxist groups were a mere rag-bag of inconsistent autodidacts, organisationally amateurish and ideologically confused.[35] Dutt was especially severe in his criticisms of 'the British- American substitute for Marxism', as he called it, and led the Communist campaign against those who dared to canvass it in the early 1920s. Indeed it was during a prolonged dispute in 1923 with the journal *Plebs* - which seemed to represent this despised home-grown variant of Marxism - that he was dubbed 'R. Pontifical Dutt' after he had savaged its textbook, the *Outline of Imperialism* with his characteristic disdain for heretics and rivals.[36]

The question of imperialism is worth dwelling on here as we attempt to explain Dutt's attraction to the Bolshevik Revolution. Dutt's early beliefs and first big political test were, after all, precisely connected with the issue of imperialism. Given his background, Dutt must be presumed to have found both the Bolshevik Revolution and Leninism especially appealing because the revolution seemed to be the first that was specifically anti-imperialist and the doctrines associated with its leader laid especial stress on the imperialist character of modern capitalism. Apart from Saklatvala[37], Dutt was perhaps the only Communist leader in Britain who attached the same importance as Lenin to this question from the beginning of his career in the movement; all the others had to be formally taught this priority. This is not to deny that all the Communist leaders would have been impressed by what the Bolsheviks had done in this regard - they had not only withdrawn Russia from the imperialist war and published the secret treaties which exposed the predatory motives of the warring states; they had also liberated former Tsarist territories (such as Finland) which now became independent states, and proclaimed the right of secession for all the peoples of the old empire. But few of them could have realised that when the Bolsheviks insisted on an uncompromising anti-colonialism and the destruction of the surviving empires through the efforts of the newly set up Communist International (Comintern) the reponsibility for this enterprise would fall on them. Dutt and Saklatvala, on the other hand, relished this responsibility, as we shall see.

While many of the intellectual leaders of European socialism quickly calculated that backward Russia was the last place in which the new society could be constructed, Dutt was impressed by evidence concerning the impending collapse of capitalism and therefore receptive to Lenin's methods, his talk of 'moribund capitalism' and his representation of Russia as merely the weakest link in the imperialist chain - the first to fall and catalyst of greater things to come. It is of the greatest psychological significance in explaining the attractions of the Communist International for Marxist war-dissidents like Dutt that Lenin succeeded in integrating all the elements of Bolshevik ideology into a theory of imperialism which simultaneously explained the perfidy of the Second International in August 1914, predicted the demise of bourgeois democracy, and provided a seemingly objective basis for revolutionary politics. The centrality of this theory for any analysis of Comintern politics requires that it be outlined here.

Although Lenin's *Imperialism The Highest Stage of Capitalism*(1916) was not published in English until 1926, its arguments pervade the theses, resolutions, and manifestos of the Comintern from its inception. Their importance for Dutt will become immediately apparent. In the first place the late war was explained as the necessary outcome of the development of monopoly or finance capitalism, which was compelled to seek new outlets for capital abroad and new overseas sources of markets, cheap labour and raw materials. The advanced capitalist nations, allegedly faced with economic stagnation as monopolies eliminated the old competitive dynamic at home, were thus engaged in a rivalry for new sources of capital accumulation which typically took the form of territorial annexations. The Great War was simply the result of dissatisfied imperialist Powers, such as Germany, coming into collision with established empires like that of Britain. Lenin was by no means very original in emphasising the economic mainsprings of imperialism - the whole argument about the struggle for markets, raw materials and investment opportunities had entered into liberal discourse in the first decade of the century, as well as the debates of the socialists. But the global spread of capitalism had led socialists such as Kautsky, Hilferding, Bebel, Haase and Jaures to believe that the extent of economic interpenetration between nations actually *reduced* the risks of war[38]; Lenin's vision, on the other hand, involved the apocalyptic forecast of an epoch characterised by wars, civil wars and revolutions. This struck an exceptionally salient note in Europe after the deluge of 1914.

But Lenin was also able to explain why the imperialist war had not been stopped by the mass workers' parties. He reasoned that the superprofits extracted from imperialism enabled the capitalists to buy off a stratum of workers, which might amount to as much as ten per cent of the proletariat and certainly involved the reformist and trade union bureaucracies that had sanctioned 'national defence'. This 'labour aristocracy' had become corrupted by virtue of its material stake in imperialism and functioned as an extension of the bourgeois state in the workers' movement.[39] Moreover, Lenin argued that the old leadership of the socialist and trade union movement had been drawn into close association with the ruling class, at the very time when that ruling class had become dominated by finance capital. Thus while the competitive capitalism of the middle nineteenth century had found parliamentary regimes an appropriate medium for the resolution of conflicts between rival fractions of capital, the era of monopoly capital could be expected to breed 'political reaction'. An authoritarian state was, on Lenin's reasoning, the appropriate form of bourgeois rule in an age when capitalism was faced with moribundity and recurring imperialist wars. The rise of fascism and the corresponding decline of democracy - not to mention the two world wars on either side of this experience - ensured that Lenin's views remained relevant well beyond the specific conjuncture in which they were written.

The conclusions Lenin reached during the war informed every

aspect of the message broadcast from Moscow after October 1917. The first, and largely symbolic, congress of the Communist International in 1919 (known as the Third International because it defined itself in opposition to the social democratic Second International) heard Trotsky declare that its very basis derived from 'the present period ... of the decomposition and collapse of the entire world capitalist system', which would lead to the 'collapse of European civilisation in general, if capitalism ... is not overthrown'.[40] He went on to denounce 'false bourgeois democracy - that hypocritical form of domination of the financial oligarchy'.[41] This was further described as 'the complete subjection of the state power to the power of finance capital' and Trotsky argued that the militarisation of both constituted 'accomplished facts' from which 'there is no turning back'.[42] Bukharin, Lenin, and Hugo Eberlein, the Spartacist delegate, all added their own variants to this theme. Lenin asserted that 'the most democratic bourgeois republic is no more than a machine for the suppression of the working-class by the bourgeoisie, for the suppression of the working people by a handful of capitalists'.[43] Although the imperialist war could not have taken place without the successful mobilisation of the working-class, this was achieved because 'the mightiest organisations of the working masses were dominated by parties which had become transformed into auxiliary organs of the bourgeois state'.[44]

Those drawn to the new International were told that the former undisputed leaders of European socialism were liars and frauds, betrayers and chauvinists; and that bourgeois democracy was a sham - doomed, in any case, as disintegrating capitalism lurched into further wars and civil wars. It was music to the ears of all those who had swum against the stream of chauvinism during the war and who, for a variety of motives, rejected mainstream opinion in European socialism; it attracted a motley band of syndicalists, utopian radicals, die-hard sectarians, Luxemburgists - even (in France) Freemasons. Those, like Dutt, who stayed the course, would discover soon enough that the new International was based on the assumption that only parties of the Bolshevik type were fit to master the conditions of the imperialist epoch and that ideological pluralism had no place within them. Indeed it is this which made the new International so attractive for so many of the militants, including Dutt himself. They were, as the Hungarian Communist intellectual Gyorgy Lukacs recalled, fired by 'a bitter hatred for capitalism and all its forms', determined 'to destroy it at all costs as quickly as possible' and transformed by their 'conversion' to Marxism at this moment of crisis to a 'messianic sectarianism'.[45] Dutt's messianism in 1919 is not to be doubted and he dated his final conversion to Lenin's new International with precision to a night of heated discussion in Geneva that December when he made his first direct contact with the Bolsheviks.

He was chairman of a delegation of four representing the USF at an International Students' Conference, with a strict mandate of neutrality as between the rival Second and Third Internationals. It became apparent immediately upon arrival in Geneva that only one question mattered to the assembled socialists - "Second or Third?"; and Dutt discovered that the real purpose of the invitation to attend the conference was to establish an international Communist students' organisation linked to the Comintern. Dutt had to explain that while he was personally entirely for the Communists the USF 'found it most useful to organise students on a unitary basis'. According to his own account:

> This created a problem; as so often in international conferences there arose an "English problem": in this case, whether to accept us in the proposed international organisation of socialist students or not. Accordingly that night a fraction meeting was called of the communist representatives ... to decide what to do with the English; we were allowed to be present as silent spectators. The discussion was held in an attic and continued into the small hours; at one point the police arrived in the house in search of the Spartakus student; we adjourned through the attic window into a neighbouring attic, and the discussion continued. The pros and cons were weighed; our organisation and line was analysed relentlessly like a body being dissected on a mortuary slab; at the end the decision went against us. As we came away in the cold air of that December night (it was Christmas), Ellen Wilkinson said to me (and she had had plenty of experience of trade union, Fabian and Labour in-fighting): 'This is the most ghastly, callous, inhuman machine I have ever witnessed'. I said to her: 'At last I have found what I have been looking for: socialists who mean business'[46].

Dutt had found an avant-garde composed of men like himself - possessed of the truth they were concerned now only with power. He continued his argument with Ellen Wilkinson, the future Labour MP, throughout the return journey focussing on the dictatorship of the proletariat until at last, as they stood on their hotel balcony in Paris on New Year's Eve - 'while the crowd danced below in the square' - the romance of the revolution temporarily overcame her initial revulsion and by the morning she had promised to join the future Communist Party when it would be formed in Britain.

NOTES

1 Most of this section is drawn from autobiographical material which Dutt was required to prepare as a delegate to the Seventh Congress of the Comintern in 1935; it is dated 26 August 1935, K4 Vol. 1935-6. See also 'Reminiscence, of Palme Dutt', *Our History Journal*, 11, January 1987.
2 S. Saklatvala, *The Fifth Commandment; biography of Shapurji Saklatvala*, Miranada Press, Manchester, 1991 p57.
3 See the interview Dutt gave to Frederick Marks, *Public Opinion*, 22 June 1951, p11.
4 Biographical Miscellany File 3.
5 D. Bose, *New Age*, 19 June 1966.
6 D. Hyde, *John Bull*, 28 May 1949, and *Evening Post*, 30 September 1950, respectively.
7 Interview, *Sunday Times*, 5 April 1970.
8 R.P. Dutt, *Lenin*, Hamish Hamilton, 1933 p19.
9 Biographical Miscellany, File 3.
10 *Ibid*, letter to Dilip Bose, 7 July 1973.
11 *Ibid*.
12 A. Boyle, *Climate of Treason*, Hutchinson, London 1979, pp40-41
13 *Ibid*, p63.
14 *Daily Mail*, 7 February 1922; R.P. Dutt, *Problems of Contemporary History* Lawrence and Wishart, London 1963, p23.
15 Dutt, *Problems of Contemporary History, op cit*, p25.
16 Letter to A.B. Rodger, editor of *Balliol College Register*, 20 August 1950, Biographical Miscellany File 3.
17 *Ibid*.
18 *Problems of Contemporary History, op cit*, p26.
19 Letter dated 21 March 1919, Biographical Miscellany File 3.
20 R.P. Dutt, 'George Bernard Shaw: A Memoir', *Labour Monthly*, 1951.
21 The declaration of the Left Wing Group of 1920 is reproduced in full in S. Saklatvala, *The Fifth Commandment, op cit*, pp122-6.
22 Quoted in Ken Coates' introduction to *British Labour and the Russian Revolution: the Leeds Convention*, Spokesman, Nottingham, nd, p7.
23 *The Call*, 15 November 1917.
24 *The Call*, 29 November and 6 December 1917.
25 *Labour Party Annual Conference Report*, June 1918, p60.
26 *Labour Party Annaul Conference Report*, June 1919, p10.
27 Quoted in S. Graubard, *British Labour and the Russian Revolution 1917-1924*, Oxford University Press, 1956, p63.
28 Quoted in S. Saklatvala, *The Fifth Commandment, op cit*, pp99- 100.
29 J. Riddell (ed), *The Communist International in Lenin's Time: The German Revolution and the Debate on Soviet Power: Documents 1918-1919*, Pathfinder, New York 1986, p410 and p412.

30 B. Webb, *The Diary of Beatrice Webb: Volume 3, 1905-1924* Virago, London 1984, p315.
31 Quoted in R.P. Dutt, *World Politics 1918-1936*, Gollancz, London 1936, pp43-44.
32 A. Rosenberg, *Democracy and Socialism*, Beacon Press, Boston 1965, p8.
33 *University Socialist Federation Bulletin*, May 1921, K6 Vol 1921-45.
34 *Manchester Guardian*, 15 September 1921.
35 See S. McIntyre, *A Proletarian Science: Marxism in Britain 1917-1933*, Cambridge University Press, 1980; and J. Ree, *Proletarian Philosophers*, Clarendon Press, Oxford 1984.
36 *Plebs*, Vol 15, 23 March and 23 April.
37 M. Squires, *Saklatvala: A Political Biography*, Lawrence and Wishart, 1990, p22.
38 G. Haupt, *Socialism and the Great War*, Clarendon Press, Oxford 1972, p149.
39 V. Lenin, *Imperialism the Highest Stage of Capitalism*, in *Collected Works*, Volume 22, Progress, Moscow 1964, pp185-304.
40 L. Trotsky, Letter of invitation to the Congress, in B. Hessel (ed), *Theses, Resolutions and Manifestos of the First Four Congresses of the Communist International*, Ink Links, 1980, p1.
41 *Ibid* p2.
42 Trotsky, Manifesto of the Communist International, *ibid*, p30.
43 *Ibid*, p8.
44 *Ibid*, p35.
45 G. Lukacs, *Record of a Life*, ed. IstvanEorsi, tr. R. Livingstone, London 1983, p60, p63 and p76.
46 Dutt, 'Confidential MS Easter 1970: Rough Draft On Some Experiences of the Communist International and the Period of Stalin's Leading Role', archive of the CPGB.

2

DISCIPLINE AND OPPORTUNISM

While the theory of the offensive was discredited in military terms on the battlefields of France the October Revolution ensured that a spirit of the offensive would inform the politics of the militant Left now drawn to the new Communist International. The Bolsheviks believed that, though objective conditions made capitalism 'rotten ripe' for socialist revolution, the 'subjective factor', the necessary political leadership, was woefully deficient in Western Europe. This could only be supplied by establishing the Comintern and its national sections on strictly Leninist principles of organisation. The collapse of the Second International in August 1914 - which, in terms of potency, could not have offered a sharper contrast with Lenin's organisation - ensured that the Bolsheviks' foreign supporters were already at least half convinced on this score when the Comintern was first created.

Even in countries like Germany, where revolutionary politics was more firmly based than in Britain, 'Bolshevisation' swept aside rival forms of Marxism inside the Communist movement - not least because the German revolution of 1919 led to the creation of the Weimar republic rather than an alternative model of socialism. In Britain, where there was no major split in the labour movement, and the Communist Party was formed from the fusion of previously unsuccessful small groups, no intellectual challenge to Leninism was possible from among those determined to join the Comintern. The Bolshevik revolution had dazzled such people everywhere; in Britain they were especially infused with a dog-like devotion. Harry Pollitt later descibed the day he met Lenin as the 'greatest of my life' and claimed, in relation to the revolution, that 'the thing that mattered to me was that lads like me had whacked the bosses and landlords':

> These were the lads and lasses I must support through thick and thin ... For me these same people could never do nor ever can do any wrong against the working class ... you cannot be a real Socialist and enemy of reaction and at the same time assist in any way to carry on a struggle against the Soviet Union.[1]

The Bolsheviks inspired a similar devotion in Shapurji Saklatvala who once told a friend that he did not allow the least criticism of what went on in Soviet Russia 'as that would be for him like a sin against the Holy Ghost'.[2] William Gallacher, a tough Clyde militant, who went to Moscow in 1920 as an opponent of Lenin's tactical line in respect of Communist involvement in Parliament, returned a convert and hero-worshipper.[3] Dutt was characteristically less emotional, and more doctrinal, in his expressions of loyalty, but no less uncritical.

He was also the first among British Communists in appreciating the real nature of the new doctrine. In 1921 he was asked to write the entry on communism for the twelfth edition of the *Encyclopaedia Britannica* and acquitted himself admirably. After proclaiming that the Bolsheviks were the 'natural leaders of the revolutionary working class movement of the world', he argued that the political agenda of communism was established by the catastrophic condition of capitalism of which the recent world war was but an early indication. The character of the Communist Party, accordingly, derived from the demands of an epoch in which civil war was an inevitability. The Party was perforce constituted upon the basis of the 'strictest internal discipline' combined with 'an external policy of revolutionary opportunism'.[4] The Comintern was 'more than a coming together of sympathetic parties in a common struggle; it is the union of different divisions in a single army, each with its own tactical problems, but all with a single ultimate directing centre'. The world war had shown, on this view, that 'it was no longer possible for the great national movements to maintain their dual allegiance at once to the existing national State which they hoped some day to control and to the international class war which they had still continued to proclaim in their resolutions'. Hard on the heels of this lesson came another as the October Revolution 'forced into the realm of actual decision the old controversies of class war or class peace, *working class government or democracy*' (my emphasis). There was no doubt where Dutt's loyalties lay in this choice between working class government *or* democracy; the Communists, he asserted, 'declare firmly that their ends can only be attained by the forcible overthrow of every obtaining order of society'.

This was exactly what the Comintern was saying openly. In 1920, as the Communist Party of Great Britain was formed, the second congress of the Comintern adopted twenty-one conditions of membership specifically to exclude any Marxists who refused to accept these tenets of Leninism. Thus to belong to the Communist movement it was necessary to believe that 'in nearly all the countries of Europe and America the class struggle is entering upon a period of civil war' and that 'the Communist Party cannot fulfill its role unless it is organised in a most centralised manner, unless an iron discipline, bordering on military discipline, is admitted, and unless its central body is armed with extensive powers and enjoys the unanimous confidence of the militants'. Clearly this was not the constitution of a debating society and those who joined the Communist Party were not looking for one. Bolshevism was for Dutt and his co-thinkers a doctrine of action, military action in politics, which though undoubtedly of great intellectual stimulation - especially by comparison with the turgid expositions of the 'materialist conception of history' which came before - was not seen as something requiring further critical elaboration or improvement.

Thus it was not a belief in economic determinism or the 'materialist conception of history' which distinguished the Communists; it was not their undoubted conviction that the world submitted to certain scientific laws. One need look no further than the gradualist elitists of the Fabian Society to find socialists who subscribed to the scientistic paraphernalia of 'historical inevitability' or even the mystical-sounding 'Life Force' of a Shaw. It was not necessary to be a Marxist to feel that optimism which came from the belief in over-arching laws of historical development; the late nineteenth century provided plenty of intellectual currents convinced on this score. Indeed it is not to be doubted that a rationalist like Dutt drew subconciously on this broader intellectual culture of the late Victorian period - he could hardly do otherwise. But it was as much the sense that the old order and principles of progress had irretrievably broken down, as faith in the all-embracing prescience of Marxism, which made intellectuals such as Dutt turn to Leninism. The conviction that the world was rotten-ripe for radical change and that the principles of Leninism provided the means to effect the change was what really mattered. This helps to explain, for all his theoretical erudition, why Dutt was a typical Communist of his generation in showing not the least concern for scholarly exegesis of Marx.

In fact a spirit of scepticism is entirely absent from any of Dutt's discussions of Leninism or Marxism, whatever the year they were published. 'The essential character of Marxism', he postulated in 1933, 'is that of a single scientific world outlook on the whole of Nature, life and activity'.[5] Before the ascendancy of Leninism, Marxists had not only disputed this view but had believed that it had no necessary bearing on the authenticity or otherwise of an activist's revolutionary credentials. Within the Comintern, however, this all-embracing Marxism was a dogmatic imperative and Dutt, for one, never questioned it. Similarly all the talk of 'revolutionary opportunism' and of Lenin's celebrated suppleness of tactics was never allowed to raise doubts about the scientific precision of the Communist line. Of course Dutt never attempted to show how this was possible; instead he was content to assert that 'there is only one correct answer for every specific situation' and that the answer was discoverable 'if the correct method and approach is used'.[6] At no point could anyone explain the basis of this magic but that did not prevent its spirit pervading the work of Communists of this generation. It has been aptly remarked of Dutt that he 'could discern an underlying rationale in the most fragmentary bits of evidence, for in his world there were no coincidences or random events, only tendencies and plots'.[7] It only needs to be added that Dutt was encouraged to think this way by the example of his hero, Lenin, and that like a good Jesuit, once convinced of his truth, he spent the rest of his life in its service.

Lenin was the man who, according to Dutt, 'had cleared Marxism from the dross of confusion and distortions which gathered after the death of Marx'.[8] Once the Augean stables had been cleaned up, the good Communist bent every effort to keep them that way. Theory, or Leninism, had to be protected from the surrounding filth of pseudo-socialisms. Even before the cult of Lenin which Stalin did so much to encourage after 1924, Communists, trained as they were in the alleged infallibility of the Bolsheviks, were convinced that Lenin stood above criticism. Writing in 1923, Dutt enthused that the Bolsheviks had prevailed because their party had 'at its head, guiding every step from start to finish, a mind and will that had succeeded in embodying in itself the spirit of revolutionary Marxism; and around that head fighters and organisers, each of whom in any other party would have won solitary prominence'.[9] It was a party of Titans who had put the mystery of their strength at the service of international socialism. For as Dutt put it the Bolsheviks had 'hit on the greatest secrets of revolutionary working class organisation - the secret of the Party as the network thrown throughout the working class'. The debt of gratitude was huge bearing in mind that the other working-class parties 'were actually becoming more and more definitely official parts of the capitalist state machine'.[10] It followed that:

> We of the other countries, when we pay our tribute on the twenty-fifth

> anniversary of the Russian Communist Party cannot do better to show the enthusiasm of our tribute than by studying afresh in the light of the history of the Russian Party the problems which we have not yet solved in our own countries - the problem of closer contact with the masses and the creation of a real revolutionary spirit.[11]

SALME MURRIK

Dutt subscribed to this dangerous formula of 'the strictest internal discipline' combined with an 'external policy of revolutionary opportunism' for the rest of his life. There is no doubt that he sincerely saw himself as little more than a soldier - a local officer no doubt - in the Communist world-army. The problem in 1920 was to create a British Bolshevism from elements which had been previously accustomed to the loosest internal discipline, combined with a rigid, yet ineffective, view of the world. In the event only the direct intervention of the Russians overcame the differences which separated Britain's would-be Bolsheviks - the British Socialist Party, Socialist Labour Party, and Workers' Socialist Federation. From these elements a British Communist Party emerged in August 1920, with a membership of around two thousand.

Dutt was heavily involved in the behind-the-scenes work which brought this about. It was while engaged on this work that he first met his future wife, Salme Murrik, a thirty-two year old Esthonian who was sent to Britain in 1920, on the direct orders of Lenin, to help in the creation of the British Party and organise the British delegation to the second congress of the Comintern. Salme was already a veteran revolutionary, who had paid for her involvement in the 1905 revolution against the Tsar with Siberian exile. She had also fought in the bloody civil war in Finland in 1919, where she became a close colleague and friend of the Finnish Communist leader Otto Kuusinen. Salme and her sister Hella were members of the Bolshevik Party and for a time they kept open house together in Helsinki, where they operated as a way-station for revolutionaries travelling between Soviet Russia and the outside world. She was married to Eino Pekkala, one of the leaders of Communism in Finland, but after petitioning Lenin to be 'sent to where the struggle was toughest' she found herself (unexpectedly) dispatched to England, which Lenin correctly judged to be the toughest nut to crack for European Communism. Dutt and Salme Murrik were married in Stockholm in 1924 but their alliance can be traced to the beginning of 1920 when they proposed to overcome the endless wranglings which delayed the formation of the Party.

To by-pass the obstructions of the tiny Marxist parties they wanted to establish provisional local committees which would recruit sympathisers and elect delegates directly to the Communist foundation congress. This proposal was defeated and, as they feared, the old organisations lingered on for a while like fossils in the new organisation.

Dutt's close friendship with Murrik may help to explain both his rapid elevation in the CPGB and his early assimilation into the Comintern apparatus. Dutt was, after all, an Oxford- educated intellectual in an organisation otherwise led by men of the working class, many of whom - like Pollitt and Gallacher - were deeply distrustful, not to say contemptuous, of intellectuals. It is true that Dutt's war record was as good - if not better - than any of theirs but his credentials as a revolutionary were in most other respects somewhat thin by comparison. As against their experience of leading industrial struggles and belonging to avowedly Marxist organisations, Dutt, just twenty-four when the British Party was formed, could only point to a certain notoriety in the small University Socialist Federation (USF) and membership of a pro-Comintern faction of the ILP.

Dutt nevertheless possessed talents of which Murrik would not otherwise see much evidence in the British Party - especially a head for theory and a grasp of international and colonial issues. His work for the Labour Research Department (LRD) had brought him into contact with Labour and trade union leaders and in 1920 he managed to get his book on *The Two internationals* published through the normal Labour channels. He was also prominent in briefing the first Labour delegation to Russia in the same year. This range of experience undoubtedly played a large part in bringing Dutt into the highest bodies of the Party. When Andrew Rothstein was asked by Bukharin and Zinoviev in October 1920 to recommend comrades best equipped to run a new journal aimed at the broad Left in Britain he mentioned Dutt, Page Arnot and Hugo Rathbone because of the contacts and knowledge they had acquired in the LRD. Arnot would have recommended Dutt in his own discussions with Otto Kuusinen and Eugene Varga when they discussed the future *Labour Monthly* in Moscow the previous summer. In January 1921 Dutt and Arnot were given the mandate to press ahead with this project when the Comintern courier Stolitsky visited Britain to convey Lenin's conception of a journal which though under Communist editorial control would have no official connection with the Party and conduct itself as a forum of the broad labour movement. Thus from the earliest days Dutt's position in the Party leadership was underpinned by the highest authority in the movement. This and the fact of his cosmopolitan background - which inhibited the scorn for intellectuals felt by men like Pollitt and Gallacher - goes a long way in explaining Dutt's early prominence in the new Party. [12] But whatever his British colleagues' thoughts on the matter Dutt's appointment in 1922, as chairman of a commission of three - Pollitt and Harry Inkpin were the others - charged with the job of reorganising the Party along Bolshevik lines, would not have happened without the support of the Comintern. The job was simply too important to be decided locally. Such a procedure would have contravened the organisational principles of the International, which gave draconian powers to an Executive Committee based in Moscow precisely to ensure that weighty matters were resolved centrally and that national sections applied them uniformly.

Dutt kept his job as International Secretary of the Labour Research Department until 1922 (when his brother Clemens took it over) - the year of his sudden propulsion to the most important job in the Party. Gallacher, who met Dutt for the first time in 1920 when preparations were in progress for the visit of the labour delegation to Russia, later claimed that he was so deeply impressed 'with his theoretical clarity and his intense revolutionary earnestness' that he himself proposed Dutt as chairman of the Organisation Commission.[13] But his enthusiasm appears to have been short-lived; we now know, thanks to the publication of the verbatim record of an especially acrimonious row in the Central Committee, that as early as 1924 Gallacher refused to serve on the Central Executive Committee of the Party if Dutt was included in its membership.[14] Unfortunately we do not know why Gallacher kicked up such a fuss; but it is evident that he was forced to climb down and the story underlines the point that Dutt's place in the party leadership - the 'Society of Friends', as it was once disparagingly referred to by a Comintern leader - did not depend on the affectionate esteem of his colleagues.

Dutt's independence of their judgment was symbolised by the foundation of *Labour Monthly* in July 1921. Its very name - nothing was accidental in such matters - suggests the 'united front' orientation which the Comintern adopted that year, in recognition of the need for the movement to find allies from within the reformist organisations. The journal was by and large successful in that task and a succession of Labour, ILP and colonial nationalist notables contributed to its pages in the 1920s - including, due in no small part to Dutt's diplomatic skills, most of the Left on the TUC General Council. The journal also found friends from 'within the ruling class' as Dutt put it. From the beginning it could count on men such as Wilfred Scawen Blunt - brother of Anthony Blunt, the Soviet spy - Harold Grenfell and Reginald Bridgeman. Bridgeman, a former official in the diplomatic service, became secretary of the League Against Imperialism in the years 1927-1937 and as an indefatigable opponent of colonialism established contacts all over the world. Grenfell had been won over to the Bolsheviks while serving - as Naval Attache - at the British Embassy in St. Petersburg and helped the Left in the civil war in Finland - an experience he shared with Dutt's wife, Salme. *Labour Monthly* was very often in need of money, as well as the contacts such people could provide, and it helped to have some wealthy supporters. Like Grenfell and Blunt, Shaw was another 'firm friend' of the journal who could be of financial assistance, as could wealthy Communists such as the founders of Collett's bookshop Olive Parsons and Eva Collett Reckitt.

Dutt was to remain in control of this journal for the next fifty years and was apt to beat off attempts to change its character or bring it under direct Party control with pointed reminders that it had been set up in its given form with the direct authority of Lenin. In a letter of 1956 he asserted that *Labour Monthly* was founded 'on the recommendation of the Communist International, as an auxiliary organ to be published not as an official organ of the Party but as an independent monthly journal of Marxism and Labour Unity ... assisting the aims of the united front'. The editorship, Dutt insisted, was entrusted 'also on the recommendation of the Communist International to Comrade Palme Dutt in association with Comrade Arnot to carry out this general line'.[15] Given that the inspiration for *Labour Monthly* came from Moscow, it is almost certain that the money to launch it made the same journey. Dutt certainly had no independent means of his own but we know that just before her departure for Britain in 1920 Otto Kuusinen gave Salme Murrik 'four large diamonds' with which to meet necessary expenses.[16] It is not inconceivable that some of the proceeds financed the launch of Dutt's journal.

The Kuusinen connection is worth dwelling on for a moment. The Finnish revolutionary became one of the few survivors of the holocaust which Stalin was to inflict, over a period of several decades, on his real or imagined rivals in the Communist movement; this durability is all the more surprising in view of the fact that, unlike Dutt, who perhaps had an accident of geography to thank for his own longevity, Kuusinen spent most of his time in Moscow. In 1920 Kuusinen's prominence in the Comintern was demonstrated by his participation in drafting its twenty-one conditions of membership, and in the following year he became secretary of its Executive Committee (ECCI). He thereafter belonged to the powerful Small Commission of the ECCI, alongside Manuilsky and Pyatnisky - the latter having responsibility for the Comintern's clandestine activities and financial affairs. Kuusinen was also chairman, from 1926, of the Comintern's Far Eastern Study Group and thus had a direct working relationship with those such as Dutt who were charged with special anti- colonial responsibilities. He achieved international notoriety during the Soviet-Finnish war in the winter of 1939-40 when Stalin briefly made him the puppet leader of Bolshevik Finland. Among foreign revolutionaries he was also unusual in belonging to Stalin's Central Committee and joined the Politburo itself in 1957.

Salme Murrik's friendship with Kuusinen ensured that Dutt's talents rapidly became known at the highest levels of the Comintern bureaucracy. Dutt first visited Moscow in 1923 but was 'already familiar' with Kuusinen when he arrived and the Finn was was to remain 'always so close a friend, so wise and so lovable' to Dutt throughout their careers in the movement.[17] Salme's sister Hella, who frequently travelled to Moscow from Finland and kept up a regular correspondence with Kuusinen throughout the inter-war years, was another link in the chain which connected her 'great brother-in-law' to the Moscow eminences of the movement.[18] Although Hella Wuolijoki had married a Social Democratic politician, her sympathies remained firmly Communist, as is made clear in the surviving correspondence to Dutt. In January 1940 she was arrested by the Finnish authorities for her clandestine attempts to negotiate an end to the war with the Soviet Union, through contact with her childhood friend Alexandra Kollontai, who was by then the Soviet ambassador to Sweden. Hella's subsequent life sentence was brought to an abrupt end with the conclusion of the second World War, and she lived to see her son, Sulo Wuolijoki, become Prime Minister of Finland.

If the testimony of Kuusinen's wife Aino is to be believed - she was herself a former Comintern agent and victim of Stalin's purges - Hella's home in Helsinki was nicknamed the 'spy centre' in the 1920s because of the constant traffic of foreigners which passed through it, including various Soviet diplomats as well as the chief of the Bolshevik military organisation in Helsinki.[19] Although Kuusinen probably never knew it, his connections with Hella brought charges of espionage against himself when Aino was interrogated in the Lefortovo prison in 1936. Who is to know whether Aino's refusal to admit these charges was the only thing which saved Salme Murrik from also being recalled to Moscow? The web of relationships which connected Salme, Dutt, Hella and Kuusinen were certainly known to Stalin's GPU. Their relevance to our story is suggested by the testimony of J.T. Walton-Newbold, the first Communist MP and subsequently a renegade from the Party, who claimed that Kuusinen and Murrik were the real power behind Dutt and Pollitt at the time of the Reorganisation Commission in 1922. Walton-Newbold, who had worked with Dutt in the Left-Wing Group of the ILP as well as in the CP leadership, could obviously speak with some authority on this matter. His wife, moreover, had stayed with members of Kuusinen's circle on her way to the second Comintern congress in 1920. He was always insistent that even in the early 1920s Dutt, whom he described as streets ahead of the other Communists in Britain, had become 'the voice of the Comintern inner circle around Kuusinen'.[20]

In forming such a close relationship with Salme, a Bolshevik with considerable revolutionary experience, Dutt came under the influence of the International before he had had any time to establish separate, independent, roots in the British Party - an absence all the more significant given his family and student background, both of which had served to remove him from the sort of first-hand experiences of political and industrial struggle which had made men like Pollitt revolutionaries. For Philip Spratt, later one of the most successful of the CPGB's agents in India, this was the key to understanding 'the paradox of the dog- like loyalty to the Comintern of this able and forceful man'. M.N. Roy, who was to cooperate closely with Dutt on Indian work, was even more specific claiming that 'the key to the puzzle was Mrs Dutt'. Spratt reported that:

> Roy assured me that when he knew them, Dutt never published an article of importance unless she had certified its orthodoxy. Roy did not say so directly, but he led me to infer that she is a member of the highly secret inner organisation of the Comintern ... desertion from which is always punished by death.[21]

The melodramatic note in this memoir invites our scepticism, though it is as well that we remember the assassination of Ignace

Reiss and the probable murder of Walter Krivitsky before it is dismissed completely. But as to the alleged dependence of husband on wife, even Dutt's friend and disciple, the Indian Communist leader P.C. Joshi, openly referred to it. Pollitt's correspondence, moreover, shows quite clearly that Murrik was regarded as an authority on Bolshevik doctrine by the young bloods of the Party.[22] We may be sure that when Dutt took on the main responsibility for 'Bolshevising' the CPGB in March 1922, Salme was a major influence.

MAKING A COMMUNIST PARTY

Formally, it was the fourth congress of the CPGB, meeting at St Pancras in March 1922, which took the decision to appoint an Organisation Commission to investigate the functioning of the Party and begin the process of its reconstitution in accordance with the principles adopted by the Third Congress of the Comintern the previous year. At St Pancras it was also agreed that the members of the commission would not come from the ranks of the Party's Executive Committee. We know, however, that the Comintern had already appointed its own commission to investigate the CPGB - the 1922 report of the Party Executive refers to it - and that this commission had made exhaustive enquiries before the Party's fourth congress. Moreover Arthur MacManus attended a special meeting of the Executive Committee of the Comintern in Moscow to discuss the problem of the CPGB in February 1922 and was back in Britain in time for the Party congress. It is almost certain that these Comintern interventions had a hand in the composition of the Organisation Commission through the medium of Gallacher. The Executive of the Party wanted a sub-committee of its own members to consider the Comintern's 'theses on organisation' but Dutt's alternative proposals, which amounted to a declaration of no confidence in the existing leadership, were carried 87 votes to 38 by the congress - after a forceful intervention on the congress floor by Gallacher. And so the members of the Commission had to be found elsewhere. Nevertheless it was the Executive which appointed Dutt, Pollitt and Harry Inkpin to do the work. The 'atmosphere of a clash between the old and the new' which Dutt remembered years later as the Commission got on with its work simply underlines the point that the Executive hardly had much self-interest in appointing individuals who would scarify its work; if Gallacher was responsible, as Dutt claimed, for persuading the

Executive to appoint him chairman of the Commission he must have been speaking with considerable authority - and that suggests the Comintern.

Pollitt's appointment is explicable in terms of his considerable experience as an organiser and agitator - dating back to the Hands off Russia campaign begun in 1919. His role in the strike in the London docks in 1920 was widely perceived to have deterred the British government from a further round of direct intervention against the Bolsheviks. Dutt's credentials, by contrast, were entirely to do with the reliability of his grasp of Bolshevik fundamentals and it was his job to draft the final report.

The Organisation Commission's work (March - September 1922) threw Dutt and Pollitt into a close working relationship for the first time and Dutt later recalled the many sleepless nights they spent together on the task in hand, after Pollitt had already put in a full day's work in the docks.[23] The fact that Dutt the theoretician and Pollitt the industrial organiser and public speaker complemented each other's talents was undoubtedly an asset in completing their task, but it should not be overstressed. The main lines of their responsibilities were already known to both of them - Lenin's contemporaneous works dwelt on organisational issues and were rapidly translated into English; by the time Dutt and Pollitt set to work the Comintern had already completed its first three congresses and was about to convene a fourth. It was only a matter of months before Dutt set to work on the reorganisation of the CPGB, that Otto Kuusinen had been charged with the responsibility for preparing the 'Draft Theses on the Organisational Structure of the Communist Parties and the Methods and Content of Their Work', which Wilhelm Koenen presented to the Third Congress of the Comintern on 12 July 1921. Dutt's work of reorganisation was thus a question of applying the 'Theses on Organisation' in Britain.

The organisational form of the Communist Parties naturally derived from a number of political considerations, including the Bolshevik experience of illegality and the organisational defects of the Second International - which on Communist reckoning had allowed social patriotic elements to betray internationalism with apparent ease in 1914. But the chief consideration was Lenin's analysis of the imperialist epoch which explained both the inevitability of such corruption within the labour movement and the necessity of civil war if capitalism was to be overcome. The Communist Party could succeed in its task of smashing the bourgeois state machine only if it was constructed on a military basis; internationalism would survive only if the Party was conceived as a subordinate national section of the 'world army'. Lenin was insistent that only the Communist Party 'is capable of leading the proletariat in a final, most ruthless and decisive struggle against the forces of capitalism', and argued that during this struggle 'all groups, parties and leaders in the working-class movement who have fully or partly adopted the stand of reformism, of the "Centre", etc., inevitably side with the bourgeoisie or join the waverers'.[24] He therefore enjoined Communists to deal with the actual organisational pluralism of the Western labour movements as follows:

> In every last organisation, league, union, association, society, or what have you - first those of the proletarian then those of the non-proletarian toiling and exploited masses - whether political, professional, military, co-operative, educational, athletic, or whatever in nature - Communist groups or cells must be planted perfectly openly, but also secretly, which will be necessary whenever they are in danger of being broken up, arrested or expelled by bourgeois elements. These cells must be tightly bound together with one another and with party headquarters, trading information and experiences, carrying on agitation, spreading propaganda, arguing, plunging into every nook and cranny of toiling workers. Through their all-embracing efforts they must systematically educate themselves, the party, their class, the mass.[25]

The Communist Party, then, claiming exclusive title as *the* working class party, had a correspondingly ubiquitous role, and Communists were necessarily required to replace the old leaders in proletarian organisations of absolutely every type.[26] This was a tall order for the CPGB with just over 2,000 paid up members in 1922 but Dutt's Commission was undeterred. The object of the reorganisation exercise was to establish that 'the principles of Communist organisation represent a complete break with the old Socialist traditions of ineffectiveness in this country'. This rupture, Dutt wrote, 'is as great a break in methods of organisation as the break in theory from democracy to dictatorship'. The analogy was chosen by Dutt with some precision because, as he immediately observed, 'our task is to create an efficient machine of the class struggle capable ... of confronting and battling with the complicated and centralised apparatus of the State'.[27]

The party was accordingly to be reconstructed on the basis of factory cells, ultimately so numerous that the entire membership of 1922 would constitute at best a single district. Its objective in the trade unions was nothing less than their transformation 'into mass organisations of the revolutionary struggle under the leadership of the Party'. Here the Communist nuclei would 'endeavour to weaken the position of the reactionary officials and leaders by pressing issues which will force them to take up an unpopular stand; it will aim at pushing the rules to their limit and so expose their unwieldy character, and work for their alteration; it will work for the election of accredited Communist candidates as officials and delegates to conference'.[28]

Nothing in Dutt's *Report*, in short, deviated in the least from established Communist principles. But this does not mean that it was free of controversy. Dutt always maintained, publicly and privately, that the Comintern agent, Michael Borodin - who was arrested and deported from Britain in 1922 - made no positive contribution to the work of Commission but actually opposed its report and engaged in a fight against its recommendations.[29] Borodin was obviously not opposed to Leninist principles and - in the absence of any explanation from Dutt - it must be assumed that his obstructiveness was motivated by a realisation that the CPGB was simply too weak to live up to the Commission's grandiose objectives and that Dutt's *Report* served to obscure this fact. What is certain is that the Party was unable to build factory branches on the scale envisaged in 1922 until the Second World War, when the circumstances of Britain's wartime alliance with the Soviet Union briefly saw Party strength rise to 55,000 with as many as 500 members in a single factory.

There is no suggestion in the *Report* that the CPGB's lack of progress since 1920 had anything to do with Comintern policies as applied in Britain. The problems identified were purely organisational; loose, federal, even autonomous branches - many of them inactive - had been cut off from Party headquarters; the Party press failed to act as a Party organiser; and the leadership itself was insufficiently centralised and had provided no clear strategic or tactical advice. To deal with these problems the Party adopted all the paraphernalia of a central Executive Committee - from which smaller bureaus (the Organisation Bureau and the Political Bureau) with their attendant special departments would be drawn - as well as an array of district committees co-ordinating residential and workplace branches. The Party congress accepted these recommendations unanimously in October 1922 and proceeded to elect an Executive with Dutt and Pollitt top of the poll ahead of older and better known comrades. The congress also voted to exclude former SLP members such as Tom Bell, Arthur MacManus and J.T. Murphy from the new 'Orgbureau' - even though they had been involved in running the Party since its formation. These individuals almost certainly sided with Borodin in thinking that the organisational changes had produced an over-elaborate apparatus which would sap the resources of the tiny Party. Nevertheless Pollitt and Dutt supported by Gallacher remained in a minority on the new Executive and were frustrated by the slow rate of change in the application of the new principles.

They saw an opportunity to put this right when the Comintern established a special commission on the situation in Britain in June 1923. Radek, Bukharin, Zinoviev and Kuusinen were all involved in the work of this commission and apart from Dutt and Pollitt the British delegation included Macmanus, Inkpin, Gallacher, Wal Hannington, T.A. Jackson, Walton Newbold, Arthur Horner, J.R. Campbell - almost the whole Executive in fact, leaving only one or two of their number back in London. This was a deeply divided delegation and Dutt was all the more isolated when Pollitt returned early to London in order to attend the Labour Party conference. He was bold enough, however, to propose at the first session that Pollitt should become General Secretary, that there should be no attempt to establish separate 'red' trade unions in Britain and that 'all international financial contributions to the party should stop'. On all three proposals Dutt was defeated but not before the commission expressed its approval for the challenge which Dutt and Pollitt represented - proof, it said, of new life stirring and of what they had been waiting for. Dutt and Pollitt were chastised, however, for impatience and deemed insufficiently experienced as yet to direct the British Party. On the matter of finance, Dutt's idea was described as a departure from the principles of internationalism while the model for trade union work which the commissioners invoked was the American Trade Union Educational League. Dutt returned from his first trip to Moscow with a new awareness of the Comintern's shortcomings in respect of the 'complicated internal situations of a particular party' and told Pollitt that they had to 'wait for a new wind in the International to carry through the necessary changes in Britain'. The reader will better appreciate the meaning of the 'new wind' if I observe here that Dutt identified it as coming at the end of 1927 with the disastrous 'New Line' discussed in chapter four.

The Party did become a stricter, more centralised and more disciplined body after 1922 - though obviously not at the rate which Dutt desired. The trade unionist, the parliamentarian, the journalist and publicist - whatever the specific role of the party member - he or she was brought more closely under the ideological and organisational control of the central apparatus. The regime was now based on democratic centralism, which required a unity in action based on conviction once a majority had been found on any issue. In practice the established Party leadership was permanent as long as it was united and backed by the Comintern. Those who could not accept the demands of ideological purity and Party discipline were forced to leave the organisation, including some of the more prominent members such as J.T. Walton-Newbold MP, Raymond Postgate, Ellen Wilkinson and A.J. Cook. Dutt returned from Moscow disappointed but with authority as the principal author of the reorganisation which the ECCI upheld. Certainly Dutt entered the Party's new five-man Political Bureau after the ECCI meeting and was able to point to the enormous success he had had as editor of the Party's newspaper. In February 1923 Dutt transformed the Communist press when *The Communist* was scrapped and *Workers' Weekly* was launched with an entirely new character.

In just eight weeks Dutt managed to boost the paper's circulation from 19,000 to 51,000. The first issue of *Workers' Weekly* declared its intention to become 'a paper by the workers for the workers' and by the end of its first year Dutt was able to claim that nearly half of the 2,500 letters and reports received from readers had been published in its columns. The journal was aimed at political activists in the trade unions and the Labour Party, as well as the CPGB membership, and Harry Pollitt's close assistance in preparing each issue undoubtedly helped the editor find the right tone and content. Together they managed to combine propaganda and agitation - for the united front, Communist affiliation to the Labour Party and the promotion of industrial struggles - with coverage of international affairs - especially concerning Germany, the British colonies, Ireland, and Soviet Russia. The tone was uncompromisingly militant with talk of 'hunger marches', 'mass murder in India', 'approaching revolution in Germany' and the grim character of 'workers life under capitalism'; articles often appeared under the legend 'censored by printer'. Up to Dutt's defeat in Moscow in June 1923 he was not averse to making factional points in the journal using the transparent code of 'Our Workers' Serial' to criticise 'the old revolutionary chiefs ... trained in a deep-lying petty sectionalism' that was antithetical to 'the new tactics and the new methods of the new party'.

And yet for all its avowals of the need for revolution, *Workers' Weekly* took a surprisingly positive view of the Labour Party when the general election of 1923 produced a hung Parliament. In answer to the question 'shall the Labour Party take power?', Dutt replied 'let them go forward unhesitatingly to form a Government on a working class programme confident in the support of the working class'.[30] This was no momentary aberration. When Ramsay MacDonald did indeed form the first, minority, Labour government some weeks later, Dutt enthused 'it is a big step in the advance of the British working class and of the working class all over the world'. This was evidence, according to Dutt, of the beginnings of proletarian class consciousness in Britain; it reflected the beginning of the awakening of the British working class to the march to power and the definite weakening of the old bourgeois politics and methods of controlling the working class.[31] Dutt's attitude faithfully expressed the prevailing view inside the CPGB - but it was roundly condemned by the Comintern as evidence of the Party's ignorance and stupidity.

THE LABOUR PARTY

At one level the Comintern's position on the mass reformist parties of Europe was easy enough to understand. Lenin had argued that 'a bourgeois labour party ... is *inevitable* and typical in *all* imperialist countries'.[32] The desperate conditions of 'moribund' capitalism suggested, that this was a temporary phenomenon - that was the reason, after all, why the Communists could look to the future with confidence. But Lenin was equally adamant that the reformist parties would not conveniently disappear just because the objective basis for reformism - capitalist expansion - no longer existed. 'On the contrary', he argued, 'the nearer the revolution approaches ... the greater will be the part the struggle of the revolutionary mass stream against the opportunist petty bourgeois stream will play in the labour movement'.[33] It was necessary, therefore, in the words of the Comintern, 'to brand not only the bourgeoisie but also its helpers, the reformists of every shade, systematically and pitilessly'. The nature of this struggle was such that 'at any moment it may and actually does substitute criticism with weapons for the weapons of criticism'.[34]

This was clear enough to anybody who bothered to read Comintern literature - including the reformists who saw the Bolsheviks putting their words into deeds inside Russia where the social democrat Mensheviks were ruthlessly persecuted. Undoubtedly a hatred for the mass reformist organisations animated the Comintern's supporters; even after they were forced to acknowledge the failure of their attempt to destroy these rivals by the policy of secession, and in the years of apparent revolutionary advance, their intransigence and hostility did not abate. Thus when in 1921 Lenin compelled his followers to see that the prospect of European revolution had receded, and that it was necessary to win supporters by means of joint action with the social democratic workers, there was no change in fundamental perspectives. The object of the 'united front', as this policy was named, was to expose and ultimately destroy social democracy by revealing its timidity and duplicity to its own supporters in the course of these joint campaigns - and it was reasoned that this could be achieved all the more easily if Communist proposals for such united efforts were refused in the first place.

The problem for the British Communists was that Lenin regarded the Labour Party as a special case from the beginning, and pleaded for a tactical orientation which many of the ultra- leftists drawn to the Communist Party found repugnant. Because of its 'unique structural link' to the trade unions and its federal organisation, which seemed to offer the opportunity for Communist affiliation, Lenin urged the CPGB to pursue from the very beginning what was, in effect, a united front policy. In fact, the relationship to the Labour Party had been one of the two dominant issues (the other was the question of Parliamentary representation) which so exercised the foundation conference of the CPGB. Although the delegates had finally agreed to support Lenin's tactical advice, their reluctance to have anything to do with the Labour Party persisted. Thus the Party's initial application for affiliation in 1920 was couched in the most provocative language and its response when duly rebuffed was positively triumphant - on both counts providing eloquent testimony of the sectarianism of its leadership, confident as they then were that the Labour Party was in any case doomed.[35] If it had been left to the Party this would have been the end of the matter; but the Comintern insisted on an ongoing campaign for affiliation, in the belief that any general radicalisation of the British working class would be channelled through the Labour Party - as yet untried and untested in government - and its affiliated trade unions. Thus, even before the adoption of the United Front policy, the CPGB had difficulty in adjusting its policy to the Labour Party.

Lenin himself was responsible for the confusion in the CPGB over the precise nature of their relationship to the Labour Party. For he had repeatedly expressed the view that the class character of a party was determined by its programme and leadership rather than by the mass of party members. 'Regarded from this, the only correct point of view', he had written in 1920, 'the Labour Party is a thoroughly bourgeois party, because although made up of workers it is led by reactionaries and the worst kind of reactionaries at that, who act quite in the spirit of the bourgeoisie, who exist to systematically dupe the workers'.[36] Dutt had come to this conclusion himself at the time when he campaigned for ILP affiliation to the Comintern in 1919-20. The fact that, in common with other CPGB leaders, he seems to have forgotten by 1924 that Labour was 'a thoroughly bourgeois party' can be understood only by reference to the Comintern's united front proddings in the intervening years. For Labour was also, confusingly, described as the 'political organisation of the trade unions'; so when the CPGB, acting on Comintern instructions, launched the Minority Movement inside the trade unions in 1924 it was perhaps reasonable to conclude that once the unions were transformed into vehicles of revolutionary struggle the Labour Party would follow suit.

The CPGB leadership may have seen, though they could hardly admit it, that there was a certain unreality in Lenin's advice to work within organisations whose leaders and programmes were openly reviled by the Communist movement. Dutt's observations on the third congress of the Comintern in 1921 certainly suggest an incomprehension in relation to the united front policy, as it was there outlined. He argued that the proceedings of this congress were 'less noteworthy than on previous occasions', and proceeded to assert that the Comintern had reconstituted itself as a 'permanent waiting opposition of revolution' which would trigger into action 'only' if there was a renewed capitalist crisis.[37] This was a total misreading of the policy and helps to explain the conciliatory tone which he adopted at the time of the first Labour Government.

In fact the reformist rot, as the Comintern saw it, was visible before the general election of 1922, when *The Communist* announced that no CP candidates would be stood in opposition to Labour candidates. In the event six Communists did stand, but only after a revolt in certain Party branches against the original policy. The Party's electoral programme was based on the perspective of transforming the Labour Party into 'an instrument of revolutionary progress', and when two Communists were returned to Parliament along with an increased Labour contingent, the Party leadership could hardly contain itself, declaring that the result had produced a new alignment of forces - with Labour as the defender of working-class interests. This verdict was disavowed by the fourth congress of the Comintern which emphasised the role of the Communist Party as the proletarian vanguard - not as a radical ginger group, the role to which it had been consigned by the CPGB's own propaganda.

Dutt took the lead in trying to correct these errors at a meeting of the Party's policy council which debated united front tactics in February 1923. Five months later he was still complaining about the Party's tendency to swing from 'reformist adaptation' to 'sectarian antagonism'. There were even 'grave cases of suppression and falsification of communism by Party members' which nothing short of 'a complete transformation of the Party' could solve.[38] No doubt his complaints were all part of the ongoing factional war in the Party leadership and evidence of the impatience which Dutt was chided for in Moscow. But if so Dutt was also aware that tactical finesse was irrelevant unless 'the masses' played the role scripted for them in the united front scenario. This was to be doubted. In 1923 he wrote:

> The deeper weakness of the situation may be summarised thus. The masses have been untouched by agitation to a degree unequalled in any other developed capitalist country outside the United States. The organised working class movement is wholly without common aim and does not recognise the class struggle. There is no party or core of conscious workers to hold the movement together and influence it with a common spirit and purpose.[39]

The united front in Britain was thus like Hamlet without the Prince of Denmark. A Labour government was 'to be expected', Dutt continued, but the effect would be 'neutralised' by 'the corrupt character of the organisation and leadership ... which acts as the machine of the bourgeoisie'. Far from radicalising the workers, in accordance with the united front scenario, Dutt concluded that a failed Labour government would do nothing of the sort; the working class was as unprepared as in the bad old days when the trade unions alone guided them under the Lib-Lab banner.[40]

When it came to the crunch and the general election of December 1923 resulted in the Labour Party emerging as the largest party in Parliament, Dutt was swept along with the euphoria like everyone else. Thus while Comintern observers pointed to the near-perfect timidity of the Labour programme and to the connivance of the established parties in contriving this safe opportunity for a minority socialist administration, Dutt referred to the 'approaching menace' and the 'unknown, dangerous, and even revolutionary factor' which it involved. He expected 'the whole fabric of British foreign policy and imperial policy (to be) profoundly shaken and an entirely new set of forces ... to come into play'.[41] 'The struggle for power is here', he announced. And he went on to urge that 'the first need of all of us at the present moment, whatever our differences ... is to unite in support of a Workers' Government and its supremacy first and foremost'.[42] It was this sort of talk which led Karl Radek to complain of a 'reformist epidemic' in the CPGB.

Why then did Dutt lead the charge down this false road? He had only recently castigated Labour's commitment to radical change as purely 'Pickwickian' when commenting on Snowden's famous Parliamentary speech on socialism.[43] His concern about the CPGB's reformist inclinations was a matter of record; indeed he had lectured the leadership on this matter and prepared a damming report for the Comintern 'on the problem of the Party' (though it was not sent). One answer is that Dutt was not immune from the problem he identified - that is the problem of belonging to a small would-be Leninist group in a barren context. Without real influence the group was forever clutching at straws. While Dutt was perfectly versed in the doctrinal principles of the united front by 1923, he was also as yet unable to completely ignore political reality. Hence his vacillations - the united front tactic was theoretically 'correct' but Dutt doubted its purchase in ideologically backward Britain. Unfortunately he was already learning to reserve his personal assessment of the actual political situation for purely internal consumption. Comintern discipline required an unqualified commitment to the 'correct line' - which was drummed into representatives of the CPGB by the ECCI at a meeting in Moscow in February 1924 - and Dutt duly deferred to it with a scathing attack on 'MacDonaldism' in May of that year.

But in exactly the same month, in an unpublished report, he took the Comintern President Zinoviev to task for the latter's criticisms of the British Party which dwelt on the opportunities for building a mass Communist movement in Britain allegedly provided by the first Labour Government. Dutt referred to the over-simplification involved in seeing this administration as the equivalent of a Menshevik Government. But worse still, according to Dutt, was the Comintern's misunderstanding of the state of class consciousness in Britain, which was far from the condition of 'revolutionary preparedness' ascribed to it, and rather more like an expression of 'primitive class solidarity' not yet divorced from liberalism. 'We can lash the ILP', Dutt reasoned, 'but we cannot lash the Labour Party', which, he argued, commanded the same sense of identification from the workers as enjoyed by the trade unions. 'We must not alienate them', he concluded:

> The letter of Comrade Zinoviev, while right in essential principles, is in all its details out of relation to and out of touch with realities in this country, so much so as even to endanger its principal lesson being misunderstood. It is impossible for us all here not to feel that more systematic attention and thought will be needed from the International, if better progress is to be made in this country ... In conclusion the Party needs above all more continuous constructive help and criticism from the International. There is no genuine Communist nucleus yet in this country.[44]

This was, of course, in addition, a judgement on his colleagues in the CPGB, many of whom, Dutt believed, continued to obstruct the 'Bolshevisation' of the organisation. But Dutt was also drawing attention to the reality, as he saw it, in Britain - a condition of political backwardness which bore no relation to the confident prophecies of impending radicalisation emanating from the Comintern. Even as he expressed these views, however, his public pronouncements conformed to the Comintern line, and any attempt to proceed from an analysis of the actual state of consciousness in the labour movement in Britain was unceremoniously dropped. In future Dutt's estimate of prospects in Britain would henceforward lean heavily on abstract doctrine and take comfort from the country's growing economic crisis which was supposedly corroding the real basis of reformism. The episode of the 1924 Labour government provided the first evidence that, in any conflict of loyalties between the International and its British section, Dutt would ultimately suppress his own convictions, if that is what loyalty to the Comintern required.

BRUSSELS 1924

Dutt's over-estimation of the Labour Party's socialist potential was a mistake he was never to make again. From May 1924 through to 1935 he was consistently the most intransigent critic of the Labour Party inside the CPGB and, because of it, earned a reputation for sectarianism among his colleagues. Although temporarily contaminated in 1924 with the commonsense view, prevalent among the Party's ordinary members, that Labour was a workers' organisation with the wrong strategy and timid leaders, Dutt was thereafter the last Communist in Britain from whom concessions to common sense could be expected. If Dutt had been infected with the euphoria and high expectations which swept through the whole labour movement at the approach of the first socialist government, it was his last experience of such contact with the popular mood for twelve years. For in 1924 he departed with Salme Murrik, first to Stockholm - where they were married - and then to Brussels, where they took up more or less permanent residence until 1936. This was another episode in his career which kept him at arm's length from his colleagues in Britain, and which gave considerable weight to the case against Dutt - brought at intervals throughout his Party career - that he was ignorant of the British labour movement and consequently a poor judge of how to operate within it.

Dutt always maintained that his abrupt departure from Britain in 1924 - just four years after the formation of the CPGB and three years since the launching of *Labour Monthly* - was occasioned by ill-health, citing 'exhaustion' and tuberculosis of the spine in particular. And it is not necessary to dismiss this explanation altogether in order to doubt that it represents the whole story. The years of Dutt's absence were among his most productive as a writer and publicist for the movement. He also retained his leadership positions within the Party and continued as editor of *Labour Monthly*, for which he invariably provided the 'Notes of the Month' - historically informed surveys of world politics in which the readership learned to discern the current Comintern line. Although his closest colleagues to this day profess ignorance about Dutt's service to the Comintern during his Brussels sojourn[45], P.C. Joshi specifically referred to Dutt's work for the West European Bureau of the Comintern during his years in the Belgian capital.[46] It was only logical that Dutt's talents should be harnessed in this way. The Bureau was particularly concerned to co-ordinate action and policy in the national sections in relation to the dominant international issues on the Comintern's agenda.[47] Dutt as an aspiring authority on India - the 'Achilles heel of British imperialism' as the Comintern preferred to see it - was an obvious recruit.

Dutt was also the British representative on the Comintern's Colonial Bureau based in Paris and worked on its behalf alongside M.N. Roy.[48] The Bureau's first meeting was in September 1924 and it is hardly coincidental that this was the year when the Comintern sternly rebuked the CPGB for neglecting its colonial responsibilities and insisted that they be given greater priority. Nor is it coincidental that Dutt spent periods of his self-imposed exile in Berlin as well as Paris and Brussels. Berlin was important for Communist politics in India - among other things it was the base for much of M.N. Roy's interventions on the subcontinent, including the publication of his journal *Vanguard*, forerunner of the *Masses of India*. It was also the seat of the committee of Indian revolutionaries led by Roy's rival Virendranath Chattopadhyaya. Clemens Dutt worked in Berlin with both men, by serving on the Foreign Bureau of the Communist Party of India which was based there, and helping Roy in the publication of *Vanguard*. Moreover, Clemens and his brother found themselves transformed from willing supporters of these older and respected revolutionaries into rival leaders and organisers, when the fifth congress of the Comintern devolved direct responsibility for its Indian work on to the slender shoulders of the CPGB in 1924. Henceforward the Party was required to establish direct links with revolutionaries in the colonies and to oversee their work.

Clemens Dutt was at first more prominent than his brother in the clandestine colonial work of the CPGB. His official position in the years 1923-6 was as editor-in-chief of the weekly journal of the Russian Trade Delegation in London; in practice he did a great deal more - including most of the editorial work for *Labour Monthly* - though the work was such that he 'hardly exist[ed] as far as the Party [was] concerned'. Certainly Clemens' name appears more frequently than Rajani's in police reports prepared for the British government and the government of India in the 1920s. For example when, after 1924, the CPGB's Colonial Commission proposed to convene an 'Oriental Conference' in Europe, with the object of bringing nationalists from the colonies into the Comintern's orbit, it was Clemens who defended the idea at a secret meeting with Roy and the Dutch Comintern agent Henk Sneevliet (Maring) in Amsterdam. But when the idea later resurfaced it was Rajani, being based in Brussels, who was able to capitalise on this work through his involvement in the discussions which surrounded the Congress of Oppressed Nationalities which the Comintern convened in the city in February 1927.

As we shall see in the next chapter this brilliant initiative was of great significance in establishing contacts with colonial nationalists - something which Roy was inclined to dismiss as 'futile' when Clemens first proposed such a conference at the

Amsterdam meeting of 1925. It was the German Communist, Willi Munzenberg, who brought the idea to fruition by arranging the Brussels Congress. Although Dutt's name does not appear on the official attendance list - which was inaccurate in any case and designed to understate the degree of Communist participation - a letter from his brother Clemens dated 19 February referred to the conference and expressed the wish that he could also be there.[49] We know that 'dozens of the delegates had been assembled in Brussels before the start of the Congress on 10 February and had participated in many informal conversations and debates with one another'.[50] It is inconceivable that Dutt was not involved in these proceedings especially since his old acquaintance, Jawaharlal Nehru, was prominent among those who put in an early appearance.

Dutt's work for the Comintern, if not entirely clandestine, was certainly not to be trumpeted from the rooftops. It is hardly surprising, then, that his doting mother - desperate for more letters from her son ('my darling bad boy') - alluded to his need for deception and tried to join it to her own need for regular correspondence:

> I am getting absolutely sick of waiting for letters ... And besides, regular, perfectly harmless letters sent straight here would I think be good tactics just now. Write any rubbish it doesn't matter what, so long as you write, do it for your sake if not mine.

A few weeks later Dutt's father alluded to their son's ban on correspondence during his first year in Brussels.[51] Surprisingly there is not a word concerning Dutt's allegedly poor health in these affectionate epistles; Mr Dutt's worry was that his son's judgement was impaired on the question of Marxist penetration of 'Asiatic' minds, these being apparently more 'spiritual' than their European counterparts. The correspondence between Dutt and Salme, on the other hand, is littered with references to the latter's ill-health. And during the twelve years of exile Dutt's wife is to be found in various parts of Germany and France - but mostly in Berlin and Paris - apparently afflicted with TB, lung trouble, heart trouble, eye trouble, bronchitis and fever, to name but a few of her complaints in the years between 1928 and 1933. During the same period Dutt once complains of a sore thumb - but nothing else. Both of them, however, were very busy - Salme for much of the time in Paris where the nature of her work was such that she expressed the worry that if anything happened to Dutt no one would know where to contact her. In fact nothing - short of writer's elbow - was likely to happen to Dutt's health in the late 1920s. Even if he had been slowed down by his exertions of the years 1920-24 it did not show in his written work which was especially incisive and voluminous in the course of the next few years. Indeed the year after his departure from Britain was the one in which he found time to establish himself as one of the Comintern's authorities on India with the completion of *Modern India* which was published on the subcontinent in 1926.

THE WORKERS' STATE AND THE BOLSHEVIK LEADERSHIP

The year 1924 was a turning point for the Comintern and the Soviet Union as well as for Dutt's career in the movement. Lenin's premature death signalled the beginning of a power struggle within the Bolshevik Party which soon spread to the International. But the fact that the CPGB was virtually unaffected by these convulsions requires explanation as does Dutt's own decision to follow Stalin.

The expressions of faith which I cited at the beginning of this chapter convey something that is significant in the mentality of the British Communist leaders towards the Soviet Union. It is as if they felt a personal indebtedness to the Bolsheviks. Left-wing politics had of course always been divided into gradualist and revolutionary wings, as if the division catered for people of different temperaments (though undoubtedly the division accommodated a great deal more than that too). But in October 1917 the erstwhile 'impossibilists' of the movement were spectacularly vindicated and overnight transformed by their association with Bolshevism from members of sects on the fringes of the movement into soldiers of a world army. What mattered was that the Bolsheviks had taken power, got rid of the old regime, and declared war on the hated capitalist ruling class everywhere. The prospects for building socialism in Russia were, at least initially, of secondary importance - as, of course, they were to the Bolsheviks themselves who were more inclined to justify the revolution as the catalyst of a European uprising. The Communists pledged their '*unconditional* support for the Soviet Republic' (my emphasis), as they were so required by the Comintern's conditions of membership, because it was unthinkable to do or say anything that would weaken the precarious workers' state or strengthen the hand of its enemies.

The entire socialist movement had in any case hitherto given hardly any thought as to what socialism would look like, much less the detailed arrangements and problems it would involve. The

Bolshevik's foreign supporters were thus all the more dependent on the precedents and precepts set by Lenin's government. Clearly the first wave of Bolshevik reforms impressed them, but it is revealing that when Lenin was forced into apparent retreat in 1921 - just a year after the formation of the CPGB - the return to capitalist principles signalled by the New Economic Policy (NEP) did not worry his British followers. It did provide, however, an opportunity to identify the essential criterion of socialist advance. British socialists had argued about this question among themselves for many years before - particularly in relation to nationalisation and the rival principle of workers' control. But the Bolsheviks taught that the real issue was whether a given tactic strengthened or weakened the working class, not whether it advanced or retarded an ideal principle of socialism.

The debate over NEP merely provided a further opportunity to repeat this point. Maurice Dobb, the CPGB's Cambridge economist, argued that 'the essential problems of today are political struggles - the struggles of rival national States and the class struggle for control of the State ... This question of where ultimate power resides is the important thing and not the mere superficial *forms* of industrial administration'. Thus, he concluded, 'however far in response to economic expediency the forms of industrial administration in Russia may be modified to a superficial resemblance to capitalist forms (eg scientific management, bonus wage-payments, credit and currency systems, etc.) Russia will remain separated by a great gulf from the capitalist world, *so long as supreme power rests with the working class'*.[52] In other words the existence of the workers' state somehow nullified even those features of capitalism which socialists had been accustomed to regard as among its most odious. It is easy to see why Communists were so little concerned to question the methods employed in the industrialisation of the USSR under Stalin.

Before the CPGB was even formed the Bolsheviks had been accused of establishing the dictatorship of their party rather than that of the working class. In replying to this accusation both Lenin and Trotsky had asserted an identity of interests between the Bolshevik Party and the Russian working class. Lenin insisted that any distinction between the two simply testified to muddled thinking, while Trotsky argued that the dictatorship of the Soviets only became possible because of the dictatorship of the Party and that 'the Communists express the fundamental interests of the working class'.[53] Well before Stalin emerged as a Bolshevik leader, even before a Communist Party was formed in Britain, the idea that the power of the Bolshevik Party was identical to the ascendancy of the Russian working class was an element of Communist faith. The conflation of the Soviet state and the Bolshevik Party was also established in Lenin's time.

In fact by the time the CPGB was formed, the image of the Bolshevik state as a pyramid of Soviets controlled from below was already false. Soviet democracy was destroyed by a combination of hostile conditions - chaos, famine, and civil war in particular - and Bolshevik principles of centralism. This was already apparent to the Labour delegation which visited the Soviet Union in 1920. Dutt, as we have seen, helped in the organisation of this visit, but its remarkably balanced report did nothing to undermine his Leninist convictions. Yet it noted a trend towards compulsion and bureaucracy in matters affecting labour and argued that the Bolsheviks' achievements had been 'bought at a very heavy price'. The price included widespread repression and the ubiquitous control of the Communist Party. Other organisations had either been outlawed or - like the unions and the co-operatives - transformed into 'a definite part of the State machinery'. The report, nevertheless, found no evidence to substantiate the wilder accusations in the capitalist press concerning such matters as the allegedly luxurious lifestyle of the Communists, the nationalisation of women and children, and streets littered with corpses. It sensibly concluded that there was no practical alternative to the Bolshevik regime and urged international coexistence with it.[54]

Of course the Communists could dismiss bourgeois propaganda against the Bolsheviks - such as Churchill's image of Lenin as 'the monster crawling down from his pyramid of skulls'[55] - as so much nonsense. Such propaganda was even used to besmirch the Labour Party in the early 1920s (by insisting on the guilt by association of all socialists) and thus was all the more easily explained as the work of the department of dirty tricks. Here vested interests were clearly involved and they were rendered transparent by the fact that such forces had done their best to strangle the revolution at birth; if they had succeeded in making the conditions of survival as difficult as possible they could hardly hope to succeed in shifting the blame on to their intended victims. But there was also the testimony and criticisms of other socialists for the Communists to contend with. Many of these were regarded as disqualified because of their social patriotic war record, which implicated them with the capitalist system as far as the Communists were concerned. When an anarchist like Emma Goldman toured the country publicising Bolshevik authoritarianism, however, to the usual Communist denials were added arguments that the repression was only aimed at counter- revolutionaries and criminals.[56] In any case, what could be more authoritarian than a revolution? To question the legitimacy of the Bolsheviks on these grounds simply missed the point as far as the Communists were concerned, and played into the hands of socialism's implacable enemies.

The chairman's address to the Labour Party conference in June 1920 showed that this latter sentiment was by no means confined to the British Bolsheviks; 'the best argument for British Labour to support Russia', it was argued, 'is that all the forces of capitalism and all the Capitalist governments have shown their determination to compass their overthrow by every means in their power'.[57] But the Labour leaders were far less sanguine than the Communists on the matter of breaking eggs to make omelettes. Labour conferences therefore denounced the Bolshevik's armed suppression of the Menshevik government in Georgia, and the death sentences which hung over 47 Socialist Revolutionaries while the Communists present at these conferences sought to justify Bolshevik policy.

In short, by 1924 Communists had already learned to live with reports of Bolshevik atrocities, with their unbridled dictatorship and their tactical retreats and policy changes. What mattered to them was that the Bolsheviks had managed to hang on to state power. They had also grown accustomed to the charge that the *raison d'etre* of the Communist Parties was simply to implement Soviet foreign policy. Indeed in 1924 Kuusinen addressed this issue head on in the pages of the Comintern's *Communist International*:

> Renegades and enemies repeatedly accused the Communist International of aiding the foreign policy of Soviet Russia. If this were true, we could only claim credit for it. To us as Communists it would be a matter of joy to be able to render efficient aid to the Socialist power of the Soviets.[58]

There was no rejoinder published to disavow Kuusinen's equation between the consolidation of the Bolshevik state and the cause of the world Communist movement. Yet the same article argued that this state was 'steadily progressing towards the realisation of Socialism' - an adumbration, perhaps, of Stalin's 'socialism in one country', a theory that would have been considered heresy in 1917. What had always been asserted since 1917 was the conviction that 'no party will stand comparison with the Russian section of the Communist International'. The myth of Bolshevik infallibility had, if anything, grown in the intervening years, as the

European Communists proved unable to emulate the success of Lenin's party. With Lenin's death in 1924, the cult of the Bolsheviks reached mystical proportions as Lenin's successors vied with one another for the legitimacy of representing the true Bolshevism. Kuusinen's article, 'Under the Leadership of Russia', gave expression to this with unconscious sycophancy, professing that 'the Russian comrades understand international solidarity in quite their own way. It is in their blood'.[59] The conflation of the party-state and the Comintern was thus well advanced by the time Lenin died.

In truth Russian control of the Comintern had been tightened in accordance with the 'Bolshevisation' policy decreed by Zinoviev at the fifth world congress in 1924. By January 1925 the campaign against Trotsky - running in parallel with this centralisation - had already progressed to the point where the 'anti-Bolshevik' character of Trotskyism had become an official position of the Russian Party. None of the British Party leaders could then have fully known what was happening or how far Trotsky had yet to fall. Nevertheless when Trotsky's book on Lenin appeared in English translation in 1925, none of the Party leaders felt able to review it and the task was farmed out to W.N. Ewer, the *Daily Herald* journalist and Party member. The fact that Trotsky's innocuous 'notes towards a biography' was savaged as the work of a 'vain, garrulous, tattler' and a 'sick, neurotic, man' provides ample evidence that Ewer was briefed to write something suitably tendentious. Ewer accused Trotsky of 'Caesarism' in 1925 so it was hardly surprising that when his next book, *Where is Britain Going?*, appeared the following year Clemens Dutt (acting editor of *Labour Monthly* in his brother's absence until 1931 when he became International Secretary of the League Against Imperialism in Berlin and editor of the *Anti-Imperialist Review*) struggled in vain for two months to find a reviewer.[60]

What is perhaps more surprising is that the job was not only, in the event, taken on by Rajani, but resulted in an extensive appreciation of Trotsky's arguments and a spirited defence of his analyses against Trotsky's British detractors who included Bertrand Russell, George Lansbury and H.N. Brailsford. Given the circumstances of Trotsky's continuing fall, Dutt's positive appraisal of *Where Is Britain Going?* points to a genuine correspondence of views on the question of revolutionary prospects in Britain. For Trotsky provided the most eloquent statement yet in print of the case for an emerging revolutionary crisis in Britain and the consequent transformation of the CPGB into a mass party. He dismissed, as a 'monstrous illusion', the idea that the non-Communist Left in the ILP and the trade unions could provide the necessary political leadership and though he was well aware of the weaknesses of the CPGB, Trotsky reasoned that the depth of the social crisis would soon put this to rights.[61] Dutt, as we shall see, was converted to a similar line after May 1924.

However, the very fact that the CPGB was perceived to be on the eve of great events weighed against any division in the Party which mirrored the quarrel in the CPSU. Furthermore those Party leaders with direct contact with the Russians knew that these Titans could be arrogant windbags (for example, Zinoviev) with little real knowledge of British affairs. Stalin, on the other hand, was good to the 'little people' of the movement and sounded sensible and realistic by comparison with many of the other leading Bolsheviks. After the prospects for European revolution had receded in 1921, he was also more at home than was Trotsky with the Comintern's reorientation towards the East, which Dutt for one must have welcomed. In fact Dutt and Stalin first met in 1923 while working together on the Comintern's commission concerned with the Polish question. According to Dutt's own testimony, 'after all the verbal pyrotechnics from the giants, Stalin spoke ... from that moment I could see that he was head and shoulders above all the others'.[62]

Incomprehensible as this sort of judgement has always been to Trotsky's admirers, Dutt's verdict was commonly expressed within the movement and as early as the fifth congress of the Comintern in 1924 Stalin impressed the younger delegates with his down-to-earth manner and contempt for revolutionary rhetoric.[63] Nevertheless the decisive reasons for the CPGB's quiesence in the face of the struggles within the CPSU must be found elsewhere. The small British Party had only just found a toe-hold in Britain; its work in the colonies had hardly begun. It was psychologically impossible for its leaders, only too conscious of these weaknesses, to take a stand on matters intimately concerned with their elders and betters - the Bolsheviks. No, they had been willing pupils from the beginning of this relationship and would form a final view on the faction fight only when the Bolshevik majority decided what that verdict would be. In the meantime they would prepare for great events in Britain.

THE IMPENDING CATASTROPHE

It is significant that Dutt's high hopes for the first minority Labour government dwelt on its foreign policy implications which he believed would be quite radical. In fact this was an area of especial disappointment, as he should have anticipated when MacDonald's choice of Ministers was made known, and a collection of former colonial governors and imperialists took all the relevant departments. Upon taking office MacDonald also gravely warned the nationalists in India - though the INC leadership was exclusively composed of constitutionalist moderates - that 'no party in Britain will be cowed by threats of force', and it soon became clear that the radical rhetoric which the party had indulged in since 1918 was just so much hot air. There was to be no revision of India's constitutional status, let alone attempts to revise the *status quo* created by Versailles. MacDonald's greatest foreign policy achievement was in helping to bring about the American Dawes Plan, which the Comintern perceived as an attempt to produce capitalist stabilisation in Europe under the hegemony of the USA.

We have seen that by May 1924 Dutt had persuaded himself - after a little encouragement from the Comintern - that 'MacDonaldism' represented 'the greatest enemy of the working class at the present stage'.[64] Once the short-lived Labour government was terminated he was apparently only too happy to announce - in flagrant contradiction to his privately expressed sentiments - that the experience had revealed that the party was now 'a broken instrument': for the workers to trust it now to look after them in the coming period of reaction and oppression would be the height of open and self-confessed folly.[65]

Dutt now predicted that, in the wake of the recent disillusionment, 'a process of separation of the workers and the Labour Party' could be expected. His analysis was heavily informed by Lenin's *Imperialism* - in short, by dogma - rather than by the embittered class relationships actually experienced in Britain since the onset of economic slump in 1921. Dutt expected 'reaction and oppression' to follow from Britain's growing economic crisis. But he also foresaw the transformation of Labour into the classic social democratic agency of capitalism, which Lenin had depicted as a universal consequence of the imperialist epoch. The working class would thus confront a party 'compelled by its whole character and position to place itself in opposition to them'. This was because 'in so far as it has any homogeneous character as a party' - and is not merely a loose electoral machine of 'all views' - 'it is the character of a social democratic party which is inevitably in opposition to the workers'.

Dutt predicted the growth of an opportunist left in the Labour Party but warned that Communists had to conduct an 'unceasing ideological warfare' against it; otherwise the masters of empty rhetoric would succeed in diverting working class militancy either into harmless resolution-mongering or dangerous dead ends. It was imperative that the Communist Party maintain 'absolute independence' from this phoney left which was bound to be discredited.[66]

The whole of Dutt's argument was much closer to Trotsky's analysis of the situation than the line favoured by Zinoviev, which imagined that a mass Communist Party would emerge from an alliance with Labour's left wing. The last days of MacDonald's government coincided with the opening of Labour's annual conference, at which the Communists not only lost the case for affiliation but also suffered the set-back of losing their eligibility for individual membership. But since the end of 1923 the Comintern had promoted great expectations of a breakthrough in Britain via the unions, which were to become 'mass organisations of revolutionary struggle' under Communist leadership. Thus in August 1924 the CPGB launched the Minority Movement with this ultimate end in view. The following month a TUC delegation to Russia agreed to set up an Anglo-Russian Committee to work for international trade union unity. One way or another the radical-sounding, but non-Communist, trade union left represented by such leaders as George Hicks, A.A. Purcell, and Alonso Swales, had to be cultivated as an essential component of the united front.

This was the gist of the critique of Dutt's views which J.T. Murphy provided to restate Comintern policy. Murphy's starting point was the realistic observation that Labour represented a growing mass movement and, more contentiously, that its left wing should be seen as 'the indicator of where friendship for our party lies'; 'if we attack the"Left-wing leaders"', he reasoned, 'we attack the mass with a similar outlook and drive them away from the Party'.[67] There was obviously a certain commonsense logic in this view, particularly as Murphy calculated that the labour movement in Britain was only just beginning its political education, and was not at the end of it, as Dutt's position now supposed. Murphy thus prescribed the maintenance of 'a united front with the left wing against the present leaders of the Labour Party, we should push this left wing forward ... and use it as a vehicle for the dissemination of our revolutionary ideas among the proletarian masses until we shall have succeeded in transforming our own party into a mass party and eventually liquidating the Labour Party'.[68] But the debate really highlighted the fact that in trying to implement the Leninist united front tactic - which prescibed merciless criticism of the non-Communist Left *and* specific collaborative work with it - its practitioners were effectively reduced to emphasising one or the other terms of the equation.

Only if an uncontrollable tide of radicalism swept the mass movement could the Communists expect to get away with such obvious duplicity. The fact that the Party was unable to prevent its exclusion from the Labour Party, could boast only one Member of Parliament (Shapurji Saklatvala), and had been unable to turn the Minority Movement into a national force was eloquent evidence of the absence of mass radicalisation. But while Dutt believed that the likes of Purcell and Swales stood in the way of its development, Murphy hoped that the revolutionary rhetoric they indulged in would encourage such an eventuality. Some things had changed for the better since 1920. A sizeable left had emerged on the General Council of the TUC, and the Parliamentary Labour Party now possessed a socialist group which included the 'Red Clydesiders'. Dutt rightly doubted that these men would pass the test of confrontation with the state which his economic analyses predicted, but Murphy, with his greater knowledge of the industrial movement, believed that they would be pushed into such confrontation because of the mounting unrest in the mines and factories.

The class conflict that had grown since 1921 was exacerbated by the return to the Gold Standard in 1925, effected by the Chancellor, Winston Churchill, at an inflated pre-war parity with the dollar - a move which almost all observers saw as a declaration of war on the living standards of the British working class. Dutt needed no particular insight to see what was happening at this level. But he was also able to survey the state of the European economy, in February and March of 1925, and forecast its coming collapse for reasons which were generally acknowledged as decisive some four years later in the wake of the Wall Street crash. The point of departure was an analysis of the Dawes Plan which found it 'demonstrably unworkable' in terms of its official rationale as a device for the painless extraction of reparations from Germany. Germany was already in deficit and would not be able to pay the

125 million pounds sterling required annually. The real point of the plan, according to Dutt, was to facilitate 'the financial subjection and colonisation of Europe' under the hegemony of the USA. As far as the control of foreign capital in Germany was concerned, this process was deemed almost completed at the cost of the intense exploitation of the German working class.[69]

Dutt conjured a vision - strikingly similar to later Communist representations of Marshall Aid - of 'Europe working under a system of financial committees whose duty it would be to transmit across the Atlantic a yearly tribute'. For now, however, capital flowed the other way. Indeed it had only been the influx of American capital to London and Europe that had permitted the temporary access of strength to sterling which formed the immediate prelude to the return to the Gold Standard. Dutt pointed out that it certainly did not reflect the strength of the British economy, whose visible trade balance was worsening. Home industries and the basic export industries in particular could only expect a further deterioration in their parlous circumstances. Return to the pre-war parity demonstrated for Dutt the strength of globally oriented finance capital in Britain, and pointed to more misery and want among its industrial workers. Yet 1925 was a year when there was much talk - even on the Left - of economic recovery and the emergence of a more organised, rationalised, capitalism susceptible to planning.

In Dutt's analysis such optimism simply rode on the back of the recent influx of American capital, whose benign influence was strictly temporary since such overseas investment:

> must immediately begin a heavy return flow of interest to America. Only so long as the new American capital put out for investment exceeds the ever-increasing volume of interest on capital invested ... only so long does the situation continue on which is based the return to the gold standard. As soon as the point is reached at which the interest and payments exceed the new investment, then, unless the whole trade and production relations of Europe and America change in the interval (so that Europe exports to America more goods than America exports to Europe - a hundred millions reversal of trade) the gold standard must crash and with it the whole restoration.[70]

For Dutt this situation would provoke a capitalist offensive involving an intensification of the exploitation of labour in Europe. By means of speed-up, industrial rationalisation, wage reductions, worsening conditions of labour - the whole cocktail of Taylorism - the employers would seek to produce a larger volume of cheaper manufactured goods. Divided, militarised, bankrupt Europe would seek to evade the American embrace by essentially futile policies which would do nothing to create markets for the increased output. 'But the whole character of the present stage of capitalist development', according to Dutt, 'is the rapid shrinkage of markets and expansion of new capitalist producing and exporting countries' - including Japan and even India, 'advancing with extreme rapidity to the detriment of British industry':[71]

> What is the net result? The net result is: first to drive the working class down in every country to greater slavery and heavier production of surplus value (producing an illusory appearance of prosperity on top); and second, to hasten the inevitable explosion which will leave 1914 a pinprick in comparison.[72]

This analysis - which incidentally helped to persuade John Strachey of the accuracy of the Communist line[73] - underscored Dutt's growing optimism for Communist prospects in Britain. Anticipation of the coming crisis swept away the caution which only a year before had advised against any challenge to a Labour government 'until we have that strength of the working class forces that are ready to set up an alternative Government'.[74] The economic analysis was on sure foundations even if the political conclusions which Dutt drew from it were not.

While contemporary opinion believed that resurrection of the Gold Standard would solve the economic problems that had persisted since the war, and symbolise a return to 'normalcy', Dutt saw the basic contradictions of the underlying reality. Most of central and eastern Europe was faced with virtually insuperable problems; the entire capitalist world was unable to escape from excess capacity; the further spread of industrialisation and increased competition which triggered the lurch to protectionism and economic nationalism was inevitable. And yet contemporaries saw 1925 as a good year, a year of recovery. As long as American capital flowed into Europe some sort of precarious balance was possible, but when it was abruptly cut back in the first half of 1929 the basic weakness in the Dawes Plan was suddenly exposed, much as Dutt expected, and Germany was plunged into financial crisis.

THE GENERAL STRIKE

In Britain the coal owners were the first to insist on the necessity of wage cuts in the wake of the return to the gold standard. But they were dramatically stopped in their tracks on 31 July 1925 - Red

Friday - when the threat of united trade union action organised by the General Council of the TUC forced the Baldwin government into a last minute intervention with the promise of a subsidy to pay wages for the next nine months. Everyone knew that this was a desperate expedient which merely deferred the inevitable confrontation and bought time for the Government to prepare its next move. Dutt confidently predicted that a general strike was on hand. The working class, according to his own calculations, was 'already twenty per cent below the [living] standard of a quarter of a century ago' and the immiseration was disproportionately large in engineering and mining. The fact that these sections of the workforce had formerly constituted two of the strongest bastions of the labour aristocracy was of capital significance for Dutt, who reasoned that their decline 'is the basis of the revolutionising of British Trade Unionism'.[75]

Profits in British industry were generally higher than ever before. but an even bigger prize was at stake - 'that predominant position in world finance which is the necessary basis of British imperialism'. This was why wage cuts were required in the exporting industries in particular. Already the Dominions had been forced to turn to Wall Street for large-scale loans and the eclipse of the City of London would continue unless the working class was forced to pay for its revival. Dutt could not see resistance coming from either the Labour Party or the ILP - the leadership of the former was 'seriously compromised with Imperialism', while the ILP stood for industrial peace through its campaign for a minimum wage. In the absence of any more positive indicators he was forced to conclude that the left on the general Council of the TUC were 'the closest indication of the advance of the British working class to Revolution'.

But his real faith was in the impersonal forces of the economy, for even if the British capitalists were successful in the present conflict, the export of capital abroad would ultimately undo them. The 'industrialisation of India' would proceed apace, as it would in other rival centres of manufacturing, and Britain would become merely 'the parasite metropolis of the imperial system'. Thus the immediate campaign to break the British unions would only result in the long-term emergence of a bigger, more militant, proletariat in other parts of the Empire. The real basis would then exist for unity between British and colonial workers.[76]

Two months after Dutt had written these analyses of the coming British crisis, he was arrested by armed detectives who broke into his Brussels apartment on 5 November. The *Daily Herald* reported that Dutt and a 'Miss Mary Moorhouse' (Salme Murrik?) - who had just returned from Moscow with 'incriminating documents' and no passport - had been engaged in establishing an agency of International Red Relief, the Communist front organisation originally created by Willi Munzenburg to coordinate assistance to relieve the Russian famine of 1921. *The Times* observed that 'fairly large sums in francs, German and Estonian marks, Swedish crowns, and Russian roubles were found in a room which they rented'. The Communist *Sunday Worker* contended that 'Miss Moorhouse' was engaged on nothing more sinister than the typing of a book - presumably Dutt's *Modern India* - but the couple were charged with 'conspiracy against the Belgian state'. In London Clemens hastily orchestrated a barrage of protest letters, including contributions from such notables of the socialist movement as John Wheatley, G.D.H. Cole and Beatrice Webb. The conviction here was that the British government had been behind Dutt's arrest and this is still the best bet. Just weeks earlier, all the leading figures in the CPGB, with the exception of Rothstein, had been arrested for seditious libel.

But while the twelve accused men in London were subsequently imprisoned, and so conveniently excluded from the run-up to the coming general strike, the charges against Dutt were dropped for lack of evidence. The police then proposed deportation on the grounds of general undesirability. Although a deportation order was issued, however, it too was cancelled by 'unanimous decision of the Belgian Cabinet' - perhaps because Dutt's forcible return to London was precisely the last thing required by the British government. The upshot of this drama was that Dutt and the mysterious 'Mary Moorhouse' were released from custody within two weeks of their arrest. The attempted decapitation of the CPGB could not, in any event, have made much difference to the Party's conduct during the general strike.

Its preparations had spanned the previous three years when it first began the campaign to centralise power in the hands of the General Council. This policy of encouraging a sort of industrial general staff was not without its dangers - as the Communists realised - but it was seemingly vindicated on Red Friday. Dutt for one, however, did not allow his obvious pleasure in these events to obscure the fact that 'the temporary retreat [of the Baldwin Government] was consciously made only in order to prepare the ground for an effective and successful conflict with the whole forces of the working class movement in the near future'. The Communists had done their best to create a militant, organised wing of the trade union movement in readiness for this confrontation, but the Minority Movement only established significant roots among the miners themselves - as symbolised by the fact that the Minority Movement candidate, A.J. Cook, was elected to the secretaryship of the Miners' Federation in January 1924. Nevertheless a mood of militancy characterised the Scarborough TUC of September 1925 and reflected growing Communist influence by supporting resolutions on the need for international trade union unity, condemnation of the Dawes Plan, the right of self-determination and secession for the British colonies, and the need to form factory cells to prepare, in concert with 'the working class party', for the overthrow of capitalism.

The Communists took the trouble to write to the Labour Party and the TUC in the voice of sweet reason - so that, as Dutt put it, even the most pacifist among them could hardly object - observing the need to 'enlighten the rank and file forces' about the nature of the struggle impending. The response was such, however, that Dutt was constrained to warn of 'the very great danger of the movement entering heavily unprepared into the coming struggle and encountering in consequence serious and heavy defeats. The danger of this, and of the consequent depression, is the most urgent danger now in front of the further progress of the movement'.[77]

This warning was amply borne out by the course of events. On 30 April 1926 the miners were locked out with the approval of the Tory government, and on 3 May the long-awaited general strike commenced. From the outset the Government, having carefully prepared for the conflict for months beforehand, defined the strike as a threat to the constitution - something which both the Labour Party and the TUC found utterly abhorrent. Although the support of the rank and file trade unionists continued to grow throughout the nine days of confrontation most of their leaders looked for an escape from the affair, which they could only conceive as an embarrassing aberration. When the conflict was called off the General Council had not even secured verbal guarantees against victimisation of the strikers; the surrender was complete and the miners - who were not consulted before the capitulation - were left to struggle in vain for another six months until they were starved into submission.

AFTERMATH

During the course of the first half of 1926 Dutt managed to talk himself into a corner with a spate of articles in the Russian and Comintern press which reflected the fevered expectations of the international leadership around Zinoviev concerning revolutionary prospects in Britain. Ever since the abortive two-day rising of the Communist Party of Germany (KPD) in October 1923 the ECCI had increasingly focussed its attention on Britain as the best prospect for the long-awaited breakthrough in Western Europe. Dutt fed these expectations in early 1926, reporting for example in *Krasnaya Gazetta* that 'a million organised workers' - in other words one-quarter of the total - had been brought 'under the banner of the Communist Party' in Britain.[78] There was no basis for this estimate except the bogus claim of the second national conference of the Minority Movement, in August 1925, to represent 750,000 workers.

But Dutt's exaggerated reports on the 'intense' crisis in Britain, constructed from his Brussels isolation, persisted in this vein until the end of the general strike. The day after the strike began Dutt characterised it as a clash between 'the organised fighting force of the whole working class' and 'the ruling capitalist dictatorship'.[79] Four days later the mass movement had apparently 'swept all before it ... the old leaders are no longer in control'. The Government had allegedly responded 'with reckless violence'; Hyde Park had become 'a vast military camp'; but 'the greatest revelation of all is the British working class. The days of Chartism are revived again, on a hundredfold greater scale ... All the years of capitalist and reformist lies and dope are flung aside ... it is already the beginning of the spirit of Bolshevism'.[80]

When the strike ended in disaster Dutt forgot his own warning of the 'consequent depression', following defeat, which he had delivered in 1925. Within a matter of days he was representing the experience as 'the greatest revolutionary advance in Britain since the days of Chartism and the sure prelude of a new revolutionary era'.[81] Just as the first Labour government's demise had supposedly exposed reformism as 'a broken reed', now he claimed that the general strike had demonstrated the collapse of an entire policy - that of the Second International. The circumstances were purportedly right for the ruthless disenchantment of the workers with the sham bourgeois democracy and 'the building up of an iron revolutionary vanguard'. The fight for a mass Communist Party - as 'the sole means to a revolutionary leadership' - could be entered in earnest. The necessary corollary of this was merciless criticism of the bogus left-wingers who had betrayed the strike.

Yet the tangible impact of the general strike upon the CPGB was only very modest. The Party had certainly thrown itself into the struggle and had emerged with enhanced prestige on the coalfields; the bulk of those arrested during the strike belonged to the Party. But the small membership of some 6,000 grew to just 10,730 by October 1926, and thereafter declined. At the Party congress of 1926, moreover, there was criticism of the line on the grounds that the slogan 'all power to the General Council' had disarmed the membership, and had delayed criticisms of the strike leaders until it was all over. Given his oft-repeated warnings about the phoney left since his debate with J.T. Murphy in 1924, such criticism of the Party leadership would not have been unwelcome to Dutt. Clemens clearly understood this and reported on the congress with the comment that J.R. Campbell's defence of Party policy had been 'horrible', amounting to no more than 'pure declamation on the wonderfulness' of the organisation.[82]

The truth is that the position of the CPGB was invariably to the right of the line advocated by the Comintern - principally because the Party leaders had to contend with the recalcitrant British reality while the Comintern dealt in abstractions. Dutt's removal from the field of conflict since 1924 made it all the easier for him to indulge in this paper Bolshevism. By his own admission (in a letter to the Political Bureau of 10 May 1926) he had been starved of Party information since the strike began; but this did not prevent him from expatiating on 'the completest exposure of capitalist democracy', warning about the approach of fascism in Britain, or arguing that the non-Communist left had been thoroughly left behind by the radicalised workers.[83] If this irritated many of his comrades in London they must have been worried to discover that before the end of 1926 the Comintern was quite settled in its conviction, that far from representing defeat the general strike had merely hastened the final showdown with reformism.[84]

This is suggested by the fact that when the full central committee reviewed the general strike at the end of May 1926 it concluded that it must continue to work with the non-Communist left in the unions. Dutt, by contrast, had argued before, during, and immediately after the strike that the TUC left had consistently betrayed and sabotaged the action by their refusal to organise for the showdown since Red Friday, and to back their rhetoric with deeds. Feeling vindicated, Dutt now allowed doctrine and wishful thinking to persuade him that the left was finished, the masses ready to follow the Communist Party. The Party leadership, far less sanguine about these prospects, and no doubt convinced that continued collaboration with Hicks, Purcell, and the rest was the best that could be hoped for, was much less combative. But when the ECCI pronounced on the subject in June, it demanded that the CPGB condemn the left on the TUC General Council in particular. Dutt's inclinations thus became authoritative and one must suppose that his greater proximity to the Comintern apparatus was of some assistance in gauging the prevalent mood of the International leadership - a matter of some concern given the continuing struggle with Trotsky and its extension to the question of the British crisis.

At all events Dutt found himself increasingly at one with the Comintern in relation to British affairs in the period between its fifth and sixth congresses. In the same years, 1924- 28, he also staked his claim as a leading authority on India. His own rise to prominence thus coincided with the rise of Stalin and the spread of Stalin's influence inside the Comintern. After the British general strike Zinoviev was removed from the Presidency of the Comintern and his successor Bukharin was already a broken man by the time of the sixth congress in 1928. Such men were replaced by devoted Stalinists like Piatnitsky, Kuusinen, Manuilsky, Knorin, and Gusev. Dutt moved into closer proximity to the Comintern apparatus in 1927 when he began to work for its West European Bureau and thus entered this sort of company. The tone at the top was set by Kuusinen and Manuilsky and at Dutt's level by the likes of Togliatti, Jacques Duclos, Walter Ulbricht, Klement Gottwald, Wilhelm Pieck, and Ernst Thaelman - Stalinists to a man. This - rather than the CPGB - was Dutt's 'society of great friends'.

NOTES

1 H. Pollitt, *Serving My Time*, Lawrence and Wishart, 1940, p139; and H. Pollitt, *Looking Ahead*, CPGB, 1947, pp41-3.
2 S. Saklatvala, *The Fifth Commandment*, *op cit*, p132.
3 W. Kendall, *The Revolutionary Movement in Britain 1900- 1921*, Weidenfeld, 1969, pp398-99.
4 R.P. Dutt, 'Communism', *Encyclopaedia Britannica*, twelfth edition 1922, pp732-3.
5 R.P. Dutt, *Lenin*, Hamish Hamilton, 1933, p10.
6 R.P. Dutt, *Leninism*, Marx Memorial Library, 1941, pp3-4.

7 S. McIntyre, *A Proletarian Science*, *op cit*, pp54-5.
8 R.P. Dutt, 'Lenin in 1944', *Daily Worker*, 18 January 1944.
9 R.P. Dutt, 'The Russian Communist Party as the Nucleus of the International Proletarian Movement', K4, Vol 1922-3, p4.
10 *Ibid*, pp4-5.
11 *Ibid*, p7.
12 Dutt prepared a 'Rough Draft On Some Experiences of the Communist International' (CPGB archive) during the Easter of 1970 with the intention of including it in his memoirs. It contains reflections on the origins of *Labour Monthly* and the dispute over Party reorganisation in the years 1922-3. Brian Pollitt suggested that Dutt's mixed 'race' background may have inhibited his colleagues from making a more severe judgement of him (interview with the author).
13 L.J. MacFarlane, *The British Communist Party: Its Origin and Development Until 1929*, MacGibbon and Kee, 1966, p76.
14 See F. King and G. Matthews (eds), *About Turn: The Communist Party and the Outbreak of the Second World War*, Lawrence and Wishart, 1990, p39.
15 As related to me by Betty Reid. But also see Dutt's letter to Fred Westacott, 21 August 1956, K4 Vol 1955-7.
15 A. Kuusinen, *Before and After Stalin*, Michael Joseph, 1974, p20; for information on Grenfell and Blunt see Dutt's tribute to Grenfell in *Labour Monthly*, 30, 4 April 1948, pp111-113.
17 Dutt, 'Rough Draft on Some Experiences of the Communist International', Easter 1970,p3 *op cit*; Dutt to Rouva Hertta Kuusinen, 19 May 1964, Files 40-42, External Correspondence.
18 Kuusinen, *Before and After Stalin*, *op cit*, p134 and note 30, p247.
19 *Ibid*, p144 and note 31 p247.
20 Newbold Papers, John Rylands Library Manchester, Autobiographical Materials; and *Railway Review*, 5 April 1940.
21 P. Spratt, *Blowing-Up India: Reminiscences and Reflections of a Former Comintern Emissary*, Prachi Prakashan, Calcutta 1955, p24.
22 P.C. Joshi, 'R.P. Dutt and Indian Communists', *Indian Left Review*, July 1971, p50; K. Morgan, *Harry Pollitt*, Manchester University Press 1993.
23 *Sunday Times*, 30 August 1970.
24 V.I. Lenin, *Collected Works*, *op cit*, Vol 31, pp187-90.
25 Quoted in B. Lazitch and M. Drachkovitch, *Lenin and the Comintern*, Stanford, California 1972, pp329-30.
25 V.I. Lenin, *Collected Works*, Vol 31, *op cit*, p191.
27 *Report on Organisation*: Presented by the Party Commission to the Annual Conference of the CPGB, 7 October 1922, p15.
28 *Ibid*, p35 and p38.
29 Dutt's comments are hand-written across a copy of the *Newsletter*, 11 July 1964, in K6, Vol 4 1960-65.
30 Editorial, *Workers' Weekly*, 14 December 1923.

31 *Workers' Weekly*, 8 February 1924.
32 V.I. Lenin, *Collected Works*, Vol 23, *op cit*, p116.
33 *Ibid*, p118.
34 B.Hessel (ed), *Theses, Resolutions, and Manifestos of the First Four Congresses of the Comintern*, *op cit*, p93 and p134.
35 See *The Communist*, 15 September 1920.
35 R. Archer (ed), *Second Congress of the Communist International: Minutes of the Proceedings*, Vol 2, New Park, 1977, pp183-4.
37 R.P. Dutt, 'Notes of the Month', *Labour Monthly*, 1,2, August 1921, pp97-99.
38 R.P. Dutt, 'Propositions on the English Question', June 1923, K4, Vol 1922-3.
39 R.P. Dutt, 'The Situation in the English Working Class Movement', May 1923, K4, Vol 1922-3.
40 *Ibid*, p8.
41 R.P. Dutt, 'The General Election and British Foreign Policy, *Labour Monthly*, 6, 1, January 1924, p23 and p17.
42 R.P. Dutt, 'Notes of the Month', ibid, p4.
43 K. Radek,'The British Labour Government', *Communist International*, Number 23, 1924, p109; R.P. Dutt, 'Socialism in the English Parliament', *Communist International*, Number 28, 1923, pp44-56.
44 R.P. Dutt, 'Conference on the British Labour Government and the Communist Party', 15 May 1924, K4, Vol 1923-4, p7.
45 Andrew Rothstein in a letter to the author claimed to know nothing of Dutt's involvement in the West European Bureau of Comintern.
45 P.C. Joshi, 'R.P. Dutt and Indian Communism', *op cit*, p50.
47 M.N. Firsov, 'G. Dimitrov and the West European Bureau of the Comintern', in *G. Dimitrov Outstanding Militant of the Comintern*, Sofia, 1972, pp 48-79.
48 A former director of the intelligence Bureau of the Government of India, Sir D. Petrie, refers to this connection in his *Communism in India, 1924-27*, Editors Inida, Calcutta 1972, p59.
49 Clemens Dutt to R.P. Dutt, 19 February 1927.
50 A.J. McKenzie, *British Marxists and the Empire*, unpublished PhD, University of London 1978, p61.
51 Anna Palme to R.P. Dutt, 21 November 1924; Upendra Krishna Dutt to R.P. Dutt, 31 December 1924.
52 M. Dobb, 'The Webbs, the State, and the Workers', *Plebs*, 15, 4, 1923, pp170-171.
53 V.I. Lenin, *Collected Works*, Vol 31, *op cit*, p41; L. Trotsky, *Terrorism and Communism*, Ann Arbor, Michigan 1961, p109.
54 *Report of the British Delegation to Russia 1920*, (Labour Party, 1920), p4, p17, p8, p25. p9.
55 quoted in R. Page Arnot, *The Impact of the Russian Revolution in Britain*, Lawrence and Wishart 1967 p20.
55 M. Durham, 'British Revolutionaries and the Suppression of the Left in

Lenin's Russia 1918-24', *Journal of Contemporary History*, Vol 20 1985, *passim*.

57 *Labour Party Annual Conference Report*, June 1920, p113.

58 O. Kuusinen, 'Under the Leadership of Russia', *Communist International*, Jubilee number 1, 1924, p134.

59 *Ibid*, p137.

60 W.N. Ewer, 'Trotsky and his "Friends"', *Labour Monthly*, 7, 6, June 1925, pp373-6; Clemens Dutt's difficulties are related in a letter to his brother dated 11 April 1926.

61 R.P. Dutt, 'Trotsky and his English Critics', *Labour Monthly*, 8, 4, April 1926.

62 Interview with R.P. Dutt in *Sunday Times* magazine, 30 August 1970.

63 A. Bullock, *Hitler and Stalin*, (Harper Collins, 1991) pp213-14.

64 R.P. Dutt, 'MacDonaldism', *Labour Monthly*, 6, 5, May 1924, p264.

65 R.P. Dutt, 'The British Working Class After the Election', *Communist International*, number 8, 1924, p25.

65 *Ibid*, pp29-30.

67 J.T. Murphy, 'How A Mass Communist Party Will Come in Britain', *Communist International*, number 9, 1924, pp13-14.

68 *Ibid*, p15.

69 R.P. Dutt, 'The Restoration of Europe', *Labour Monthly*, 7, 2, February 1925, pp67-72.

70 R.P. Dutt, 'The Gold Standard', *Labour Monthly*, 7, 3, March 1925, pp144-5.

71 *Ibid*, pp147-8.

72 *Ibid*, p149.

73 See J. Strachey, 'Fifteen Years of *Labour Monthly*, *Labour Monthly*, 18, 7, July 1936, p398.

74 See *Communist Review*, April 1924, pp518-19

75 R.P. Dutt, 'The Capitalist Offensive in Britain', *Inprecorr*, 5, 62, 5 August 1925, p853 and p855.

75 R.P. Dutt, 'Red Friday and After', *Communist International*, number 16, 1925, p68 and p77.

77 *Ibid* pp85-6.

78 R.P. Dutt, 'The Coming Conflict in Britain', K4 Vol 1926.

79 R.P. Dutt, 'The First British General Strike', *Inprecorr*, 4 May 1926, p1; See also R.P.Dutt, 'Two Processions', *Krasnaya Gazette*, 3 May 1926, K4, Vol 1926.

80 R.P. Dutt, 'The British Workers in Battle', *Krasnaya Gazette*, 8 May 1926, K4, Vol 1926.

81 R.P. Dutt, 'The First British General Strike', *Communist International*, number 21, June 1926, p3.

82 Clemens Dutt to R.P. Dutt, 15 November 1926.

83 R.P. Dutt, 'To the Political Bureau', 10 May 1926, K4, Vol 1926.

84 See J. Pepper, 'Britain's Balance Sheet For 1926', *Communist International*, 3, 5, 15 December 1926, p13.

3
THE ANTI-IMPERIALIST STRUGGLE

It became an axiom of Communist politics, from the inception of the movement in 1919, that socialists who failed to conduct anti-colonialist campaigns in their own countries were simply 'scoundrels and imperialists' themselves. A supporter of Indian independence such as Dutt naturally found this attitude hugely attractive. The pre-war record of the Second International in relation to imperialism had been at best equivocal - it certainly seemed so to many socialists, not to mention nationalists such as Nehru. By the end of the imperialist war it was much easier for such people to see the reformist parties as actually implicated in the maintenance of empire. The record of the Bolsheviks, on the other hand, offered the sharpest possible contrast to this policy of collaboration with the imperialist states. Lenin had long advocated the right of nations to self- determination and specifically applied this principle to the colonies and dependent territories as well as in Eastern Europe. In both cases he saw nationalism as a historically progressive force which could weaken the imperialist *status quo*; it was, in his own words, 'inflammable material in world politics'. By the end of 1917 the Bolsheviks could not only point to their revolutionary anti-war record but also to the October Revolution itself as proof positive of their anti-imperialist credentials.

But the revolution also gave the young Soviet state the conundrum of having to co-exist with more powerful hostile states while standing at the head of a world movement dedicated to their overthrow. While the Bolsheviks had an obvious vested interest in anti-colonialism insofar as this stance weakened their enemies, the Soviet state was also forced to seek some sort of *modus vivendi* with the hostile Powers. Britain, the leading imperialist power, was perceived as the spearhead of the anti-Soviet coalition and thus the main foreign enemy - hopefully also the most vulnerable to colonial revolts. This is why Bukharin urged the Bolsheviks to support 'the most outright nationalist movement' if 'it contributes to the destruction of English imperialism'.[1]

Matters were not quite so simple, however. The issue was

complicated in both practice and theory. The Communists' overiding goal was the socialist revolution by means of a civil war in which the Party would lead the working class. It was not obvious that this ultimate goal would be served in the colonies if the Communists merely latched on to existing popular movements, which might feed off and encourage communalist, racist, obscurantist and tribal loyalties and prejudices. Successful Pan-Islamic or Pan-Turanian sentiments, for example, might obstruct the spread of Communism while undoubtedly constituting a real threat to the imperialist *status quo*. In Indonesia the Communist penetration of Sarekat Islam, the mass nationalist movement, was jeopardised by Comintern denunciations of Pan-Islamic ideas - or so the local militants believed. Yet only a year earlier, Zinoviev had appealed to Islamic sentiment when calling for a holy war against British imperialism at Baku in 1920. When they subjected situations to close scrutiny, the Communists were confronted with dozens of dilemmas of this sort.

On the basis of the Comintern's first pronouncements on the colonial question it was not even obvious how the Communists would relate to bourgeois nationalists in countries such as India. Was it necessary to put back the socialist revolution indefinitely in China, Indonesia, and India until the bourgeois revolution was accomplished or could these countries skip an historical stage? Perhaps the Western labour movements were now so corrupted by imperialism that the prospects for socialism actually depended on the prior liberation of the colonies - some Communists certainly thought so. But given the artificiality of colonial boundaries, which may or may not have coincided with ethnic and other loyalties, it was far from self evident that a single nationalist movement would emerge in any colony - rival nationalisms might awaken in the course of a prolonged conflict with the imperial power. Would the Communists ruthlessly exploit regionalist and separatist movements or take a 'principled' stand in favour of maintaining the territorial integrity of the country concerned? It was a problem made more complicated once the defence interests of the Soviet state entered the equation. In short, the Communist movement was compelled to deal, one way or another, with all these local difficulties while purporting to see sufficient homogeneity in world politics to justify its centralised command structure and disciplined adherence to 'the line'.

Some of these questions were first debated at the Comintern's second congress in 1920, where a division of opinion immediately appeared between Lenin and M.N. Roy, the Indian revolutionary and former Bengali terrorist. Lenin's views on imperialism were already somewhat eccentric for a Marxist, in that he depicted the relationship between the advanced capitalist countries and their colonies as parasitic, and working to arrest their economic development. It was an argument which nationalist intellectuals such as Romesh Chandra Dutt had theorised independently as the 'economic drain'. But Lenin was orthodox enough in thinking that the national movement in the colonies would necessarily assume a bourgeois democratic character because of the overwhelming preponderance of the peasantry and the negligible size of the working class in these economically backward territories. Roy insisted, however, that this analysis underestimated the rapid industrialisation of countries such as India and Egypt, where the size of the proletariat was growing fast and an army of landless peasants existed as potential allies. This meant a much bigger base existed for independent Communist organisation than perhaps Lenin supposed. And if, as Roy thought probable, the national bourgeoisie reached a mutually satisfactory deal with imperialism, independent Communist organisation and leadership in the nationalist struggle was necessary to secure an unrelenting campaign for independence.

This debate produced a compromise formula at the second congress which only served to underline the rudimentary stage of Communist thinking on this subject; 'as communists', it read, 'we will only support the bourgeois freedom movements in the colonial countries if these movements are really revolutionary and if their representatives are not opposed to us training and organising the peasantry in a revolutionary way'.[2] There was thus endless scope provided by this thesis for futile debate and destructive changes of tack about what was 'really revolutionary'. It also insisted on the impossible condition that a bourgeois movement should tolerate activities designed to undermine bourgeois interests. The first Comintern debate on the colonial problem also saw Lenin further complicate the picture by characterising the main axis of conflict in world politics as one which pitched a small number of imperialist nations against 'the Soviet movement and the Soviet powers with Soviet Russia at their head'. This would allegedly govern the 'mutual relations between states'. Lenin thus argued that 'our policy must be to bring into being a close alliance of all national and colonial liberation movements with Soviet Russia; the forms taken by this alliance will be determined by the stage of development reached by the communist movement of each country or by the revolutionary liberation movement in the undeveloped countries and among backward nationalities'.[3]

With hindsight one can see in this formula an excuse for each and every subsequent twist of Comintern and Soviet state policy under Stalin's leadership, as well as evidence of Lenin's own responsibility for sometimes equating Soviet state interests with those of the Communist movement. In practice, as is well known, the young Soviet state was occasionally forced to subordinate the interests of world revolution to the cause of its own survival; the requirements of trade and defence led, for example, to some dampening down of anti-imperialist activity in Soviet central Asia during 1921 in order to appease the British foreign office; and the Bolsheviks were compelled to deal in the same year with Turkey despite the nationalist regime's recent savage repression against the local Communist Party.[4] But Lenin also brought this question of the defence of Soviet power to the direct attention of the second congress of the Comintern. Addressing a movement composed of men and women who believed without question in the necessity of preserving the Bolshevik state, he argued that it was only from the standpoint of the configuration of the world system of states, around the pro- and anti-Soviet axis described above, 'that the political questions of the Communist Parties, not only in the civilised but also in the backward countries can be be posed and answered correctly'.[5]

Dutt always subscribed to this presentation of the problem and his contributions to *Labour Monthly*, in particular, contrived to situate Communist policy within this framework. The second congress of the Comintern had done no more, however, than provide the first tentative outline of a Communist colonial policy and an aspiring expert on international politics such as Dutt still had plenty of scope for providing the detail. Though he had never so much as visited India, the subcontinent was Dutt's obvious field of specialism in anti-colonial work. India was Britain's most important possession and the nationalist movement there had sprung into life at the close of the imperialist war, thanks to Gandhi's ability to inspire the rural masses. Dutt's father might express some scepticism about the prospects for success of his son's secular ideas in the face of Eastern spiritualism but he was prepared to acknowledge Rajani's greater knowledge of the economic and social forces now sweeping India. Certainly a more auspicious moment for socialist intervention in Indian politics could not have been imagined - the joint impact of the world war and the Bolshevik revolution having only recently worked their destabilising influence.

DUTT AND M.N. ROY

M.N. Roy, for one, was convinced on this score. As a former terrorist he had always taken a dim view of the timid Indian National Congress (INC). Now, as a Marxist, he sought to marshall economic and class data on the new India to support his penchant for a revolutionary strategy which did not depend on the perfidious, bourgeois nationalists. But he too was prepared to acknowledge Gandhi's decisive role in helping to transform the old debating society of the INC into a mass movement of many millions. By the beginning of 1922 something like 30,000 Indians had been imprisoned in the course of nationalist agitation around Gandhi's appeal for a boycott of imported cloth. Indeed the boycott movement in the countryside spontaneously extended to the non-payment of rent and outbreaks of violence - neither of which had been specifically sanctioned by Gandhi. One such incident at Chauri Chaura in the United Provinces led to the deaths of 22 policemen in February 1922 and became forever associated with Gandhi's 'Bardoli decision,' which effectively called off the campaign and, in demobilising the peasantry, paved the way for a downturn in nationalist agitation. This left the disoriented movement defenceless against the repression that followed. Roy was thus spectacularly vindicated - the national bourgeoisie had deserted the independence cause at the first sign of a threat to their own property; Gandhi had scuppered the non-co-operation campaign to protect the class interests of the landowners and the bourgeoisie in the INC leadership.

Roy and his American wife and co-thinker, Evelyn Trent, now announced that Gandhi had no further role to play in the national struggle. His leadership had lacked political acumen and displayed blindness to the social and economic demands of the masses while his philosophy - preaching non-violence, personal poverty, celibacy and a rejection of modern technology - marked him out as an obscurantist who had functioned as the 'unconcious agent of reaction'. The Communist press, and *Labour Monthly* in particular, was bombarded with this thesis from 1922.[6] Alongside it the Roy's played up the political capacity of the Indian working class. The puny All-India Trade Union Congress, for example, was given exaggerated importance as the organisation of the class conscious workers fighting for the social and economic programme which the Gandhians ignored, even though its only real function since 1921 was to secure Indian representation at the International Labour Organisation. The 'rapid industrialisation' of India was invoked as the ultimate source of the political strength of the workers and the real basis of the 'increasing intensity of the nationalist campaign'.[7] M.N. Roy perceived in all of this a politically weak bourgeoisie allied to foreign finance capital confronted by a growing proletariat, which would sweep religious fanaticism aside on the basis of advancing class consciousness, and a hegemonic workers' party capable of simultaneously defeating imperialism and the national bourgeoisie.[8]

Between the third and fourth congresses of the Comintern Roy developed his ideas in *India in Transition* (1922) where the 'rapid industrialisation' thesis was given its fullest treatment to date. In Britain, Shapurji Saklatvala had already drawn attention to changes in government policy regarding Indian economic development, which had been occasioned by the world war. He pointed out in 1921 that the change had been signalled in 1916 with the appointment of the Indian Industrial Commission, whose subsequent report recommended an active policy of industrialisation on the subcontinent.[9] The political counterpart to this strategy was supposed to be outlined in the Montagu-Chelmsford Report of 1917 which recommended constitutional changes amounting to a limited form of self-government, or dyarchy - the first step towards power-sharing between the British and Indian capitalists as the Communists saw it. The very real measures of industrialisation which the war stimulated in India, combined with the obvious political moderation of the Indian nationalist leaders - very far, as yet, from demanding independence - provided sufficient evidence to convince Dutt, Roy, and Saklatvala that a compromise between the British and Indian capitalists was on the agenda. Dutt later claimed to have originated this thesis and in view of Saklatvala's minor role as a theorist the claim should not be dismissed.[10] But it was Roy who first developed it into a full-blown treatise on paper.

The common ground between Communists and nationalists such as Romesh Dutt lay in the conviction that - until the world war at least - the political impact of British rule on the subcontinent had been disastrous for its economic development. Manufacturers had been destroyed as an act of policy in order to eliminate India as a competitor, especially in the textile industry. Going even further back the Permanent Land Settlement of 1793, by turning the tax-collecting zamindars into landlords, had created a class with no interest in industrial development, but one that leached the agricultural surplus that might otherwise have funded economic development. The Raj also reinforced the feudal aristocracy as a mainstay of British power and fostered religious and communal divisions for the same purpose.

Roy argued that a retardation of the 'normal' transition to the machine age had occurred. The rural artisan class had been destroyed under the impact of the superior capitalist techniques used in Britain. But India was prevented from developing its own modern machine industry. Thus British policy acted to prevent the emergence of an urban working class in India and instead consigned the redundant artisans to the countryside. The proportion of the population dependent on a backward agriculture thus grew. So too did the class of rural wage-earners - scattered throughout the land and permanently threatened with unemployment. In the towns the needs of commerce and bureaucracy created a class of 'petty intellectual workers', certainly more numerous than the tiny factory proletariat, but, in the absence of industrial development, this sector was unable to absorb the growing surplus population of rural poor. Until the closing decades of the nineteenth century, India's agriculture thus groaned under the weight of both parasitic tax-farmers and a burgeoning debt, in the context of backward, small-scale methods of production and a growing population of labourers, many of whom were superfluous to requirements. Roy argued that nothing short of 'a complete agrarian revolution' could solve the problem - the rural population being so vast that even a massive expansion of industry could not absorb the mass of unemployed.[11]

This then was the picture of retarded development which Roy ascribed to the impact of British imperialism up to the close of the nineteenth century. A 'spectacular growth' in industry had nevertheless occurred, according to Roy, in the twentieth century and particularly during and after the war, when a change in British policy became noticeable. Nine million workers were allegedly employed in large capitalist concerns by 1921, as compared to only three million before the war began; 14.4 million all told could be found in transport, textiles and mining; 42 million now lived on agricultural wages of whom 25.8 million 'are actual workers'.[12] The statistics need not detain us - Roy later admitted that they were bogus, but blamed his assistant Abani Mukherji for the misleading magnification. The real issue before us concerns the political conclusions which Roy drew with the assistance of these figures.

First it had been made plain to the Indian bourgeoisie, according to Roy, that 'it was no longer impossible to realise its ambitions under bourgeois rule'. Second, 'the conditions for a bourgeois revolution do not exist in India':

> The Indian national movement is not a struggle of the commercial and industrial middle class against decrepit feudalism. The Indian bourgeoisie is not engaged in a class struggle. The basis of the national movement is the rivalry of a weak and suppressed bourgeoisie against its immensely stronger imperialist prototype controlling the state power ... The present fight of the Indian bourgeoisie cannot be, therefore, unrelenting. Its growth and prosperity are not necessarily conditional upon the total destruction of its present enemy ... [it] is bound to be compromising ... the British rule, in spite of itself, promises protection to the advent of capitalist civilisation in India.[13]

The bourgeoisie could therefore be expected to mobilise the masses around nationalism in order to extract concessions from the British, but to demobilise the movement when it assumed the character of a struggle for the social and economic demands of these same masses.

By 1926 Roy was able to boast that 'bourgeois nationalism in India has ended in a complete compromise with imperialism as was predicted years ago by those who judged the situation with Marxian realism'.[14] This was, he argued, because class struggle had predominated over the programme of nationalism as expressed by the INC - which under the leadership of the bourgeoisie was capable of only 'a feeble protest against the "unfair" distribution of the booty'. The war-inspired policy of British encouragement for Indian industrialisation had been further reinforced, according to Roy, in 1923 when the Government of India accepted the principle of discriminating protection for the industries of the subcontinent, although this was a device, primarily, for excluding the Japanese capitalists. Now that Indian industrialisation was 'a joint Anglo-Indian affair', 'the antagonism between imperialism and Indian capitalism has been, at least for the time being, almost eliminated'.[15] But the conditional clause in the last sentence was actually redundant; Roy believed that the Indian working class had to become hegemonic in the national struggle, through the Communist Party acting 'side by side' with revolutionary nationalist elements.

Roy also denounced Gandhism as 'the acutest and the most desperate manifestation of the forces of reaction', because it stood in opposition even to those objectively revolutionary elements in bourgeois liberalism.[16] Post-British India could not and would not become pre-British India, in spite of the efforts of the 'counter-revolutionary leadership' of the Gandhians.[17] The upheaval which began in 1918 was, for Roy, in large measure a rebellion against exploitation, but the revival of the spiritual civilisation of India which Gandhi, and before him Tilak, had championed could not articulate it. In *What Do We Want?* (1922), Roy made clear that political independence was only the first step to economic freedom and social emancipation. There would have to be an end 'to all economic slavery and social bondage', in short an 'end to all class rule'. These objectives could not be achieved by the bourgeoisie - no matter how vigorously it pursued independence from Britain.

When the INC met at Gaya in 1923, a list of more modest immediate demands prepared by Roy was put before the nationalists. Already the Communists were clear that the goal was 'complete national independence' and the election by universal suffrage of a National Assembly. This would lead to the establishment of a Federated Republic of India. The bulk of the immediate demands concerned economic and social reforms including a minimum wage, an eight-hour day, the reduction of land-rents to a fixed minimum, the abolition of landlordism, the recognition of trade unions and the right to strike, free and compulsory education, separation of state and religion and full social, economic and political rights for women. The Communists also wanted nationalisation of the railways, mines and waterways and the state modernisation of agriculture and industry.[18]

One would never guess from Roy's pronouncements on the matter that Indian Communism was represented by no more than a handful of individuals at this time. In fact the CPGB became aware of the real state of play in 1925, when Percy Glading (who was to be convicted of espionage and imprisoned in 1938) returned from a reconnoitre of the subcontinent to report that he could find no evidence whatever of Party organisation. Glading's evidence was among the items discussed at an acrimonious meeting in Amsterdam convened by the CPGB's Colonial Committee, which revealed considerable friction between Roy and the British Indian experts.[19] One of the main areas of contention concerned Communist collaboration with nationalist elements which the CPGB, in accordance with Comintern policy, wished to foster. This co-operation was the essence of the political line which Dutt elaborated in his first major book on India.

Thus while Dutt's *Modern India* restated the rapid industrialisation thesis, the bulk of the argument was concerned with the politics of the national struggle and in this Dutt was significantly more cautious than Roy - perhaps in part because he estimated the number of industrial wage workers in India at a sober two million.[20] Dutt saw the industrialisation process taking place 'under British control', in any case, and this left the Indian capitalists merely as the 'subordinate partner'. There was thus scope for even sections of the bourgeoisie to fight for complete independence.[21] Dutt was also noticeably more positive than Roy about the role of Gandhi. He realised that 'the personality of Gandhi has woven its way into the hearts of millions', and that his achievement was bigger than all his 'idiosyncracies and weaknesses'. Gandhi had not only mobilised the masses but had provided them with a policy. And Dutt saw that this policy was the very 'opposite' of the non-violent rhetoric in which Gandhi sometimes indulged. Mass civil disobedience was 'the attempt to *force* the Government to submit ... it [was] a question of *power*' and Ghandi, according to Dutt, was often perfectly clear about this.[22] Thus it was not violence which led to the Bardoli decision, as any scrutiny of the resolution which called off the campaign in 1922 would reveal: it was the threat to property.

But if Gandhi had succumbed to bourgeois pressure, this did not mean that the Indian National Congress was actually led by the bourgeoisie. Dutt specifically denied this and argued that the big bourgeoisie remained outside the whole non-co-operation campaign. The leadership of the INC was, for Dutt, a leadership of 'petty bourgeois intellectual elements'.[23] The clear implication was that such a leadership would succumb to pressure from whichever of the two big social forces in India - reactionary or progressive - exerted the larger force. Dutt insisted that 'the Congress, so far, is and has been the only approach to a mass organisation throughout the Indian people'.[24] Indeed much of his argument in *Modern India* was dedicated to the thesis that the Congress would exert no influence at all in the absence of a mass organisation. What was required, therefore, was a structure which would properly harness the masses, and a programme that would articulate their interests. On the latter, Dutt's proposals were essentially those promoted by Roy at the Gaya Congress of 1923, focussing on civil rights, immediate economic and social demands and the land question. Dutt's organisational recommendations were designed to democratise Congress and incorporate workers' and peasants' associations. 'The immediate important task', he concluded, was 'to carry on a battle of clarification within the existing movement and organisations'.[25]

In practice, of course, Dutt was well aware of how far this process had yet to go if the nationalist movement was to be refashioned as a secular mass force committed to complete independence, let alone as a champion of the social and economic programme put forward by the Communists. It was still unable to define its political goals, and had committed the 'Himalayan mistake' of reviving and intensifying the religious and racial traditions of the people, hoping at some later date to obtain a sectional combination in the form of Hindu-Moslem Unity:

> How did this conception arise? The conception was introduced by the Extremists in opposition to the old moderate Nationalists. The Extremists saw the old upper class Nationalists saturated with the 'denationalised' outlook and methods, learning, social life and politics of the British bourgeoisie. Against this 'denationalisation' or capitulation to British culture, they sought to lead a revolt. But on what basis could they lead a revolt?
>
> They were themselves tied to the narrow range of the bourgeois outlook, and could not see the workings of capitalism. In consequence they could not see that the so-called 'British' culture they were inveighing against was in reality the culture of capitalism, and that the only real opposition to this culture could come from the working class. They could not, on the basis of experience then in India, have any conception of the rising working class outlook and culture which alone can be the alternative and successor to bourgeois culture, going beyond it, taking what is of value and leaving the rest. Therefore, when they came to look for a firm ground of opposition to the conquerors' culture, they could only find for a basis the pre- capitalist culture of India before the conquest.
>
> So, from the existing foul welter of decaying and corrupt metaphysics, from the broken relics of the shattered village system, from the dead remains of court splendours of a vanished civilisation, they sought to fabricate and build up and reconstitute a golden dream of Hindu culture - a 'purified' Hindu culture - which they could hold up as an ideal and a guiding light.
>
> Against the overwhelming flood of British bourgeois culture and ideology, that is to say of the culture and ideology of capitalist robbery which was completely conquering the Indian bourgeoisie and intelligentsia, they sought to hold forward the feeble shield of a reconstructed Hindu ideology which had no longer any natural basis for its existence in actual life conditions. All social and scientific development was condemned as the conquerors' culture: every form of antiquated tradition, abuse, privilege and obscurantism was treated with veneration

> and respect.
>
> So it came about that the national leaders of the people, who should have been leading the people forward along the path of emancipation and understanding, away from all the evil relics of the past, appeared instead as the champions of reaction and superstition, caste privilege and division, as the allies of all the 'black' forces, seeking to hold down the fetters upon the people.
>
> The Extremists believed that in this way they were building up the masses. Only so can it be explained that a man of the intellectual calibre of Tilak should have lent himself to such agitations as his campaigns in defence of child-marriage or his Anti Cow Killing Society.
>
> But the policy was not only vicious in principle, but also mistaken in tactics. The path to the masses does not lie through the superstitions which are their enemy.[26]

Dutt could see that Gandhi continued this 'vicious' policy in so far as he invoked the images and myths of religion to arouse the people, or turned his back on advanced technology and endorsed the caste system (in spite of his campaign against untouchability). The Communists always criticised the failure of the Congress leadership to break completely with religion and the communal antagonisms associated with it. But they reserved their most furious polemics for British encouragement of communalism and for the chief political beneficiary of this policy in India, the Moslem League. Racial and religious conflicts were seen almost exclusively as either the disguised form of current economic antagonisms or cultural survivals of a bygone material reality which were artificially stirred back into life as one of the 'desperate expedients' of a declining capitalist civilisation. Neither Dutt nor Roy could admit that Gandhi was able to link the peasantry to powerful sections of the bourgeoisie by means of the very thing they disliked so much - his reactionary social and economic doctrines. It was precisely because Hindu culture was not merely composed of evil 'relics', but was on the contrary a living part of the complex by which caste, religion and agrarian conditions reinforced one another, that Gandhi was able to mobilise the peasants without seriously threatening Indian property interests. But while Dutt and Roy may not have seen the potency of this strategy, they deserve credit for seeing that it was inimical to Indian social and economic progress and fighting remorselessly against it.

Gandhi did indeed use his influence to oppose political and economic strikes, and to deflect the struggle away from class antagonisms, but his success was firmly rooted in the cultural and economic conditions of India's 500,000 villages and the ingrained hierarchical submission which they maintained. The attempt to inject Communist politics into this situation was nothing short of heroic. But Dutt's Marxist vision even enabled him to imagine that India might avoid having to repeat all the stages of economic development of Western Europe, and to reach socialism by a shorter route. His optimism derived from the conviction that the modernisation of the subcontinent had at least started because of 'the modern world development of imperialism' - that is because it was required by the needs of a system grown fat and stagnant in the countries of its birth. Perhaps this is why he underestimated the power of Gandhi's particular nationalist strategy. For Dutt's conception of the imperialist epoch meant that the economic development of India did not depend on the existence of a vigorous internal dynamic but on extraneous factors - essentially the export of capital to the subcontinent. Unlike Lenin, then, Dutt - and Roy for that matter - subscribed to Marx's vision of capitalism reaching out to and developing all corners of the globe. But this was as far as the disagreement with Lenin went.

For in the thesis of the 'rapid industrialisation' of India they believed, paradoxically, that they had found evidence to support Lenin's general theory of the demise of capitalism. Dutt envisaged British financed capitalism in India would undercut wages and employment at home, so that 'the Empire, which was previously a source of limited advantage to a section of the working class, is now becoming a source of impoverishment and weakness to all sections, including the former aristocracy of labour'.[27] Though Roy had been slapped down at the second congress of the Comintern for wanting to go one better and argue that revolution in the West depended upon the prior liberation of the colonies, the conviction that the social revolution in Europe was intimately related to colonial developments survived. It was therefore a matter of signal importance to make the workers in Britain see this connection.

AGAINST THE STREAM

This was a tall order. An essential part of the *raison d'etre* of the Communist movement was the conviction - there is no reason to doubt its sincerity - that a significant layer of the working class had been corrupted by imperialism, as demonstrated by the collaboration of the mass reformist organisations in the prosecution of the war of 1914-18. In Britain the socialist movement had produced prominent imperialists such as Robert Blatchford and

Henry Mayers Hyndman, whom even the pre-war Second International had taken to task for their expressions of chauvinism. And as these examples show, the problem was not confined to the moderate wing of the movement - though some of the worst imperialists and racists undoubtedly belonged to its respectable components such as the Fabian Society (one has only to think of H.G. Wells and the Webbs). But to return to the first point we need look no further than Tom Quelch of the British Socialist Party - later a founder-member of the CPGB - who once referred to 'jolly coons' in an article in the socialist press on the use of black labourers in the London docks. The same piece expressed the archetypal racist fear that these black 'Othellos' were a danger to British women. It is perhaps significant that when Quelch was challenged about these views, the objection was raised by the Bolshevik Chicherin, then resident in London, rather than by a British socialist.[28]

The point is underlined by an episode which occurred in 1920, when E.D. Morel raised a hue and cry about 'the black horror on the Rhine' - a reference to the Moroccan troops used by France when it occupied that part of Germany. Morel's articles talked about 'black savages' and their 'barely restrainable beastiality', the threat of the spread of syphilis, the danger to white women in view of the fact that for 'well-known physiological reasons' rape by a black man nearly always results in injury or death to the white victim.'[29] The pervasiveness of racism in Britain may be judged from the fact that Morel - far from being an ordinary reactionary - had an honourable reputation as an opponent of imperialist oppression in Africa. The article, moreover, was originally published in the socialist *Daily Herald* and its editor, George Lansbury, specifically drew the attention of its female readership to Morel's account of the 'sexual outrages' allegedly perpetrated by the black soldiers. The issue was allowed to drag on through the spring and summer of 1920. An equally racist follow-up pamphlet was favourably reviewed in the ILP press and presented to each delegate at the 1920 TUC. Resolutions were passed by branches of the unions, the Labour Party and the ILP, dwelling on the 'degrading and dangerous' practice of using black troops. Though the German Communist Party denounced the racism which informed a similarly sensationalist outcry at home, the CPGB - in common with most of the British Left - remained silent.

It is hardly surprising, given this background, that the British delegation to the second congress of the Comintern in 1920 was reluctant to assume any special responsibility for anti- imperialist work in Britain. Tom Quelch insisted that the British workers would regard it as treason - an argument which other delegates quoted as evidence of the social patriotism characteristic of the British labour movement. Quelch and company were told that 'the Comintern will judge the British comrades not by their articles in favour of liberation, but by the numbers of them imprisoned for agitation in Ireland, Egypt, or India'.[30] In fact it took several more years of constant chiding before the British Party was brought up to scratch on this issue; years in which serious anti-imperialists like the Dutt brothers, Robin Page Arnot, and Saklatvala replaced men of the old Marxist left such as Quelch.

It can hardly be doubted, however, that but for the constant pressure of the Comintern, the CPGB's colonial work would have sunk to the bottom of its list of priorities. As it was, the ECCI complained as late as 1924 that the Party had done 'as good as nothing' in the colonies. This was the year, of course, when the Comintern sharply reminded Dutt and his colleagues that the Labour government was 'a bourgeois- imperialist government'. It was also the year when a draft programme on Communist colonial policy submitted by the British Party for the Comintern's consideration was rejected as 'not enough', because though it envisaged the complete political and economic freedom of Britain's colonies, it also said that they were to remain 'within the confines of the Empire'.[31] Later in 1924 Manuilsky, the chairman of the ECCI Commission on National and Colonial Questions, was moved to criticise the British Party's attitude to the colonies as 'passive' and specifically condemned the fact that not one of the documents which he had scrutinised on this issue 'contains a single word by which the English Party declares itself unequivocally for the separation of the colonies from the British Empire'.[32] The pressure continued in 1925, with the Party enjoined to increase its agitation against the imperialist sentiments of the British labour aristocracy.

Now, given Dutt's exposure to Indian nationalism since childhood, it is clear enough that an important element in his loyalty to the Comintern derived from its position on colonial issues: thanks to this externally imposed discipline, the CPGB was in time the only socialist party in Britain which accorded the anti-imperialist struggle the importance Dutt himself attached to it. In the related matter of 'race' equality, which touched Dutt personally of course, there was another reason to give thanks to the Soviet state. Many examples could be given to show that the Bolsheviks commanded a respect and affection by virtue of their radical stand on this issue. M.N. Roy testified to this many years after his expulsion from the Communist movement, when he recalled his first Comintern congress where, 'for the first time, brown and yellow men met white men who were not overbearing imperialists but friends and comrades, eager to make amends for the evils of colonialism'.[33] The Trinidadian ex-Communist, George Padmore, in a book published in 1956 which excoriated Communist policy, nevertheless observed that among black Americans the reputation of the Soviet Union stood high 'because they hear that colour bar and racial discrimination is illegal and severely punished in the USSR'. Padmore, who for a time lived in Russia, affirmed the existence of this 'absolute racial equality'.[34]

Such views seem to have some validity: while visitors to the Soviet Union might easily be misled over such matters as working conditions and pay - by careful screening and visits to model factories - racism could not be so easily camouflaged - certainly not for men and women who had been its victims. Almost thirty years after his first visit to the USSR in 1934, Paul Robeson remembered that there for the first time in his life he walked in full human dignity.[35] The Robesons were told by all the black Americans they met in the USSR that it 'was entirely free of racial prejudice'. It may well be that this had more to do with Russian culture than Bolshevik doctrine, though one can easily understand why socialists would be blind to this distinction. But what also impressed such people was the fact that the Bolshevik state punished racism at a time when the Western states either turned a blind eye to it or fanned its flames. Many socialists and colonial nationalists also believed, as Dutt never failed to trumpet, that the USSR had solved the problem of national minorities and achieved a degree of social and economic advance in the lives of the erstwhile backward peoples of the Union such as was not believed possible of attainment in the dependent territories of the capitalist empires.

There was enough truth in these assertions to satisfy people looking for radical solutions to problems that might well be considered intractable by 'sensible' conservatives fond of invoking human nature. In education, employment and health the Soviet Union did make real progress, while similar initial conditions were cited as being too much for the British in India to overcome. And, as nationalists like Nehru were only too well aware, there was also 'the haughty superciliousness, arrogance and even insolence of behaviour' of the white colonists and their administrators to contend with.[36] By contrast, the Communists everywhere made strenuous efforts to combat racism. In the Communist Party of the USA, for example, 'white Party members were pressed theoretically, practically, and personally to wrestle with the Black question, to encourage Blacks and to treat them with perfect equality or risk censure and expulsion'.[37] This was much more than just consciousness-raising; if the circumstances arose, the lives and liberty of the Party members were put on the line. In South Africa, for example, as George Padmore conceded, 'the only Europeans ... who have taken an uncompromising stand on behalf of racial equality for non-Europeans are the Communists. On the question of human rights for Africans, the Communists have never faltered'.[38] And there was obviously a price to be paid for such courage.

For the Communists it was not enough to support pious resolutions for colonial independence; it was necessary to operationalise this commitment. In the British labour movement matters were rather different. As an indication of the Labour Party's concern for the colonies, it is significant that it was not until 1949 that its International Department finally created a 'Colonial Assistant', and even then the job was mainly diplomatic in content. A Commonwealth Department had to wait until 1958.[39] The CPGB, on the other hand, created a Colonial Committee, under Clemens Dutt's supervision, as early as 1925. By this time the Party leadership claimed that it had already made contact with Communist Parties and revolutionary groups in 'most' of the colonies and Crown Dominions.[40] British Party members also took part in discussions in Berlin at the beginning of 1923 which led to the formation of an Indian Labour Bureau which was to act as a legal link with nascent trade unionism in India.[41] The centrality of India in the Party's anti-colonial work was evident from the beginning.

Its work among Indian students in Britain enabled the Party to compile a report on the political composition of the Majlis (the Indian students' society) at Oxford University as early as 1924. Saklatvala used the Indian Labour Bureau in London to bring the Leftists among them under the Party's direction. Work among students from the colonies remained an important component of the CPGB's international responsibilities throughout the inter-war years, and indeed into the 1960s. So far as India was concerned, the high-point of the attempt to find converts among the educated elite was probably reached in the 1930s. By this time Dutt was back in the country and able to play a direct role in the affairs of the Federation of Indian Students. In 1974 Ashok Mitra, an Indian academic, was able to refer to a group photograph of members of the Federation, taken in 1939, which showed Dutt squatting, first row, centre, 'flanked by his young admirers - budding lawyers, economists, historians, political scientists, engineers, statisticians, and others'. They included 'the son of a taluqdar [wealthy landowner], the daughter of a princeling [and] Mazhar Ali Khan of Lahore, rich and debonair, now better known as the father of Tariq Ali'. In another corner of the photograph is 'one who subsequently became chairman and managing director of several industrial and commercial firms in the country ... In the third row, fourth from left, is ... the namesake of the great Dutt, Rajani Patel, boss of the Bombay Congress ... In the next row, the present Secretary-General of the World Peace Congress'.[42]

Some surprising allies indeed - even allowing for the Popular Front policy of the time. But perhaps not so surprising in view of the low opinion which many colonial nationalists had of the Labour Party. Nehru, for example, claimed that 'the whole record of the Second International from the war onward filled me distaste,' and admitted that his sympathies lay with the Communists.[43] His biographer explained that Nehru's first-hand contacts with British Labour leaders had filled him with particular contempt for what he called 'these sanctimonious and canting humbugs'.[44] Middle class nationalists in India were not the only colonial leaders who saw matters this way; had it not been for the ILP even more of them would have viewed the Communists as their best friends in Britain.

The Communists were nevertheless more interested in establishing workers' and peasants' organisations in the colonies than in cultivating links with bourgeois nationalists. A variety of expedients were adopted with this end in view. Saklatvala, for example, was instructed to establish an Indian Seamen's Union in London on the orders of the Red International of Labour Unions (Profintern). In their struggle against the Tsarist state the Bolsheviks had learned to use seamen as couriers between the emigres in Western Europe and the illegal party organisations in Russia. The lesson was learned by the Communist Parties, which established appropriate organisations for this purpose in important ports such as Hamburg, Marseilles and London. Saklatvala's involvement with the London based Workers' Welfare League of India (WWL) provided a useful bridge into such work. The WWL had agitated since 1917 for trade union rights in India, and improvements in the regulation and conditions of work on the subcontinent. Although it was not founded under Communist auspices, with Saklatvala as

Secretary the WWL was able to become the London agent of the All-India Trade Union Congress from 1925, thus providing Party members with enhanced legitimacy in their work among Indian sailors in the London docks. The British police regularly observed Saklatvala addressing open air meetings of up to several hundred seafarers.

Since Comintern publications were generally banned on the subcontinent - as elsewhere in the British colonies - it was vitally important that reliable means were established for the smuggling of its literature - such as Roy's *Masses of India* on which Clemens Dutt worked in Berlin. Clemens also served with Roy on the so called Foreign Bureau of the CPI based in the German capital. In Moscow the British representative engaged on Indian work was Ralph Fox who was sent there in September 1925. Exactly a year earlier the Comintern had launched a Colonial Bureau in Paris, in which Palme Dutt was involved.

To be really effective, of course, it was necessary to get Communist agents into the colonies directly. The first attempts to establish emissaries of the British Party in India were foiled by the police, but in April 1926 George Allison arrived undetected in Bombay and was able to begin the work of organising a Left inside the All India TUC, until his arrest in January 1927. And by the time Allison was sentenced to eighteen months imprisonment and deportation, Philip Spratt, a graduate of Downing College Cambridge, was ready to replace him. Some months later he was joined by Ben Bradley who arrived under cover of his brother's 'underdrain tile company'. Between them Spratt and Bradley managed to establish a functioning Communist Party in India.

In his memoirs Spratt recalled the 'sudden enlightenment and tough exhilaration when I grasped the idea of the party; whole-time, professional, dedicated, under military discipline with but one goal-power'.[45] He had no idea, however, that at the time of his departure for India this was still an impossibly remote ideal on the subcontinent. Communist organisation was still a shambles. And it was suffering, not simply from a negligible membership - fifteen or twenty nominal members according to Spratt at the time of his arrival in December 1926 - but also because of the conflict and confusion around Communist policy at the highest levels of the Comintern.

CPGB POLICY IN INDIA

Personal rivalries as well as political differences separated Roy from the other influential figures directly concerned with Indian Communism. His clash with Lenin at the second congress of the Comintern, and the resulting compromise, did nothing, however, to harm Roy's prestige or to alter his hostility to bourgeois nationalism. He persisted in exaggerating the size of the Indian working class and boasted that 'in most of the colonies there already exist organised revolutionary parties'. While Lenin spoke of close collaboration with bourgeois nationalists, Roy only envisaged a grudging co-operation, and repeatedly emphasised the 'counter-revolutionary' tendency of the Indian National Congress.[46] His personal predilections were given vent in 1920 when, as a representative of the Comintern's Central Asiatic Bureau, he established an Indian Military School in Tashkent, with the intention of raising an army in Afghanistan for direct intervention on the subcontinent. In the event Roy did manage to convert a handful of Muslim militants bound for Turkey - seat of the Caliphate which they wanted to restore - but under pressure from the British Foreign Office his military enterprise was abandoned by Moscow in May 1921. He returned to Moscow, however, as the founder of a Communist Party of India. This had been been formed in Tashkent towards the end of 1920 with a membership composed of seven individuals from his immediate retinue - and had no basis in India.

Early in 1921 Roy met with members of the Berlin based Indian Revolutionary Committee in Moscow. Several of the most important of these 'derelicts of German intrigue', as he once called them, had actually been converted from nationalism to Bolshevism. None was more important than Virendranath Chattopadhyaya. At the Moscow meeting it soon became apparent that Chatto's group were 'openly hostile' to Roy's pseudo Party and indeed to the central ideas of the thesis which Roy had put before the second congress of the Comintern.[47] This was all the more unfortunate in view of Roy's transfer to Berlin in April 1922, and the fact that the Comintern was still prepared to trust his judgement of the size of the revolutionary forces on the subcontinent. By November 1922, 120,000 pounds sterling had passed through his hands - much of it pocketed by intermediaries and terrorist groups more interested in Russian money than Comintern politics.[48]

The Comintern's patience with Roy began to run out by

1924, when the fifth congress decided, against his advice, on the necessity of direct contact between itself and mainstream nationalists. Roy was specifically charged with exaggerating the social movement in the colonies to the detriment of the nationalist movement - a mistake which Dutt could avoid as he prepared *Modern India* in the wake of this censure. Undeterred, Roy wrote an appeal for the establishment of a 'Revolutionary Nationalist Party' to replace the INC soon after the fifth congress had dissolved. But since the same congress had devolved responsibility for India to the CPGB, Roy's influence was already fading. The CPGB was instructed to forge 'very close contact' with the Indian nationalists and was soon preparing an 'Oriental Conference' with this goal in mind. When the idea was floated at a meeting with Roy and the Dutch Communist Henk Sneevliet in Amsterdam, Clemens Dutt was told that the project was futile and that only 'unreliable elements' would answer the call. In reply it was revealed that the CPGB had been unable to find any 'real revolutionaries' in India. The meeting then moved on to a list of complaints which Roy harboured against the CPGB.

Thus, in spite of the allegedly good relations which existed between Roy and the Dutt brothers, the former complained of the Party's tardiness in establishing an Indian Seamen's Union; of its witholding of information and interception of Roy's mail; of its 'imperialism' in seeking to monopolise the responsibility for India;and of Rajani Palme Dutt's failure to attend meetings of the Colonial Bureau in Paris.[49]

The differences between Roy and Palme Dutt were also communicated to the tiny Communist groups based in Bombay, Calcutta, Madras, Lahore, and the United Provinces. By December 1925 some 78 Communists were able to announce the formation of an Indian Party (apparently Clemens Dutt did not know whether to laugh or cry - but was certainly suspicious about this initiative). When Spratt was briefed by Clemens and D. Petrovsky - the Comintern's representative in the British Party - before leaving for India, the message conveyed was that the Communists should imitate their Chinese counterparts whose alliance with the bourgeois nationalists was as intimate as could be. The Indian Communists were thus required to work within the INC, infiltrate the existing trade unions and create Workers' and Peasants' Parties (WPP) as a 'legal cover' for the tiny Communist Party.[50] But at least until the time when Spratt and Bradley established themselves at the head of the CPI, conflict and confusion reigned because of the contradictory messages contained in Roy's *Future of Indian Politics* and Dutt's *Modern India*, which was published in Bombay in 1926.[51]

The first WPP was created in Bengal in February 1926, and held a second conference in December, just before the start of Saklatvala's successful tour of the country. The rapturous welcome with which Saklatvala was received undoubtedly helped the Communists. The British MP was able to address thousands of people at public rallies - particularly in Bombay - and engaged Gandhi in a highly-publicised epistolatory debate in which he exhorted the 'great soul' to renounce his reactionary social philosophy. When, after three months Saklatvala returned to Britain, his passport was modified to prevent a repetition of this episode. But the damage was done. More WPPs were set up in the course of 1927 and by 1928 the Communists had made real progress in the trade unions - particularly among the Bombay textile workers whom Saklatvala had addressed.

The Communist-led Girni Kamgar Union increased its membership from 324 to 54,000 during a six-month strike which ended in September 1928. Communist influence also spread to the railway workers, to the Burma Oil Company in Madras, and to the jute mills, paper mills, and municipalities in Bengal and Bombay. The Communist 'Broad Left' became the dominant wing of the AITUC in the same year, and Communists found their way on to its executive and on to the national committee of the INC. The Government of India now lamented that 'there was hardly a single public utility or industry which had not been affected in whole or in part by the wave of communism which had swept the country'.[52] Of the two hundred or so industrial disputes recorded in 1928, over one hundred took place in Bombay. The Viceroy, Lord Irwin, publicly expressed alarm at the growing Communist influence and served notice that he intended to stamp it out. At the end of the year an intercepted letter from M.N. Roy to the CPI was read to the Legislative Assembly. This fuelled the Red scare by revealing the Communists' tactic of hiding behind the WPPs. Though Clemens Dutt despatched this 'Assembly Letter' on Roy's behalf, the latter evidently could not resist another swipe at the CPGB in the course of his lecture on tactics.

By December 1928 the WPPs were based in Delhi, Meerut, Gorakhpur, Jhansi and Allahabad and the time was ripe to launch them on an all-India footing. The authorities, however, had already nipped in the bud a previous attempt at the establishment of strong

Communist organisation, when the Cawnpore Conspiracy Case of 1924 saw four defendants receive sentences of imprisonment - from the same judge who had sentenced 172 people to death after Chauri Chaura. Another crackdown might have been expected, and in March 1929 the Government acted - arresting 31 militants, including Spratt and Bradley, in different parts of the country. This proved to be the beginning of the Meerut Conspiracy Trial, which dragged on for over four years, much of the time during the period of the second Labour government. The Communists, naturally enough, did their best to publicise the repression as an aspect of social imperialism.

EMPIRE SOCIALISM

Even before the Meerut Trial the British Left had begun to take an interest in the empire, largely because of the defects of the Labour government. MacDonald's first administration exposed the absence of any distinctive Labour policy on the future of the colonies, and during the course of 1925, Lansbury, G. D. H. Cole, and John Wheatley were prominent among a group of leading left- wingers in the party who tried to find one. Lansbury argued that the approaching political dominance of the workers in Britain brought with it the responsibility 'to set before mankind a new idea of International relationships based on the commonweal'. Invoking the Soviet state as a model of multi-national, voluntary co-operation he concluded that:

> There is no reason for breaking up the British Empire any more than there is a reason for smashing our own national institutions. Our duty is to transform the British Empire of Domination into a Commonwealth of free nations, including within this Commonwealth those people who themselves desire to join us.

Lansbury went on to lay out the grandiose prospect before his readers of a system which 'at least within the Commonwealth ... production, distribution, and exchange of goods shall be organised for and on behalf of the community.'[53]

For the Communists it was axiomatic that this was all nonsense; the fact that the British Party had entertained similar thoughts in 1924 was now forgotten, and had the Communists been reminded of it, they would only have replied that it was evidence that the infant Party had hardly understood the first principles of Leninism. By the end of MacDonald's first government, Dutt at least had begun to rectify some of these shortcomings and was already talking as if the principle problem in British politics was the destruction of the Labour Left. If reformism was finished, or so he reasoned, the only people who stood between the British workers and revolution were those on the left who sounded radical but acted with respectful compliance to the *status quo*. Imperial policy was only a special case of this general principle - he had already concluded in 1924 that the Labour Left, 'when it comes to policy and expression ... are as much the slaves of the nation and the "Empire" and the rest of the cant as any'.[54] For Dutt, Lansbury's talk of socialising the empire was the nonsensical equivalent of socialising slavery since it neatly ignored the crucial relations of dominance on which the whole edifice had been constructed.[55]

This was by no means the end of the matter. The transformation of the empire into a commonwealth enshrining socialist principles was a prospect which appealed to the reformist Left, according to Dutt, because in reality the only way they could imagine dragging Britain out of the depressed, bellicose, cut-throat world of actually existing capitalism was by utilising the empire as a protected trading bloc. But Wheatley and his co-thinkers were influenced by the work of the maverick economist, J.A. Hobson, who had long believed that unemployment was a problem of 'underconsumption' - the lack of effective mass demand. This maldistribution of income, so the argument went, also blocked investment opportunities in the home market and drove surplus savings abroad in search of alternative outlets. Thus the existence of empire in its current form was inimical to conditions for the working class. By 1925 the ILP was converted to this view in so far as it now linked the problem of poverty in Britain to the growth of colonial competitors whose lower wage costs undercut domestic industries. Dutt could obviously agree, thus far, since he had deduced such a relationship for himself. But Wheatley, and others like him, reasoned that the only way British unemployment could be tackled in such a world was by turning the empire into a 'bloc against world capitalism'.[56] Thinking along these lines led some members of the left-wing Clyde group of MPs to vote in favour of imperial protection in the summer of 1925.

Empire socialism was thus for Dutt either a long-term woolly mystification or a short-term cover for social imperialism. And to make matters worse, in the same way that these nostrums for the colonial world ignored the power relationships of empire, the ILP developed a domestic programme for a 'Living Wage' in 1925, which also ignored the class relations of dominance. Dutt and his co-thinkers saw this class dominance as increasingly oppressive in the run up towards the General Strike. At the very time when all the economic indicators pointed, for capitalists, to wage cuts, unemployment, industrial speed-up, rationalisation, and a lurch into protectionism; the ILP conference had adopted the Living Wage programme or, as the Communists put it, the policy of 'socialism by kind permission'. On the very eve of the General Strike - a moment of great intensification of the class struggle for the Communists and an opportunity to nurture a revolutionary class consciousness - the ILP proposed to remedy unemployment by a future Labour government tackling defective demand with higher money wages and a programme of social reforms. This looked to Dutt like a wilful refusal to recognise the absence of any reformist opportunities in the deteriorating British economy. All the ILP programme could hope to achieve was to spread illusions in a spent reformism and thus prevent the militants from preparing with the Communists for the gathering storm.

After the defeat of the General Strike, the ILP itself injected a stronger class struggle rhetoric into the Living Wage proposals. But by now, of course, the British Communists - prodded incessantly by the Comintern - had turned to the offensive against their former allies in the labour movement. We saw in the previous chapter that Dutt was adamant that the General Strike had served to radicalise the British working class. Since May 1924, moreover, Dutt had championed the idea that reformism was so bankrupt that any close relationship with the socialist Left could be viewed as a contamination of the Communist Party. He needed no prompting from the Comintern therefore to stress, in the wake of the strike's defeat, that the Communists must prepare for a polarisation in British politics which would pit them against all shades of reformism as well as their more obvious enemies. The working class was now allegedly well in advance of the non-Communist Left on the road to revolutionary class conciousness.

After his public clash with J.T. Murphy on this issue in 1924, Dutt grounded his case in an economic analysis which - while obviously based on Lenin's apocalyptic prognoses for the imperialist epoch - focussed on the British conjuncture and the implications of the return to the Gold Standard. He was right, of course, to predict worsening economic conditions, and he foresaw a European-wide slump once American capital exports dried up, as abruptly became the case after the Wall Street crash of 1929. And Dutt also tried to make connections between these economic perspectives and developments in the colonies, particularly in India, where he expected the further advance of capitalist industry on the basis of capital exports from the increasingly stagnant developed economies of the West. Thus the old labour aristocracy was expected to fall from grace in Britain, precisely because a super-exploited proletariat was arising in India which rendered the labour aristocracy's relatively high wages a redundant luxury. On this basis the prospect for international working class solidarity and the erosion of imperialism was supposed to advance.

Given Dutt's guiding assumptions, then, his attempt to fuse domestic and imperial perspectives achieved a measure of success. But there the harmony ended. For while he prescribed an ultra- left stance in Britain, on the assumption of an explosion of class consciousness, Dutt was an advocate of continued collaboration with non-Communists in the colonial world. *Modern India* elaborated the orthodox Comintern strategy in relation to colonial nationalism despite its stress on the rapid industrialisation of the subcontinent; and meanwhile the policy of the CPGB sought to implement this policy in practice in India.

The CPGB's efforts to make contact with radicals abroad had resulted in rudimentary contacts with small groups in Egypt, India, Palestine and Ireland by 1925; and it was the British Party which first conceived of the idea of a grand congress in Europe which would bring nationalist elements from the colonies into contact with the metropolitan Left. Dutt was present in Brussels when this project was taken a stage further by the Congress of Oppressed Nationalities in February 1927. The preparatory work of establishing contact with nationalists was extended at the Brussels congress to include radicals from North Africa, Indonesia, Central America and the Caribbean. Such big fish as Nehru, Mohammed Hatta of Sarekat Islam, and the leaders of the Kuomintang in China had been drawn into the net in Brussels, alongside less well known nationalists such as Jomo Kenyatta of Kenya and General Sandino of Nicaragua. Though they kept chiefly to the background, the Brussels conference enabled Communists like Dutt and Ho Chi Minh to acquaint themselves with important figures in colonial politics.

None of them could have known that this network would soon be blown apart by a sharp change in Comintern policy. The next chapter will focus on this 'Third Period' in Comintern politics and show how the CPGB fought against its inauguration.

NOTES

1 At the eighth congress of the Russian Communist Party. See J. Degras (ed), *The Communist International, 1919-43*, Vol 1 1919-22, Cass, 1971, p139.
2 R. Archer, trans., *The Second Congress of the Communist International*, Vol 1, *op cit*, p111.
3 J. Degras (ed), *The Communist International*, *op cit*, p141.
4 F. Claudin, *The Communist Movement*, Penguin, Harmondsworth 1975, pp250-252; C. Keeble; *Britain and the Soviet Union 1917-89*, Macmillan 1990, pp82-3.
5 R. Archer, *op cit*, p110.
6 See M.N. Roy, 'The Empire and Revolution', *Labour Monthly*, 3, 4, October 1922, pp222-3; E. Roy, 'The Crisis of Indian Nationalism', *Labour Monthly*, 2, 2, February 1922, pp146-8; E. Roy, 'The Debacle of Gandhism', *Labour Monthly*, 3, 1, July 1922, pp32-43; E. Roy, 'The Awakening of India', *Inprecorr*, 2, 32-3, 5 May 1922; M.N. Roy,'The New Trend of Indian Nationalism', *Labour Monthly*, 6, 2, February 1924, pp 97-106.
7 E. Roy, 'The Awakening of India', *op cit*, p247.
8 M.N. Roy, 'The Empire and Revolution', *op cit*, pp222-3.
9 S. Saklatvala, 'India in the Labour World', *Labour Monthly*, 1, 5, November 1921, pp400-451.
10 Dutt made this claim in a letter to M. Ahmed reproduced in M. Ahmed, *Myself and the Communist Party of India*, National Book Agency, Calcutta 1970, pp479-80.
11 M.N. Roy, *India in Transition*, Nachiketa Publishers, Bombay 1971, pp84-5.
12 *Ibid*, p119 and p54.
13 *Ibid*, p40 and p204.
14 M.N. Roy, *The Future of Indian Politics*, Bishop, 1926 p9.
15 *Ibid*, p43.
16 M.N. Roy, *India in Transition*, *op cit*, pp203-4.
17 M.N. Roy, *The Future of Inidan Politics*, *op cit*, p47.
18 M.N. Roy, *The Aftermath of Non-Co-operation*, CPGB 1926, p83.
19 HMSO, *Communist Papers*, CMND 2682, 1926, pp83-4.
20 R.P. Dutt, *Modern India*, CPGB, 1927, p19.
21 *Ibid*, p30, p63, p129.
22 *Ibid*, pp73-4.
23 *Ibid*, p81.
24 *Ibid*, p88.
25 *Ibid*, p148.
26 *Ibid*, pp111-112.
27 *Ibid*, p172.
28 See S. McIntyre, *Imperialism and the British Labour Movement in the 1920s*, CPGB, 1974.

29 See R.C. Reinders, 'Racialism on the Left: E. D. Morel and the "Black Horror on the Rhine"', *International Review of Social History*, Vol 13, 1968, pp1-28.
30 J. Degras (ed), *The Communist International*, Vol 1, *op cit*, p139.
31 See 'The Draft Programme of the CPGB to the Comintern', *Communist Review*, 5, 1, May 1924, pp99-100.
32 See E.T. Wilson, *Russia and Black Africa Before World War Two*, Holmes and Meier, New York 1974, p140.
33 M.N. Roy, *Memoirs*, Allied Publishers, Bombay 1964, p348.
34 G. Padmore, Pan-Africanism or Communism? Dobson 1956, p313.
35 M. Bauml Duberman, *Paul Robeson*, Bodley Head 1989, p190.
36 P. Fryer, *Black People in the British Empire*, Pluto 1988, pp52- 3.
37 P. Buhle, *Marxism in the USA*, Verso 1987, p139.
38 G. Padmore, *Pan-Africanism or Communism?*, *op cit*, p346.
39 D. Goldsworthy, *Colonial Issues in British Politics, 1945-61* Clarendon, Oxford 1971, pp146-7.
40 *Report of the National Executive Committee*, presented to the National Party Congress May 17-19 1924, p24.
41 M. Squires, *Saklatvala*, *op cit*, p147.
42 A. Mitra, 'Middle Class Movement', *Seminar* New Delhi, Number 178: Marxism in India, June 1974, pp43-44.
43 D. Norman (ed), *Nehru: The First Sixty Years* Bodley Head 1965, p126.
44 S. Gopal, *Jawaharlal Nehru: A Biography*, Vol I, Cape 1975, p111.
45 P. Spratt, *Blowing-Up India*, *op cit*, pp21-2.
46 J.P. Haithcox, *Communism and Nationalism in India*, Princeton 1971, p15.
47 M.N. Roy, *Memoirs*, *op cit*, pp478-90.
48 J.P. Haithcox, *op cit*, pp28-32.
49 HMSO, *Communist Papers*, *op cit*, pp83-8.
50 P. Spratt, *op cit*, pp29-30.
51 S.R. Chowdhuri, *Leftist Movements in India, 1917-47*, South Asia Books, Calcutta 1976, p73; See also P.C. Joshi, 'R.P. Dutt and Indian Communists', *op cit*, p49.
52 B. Chandra *et al*, *India's Struggle For Independence*, Penguin, Harmondsworth 1989, p219.
53 G. Lansbury, 'Empire Day', *Lansbury's Labour Weekly*, 23 May 1925; Similar points were made by G.D.H. Cole in *Lansbury's Labour Weekly*, 26 Feb 1927.
54 R.P. Dutt, 'Notes of the Month', *Labour Monthly*, 6, 5,May 1924, p266.
55 R.P. Dutt, *Empire "Socialism"*, CPGB 1925, *passim*.
56 See D. Howell, *A Lost Left*, Manchester University Press, 1986, pp261-2.

4

COMMUNISTS ALONE

Even before the end of 1926, J.T. Murphy, erstwhile advocate of Communist collaboration with the left in the labour movement, had written off the ILP as the 'left-wing party of the bourgeoisie'.[1] Clearly, dissatisfaction with the united front policy was not confined to Dutt. On the contrary, a questioning of the old policy had spread within the Party leadership. It is significant, for example, that the Party's sole MP, Shapurji Saklatvala, and Harry Pollitt - arguably its most experienced member in the field of trade union work - were prominent in championing a more intransigent line in the course of 1927; these men were growing tired of a political line which took no account of the increasingly hostile measures which the labour and trade union organisations were taking against the Communists.

Of course the Comintern had sanctioned sweeping attacks on the Communists' former allies by insisting that 'the masses' were now well to the left of the likes of Maxton, Cook, Purcell, and company, and this hardly made the united front policy any easier to apply. But if the fiction of mass radicalisation had been made official, it was at least consistent with the implicit logic of the united front since the whole policy presupposed that the Communists would actually gain support by opposing the official leaders from the far left. The difference, by the end of 1927, was that Dutt - supported by Pollitt and Saklatvala - was no longer cautioning, as he had in 1924, that mass political consciousness in Britain lagged well behind the expectations of the Comintern. In all probability, however, support for the Comintern's perspectives in the British Party derived, not so much from a real conviction of a mass surge to the Left, but - as the examples of Saklatvala and Pollitt suggest - from the frustration and anger of having to operate in a country where the leadership of the labour movement grew more conservative as the 'objective' situation, according to theory, predicted class polarisation.

As early as October 1926 Dutt had been moved to compose a letter to the miner's leader A.J. Cook which, while expressing 'deep affection' and his 'joy and appreciation' at all Cook had achieved, was chiefly concerned to warn him against a continuing drift to the

Right.[2] In other words even Cook, who needed no lessons in class consciousness from Dutt, had not been prepared to follow the Communist line in a ruthless denunciation of the General Council of the TUC. In the absence then of any evidence from such militants as Cook of an advancing militancy, Dutt leaned heavily on predictions of approaching catastrophe - the development of an economic crisis which must result, sooner or later, in an explosion of mass discontent.

In 1927 he estimated that British workers had lost some five billion pounds in wage reductions since 1921. The root of British economic problems, Dutt reasoned, was the contraction of the world market as rival imperialist powers and new sources of capitalist industry (such as India) encroached on what was left of global trade, in the context of an international lurch into protectionism. Britain's initial leadership in industrialisation, moreover, had become a handicap, because the legacy of outdated capital and technique, far from leading to a national strategy of modernisation, was allowed to weigh heavily on the country's powers of recuperation. According to Dutt, the preponderance of Britain's world financial and imperial interests precluded the necessary investment in domestic industries. Unlike Keynes, Dutt refused to see these problems as essentially short-term structural adjustments in the transition to new industries, because he believed that any new international division of labour was predicated on the stability of imperialism - a contradiction in terms for a Leninist. He concluded from all of this that:

> *In the period of capitalist decline a reformist leadership and party has no longer any basis, and can only maintain itself for a while by acting more and more openly as the decoy agent of the capitalist class in the tasks of repression and stabilisation on the backs of the workers, that is, in the tasks of capitalism in its decline* (emphasis in original).[3]

Thus it will be seen immediately that, although Dutt's analysis invoked conjunctural evidence and structural problems peculiar to Britain, his argument ultimately rested on the arguments in Lenin's *Imperialism*. I have already stressed the importance of these arguments for the very *raison d'etre* of the Communist movement, so I will not labour the point here. Nevertheless we can better appreciate the importance which Dutt's generation attached to this *weltenschauung* - with its verdict on the moribundity of capitalism and corresponding redundancy of reformism and parliamentary democracy - by glancing at a letter Dutt received from his wife in 1928:

> I have just been reading Lenin's *Imperialism*'. I just devoured it. What a long time it has been witheld from me! I don't believe that it has been properly read. Such a fountain of crystal clearness. And - oh God - how all the modern problems have been worrying us and there is nothing to worry [*sic*]. Once Lenin is properly understood the subsequent simply follows. Only we must learn to look with Lenin's eyes. What a lot of unnecessary thinking work we had done.[4]

It only needs to be added that the hero worship of Lenin, and the faith in the written word, exhibited here was not that of a starry eyed adolescent but of an experienced revolutionary and cosmopolitan intellectual.

Not all the British Communist leaders were in the same league of gnostic insight as the exiled Dutts, but they certainly shared the conviction that the inevitability of Communist mass support stemmed from the futility of all rival socialist strategies in a context of epochal capitalist decline. The Comintern identified fascism in 1923 as 'an international phenomenon' based on 'petty bourgeois reaction' which the ruling class was prepared to utilise in order to save itself from the socialist revolution; and this only served to emphasise that it was the crisis of liberal capitalism rather than the advent of socialism which the Communists regarded as inevitable.[5] Fascism was recognised, in short, as a last resort which signified the absolute sway of capitalism 'in its bloodiest form'. To this extent, fascism provided evidence to support Lenin's belief that bourgeois democracies would be replaced by openly authoritarian forms of bourgeois rule. And in 1924 fascism was linked with social democracy, when the Comintern ruled that they were 'two sides of a single instrument of capitalist dictatorship'. Such a conclusion was perfectly consistent with Lenin's depiction of reformism as an auxiliary of the bourgeois state inside the workers' movement. Later in 1924 Stalin added his own twist to this debate when he pronounced fascism and social democracy 'twins' - complementary instruments of capitalist stabilisation.[6]

The apocalyptic world inhabited by the Communists was far from being confined to their own imaginations. On any particularpoint of Leninist doctrine there was no shortage of supporting evidence. Social democratic violence against the German Communist Party (KPD) in 1919, for example, lent credence to the Comintern's dismal view of reformism, as did the subsequent forced removal from office of the provincial government in Saxony in 1923, not to mention the failure of reformist movements everywhere to begin the transition to socialism. In 1936, Dutt was able to look back on the events which succeeded the post-war revolutionary wave and find a period of unstable equilibrium of revolution and counter revolution involving an 'unbroken chain' of deep-seated revolutionary unrest and intense class struggle. The armed suppression of the Workers' Governments in Saxony and Thuringia, he observed, 'was followed by the Esthonian uprising in 1924, the colonial struggles in Syria and Morocco in 1925, the advance of the Chinese revolution through 1925-1927, the British General Strike of 1926, the Vienna rising of 1927, the sharpening German situation of partial civil war through 1929-1933, the Indian mass struggle of 1930-1934, the Spanish Revolution from 1931, the February days in France in 1934, the armed fighting in Austria and in the Asturias in 1934, and the new stage of the Spanish Revolution to-day'.[7]

With the exception of the General Strike, however, the British case stubbornly refused to fit in with Communist expectations. Yet this did not prevent Dutt from predicting in 1925 that fascism 'will play a very big role in Britain'. As usual Dutt's analysis showed him to be a far better analyst of the ideologies, motivations and interests of elements in the British ruling class than of 'the masses'; thus evidence of embryonic fascism was found in everything from the Boy Scouts to the celebration of Empire Day. Dutt's biggest problem of incomprehension was, of course, the Labour Party, which he never understood, whether he was concerned with leaders or led. The compass of Comintern theory was too narrow to cope with national 'peculiarities' on this scale. Hence, following the International's lead in the analysis of European social democracy, he purported to find evidence of Labour's 'direct friendliness to Fascism', but was reduced to the tortuous argument that it had nurtured the problem by encouraging exaggerated hopes for peaceful, constitutional change.[8] In fact the British Communists were more often to be found arguing the opposite of this - damning Labour for its timidity and retreat from the reform programme of 1923.

What had most certainly changed since the first MacDonald government was the Labour method of treating the Communists. The drive to expel communists from the Labour Party began in 1924, when Party members were debarred from individual membership of the Labour Party and trade unions were asked not to nominate Communists as delegates to Labour organisations. These measures having failed to exclude the Communists, the Labour Party next resorted to the disaffiliation of its local organisations where these had refused to comply with the 1924 ruling. The resulting campaign saw twenty seven borough or divisional Labour parties expelled by 1929, most of them going in 1926 and 1927. The same aversion to the Communists was displayed in relation to the National Unemployed Workers' Committee Movement, which had been organising 'hunger marches' of the unemployed under Communist leadership since 1922. The atmosphere changed in the wake of theGeneral Strike and any hope of joint action with the TUC was quashed. Similarly the Minority Movement was anathematised by the TUC. In 1926 the General Council ordered trades councils to refrain from affiliation to the Minority Movement and in 1927 the General and Municipal Workers Union suspended Communists and disenfranchised dissident branches. More unions followed suit in 1928.

The weakening of the militant left after the defeat of the General Strike was not confined to the Labour Party's drive against the Communists. After all, the outcome of the confrontation enabled many employers to victimise militants with impunity, and the Conservative government exploited the situation by introducing the Trade Disputes Act in 1927 to restrict picketing and secondary strikes and weaken the unions' links with the Labour Party. Between 1927 and 1929 the number of recorded strikes and working days lost through strikes fell to the lowest figure since such records had begun forty years earlier. In the context of defeat and retreat, the leadership of the unions sought influence by proposing joint talks with the employers in 1927 so that they could together 'speak for industry as a whole'. For the Communists this was class collaboration at its most blatant. Even leading socialist intellectuals on the left of the movement were infected by the new realism, and openly questioned the validity of slogans such as the right to work or proposals for nationalisation; in the context of economic depression there was simply no point, it was now reasoned, in taking over bankrupt industries or advocating 'the useless employment of redundant labour'.[9] There was thus an evident lack of socialist direction which culminated, of course, in the paralysis of the second, disastrous, Labour government of 1929-1931.

Dutt was quick to detect a trend to more authoritarian arrangements in these various developments - whether in the corporatist talk of the TUC, the campaigns against the Communists, the merger boom of 1927 and accompanying proposals for massive industrial rationalisation, the legislation restricting strikes, or the international drift towards protectionism. They seemed all of a piece with state capitalism and an attempt to resolve the post-war world crisis by a combination of domestic repression and an international drive towards war. The Russians fed this perspective of impending catastrophe with their own warnings of anti-Soviet war preparations, which reached fever-pitch when Britain severed diplomatic relations in 1927 and the Anglo-Russian Joint Advisory Committee was suspended by the TUC. But the international picture as presented by the Comintern was also pregnant with Anglo- American conflict, tension among the European Powers and a war involving Japan for dominance of the Pacific.[10]

While the original Communist world-view of 'crisis-class polarisation-civil war' remained as relevant as ever on paper, in practice few in the British Party thought in terms of the 'actuality of the revolution'. Dutt's writings from the summer of 1924 suggest that he was the exception. When the Party as a whole met for its ninth congress in October 1927, it reiterated familiar perspectives envisaging the return of a Labour government with 'a more definite Socialist programme'. In so doing, they had placed themselves at odds with the official Comintern strategy but it was only after this congress had finished that a delayed telegram from the Comintern arrived,followed by a letter from Bukharin, which called for a reconsideration of the Party's relationship with the Labour Party. On 15 December 1927 leaders of the CPGB were called to a meeting of the Presidium of the ECCI in Moscow where they were told that the Party must demand 'a revolutionary workers' Government' - a position based on the assumption of rising class consciousness and struggle. This bore 'no relation whatever to the situation actually in existence in Britain', as Gallacher remarked, but was based on settled conclusions which the Comintern had reached well before the arrival of the British representatives in Moscow.[11] But the objections of Gallacher and Albert Inkpin only succeeded in deferring the required changes until February 1928 when a special Commission could be convened to settle the matter at the Ninth Plenum of the ECCI.

In the meantime, a majority of the Central Committee of the CPGB decided on 9 January 1928, after a three-day debate, to continue to call for a Labour government and reinstatement of the Communists inside the labour movement. Communists would only oppose Labour candidates in exceptional circumstances. There was, according to the central committee, no difference between the circumstances of 1928 and those of 1920 to warrant dumping the united front tactics originally advocated by Lenin. If anything, 1928 was not so 'objectively' revolutionary as 1920 had been.[12] This position was upheld by 17 votes to 6, with Pollitt, Saklatvala and J.T. Murphy the most prominent dissidents. Pollitt revealed at this meeting that Stalin and Bukharin had both called for a new line on the Labour Party as early as October 1927, during private discussions in Moscow. It was at this meeting, as the central committee minutes show, that Pollitt learned to regard Labour as 'a third bourgeois party'. Dutt's greater proximity to the Comintern apparatus would suggest that he also picked up on the hardening mentality in Moscow at an early stage in the process - a development even more likely in the case of Murphy who was just coming to the end of a two year stint with the Comintern secretariat in Moscow. It only needs to be added that in Dutt's case the trend within the Comintern chimed in with his own sectarian views.

Dutt, therefore, was quick to elaborate the new alternative position - no doubt guided by the attitude of the ECCI's Small Commission, which had been made known in December 1927. On 19 January 1928 he explained to Pollitt that the continued decline of capitalism in Britain had vindicated the 'basic position' of the Minority Movement - namely that it was faced with 'revolutionary tasks' which demanded for their accomplishment 'the complete transformation of existing trade union organisation and leadership from the old basis of veiled collaboration with capitalism to a new basis of revolutionary class struggle'. Furthermore, he insisted that the Minority Movement had become the 'sole opposition' and that its 'supreme objective' was to win over the trade unions to the struggle for a 'Revolutionary Workers' Government'. The most important weapon in this struggle would be the political General Strike. On Dutt's reckoning, 'the exposure of the pseudo-left leadership since the betrayal of 12 May is complete ... they now stand out openly as supporters of Industrial Peace and allies of capitalism'. For good measure he reinforced his apocalyptic vision with a reminder that 'Britainis driving most powerfully in the direction of war'. He also added, when Pollitt came to visit him in Brussels, that if they won their battle - now with the support of the Comintern - he 'would guarantee that he [Pollitt] would be General Secretary of the Party in twelve months'.[13]

Pollitt, thus briefed, now scripted a minority statement on 24 January briefly outlining the position that Labour had become a third capitalist party with which the CP should should have no truck - abandoning the affiliation campaign, the National Left

Wing Movement, and electoral support for Labour candidates in recognition of this transformation. A copy of this statement was sent to Dutt who drafted his reply two days later. Dutt supported Pollitt's position invoking 'the continuous revolutionisation of the British working class, as pointed out in every International Thesis on the British situation during the present period'. The appropriate position on the Labour Party was to be determined by recognition of this process, in conjunction with the fact - as Bukharin had pointed out at the fifteenth congress of the CPSU - that Labour had tasted power and had thus been exposed as a prop to the system it was meant to oppose. Disillusionment with Labour proceeded from this ignominous experience of office, but to wait until the majority of the working class had arrived at this point would amount to 'a dangerously passive, defeatist view of our role': Dutt thus proposed CP opposition to prominent Labour candidates to the maximum extent of the Party's resources. But noting the Small Commission's lack of clarity on this issue, he argued that where the CP was unable to field candidates the correct line to be adopted in such constituencies would require further discussion. His own preference was conditional support for Labour candidates where Communists could not be found to stand - the condition being that they should support the Communist Party's demands. This was tantamount to a policy of abstention - though Dutt's blindness to the political realities in Britain may have prevented him from seeing that his conditions would be universally rejected by Labour candidates. Dutt was convinced that the policy of affiliation was 'finished' and also wanted the Party to oppose the trade union political levy and demand that it be given instead to the CP. This latter demand, more than anything else, displayed the extent to which he misunderstood the situation in Britain.

Unlike Pollitt, however, Dutt saw merit in persisting with the CP's entryist operation as co-ordinated by the National Left Wing Movement. The Party had set this up after the Labour Party's annual conference of 1925, when the exclusion of Communists from individual membership had been upheld from the previous year. It was designed to seduce the Labour Left into joint work with the Communists and succeeded, up to the General Strike, in fostering some sort of united front; in 1926 the circulation of the CP's *Sunday Worker*, which was the voice of the Left Wing Movement, rose to 85,000. It thus reached over eight times as many people as the Party's peak membership for that year. Dutt had never been happy with the dilution of Communist principles which he perceived in all of this, but now recommended persistence with the entryist groups in order to expose reformism from within. This required tighter Party control over such groups and a recruitment drive to bring the periphery of supporters into the Communist ranks.[14]

This was all of a piece with the declaration of war which headvocated in his earlier missive to Pollitt, on the role of the Minority Movement. Dutt's aim was to effect 'a complete change of leadership ... a complete purge of the reformist traitors in office, both locally and nationally'.[15] Without regard to the actual politics of the British labour movement, Dutt was in effect restating the perspectives on which the Communist movement had initially been launched. The best that can be said in his defence is that these perspectives derived from a purportedly scientific analysis of the imperialist epoch, which the Comintern never revised and which was now revived as an immediate guide to tactics by the most authoritative leaders of the movement in the shape of Stalin and Bukharin. Pollitt, no doubt motivated by the adverse practical problems which Communists encountered in the labour and trade union organisations in Britain, simply deferred to Dutt's version of the new Moscow line, and appended his own signature to the document drafted in Brussels on 26 January. He thereby became an advocate of the Moscow fiction - first articulated by Dutt in May 1926 - of mass 'revolutionisation' in Britain, a position Pollitt had omitted to mention in his statement of 24 January. The Dutt- Pollitt 'Alternative Proposals' were then put before the Party leadership.

Dutt, however, prejudged the issue, and committed the ultimate sin - breaking Party discipline - by publicly announcing the advent of a 'New Phase of the Labour Party' in the pages of *Labour Monthly* at the end of the month. More than anything else this statement - which in the circumstances was no more than a 'factional' view and was angrily denounced as such by Rothstein - testifies to his confidence that the minority position in the British Party was already the 'official' view in Moscow. Thus he confidently asserted that the 'final testing and discrediting' of reformism was underway, and that the radicalisation of the masses proceeded from the closing down of every avenue for peaceful, constitutional change. Labour had allegedly already displayed its 'essential unity with the whole mechanism of State and foreign policy and empire'. It was thus 'the third party of the bourgeoisie' and it was necessary to 'advance to the offensive against it'. As usual, Dutt struck a note of logical necessity, and even managed to find support for his arguments in the evidence of Labour's actual growth:

> From the liberal-constitutionalist-democratic outlook must necessarily follow, more and more clearly as the party grows larger, acceptance of the existing order (pending constitutional change), acceptance of the existing state, acceptance of the task of maintaining law and order, and so finally complete acceptance of capitalism, imperialism, class co-operation and coalition - in complete contradiction of the original aspiration of independent working class politics.[16]

Furious charges of factionalism greeted this piece from the majority of the CP's leaders and Dutt was censured by the Party Executive. Two months later the vote of censure was rescinded in response to pressure from the Comintern.[17]

The objections of the Party leadership were thus to no avail. Gallacher and J.R. Campbell did their best to defend the CPGB's position at the Ninth Plenum in Moscow in February 1928, but they found themselves up against the Russians, supported by leaders of the Comintern apparatus such as Togliatti, as well as the British minority for whom Page Arnot was the spokesman. The CPGB emerged from this meeting obliged to call for a'Revolutionary Workers' Government' and required to denounce Labour as an auxiliary of the bourgeoisie, and to campaign for local control of the politicial levy which the unions paid to the Labour Party. But while the Plenum ruled in favour of standing Communists against leading 'traitors' in the Labour Party, the proposal to abstain in constituencies where there was no Communist candidate was rejected, as was Dutt's argument to drop the affiliation campaign. This was by no means the end of the matter, however.

The real authors of the New Line in Moscow had their own agenda, with Stalin's faction moving towards a policy of all-out terror against the peasantry and rapid industrialisation of the Soviet economy. Opponents of this policy inside the CPSU, organised around Bukharin, would be utterly crushed in due course, but Stalin would not emerge as the omnipotent general secretary until 1929. During 1928 this internal struggle over a move to a more sectarian, leftist position in the Soviet Union, overlapped with the changes in Comintern policy described above; the Stalinists were pressing for the most intransigent line, and Bukharin's leadership of the Comintern was already being undermined when he presided over the sixth congress of the International (17 July-1 September 1928). In reality this meeting was the occasion of two congresses. As Stephen Cohen observes, 'rumours swept the congress as Stalin's agents whispered of Bukharin's "right deviation" and "political syphilis", and that he was condemned to Alma Ata, Trotsky's place of exile.[18] After two weeks the 'corridor congress' had grown so clamorous that the Soviet Politburo felt compelled to issue a collective denial of a split in its ranks. No one seems to have believed the disclaimer, and the "anti-Bukharin caucus" went on unabated. Thus the move to the 'left' was still in process when the congress ended, and the New Line was subject to repeated modification in the course of 1929, as the Stalinists consolidated their grip in Russia.

The external impetus for sectarianism does not mean, however, that genuine supporters of an intransigent leftism were absent from the Communist Parties. In Britain it is clear that a majority of the London district of the CPGB - led by such people as Reg Groves of the Balham branch - wanted to go further than the Ninth Plenum, and in April 1928 they demanded the liquidation of the National Left Wing Movement, as well as abstention in constituencies where there was no Communist candidate, and an end to the affiliation campaign and the payment of the political levy. These demands were raised again at the July central committee only to be rejected. By the autumn, however, the Party leadership was compelled to open a discussion on these issues in the run up to the British Party's tenth congress of January 1929. By this time, the Comintern itself had ruled against voting for Labour candidates, at its sixth congress, and an article by Murphy, who had recently returned from Moscow, signalled in November 1928 that a change was required on the issues of affiliation, the political levy and the National Left Wing Movement.[19] In the same month the central committee gave way over affiliation, but the ultra-leftists in the Party were still not satisfied and - no doubt emboldened by the drive against the 'Right danger' inside the Comintern - insisted on the liquidation of the National Left Wing Movement and opposition tothe payment of the political levy. In January 1929 Dutt for the first time openly announced his change of mind, by adding his voice to the clamour against the National Left Wing Movement.[20]

There can be no doubt that throughout this period the sectarian minority inside the CPGB was continuously prodded along by the Stalinists in the Comintern leadership. Murphy was a useful medium in this respect having been resident in Moscow during the crucial period. So too was Dutt's protegé William Rust of the Young Communist League (YCL), also attached to the 'centre' as a member of the secretariat of the Young Communist International. Along with Pollitt, Rust was one of only three British Communists on the

Presidium of the ECCI. One has only to add that Pollitt and Dutt emerged in 1929, as the leaders of the Party and the picture seems complete; obedient Stalinists rewarded for services rendered. But this conclusion is a little too simple.

CONTROVERSY OVER INDIA

We have already seen that the ultra-leftism sanctioned by the Comintern had genuine supporters inside the CPGB - none more so than Dutt. But even as the Comintern was transformed into an instrument of Stalin's faction of the CPSU, British Communists asserted themselves in open opposition to the international leadership over the question of colonial policy. This was not the behaviour of automatons.

The debate was opened by the Comintern economist Eugene Varga in March 1928, when he attacked the Dutt-Roy thesis concerning the alleged rapid industrialisation of India arguing instead that imperialism acted as an obstacle to modernisation in the colonies. At the same time Varga insisted that the colonial bourgeoisie was unfit to lead the anti-imperialist struggle, a role which the working class (that is, the Communists) would have to assume directly.[21] At the eighth congress of the CPGB in 1926, however, the British Party had reaffirmed its commitment to the tactical line associated with Lenin:

> The forces of the movement for emancipation in the colonies are not limited to a sentiment amongst the toilers or to small circles or parties of the Comintern ... Revolutionary nationalist democratic movements exist side by side with the revolutionary proletarian organisations ... We must at all times look for a united front with those who are oppressed and are honestly fighting oppression.[22]

As against Roy, Dutt had always maintained that Gandhi represented petty bourgeois rather than feudal and big capitalist interests in the leadership of the Indian National Congress; indeed this was the position hitherto upheld by the Russians, and even included in the *Large Soviet Encyclopaedia* of 1929.[23] Dutt now reaffirmed this long-standing orientation in his reply to Varga in June 1928, claiming that the national bourgeoisie, and especially the petty bourgeoisie, had a leading role to play in the anti-imperialist struggle. He was equally adamant that India was subject to a process of industrialisation, observing that this was responsible for the growth of the Indian working class.[24]

But Varga's argument proved to be merely the opening shot in a campaign to discredit the anti-imperialist united front and to justify a policy of intransigent opposition to all who refused to follow the Communist line in the colonies. It reproduced, in other words, the essentials of the New Line as applied to advanced capitalist countries. Just as the one denounced reformists and especially left reformists as social fascists, so did the other denounce the nationalists and especially the leftnationalists as collaborators with imperialism. The direct inspiration for this new colonial policy was the recent collapse of the Comintern's policy in China where the Party had been allied to the nationalist Kuomintang until the latter began to shoot Communists in 1927. Stalin had been an enthusiastic supporter of the earlier policy but was now distancing himself from it.

But it is arguable that the intimate alliance with nationalists, first fashioned by the Communists in Indonesia within Sarekat Islam, and known in Comintern jargon as the 'bloc within' - should never have been reproduced in China, where the Kuomintang controlled the armed forces of the nationalist movement.[25] The tactic of working within a nationalist movement in order to capture it from the inside had certainly been an effective strategy in Indonesia, where Communist influence had grown rapidly. But, as Stalin observed, the purpose of the exercise had been to squeeze the nationalist movement like a lemon until it was ready to be tossed aside. The trouble was that in China it was the nationalists who controlled the armed forces and it was the Communists who were tossed aside. In reality this experience was a vivid example showing that tactics successfully adopted in one region could not be easily applied in another. But this specificity was ignored by the Comintern. The debacle in China - which incidentally was blamed on the local leadership, including M.N. Roy, who had the misfortune to be on the spot as a member of Borodin's team of Comintern agents - prompted a repudiation of the alliance strategy and the wholesale adoption of an ultra-leftist orientation similar, ironically, to the one which had been advocated by M.N. Roy in 1920.

Yet in India, as we saw in chapter three, the alliance strategy was making real progress by the end of 1928, notwithstanding government repression which had only served to increase the prestige of the Communists in nationalist circles. Dutt's position had been vindicated. Although insistent that British policy was to industrialise India under the control of British finance capital, he had allowed for such contradictions in the policy as to permit the Indian bourgeoisie a genuine, though unreliable, role in the nationalist struggle. But in 1928 his Comintern detractors lumped Dutt in with Roy as an exponent of an economic theory of 'decolonisation', according to which the industrialisation of India would lead to the relaxation of British rule and eventual self-government. Dutt had never argued this position, but that did not prevent an official repudiation of *Modern India* on these grounds at the sixth congress of the Comintern. By a Byzantine twist, Dutt himself had been asked to present the theses which contained this rebuttal, but he managed to evade the responsibility on health grounds and the task fell to Kuusinen.[26]

The argument which the sixth congress endorsed, frankly, made no sense. Kuusinen told the delegates that capitalism had a vested interest in keeping the colonies in a condition of economic backwardness and dependence and was only interested in cheap raw materials and markets for industrial goods from the metropolis. But if this was the case, why should the colonial bourgeoisie collaborate with imperialism, and how could the colonial working class grow to become a hegemonic force in the independence struggle? With the exception of Murphy, the British Party leaders stuck to their guns, pointing out these contradictions in Kuusinen's theses, and countering with the argument that it was a 'general law of capitalist development' that the export of capital from the advanced sectors of the world economy involuntarily creates future economic rivals out of the backward colonies.[27] All but four of the eighteen members of the British delegation voted against Kuusinen's theses.

Macfarlane tells us that British opposition to Kuusinen's *The Revolutionary Movement in the Colonies* was not based on the inapplicability of the New Line to the colonies, but rather on the grounds that Kuusinen's political requirements - strengthening of the working class inside the Indian Communist Party, proletarian leadership of the peasantry, exposure of reformists in the Congress leadership - were consistent with their own economic analyses, not those adopted by the Comintern.[28] But while some members of the British delegation certainly found this a useful debating point, it is clear from Dutt's reply to Varga in June 1928 that he was as equally opposed to the change in tactics as to the economic analysis that went with it. Not only had he asserted that industrialisation was 'inevitable', even if it had latterly slowed down, he had insisted that British policy was determined to keep the process *'under British control'*, and that political friction between the capitalists of both countries derived from this fact, as well as the short-term factors responsible for the recent diminution of British capital exports.[29] Dutt even detected a 'sharpening of opposition' signified by the swing to the left at the Madras Congress in 1927, the recent adoption of the language of 'complete national independence', the decision to affiliate to the League Against Imperialism, and the nationalist condemnation of British war preparations against the Soviet Union.

Dutt was, of course, perfectly right. The nationalist movement in India was stung into action by Lord Birkenhead's announcement in 1927 of a commission of constitutional enquiry under Sir John Simon, to investigate the possibilities of further political reform on the subcontinent. Not one Indian was to serve on the Simon Commission, and its work was duly boycotted by the Congress. The British Labour Party discredited itself in the eyes of the nationalists by agreeing to participate (in the person of Clement Attlee), a decision which for Jawaharlal Nehru, at least, could only reinforce the impression of the Labour leaders as sanctimonious and canting humbugs.[30] Dutt was well aware of Nehru's growing radicalism. The Brussels Congress of Oppressed Nationalities had helped enormously in converting him to a Leninist theory of imperialism[31] and the following autumn Nehru returned from Moscow 'deeply impressed' by the achievements of the Bolsheviks.[32] By the end of 1927 Nehru was ready to join forces with other radical elements in the INC - notably Subhas Chandra Bose - to form the Independence for India League, to act as a pressure group within the nationalist movement campaigning for complete independence.

Progress in India could also be measured by the growth of Communist influence in the nascent unions during 1928, and even by the crackdown heralded by the Meerut Conspiracy Trial, which succeeded in projecting Dutt and Roy as behind-the-scenes plotters for independence - heroes, in short. Nehru acted for the Communist defendants at Meerut, and unsuccessfully lobbied theBritish TUC to come to the aid of Indian trade unionism. Meanwhile the CPGB's Meerut propaganda made much of the second Labour government's 'social imperialism' and worried the Party's enemies.[33] Dutt and his colleagues could derive some satisfaction from all of this, but their greatest achievement was to have managed, by 1928, to launch the long-planned All-India Workers' and Peasants' Party (WPP). But even before the end of the sixth Comintern congress in 1928 it was clear that the Kuusinen policy was determined to throw all this away. And by 1929, when the new sectarianism was in full flood, the Communists succeeded in driving their allies out of the League Against Imperialism, and out of the unions which the Communists controlled; the new policy also led to the abandonment of the WPPs on the grounds that they were always likely to degenerate into petty bourgeois organisations. Stalin announced to the sixteenth congress of the CPSU that Gandhi was and always had been an assistant of the bourgeoisie and that Gandhism represented 'the teachings of the cowardly anti-revolutionary bourgeoisie, linked up with the landlord system and in deadly fear of a national revolution'.[34]

In fact, just as Stalin came to these conclusions, Gandhi was ready to issue an ultimatum to the effect that unless dominion status arrived by the end of 1929 Congress would campaign for complete independence. The Communists had thus been handed an unprecedented agitational opportunity, which the Comintern's new policy prevented them from exploiting. When the second great non-co-operation campaign began at the beginning of 1930, the Communists stood aloof, while denouncing the Independence for India League's programme as all 'confusion and twaddle'.

THE THIRD PERIOD

The British Party came to heel in relation to the new colonial policy, because there was no choice for the individuals concerned other than to leave the movement or be expelled from it. Roy himself was expelled in July 1929, a victim of Stalin's struggle with Bukharin, and his own, ill-timed, conversion to the united front. Here was a lesson for any doubters elsewhere, all the more poignant in view of Roy's continued admiration for Stalin and the Soviet Union, despite his occupation of the political wilderness beyond the Party. Discipline required active support of the line - even sullen acquiesence would not do (though it is noteworthy that the usually prolific Dutt was less effusive about the Comintern's colonial line in the period 1929-35 than he was either before or after).

Some indication of this is provided by the fact that, of the thirty six articles on India published in *Labour Monthly* between January 1929 and December 1935, Dutt provided just one. Yet in these years the Comintern line drove away socialist and nationalist contributors - the sort Dutt had carefully cultivated since the journal's inception - and made *Labour Monthly* more than ever dependent on Communist writers. Having been publicly rebuked for *Modern India* by the Comintern, Dutt may well have genuinely reconsidered the economics of imperialism. Certainly when questioned years later about this episode Dutt accepted that he had been wrong to believe that the industrialisation of India was possible under imperialism. According to an account which Dutt gave to the Indian Communist Muzzafar Ali, Roy visited him in Brussels immediately after the sixth congress, proposing to fight the international leadership in an alliance with other dissidents around Brandler in Germany and Doriot in France. Dutt refused to join the faction and 'informed him that [he] considered the criticism and line of the Sixth Congress to be correct'.[35] On the matter of the tactics to be pursued in India, however, Dutt had vigorously opposed the Comintern, as we have seen.

No doubt Kuusinen's international analysis helped Dutt and his co-thinkers to suspend their disbelief about the new tactical orientation in the colonies. Like Lenin before him, Kuusinen was careful to situate the tactical issue in the context of the overarching conflict between the Soviet Union and the capitalist states. This was the paramount factor, and the good Communist would do nothing to weaken the Soviet side, now perceived to be in especial danger from imperialist attack. It was time to take to the offensive - and nobody had been more adamant about this than Dutt, convinced as he was that a breakthrough was in the making in Britain.

The sense of urgency, danger, and escalating crisis - always present in Dutt's writings - now reached fever pitch. Even in so pedestrian and nebulous a document as *Labour and the Nation*, the Labour Party's new programme of 1928, Dutt found evidence 'of the whole present line of the Second International, and of the whole present tendency of World Capitalism'. Readers of the *Sunday Worker* in June 1928 may have been alarmed to discover that the programme, largely written by the moralist R.H. Tawney, was 'a programme of State Capitalism'. World capitalism, warned Dutt, sought 'reorganisation, amalgamation and intensified large-scale technique' and would produce 'intensified world competition, intensified war preparation and eventually - as the necessary culminating step of capitalist world stabilisation - war on the Soviet Union'.[36] Thus, in the tea leaves provided by Tawney, Dutt purportedly discovered 'the meaning of the new Labour programme' - 'Coalition-State Capitalism-War'.

This was the line of approaching cataclysm that Dutt had been preaching ever since he began his exile in Brussels. The sixth congress merely sanctioned it and provided Dutt with the authority to harangue his less sectarian colleagues. And the opportunity for Dutt to assume the role of theoretical guide was provided by the continuing uncertainty about where the New Line would lead, as well as his unwavering conviction that revolutionary openings were brewing. Dutt thus played a prominent role in harassing the hapless realists of the British central committee as the new policy took shape. Throughout 1928 his Notes of the Month stridently insisted on the growing polarisation in Britain, where a leftward-moving working class was bound to separate from an increasingly authoritarian and pro-capitalist Labour bureaucracy.

Dutt deftly depicted the transformation of Labour as inextricably connected to the state capitalist reorganisation of the economy. As the year drew to an end he used press predictions of a future coalition government to signify that 'the three parties ... are turned in reality into a single factor - the different component elements of the single capitalist bloc'.[37] The ILP, meanwhile, had merely demonstrated the futility of a loyal oppositionist policy within the Labour Party, emerging from a year-long 'Hamlet-like process of introspection and self-questioning' only to discover that the scope for dissidence was 'more and more exiguous and precarious'.[38] Former major figures of the ILP, such as Snowden, were now taking their leave of it; having secured a place in 'the world ofbourgeois statesmanship' they were now ready to kick away the ladder that helped to get them there - 'the ladder humbly craving', Dutt sneered, 'that they may still be "personal friends"'. That Maxton and Brockway had frightened off the likes of Snowden by consorting with A.J. Cook and indulging in radical rhetoric, only served, according to Dutt, to support Oswald Mosley's observation of 'faded cynicism', that 'MacDonald made an appeal to one section of the community with incomparable skill, and Maxton and Cook appealed to the working class as no one else could'.[39] In reality, Dutt insisted, MacDonald's policy was identical to ILP policy save only for the 'familiar eunuch resolutions'. The best that could be said for the revived Cook- Maxton campaign for a real socialist policy was that it made an unwitting contribution to 'hastening the disintegration of the Independent Labour Party [by] raising issues which it cannot itself solve'. It all added up to the Communist Party as 'the sole independent political force in opposition to the bourgeoisie'.

Even the ECCI could see that the majority of the CPGB leadership grounded their resistance to Dutt and the New Line by stressing the circumstances of defeat following the General Strike. This was expressed in such factors as the decline of trade union membership and strike activity. And the rise in unemployment, and a corresponding loss of confidence, made the prospect of another Labour government an object of working class hope, and symbol of progress, rather than the disaster which the Comintern depicted. But in its 'Closed Letter' of 27 February 1929, following the British Party's tenth congress, the Presidium of the ECCI found this local analysis to be proof of 'serious deficiencies' in the CPGB leadership.

The Party was reminded that the sixth congress of the Comintern had characterised the immediate conjuncture as 'the third period' of the 'general crisis of capitalism'. It was, according to the ECCI:

> a period of technical progress, growth of cartels and trusts and tendencies to State Capitalism but at the same time, a period of sharp accentuation of the general crisis of capitalism, radicalisation of the masses, acute class struggles, growth of the revolutionary movement in the colonies and the growing danger of imperialist war - leading to the further shattering of capitalist stabilisation and tremendous revolutionary class conflicts.[40]

In the light of this, the ECCI reiterated the Comintern's claim that the chief danger facing the Communist Parties was the 'right danger'. But despite criticism of the British central committee at the Party's tenth congress, the erring leaders had been re-elected as if to vindicate the Comintern's diagnosis. The Presidium now demanded the immediate inclusion of some of the central committee's critics into the Party's highest bodies, to be followed by a campaign within the Party for the Presidium's positions, as contained in the 'Closed Letter'. It called for even bigger changes of personnel at the next Party congress. The British leaders - especially Campbell and Rothstein - were thus exposed to constant attack throughout 1929, on the grounds of their lack of conviction, their defeatism and their excessive insularity. Discipline was not enough; the British Party had to be led by comrades who believed that a revolution was just around the corner.

From Brussels Dutt was now emboldened to orchestrate the campaign against the 'right danger' in the CPGB, engaging infactional activity by correspondence with the likes of Reg Groves and zealots in the Young Communist League such as William Rust and Dave Springhall, while constantly hectoring the leadership. In the general election, at the end of May, the Party trawled a meagre 50,000 votes from 25 constituencies, a result which Dutt admitted was 'fit only to excite laughter'. But such a superficial response allegedly missed 'the gathering contradictions' revealed by Marxist analysis, which allowed Dutt to see that 'the present period is not a period of harmonious capitalist development and stabilisation, but of sharpening class antagonism, gathering economic and political struggles, intensified capitalist contradictions, and the approach to war'.[41] Many in the Party remained sceptical about the Comintern line - not least those in the shrinking ordinary membership, as Clemens Dutt was forced to admit .[42] Yet in July 1929 the Comintern's Tenth Plenum made matters worse by deciding that the trade unions had also become enemy organisations; in August of that year the sixth annual conference of the Minority Movement accordingly resolved that its puny forces would seek to bring the union rank and file directly under its leadership, in preparation for a complete break with the reformists. This was the line adopted at the CPGB's eleventh congress at Leeds in November 1929.

The eleventh Congress enabled the Comintern to install the ultras on the Central Committee - twenty-three newcomers in all, to stiffen the Party's resolve. These were elected after a Congress committee had prepared a list of names which the delegates were invited to elect en bloc - a device designed to reduce the influence of the old 'moderate' leadership. Henceforward this 'panel system', the 'recommended list', became the means by which the retiring leadership ensured its self- perpetuation, thus further centralising - and insulating - the Party leaders.

But if the Party's isolation grew even as the New Line was accepted, Dutt remained convinced that errors of leadership were to blame. Throughout 1929 he repeated the Comintern notion that the Party's failure to grow was due to a lack of conviction. announcing in a letter to the Central Committee in August, for example, that it was not enough to formally accept the New Line while recognising past 'mistakes'; 'it is necessary to draw out by the roots the *tendency* revealed by the mistakes and brand it. If after correction, similar mistakes are repeated, then we have to recognise that we are faced with a fully *formed tendency* which we have to fight; and we have to be prepared to draw the necessary conclusions, including with regard to changes of leadership'.[43] Like the ECCI, Dutt banged the drum for immediate changes of personnel, and proposed the names of several ultra-revolutionaries in the London district - Groves, Purkis, Mahon and Shepherd - together with others from Tyneside, Greenock and Fife. He quite openly admitted that he believed in the existence of 'a definite continuous Right Wing tendency within the Party which must be fought'. This was a complaint he had voiced before and he believed the tendency to be based on a lack of Bolshevik understanding, especially internationalist understanding, in the CPGB. Not for last time he observed that:

> There are very dangerous signs of a lack of understanding of the principles of international centralism and of the leading role of the International Executive in relation to all questionsof the Party ... It is the full province of the ECCI as the direct leader of all sections of the International to intervene in all questions affecting the Party, not only political, but also of organisation, including questions of leadership.[44]

The alternative could only be 'national exclusivism' - a disease which had broken out throughout the Comintern under stress of the New Line.

Dutt never made the mistake again of allowing local, British conditions to affect his judgement, as they had, briefly, in 1924. This earned him the accolade from G. Safarov - the Comintern's colonial expert and one of Lenin's closest collaborators no less - as 'one of the most steadfast and conscious fighters for the Comintern in Britain'. This was all the more gratifying, no doubt, in view of the fact that Safarov had recently anathematised Roy as 'an unmasked and discredited symbol' of the Indian masses, who had gone over to the theory of 'bourgeois progress'.[45] But Dutt's closeness to the Comintern also brought charges of armchair Bolshevism from Party members, who said that he was 'not only divorced from the masses [but] he has also been divorced from the actual life of the Party for a considerable time ... He knows only resolutions, theses, ballot results ... newspaper cuttings etc'.[46] But even his detractors could not deny that Dutt made impressive use of the information at his disposal in weaving a coherent line for his Notes of the Month. As 'RPD' he had become, according to Clemens' correspondence, a legend among the Party's worker- activists. Such was the mystery surrounding Dutt that John Strachey, one of his avid readers at this time, even thought that the legend was dying somewhere in Paris. In fact the vast bulk of Party members, let alone ILP-ers like Strachey, had to be told by *Communist Review* that the mysterious recluse was an 'outstanding Party theoretician' who 'plays a decisive part in central committee discussions through his articles and letters'.[47]

This information was made necessary by repeated references to Dutt, as well as missives from Dutt, in the Party's publications as the factional disputes rumbled on; even as late as March 1933, allegations of Dutt's factionalism were still heard among the leadership.[48] The allegations were well founded. In the run up to the Party's eleventh congress of November 1929, the leadership was having to come to terms with the Tenth Plenum's depiction of the trade unions as essential apparatuses of the capitalist state, as well as the increasingly violent denunciations of social democrats , both left and right, as 'social fascists'. The CPGB Political Bureau - responding in kind to the escalating rhetoric - now discovered that 'the situation (in Britain) is becoming acutely revolutionary' - only to find Dutt once more on its back accusing it of parody.[49] The tenth Plenum in July had heard Manuilsky disparagingly refer to the Party as 'a society of great friends', whose lamentable lack of division was contrasted with 'the German comrades [who] weigh every word spoken by anybody [and] allow no deviation from the line'. Though the Comintern approved Pollit's election to the General Secretaryship, only Dutt was in a position to emulate the Germans and, in Manuilsky's words, 'attack the least deviation, respecting no persons'; only Dutt possessed the requisite qualities of scholasticism, emotional detachment and 'internationalism'.

Dutt's weak point, of course, resided in the fact that the Comintern line was not always clear - in fact it was becoming increasingly capricious and contradictory. An example is afforded by the line on the trade unions adopted at the CPGB's eleventh congress which, in accordance with the Comintern's ruling, talked of the 'ever-growing fascisation of the trade union apparatus'. The Party was thus committed to constructing an alternative trade union leadership, and noone supported this more enthusiastically than Dutt. The policy was such a disaster, however, that yet another British Commission in Moscow in December 1931, was forced to retreat, by allowing for the transformation of the existing unions; this was done, however, specifically repudiating the earlier line. The upshot was that Pollitt, supported by Gallacher, agitated for a clear commitment to the transformation of the existing unions, while Dutt, with the backing of sectarians in the Balham branch of the Party, publicly defended the Leeds congress argument that the unions were irredeemably corrupt and reformist. The dispute dragged on in the pages of the *Daily Worker* until the twelfth congress in November 1932, where Dutt's position was repudiated.

It is an interesting sidelight on Dutt's factional activities to note that the young ultra-lefts he promoted - Groves, Mahon, Purkis and Ferguson - contributed fourteen articles between them to *Labour Monthly* in 1929-30. It is clear evidence that he was consciously building them up - nothing had been heard from them before the binge of ultra-leftism. But by the end of 1932 Dutt was forced to drop Groves and his co- thinkers in the Balham branch. The latter had which persisted in its 'revolution now' mentality, and was expelled from the Party altogether after the twelfth congress. Thus, from these puerile beginnings, was British Trotskyism born.

Undeterred by such gaffs, Dutt's 'letters from afar', from 1929 up to his return to Britain in 1936, show by their tone, as much as by their content, that he regarded the leadership of the Party as dependent on his advice and guidance. When a specimen of the forthcoming Party paper, the *Daily Worker*, was produced in November 1929, Dutt told the Political Bureau that 'the whole of this humiliating production ... is an insult to every Communist'.[50] At the same time he wrote to Groves denouncing the paper as 'a weak imitation of the *Daily Herald*', and argued that 'we must demand ... elimination of all elements associated with Fleet Street and *Daily Herald* traditions'; 'the whole tone', Dutt fumed, 'is not a political mass tone but a gossipy clique tone [with] exactly the same type of stunt headings as in the ... capitalist press'. A long disquisition on the iniquities of capitalist sport followed with Dutt, self- confessed sports refusenik that he was, citing the paper's sports coverage as just one of the paper's many concessions to the dominant ideology. Dutt declaimed against bourgeois domination and ideology in mass spectator sports, and the promotion of corruption, passivity and gambling in the onlookers, who were thus sold an 'alternative' to class struggle.[51] This was an issue which exercised him more than once in these years, and provided further opportunities for his shallow functionalist tirades.

But, more to the point, Dutt's polemic was of a piece with his persistent search for an elusive doctrinal and organisational purity - the missing links in an otherwise favourable situation. In a long letter to the Comintern's commission of enquiry into the state of the British Party in August 1930, for example, Dutt puzzled over the organisation's weakness 'in a rapidly advancing objective situation, the whole character of which plays into our hands'. He could only find an explanation for this in defective methods of work together with confusion and uncertainties over the line. Dutt could see that 'the reality ... is not that of a revolutionary advance-guard organically connected with further sections of the workers and through them extending its leadership; the reality is that of a small group of workers throwing out calls and leads into the air, but *without contact with the workers*'[original emphasis]. But he could not see that this was derived from the small size of the

Party - total membership just 2,555 at the end of 1930 - and the self- destructive character of its sectarianism.[52] Instead he dwelt at length on methods, and the dangers of capitalist ideology. This is a point that would hardly be worth mentioning had it not been so characteristic of Leninists to habitually invert the Marxist method, by stressing such factors as will, leadership, conviction, and the like while ignoring uncomfortable material reality.

The following year, with the Party's situation having deteriorated further, Dutt's complaints were addressed to Manuilsky, who was told that the membership of the Party consisted of a high proportion of 'lumpen' elements divorced from the working class. (In fact about one-third of the membership was unemployed.) In March 1931 Dutt also found evidence of right-wing factionalism in the form of a document, *Towards a New Party*, circulated amongst Party members and probably derived from the ILP. Once again Manuilsky was informed.[53] But when, in August 1932, Dutt learned of a proposal for a 'society of intellectual workers' inside the Party, he dealt with it himself by reminding its sponsors - Maurice Dobb and D.S. Mirsky - that 'the first role of intellectuals who have joined the Party is to forget they are intellectuals and act as Communists, that is enter fully into the Party fight'. The alternative was that they would be found 'chasing after foolish or dangerous theories by themselves'. With the exception of 'student groups', there were to be no special organisations within the Party if Dutt had his way. The bourgeois intellectual in particular had to 'un-learn from the roots, to break all ties with their old associations'; he [sic] had to 'strip himself at the outset of the notion that he comes with superior wisdom and important new theories when he is only trotting out old fallacies and exposing his ignorance'.[54]

The confrontationalist course of the New Line was the nearest Dutt had been to the harsh struggle promised in 1919 when he was first drawn to the Comintern; it reminded him of the need for discipline and purity of purpose. As Brecht was to write:

> He who fights for Communism
> Must be able to fight and not fight
> Must tell the truth and not tell the truth
> Render service and not render service
> Place himself in danger and avoid danger
> Be recognisable and be unrecognisable.
> He who fights for Communism
> Has of all virtues only one
> That he fights for Communism[55]

The situation was perceived to be so grave, after all, that commitment to the cause had to be total and ruthless. Viewed internationally - the only proper way of assessing the situation for Dutt - the Communist Party was fighting for its life - and, in the event, a number of its national sections were practically destroyed in the years of the Third Period, most of them by Fascism. The *Daily Worker* - run by the ultras such as Rust and Walter Tapsell - accurately reflected this embattled condition when it finally appeared in January 1930, with news of Communists 'tortured in fever-ridden jails' in Indonesia, of the Meerut prisoners persecuted for trying to establish trade unions in India, of the 'war psychology' which the Labour government was allegedly stoking up against the Soviet Union, and of Labour's 'brutal repression in the colonies'. In the first issue Dutt announced that 'capitalism is today in decline all over the world and nowhere more so than in Britain', where a Labour government was doing its best - 'in exactly the same way as any previous capitalist government' - to maintain the bourgeois order.[56]

In much of the detail in Dutt's analysis there was enough that was accurate to lend credence to the Communists' catastrophist mentality. From the beginning of this second Labour administration he predicted a policy of 'sound finance' as the government struggled to maintain the 'precarious position of the gold standard'. He also foresaw recourse to protectionism while conceding that it might be left to the Conservatives to carry it out. This would represent, he argued, a turning inwards, 'a last parasitic attempt to clutch at what remains of a diminishing world domination'.[57] All these strategems would be to no avail in Dutt's scenario, dominated as this was by an impending world economic crash - which of course actually came after the stock market collapse on Wall Street, just months after the return of the Labour government. Dutt was also right to see that the ILP's critics of MacDonald were too closely tied to the Party leader to be able to break free from Labour in time; instead, when the break came in 1932, the world crisis had already deepened and the Labour government had ended in ignominous rout.

The Communist hope was that the intensification of the world crisis would cause the real political choice to be 'not between the Labour Party and fascism, but between the revolutionary class struggle and capitalism, which includes both fascism and the Labour Party'.[58] In accordance with the Comintern's hardening attitude, Dutt asserted in November 1930 that, 'Social Democracy is the instrument of transition to the new fascist type of state that is being evolved'.[59] This mentality is, of course, still difficult to understand - evidence of Labour's actual conversion to fascism defeated even Dutt's powers of fabrication. But perhaps the underlying logic was best expressed by Trotsky at the end of the decade, when he wrote:

> Naturally there exists a difference between the political regimes in bourgeois society just as there is a difference in comfort between various cars in a railway train. But when the whole train is plunging into an abyss, the distinction between decaying democracy and murderous fascism disappears in the face of the collapse of the entire capitalist system.[60]

For Dutt the whole train was already plunging into an abyss in 1930. When the Labour government collapsed the following year, he could in truth remind the readers of *Labour Monthly* that:

> For ten years we have spoken continuously of the central fact of the decline of capitalism in Britain, of its deeper permanent causes, of its chronic and accelerating character, of the consequent illusion of all the reform programmes and programmes of capitalist reconstruction and the inevitable revolutionary issue confronting the working class.[61]

What lay ahead, according to Dutt, was 'impoverishment and starvation on a scale still undreamt of'. The Communist might have private reservations concerning the Comintern's tactics and its 'social fascist' thesis - we have seen that British Party leaders certainly did - but if the capitalist system was moribund and the real political alternatives accordingly whittled down to a choice of socialism or fascism, such reservations were easy to rationalise away. And it helped to know that Lenin had all along imagined that the Communists alone - give or take the occasional tactical adjustment - could ultimately solve the crisis of capitalist decline in a socialist direction. In the present period of sectarianism Dutt thus openly scoffed at the ILP's secession from the Labour Party in 1932 as 'a red herring', and suggested that unity of the ILP and the Communists was as preposterous as calling for unity between capitalism and the working class.[62]

In fact when Dutt came to write his *magnum opus* of the 'third period' - *Fascism and Social Revolution* (1934) - he set out with the intention, as he told Pollitt, of constructing a sort of sequel to Lenin's *Imperialism*.[63] His purpose was to show that fascism was 'the most complete expression of the whole modern tendency of capitalism in decay ... the final attempt to defeat the working class revolution'.[64] He wrote the book after the accession of Hitler in Germany. Within a month of its publication a pact between the

French socialists and the Communist Party was cemented (27 July 1934) which heralded the inauguration of the People's Front, and the beginning of a period in which the Communists, in a reversal of their policy during the 'third period', would work alongside any group committed to anti-fascism. *Fascism and Social Revolution* was thus instantly out of date in relation to Communist tactics; but it is a very accurate statement of Dutt's deepest convictions and a mental universe which remained relevant for Communists throughout the 1930s.

His starting point is the contention that 1914 marked the opening of the general crisis of capitalism, the final phase of imperialism characterised by the normalisation of economic depression - broken only by short recoveries - and violent social and political upheavals. Attempts to stabilise Europe had passed from schemes such as the Dawes and Young plans, and security arrangements such as the Locarno Pact, to dreams of an organised capitalism and the contemporaneous emergence of an authoritarian state capitalism. Dutt described even the wishful thinking of a planned capitalism, which had affected elements in the labour movement, as 'an unconscious groping after Fascism without facing its logical implications'.[65] He reminded his readers that, as Lenin had pointed out in 1916, corresponding to the realities of monopoly capitalism, the routine of government was in fact already in the hands of an increasingly strengthened and centralised bureaucracy; effective power and the decision of policy lay with the handful of leaders of finance capitalism; 'while the puppet-show of Parliament, responsible Ministers, elections and nominally opposing parties, became increasingly recognised as a 'decorative appendage of the Constitution for the purposes of window-dressing'.[66]

The distinguishing feature of the present conjuncture, Dutt reasoned, was that the bourgeoisie was increasingly compelled to resort to more direct and open forms of coercion. This followed from the fact, as he saw it, of the extreme crisis of capitalism and the failure of reformism. Together these developments had undermined confidence in parliamentarism, created a mass of disaffected petty-bourgeois elements susceptible to national and social demagogy, demobilised and disoriented the workers' organisations, and provided the necessity as well the opportunity for the big bourgeoisie to crush living standards and labour defence organisations. The National Government formed after the general election of 1932 suggested to Dutt that Britain had reached a stage on the road to fascism comparable with that represented by the

Bruning government during the twilight months of Weimar. The overwhelming Parliamentary majority, the enfeeblement of the Labour Opposition and the defection of its leaders to the bourgeoisie - all this was bad enough; but the Government's authoritarianism had been signalled from the outset with the introduction of the Means Test, the reorganisation and centralisation of the police, and the Unemployment Act with its provision for 'training centres' (read labour camps) of the unemployed.

It remained a settled conviction with the Communists, up to the Second World War, that the National Government marked a stage on the road to fascism in Britain. Lenin had argued that moribund capitalism would resort to increasingly open forms of authoritarianism; Dutt simply insisted that its name was fascism. His purpose was to stress that in Western Europe, and especially in Britain (where the 'parliamentary institutions of deception' had been more securely based thanks to unrivalled wealth and power - an effect of the privileged position of the imperialist powers), the benign influences that had sustained democracy were no longer operant. Instead an 'encroaching fascism' was set to fill the void as long as the dope of reformism prevented the workers from adopting the only alternative - the Communist revolution.

In this sense, and on these assumptions, it was only a question of simple deduction for Dutt to demonstrate the culpability of the Labour Party. Here again he was on the established ground of Communist theory. The Comintern had always subscribed to the view that capitalism survived the immediate post-war crisis thanks largely to the social democratic parties' reformist leaderships. If fascism was developing organically out of a decaying capitalist civilisation, those who artificially prolonged its life by gulling the masses with reformism were guilty of aiding and abetting the extreme right. Dutt provided the empirical 'evidence' to support these assertions with the cases of Italy and Austria, where the reformist leaderships offered no resistance to the fascists. And by omitting any reference to Communist tactics he could show the same was true in Germany - the reformists bore a special responsibility for the rise of fascism.

All this was accomplished across nearly three hundred pages of text, with only one reference to Stalin and no mention of social fascism. Dutt stressed that the 'sole new feature of the fascist Corporate state', upon which its 'iron-fisted harmony' was based, was the 'violent destruction of the workers' independent organisations and the complete abolition of the right to strike'.[67] The dual purpose of this state was to crush working-class living standards and prepare for wars of imperialist expansion. Social Democracy desired neither of these outcomes, according to Dutt, but nevertheless prepared the way for them, because of its insistence on conducting its opposition to fascism on the basis of bourgeois democracy. Dutt was adamant that it was useless to counterpose the democracies against the dictatorships since the latter only expressed in an extreme form symptoms and tendencies common to all of them. If France and Britain were not yet fascist, the germ was already there; if they did not propose wars of imperialist expansion, it was because they were relatively sated imperialist powers; if they appeased the fascist states it was because they sympathised with their attempt to crush the social revolution and looked kindly on an anti-Bolshevik crusade spearheaded by Germany and Japan.[68] The real alternatives were clear; either social revolution or fascism - there was to be no comfortable repose in liberal democracy; capitalism with a human face was dead.

NOTES

1 J.T. Murphy, 'Socialism By Kind Permission', *Communist International*, 3, 1, 15 October 1926, p18.
2 Dutt to A.J. Cook, 23.10.26, K4 Vol 1922-27.
3 R.P. Dutt, *Socialism and the Living Wage*, CPGB, 1927, p75.
4 Salme Murrik to Dutt, 8.6.28, File 6.
5 K. Radek, 'International Fascism and the Communist International', *Inprecorr*, 3, 53, 26 July 1923, pp559-600.
6 See D. Beetham, *Marxists in the Face of Fascism*, Manchester University Press, 1983, p19.
7 R.P. Dutt, *World Politics*, Gollancz, 1936, p51.
8 R.P. Dutt, 'Fascism in Britain', *Inprecorr*, 5, 53, 25 June 1925, pp 726-7.
9 G.D.H. Cole, *The Next Ten Years in British Social and Economic Policy*, Macmillan, 1929, p 7, p63, and p139.
10 R. Page Arnot, Anglo-American Rivalry, *Labour Monthly*, 9, 10, October 1927, pp580-588.
11 N. Branson, *History of the Communist Party of Great Britain, 1927-1941*, Lawrence and Wishart, 1985, p19.
12 R.P. Dutt, *Memorandum on the Theses on the Labour Party adopted by the CC on 9 January 1928 and Alternative Proposals*, 26 January 1928, K4 Vol 1928-1929.
13 R.P. Dutt, *The Situation in Great Britain and the Tasks of the Trade Union Movement: Draft Theses for Submission to RILU Congress in March 1928*, 19 January 1928, pp1-5, ibid; the forecast concerning

Pollitt's promotion is mentioned in Dutt's 'Rough Draft on Some Experiences of the Communist International', Easter 1970 (CPGB archive) p5.

14 R.P. Dutt, *Memorandum on the Theses on the Labour Party, op cit*, pp15-16.

15 R.P. Dutt, *The Situation in Great Britain, op cit*, p7.

16 R.P. Dutt, 'The New Phase of the Labour Party and OurTasks', *Labour Monthly*, 10, 1, January 1928, p7 and p16.

17 Clemens Dutt to R.P. Dutt, 9 February 1928.

18 S. Cohen, *Bukharin and the Bolshevik Revolution*, Wildwood House, 1974, pp293-4.

19 J.T. Murphy, 'Is There A Right Danger in Our Party?', *The Communist*, 16 November 1928.

20 R.P. Dutt, 'Questions Before the Party Congress', *Communist Review*, January 1929.

21 E. Varga, 'Economic Policy in the Fourth Quarter', *Inprecorr*, 8, 3, March 1928, pp285-310.

22 See *Eighth Congress of the Communist Party of Great Britain*, CPGB, 1927, p81.

23 S. Ghose, *Socialism and Communism in India*, Allied Publishers, Bombay, 1971, pp124-125.

24 R.P. Dutt, 'The Indian Awakening', *Labour Monthly*, 10, 6, June 1928, pp323-341.

25 R.T. McVey, *The Rise of Indonesian Communism*, Cornell University, New York, 1965, p xiii and p82.

26 M. Ahmed, *Myself and the Communist Party of India*, National Book Agency, Calcutta, 1970, p478.

27 *Inprecorr*, 8, 8, 1928, pp1225-1542.

28 L.J. Macfarlane, *The British Communist Party*, MacGibbon and Kee, 1966, p208.

29 R.P. Dutt, 'The Indian Awakening', *op cit*, p325 and p329.

30 S. Gopal, *Jawaharlal Nehru: A Biography*, Cape, 1974, Volume 1, p111.

31 *Ibid*, pp101-105.

32 M.J. Akbar, *Nehru: The Making of India*, Penguin Books, Harmondsworth, 1988, p199.

33 Such as Walter Citrine; see A.J. Williams, *Labour and Russia*, Manchester University Press, 1989, p83.

34 S. Ghose, *Socialism and Communism in India, op cit*, p127.

35 In a letter quoted in full in M. Ahmed, *Myself and the Communist Party of India, op cit*, pp479-480.

36 R.P. Dutt, 'Coalition-State Capitalism-War: The Meaning of the New Labour Programme, *Sunday Worker*, 5.6.28, pp1-2.

37 R.P.Dutt, 'The General Election and the Working Class', *Labour Monthly*, 10, 11, November 1928, p644.

38 R.P. Dutt, 'The ILP and Communism', *Labour Monthly*, 10, 5, May 1928, p262.

39 R.P. Dutt, 'The Maxton-Cook Revival', *Labour Monthly*, 10, 8, August 1928, p461.

40 The Closed Letter, 27 February 1929, reproduced in full in L.J. Macfarlane, *The British Communist Party, op cit*, pp308-319.
41 R.P. Dutt, 'The Second Labour Government', *Labour Monthly*, 11, 7, July 1929, p393.
42 Clemens Dutt to R.P. Dutt, 7.3.1928 and 28.8.1929.
43 R.P. Dutt to Central Committee, 3.8.1929, K4 Vol 1928-9.
44 *Ibid*, p3.
45 Press Cuttings K6 Volume 1, 1921-45, from *Communist International*, 13.1.1930. See G. Safarov, 'The End of Mr.Roy', *Communist International*, Vol 6, 1930, pp1108-1116.
46 *Worker's Life*, 29.11.1929.
47 *Communist Review*, January 1931, p12; See also H. Thomas, *J.Strachey*, Eyre Methuen, 1973, p65.
48 Salme Murrik to Dutt, 14.3.33.
49 R.P. Dutt to Political Bureau, 25.9.29, K4, Volume 1928-9.
50 R.P. Dutt to Political Bureau, 26.11.29, *ibid*.
51 R.P. Dutt to Reg Groves, 26.11.29, *ibid*.
52 R.P. Dutt, *To the Anglo-American Secretariat*, 4.8.30,K4 1930-1932.
53 Dutt's letters to Manuilsky of 9.1.31 and 17.3.31, *ibid*.
54 R.P. Dutt, *Memorandum on NCLC and Intellectuals*, 7.8.32, *ibid*; See also his 'Bourgeois Journalism and Our Press', *Communist Review*, Volume 4, July 1932, pp325-331.
55 B. Brecht, *The Measures Taken and Other Lehrstucke*, Eyre Methuen, 1977, p13.
56 R.P. Dutt, 'War and the Labour Government', *Daily Worker*, 1.1.30.
57 R.P. Dutt, 'The Second Labour Government', *op cit*; and his 'The New Empire Socialism', *Labour Monthly*, 12, 9, September 1930, pp525-7.
58 R.P. Dutt, 'Fascism, Empire and the Labour Party', *Labour Monthly*, 12, 11, November 1930, p643.
59 *Ibid* p643.
60 L.D. Trotsky, 'Imperialist War and the Proletarian World Revolution', in W. Reisner (ed), *Documents of the Fourth International: The Formative Years*, Pathfinder, New York, 1973, p349.
61 R.P. Dutt, 'Towards National Coalition', *Labour Monthly*, 13, 9, September 1931, pp534-5.
62 R.P. Dutt, 'The Labour Monthly Conference - A Review', *Labour Monthly*, 14, 2, February 1932; see also 'The Burning Question of Working Class Unity', *Labour Monthly*, 14, 7, July 1932, pp421-2.
63 Dutt to Pollitt, 20.7.34, K4 Volume 1933-4.
64 R.P. Dutt, *Fascism and Social Revolution*, second edition, Martin Lawrence, June 1935, pxiv.
65 *Ibid*, pxix.
66 *Ibid*, p59.
67 *Ibid*, p203.
68 *Ibid*, pp216-217.

5

Enemies of Fascism, Friends of the Soviet Union

The ultra-revolutionary policies which the Comintern adopted from the summer of 1928 found their main testing-ground in Germany, where the divided Left looked on helplessly when Hitler assumed the Chancellorship on 30 January 1933, and the Nazis took 43.9 per cent of the vote in the elections of 5 March. On the same day the ECCI, while upholding the Communist policies that had contributed to this unprecedented disaster, called upon 'all communist parties to make a further [*sic*] attempt to establish a united fighting front with the social-democratic working masses through the social-democratic parties'. Eight days later Dutt - the cracked gramophone of ultra-leftism in the British Party - told Pollitt:

> It's a damned good thing and long urgently due. The only pity is that we could not have reached it sooner, that is in front of the Hitler coup and so that the Seven-Party small fry could not strut about now as having started it all.[1]

It seems incredible that even now Dutt could be so lacking in a sense of proportion that petty sectarian considerations remained uppermost in his mind. But the advent of Hitler had by no means forced a complete reappraisal of the previous policy - even in off-the-record correspondence - and Dutt was careful to stress that the united front changed little. Pollitt was instructed that it was in fact not a new policy at all and there was 'no question of electoral opportunist combinations' - a point 'too obvious to mention had you not written of it being raised'. The leader was enjoined to 'study carefully' the 1922 Berlin negotiations in which the three Internationals (the 2nd, '2½'and 3rd Internationals), considered joint action at the highest levels. These acrimonious discussions were apparently notable in Dutt's mind only because Lenin had raged against the Communist delegations' concessions in the face of Social Democratic criticism of the Soviet government's repression in Georgia. Dutt reminded Pollitt that Lenin had judged that the Communists had paid too high a price in the negotiations, and was obviously concerned to prevent Pollitt from repeating the mistake.

Interestingly, since he was 'certain' that the Labour Party and the TUC would reject the Communists' overtures, it was relations with the ILP - the biggest of the 'Seven-Party small fry' - which Dutt had in mind.

To understand why the ILP would in Dutt's words 'obviously agree' with the Communist demand for a united front, one has to appreciate that for many left activists the sins of the Communist Party and the Comintern were dwarfed by the fascist danger which threatened war and terror against the labour movement. The ILP had also grown impatient with gradualism in the context of the persistence of mass unemployment in Britain, and of the inability of the second Labour government to do anything about it. The collapse of that government, and the departure of MacDonald and Snowden for the National Government, finally convinced a majority of the ILP's leaders that the world economic crisis demanded a revolutionary policy and secession from the Labour Party. Maxton and Brockway thus sought 'unity of revolutionary socialist forces' when the ILP split from Labour in July 1932, and they shared the Communist conviction that reformism was effectively finished. Even those former ILP members who refused to support disaffiliation, and now organised themselves as the Socialist League within the Labour Party, had grave misgivings about the prospects for parliamentary reformism at a time when the world was plunged into the interconnected catastrophes of slump, fascism, and war. Consequently the activist left, both inside and outside the Labour Party, was increasingly receptive to Communist calls for joint expressions of militancy.

The ILP, having signed an appeal for the unity of the Second and Third Internationals for a common front against Nazism in February 1933, accepted united front activity with the CPGB the following month - a matter of days after the correspondence between Dutt and Pollitt cited above. Though the ILP was probably the larger party (16,773 members in 1931, falling to just over 4,000 in 1935), the Communists made no secret of their belief that the object of the exercise was to absorb it into the Communist Party - two revolutionary parties of the working class being a self-evident absurdity to any Leninist. A letter from Dutt was read to a *Labour Monthly* conference on revolutionary policy in April in which he emphasised this point: 'there can only be one line of the revolutionary working class'; there was no 'third road', no room for two Marxist parties. But one issue above all else stood out:

> it is the issue of revolutionary discipline, of centralism, both nationally and

> internationally, of democratic centralism. Here [in Britain] the old social democratic conceptions of a loose, parliamentary and propagandistic party die hard. The Leninist conception of the revolutionary workers' party, of its leading role in every phase of the workers' struggle, of its necessary basis in the workers' industry, of its combination of democracy and centralism, needs to be explained again and again, especially in England where it is still largely unfamiliar save in the current bourgeois and social democratic caricatures of 'machine discipline', 'dictatorship', 'Moscow orders' and co.
>
> There are also present remains of national prejudices, which express themselves in insistence on the peculiarity of British conditions as a reason for opposition to international ('Russian') control; here, opposition to the principle of a centralised international takes on a British national guise.

Within the heavily factionalised ILP, a so-called Revolutionary Policy Committee, led by the lawyer Jack Gaster and Dr. C. K. Cullen, Medical Officer of Health for Poplar, also stood for a united Communist Party. Dutt advised Pollitt in November 1933 that Gaster and Cullen, with whom Pollitt had been in direct contact since the previous summer, were 'ambiguous, evasive left types', who should be instructed to immediately form a 'committee for affiliation' to the Comintern.[2] Thus was begun an agitation which peaked at the ILP Easter conference of 1934, and ended only when the 'ambiguous, evasive, left types' - as many as one hundred of them - resigned en bloc from the party in October 1935, taking themselves into the CPGB.

Dutt's suspicion of non-Party socialists was the corollary, of course, of the Leninist conception of Marxism as an exact science monopolised by the Party. It was inevitably at its most severe when confronted with individuals like Gaster and Cullen, giving themselves over to revolutionary views. Given his own Jesuitical tendencies, furthermore, it is likely that few of Dutt's comrades met these severe standards of theoretical rigour. Pollitt, the leader, was constantly treated to Dutt's patronising, sometimes minatory advice and guidance, as we have seen. Saklatvala and Ben Bradley - men whom Dutt actually liked - were described respectively as 'full of touches of opportunism' and 'not a politician'. Bradley, though 'a triumph of theory over nature', as a leader of the CPI lacked acumen for theory, according to Dutt and Clemens was advised that 'for the line, don't go to him'.[3] The truth is that Dutt had no intellectual peer in either the British or the Indian Party, an absence which, while heightening the sense of his own indispensability also, in reality, adversely affected his own work. He wrote too much and was forever 'improving' the work of the Party leadership.

'We believe that in Marxism, in Communism', he told a

Communist students' conference in September 1933, 'we hold the key to all burning problems which confront every serious thinking student'. This was Dutt's other problem - he believed that in 'Marxism-Leninism' he had all the answers. Communism was quite simply 'a complete world conception covering every aspect of life, and transforming all our thinking and activity'.[4] This left nothing to chance; the line was rarely, if ever, wrong, but could become 'out of date' as the balance of class forces shifted. This was how Dutt now read the situation since the Nazi success in Germany. In October 1933 he told Pollitt that the Party 'must beware of merely rehashing the old Lenin arguments on bourgeois democracy and proletarian dictatorship. This is no longer adequate because the whole situation is changed ... the workers naturally feel, when face to face with Hitler-Germany, that the rights of organisation, press, meeting, etc even under very limited capitalist conditions are extremely important'. That this shift in propaganda was purely tactical, however, Dutt was never in doubt; 'Fascism', he reminded Pollitt, 'grows out of "democracy" - that is the heart of the issue. The workers are chloroformed by talk of democracy'.[5]

By this time, of course, Hitler had completely destroyed German democracy. But Dutt was not impressed. When Hitler turned against the SA leaders at the end of June 1934 he told Pollitt that this was evidence of a:

> ripening revolutionary crisis in Germany, of Hitler losing mass support and compelled to destroy the main part of his previous mass basis and replace [it] by more and more openly revolutionary terrorist regime - therefore of growth of revolutionary forces and possible future fall of Fascism. But fall of Fascism offers strong likelihood of victory of Communism. This is the spectre which June 30 has raised for international bourgeoisie.[6]

Dutt's fidelity to the Comintern line was not, however, always reflected in the attitudes of Party members, including some of those in the leadership - a fact which could only reinforce his low opinion of them. Much of the correspondence to Pollitt was clearly designed to prevent the Party leader from wandering into deviation, as when he referred in an article to the destruction of the German Communist Party and had to be told, in January 1935, that on the contrary it 'lives and fights, is stronger than ever, will conquer'. Pollitt's problem, according to Dutt, was that he did 'not really see the whole international field and complexity of the problem, but reflects mainly the special position in Britain'. It was the old problem and Dutt must have felt like Sisyphus in his labours to correct it; in general, he concluded on this occasion, 'we have to be very sure of our ground, very clear on the international line'.[7]

Dutt was likewise shocked to hear that a member of the Political Bureau no less had raised doubts about the theory of social fascism. This was evidence that comrades had not understood 'the real purpose and value' of his *Fascism and Social Revolution*: 'they do not see that the real aim is to make understood the present period, to lay bare economics and politics of extreme latest stage of imperialism - it is twenty years since Lenin's *Imperialism* and much has happened since then - which makes clear why issue of fascism inevitably develops at present stage'.[8]

Dutt's updating of Lenin, though not in the least innovative, produced some counter-intuitive conclusions that could only baffle the more commonsensical militants in the Party. And yet apart from the obvious fact that his analysis of fascism was derived from the Comintern's publications, the continuities with Lenin's characterisation of the imperialist epoch stand out in *Fascism and Social Revolution*, not new departures. This is important to remember, because it points to the fact that there was no revision of the original rationale for the Communist International at any time in the Comintern's life. The characteristic form of bourgeois rule during the period of its general crisis was now said to be fascism, where Lenin in 1916 had predicted a general authoritarianism as the successor to parliamentary democracy. In both versions of the argument, the intense economic contradictions of imperialism were responsible for recurring slumps of growing intensity, accompanied by social and political instability and the ever-present threat of war. The objective conditions of the period thus favoured the social revolution and it was in order to suppress this that the imperialist bourgeoisie turned to fascism. There was nothing peculiar about fascism then, for Dutt and the Comintern; it was basically an epiphenomenon of decaying capitalist civilisation - an instrument of the big bourgeoisie, assuredly, but by no means an independent movement of the middle and lower middle class. The move to fascism was an organic outgrowth of moribund capitalism which affected every capitalist state.

In Britain this analysis inevitably pointed to the National Government as a stage in the 'fascisation', of the state as well as to the more obvious activities of Mosley's British Union of Fascists (BUF). Bourgeois democracy was no defence against the BUF when, as Dutt argued, fascism grew out of democracy. The fight against fascism involved therefore not only the street battles against the Mosleyites - a declining force after 1937 and never a genuine mass movement - but also a continuous campaign against the National Government's policies. Throughout the 1930s Dutt's interventions in Party discussions constantly reminded his colleagues that the chief fascist danger, and therefore the chief war danger of especial concern to the British Party, emanated from the National Government. This was especially difficult for the Party to absorb, because much of its propaganda after 1933 was devoted to a campaign to get Britain aligned with the Soviet Union against the war danger from Hitler's Germany. Dutt, good Leninist that he was, instinctively saw that his duty was chiefly to destroy the (anti-Soviet) bourgeoisie at home. Thus when the Central Committee published a *Manifesto on the War danger* in the *Daily Worker* on 21 March 1935, Dutt fulminated that it presented British imperialism as 'poor innocent babes in the wood deluded and led by the nose by the "German militarists" who play on their "weak" point of hatred for the Soviet Union'. The reality was rather different, 'Our fight is primarily and specifically against British Imperialism ... because [it] is openly the leader behind the whole present war-plot, as we have consistently pointed out for two years ever since Hitler'.[9]

It only needs to be added that, had the National Government concluded a defensive pact with the Soviet Union, none of the arguments mentioned above would have remained relevant. In these circumstances Dutt would have been the first to alert the Party to the new balance of 'class' forces.

The Party's inability to make proper use of Dutt's theoretical works was a settled conviction in the Dutt household - Salme is still to be found complaining about it to Pollitt in 1939. Yet the organisation's dependence on his propaganda work was never in doubt, and explains Clemens' reference to the 'myth- like halo' which surrounded his brother's name among the Party rank and file.[10] Figures for 1931, for example, show that Dutt was the author of nearly 40 per cent of the pamphlets sold by the Party, according to a *Daily Worker* survey.[11] By December 1934 he was also able to boast that he had written 'the majority of leading party documents' during the previous six months. And yet he continued to be dogged by 'semi-private attacks' to the effect that he was out of touch with the Party. These had 'always been going on for many years now; and there is really nothing to be done about it', he told Clemens at the end of 1934.[12]

There was nothing to be done about it because Dutt was still living in Brussels. To entreaties from the Party that he should return to Britain, he would explain that Salme, with no passport, would be refused entry. This sort of problem was of course routinely surmounted when the Comintern required it, though Salme's status as a Comintern agent may well have given rise to very real fears that she would be arrested upon re-entry to Britain. At all events, Dutt's anomalous position was allowed to continue for twelve years in all, despite his undoubted centrality in the Party's policy-making from at least 1928. Nevertheless he would remain a loner by choice after his return to Britain, the one Party leader invariably absent when the others socialised. This personal reserve probably came naturally to Dutt, but it was also useful in his role as the Comintern's unofficial watchdog; and his conscious cultivation of a certain air of mystery should not be excluded either.

Dutt's position as the Party's leading theorist was perfectly obvious even to an outsider such as John Strachey who, turning to Marxism after his brief flirtation with Oswald Moseley's New Party, looked to the Brussels emigré for further enlightenment at the end of 1931. He thereby began a close collaboration which lasted nearly ten years. Strachey wrote that he:

> wanted very much to discuss the general British position with you. Like so many other people, I have been deeply impressed by your notes in *Labour Monthly* and the undeniable accuracy of your prognosis. I find myself unable any longer to deny the accuracy of the Communist diagnosis and the correctness of the communist line in Britain.[13]

That Strachey could be converted to the doom and gloom of Dutt's message only goes to show the depth of his depressed spirits - and those of many fellow socialists - in the wake of the 1931 general election. But his turn to the Communists may also be connected to the growing perception of the success of planning in the USSR. The only other ray of hope was the conviction that 'objectively' the situation was rotten ripe for revolution. But even Strachey could see that the Party was totally isolated - the membership of 2,724 in June rising to 6,279 in November. Undeterred by what he called his pessimism about the Party's ability to get any grip on the mass movement, he was nevertheless able to send Dutt the manuscript of the apocalyptically entitled *The Coming Struggle For Power*, the following summer with its prophecy of imperialist war or socialist revolution. Dutt's corrections to this text - it was an argument, after all, which he had honed to perfection - were incorporated into the final version and Strachey thanked him on returning from Brussels for 'one of the most intellectually exciting conversations [he] had ever had'.[14]

At Dutt's insistence there was no acknowledgement of his contribution in the preface to the book; Strachey's value to the Party was enhanced by his maintaining a certain distance from it. In any case, after talking a great deal about the relationship between Marxist and Freudian ideas at the beginning of 1932, he was not at all sure that Strachey was ready to join the Party (presumably because Strachey enthused about Freud). It was time for his homily on commitment:

> It is one thing to reach a certain intellectual agreement with the correctness of the Communist analysis, as demonstrated by events. It is another thing to reach real revolutionary consciousness, so that the question of entering the revolutionary movement no longer appears as a question of making sacrifices, losing valuable opportunities of work etc, but on the contrary, as the only possible basis of work and realisation.[15]

It was a sermon which carried force precisely because of Dutt's own selfless asceticism - he was the very model of Communist restraint, rectitude, industry and courage. Lenin was the prototype, of course, but it was perfectly possible for any group of Communists - at the end of a *Labour Monthly* editorial board meeting, for example - to swap stories and jokes of common hardships such as their experiences of prison. (Dutt is remembered, incidentally, as having enjoyed the banter but without contributing to it.) In any case the life of single- minded devotion could inspire admiration in one such as Strachey - always conscious of Dutt's capacity to live on tea, bread and sardines during the period of their collaboration, while he himself expected rather more of the world's material comforts. Victor Gollancz was similarly impressed and remembered Dutt's life of austerity for the cause with affection even after their political separation. It must be said, however, that this had its drawbacks for those closer to Dutt like his more passionate brother - whose amorous entanglements produced only a disapproving coldness - or Salme who appears to have been oppressed by her husband's regime of work towards the end of her life.[16] Dutt's natural mode was didactic and in this capacity he excelled in the service of those like Strachey (and during the second World War, D.N. Pritt) who wanted a Marxist mentor.

While Dutt was happy to use Strachey - during the course of 1932, for example, he was directed to the task of luring the restless elements inside the ILP over to the Party - he was also instrumental in keeping him out of the Party, or so Strachey complained that November.[17] In spite of this, it was with Dutt's help that Strachey made a name for himself as the most gifted expositor of Marxism in the English language during the next few years, through such books as *The Menace of Fascism* (1933), *The Nature of Capitalist Crisis* (1934), and *The Theory and Practice of Socialism* (1936). Again there was no acknowledgement of Dutt's input, although this had been substantial and led, in the case of *The Nature of Capitalist Crisis*, to Strachey having 'drastically reformulated the "crisis analysis" part of [the] book as a result of our discussions'.[18] In March 1935 Dutt told Eugene Varga, the Comintern's leading economist, that Strachey had 'now either joined the party or is at any rate regarding himself as under the same responsibility', but added that 'his theoretical competence is not yet quite secure'. It was all the more important that Varga, therefore, should review *The Nature of Capitalist Crisis*, there being according to Dutt - taking another swipe at Maurice Dobb - 'no one in our ranks fully competent enough in economic theory'.[19]

THE SEVENTH CONGRESS OF THE COMINTERN

In 1934 the Soviet Union joined the League of Nations - erstwhile 'thieves kitchen' of Leninist lore - and thereby signalled Stalin's determination to find allies from among the bourgeois states and to achieve collective security against the Nazis and their allies. On 27 July 1934 the French Left concluded a pact which created the People's Front for much the same purpose; Communists and former 'social fascists' were united against the real fascists. These steps are now taken as evidence of a major tactical shift within the Communist movement which culminated with the last Comintern congress, the seventh, in August 1935, at which the ultra-leftism of the previous six years was severely modified, rather than dropped or repudiated. Just as the Soviet Union was right to seek alliances with the bourgeois democracies to protect itself against the fascist states, so it now behoved the Communist Parties to seek anti-fascist alliances with any organisations prepared to enter into such an arrangement.

Georgi Dimitrov, the Bulgarian Communist who gave the main report to the seventh congress, was accordingly able to emphasise the peculiarities of the fascist dictatorship - narrowly defined as 'the open terrorist dictatorship of the most reactionary, most chauvinistic and most imperialist elements of finance capital' - in such a way as to differentiate it from other forms of bourgeois rule. The point was made, for example, that the democratic liberties enjoyed in some capitalist states had often been wrested from the bourgeoisie historically by the workers' movement itself. The qualitative difference between fascism and bourgeois democracy, that had hitherto been specifically denied, was now acknowledged. Social democracy, under pressure of the events of the last few years, it was now said, was no longer the main bulwark of the bourgeoisie and could be won over to the anti-fascist front. The choice, said Dimitrov, was not between proletarian dictatorship and bourgeois democracy but between bourgeois democracy and fascism.[20]

However Dimitrov also observed that the bourgeoisie in certain countries had paved the way to fascism through governments - such as the National Government in Britain - committed to reactionary policies. The eight days of discussion devoted to Dimitrov's report thus had to cope with a policy which combined old ideas with new departures. The needs of Soviet foreign policy, which of course informed the entire congress, could not - in the nature of the complex international situation unfolding - give rise to a single, clear analysis. Thus the debate explored different meanings in Dimitrov's report. The unprecedented policy of collaboration with bourgeois parties might lead the Communists to support their 'own' capitalist state if it proved sufficiently committed to an alliance with the Soviet Union. Alternatively, the perspective of revolutionary change could remain relevant in cases where any co-operation with the Soviet Union was opposed by the bourgeoisie and also where a radical upheavel was a real possibility. In both cases the primary object of the exercise was the defence of the Soviet Union and the prevention of an anti-Soviet war. This was the only stable factor in the analysis, all else was tactical. In the heat of battle it was of course possible to forget this and on these occasions Dutt was on hand to expose the error.

Dutt's own contribution to the debate - in what was his first, and last, appearance at a Comintern congress - included a mealy-mouthed self-criticism to the effect that, 'in our agitation and propaganda we were sometimes inclined to call practically anything outside the communist camp fascist'. Dutt now belatedly acknowledged that the formation of the Nazi Government was 'a turning-point of decisive importance'. But he also persisted with the perspective, while acknowledging the essentially 'defensive' character of much of what Dimitrov had had to say, of 'approaching revolutionary crisis':

> The blow of fascism is also the sign of the approaching revolutionary crisis, the sign that the latent civil war in class society is coming out into the open

> ... in all the leading countries the majority of the population is becoming more and more divided into two camps.[21]

Only four months before the seventh congress, Dutt had instructed the Secretariat of the CPGB that the slogan 'For Soviet Power' had to be central to the Party's propaganda. After the seventh congress he is remembered as having been still inclined to drag his feet on the more flexible, less sectarian approach which it inaugurated, as opposed to Gallacher and Pollitt who were enthusiastic advocates of broad anti-fascist alliances.[22] Thus it is not surprising that, as the delegates from some of the CPs were striking a patriotic note and discovering themselves to be the heirs of Kant, Fichte and Hegel, or Abraham Lincoln, or the Encyclopedists, Dutt's speech to the seventh congress emphasised rupture rather than continuity with the past.

In one of the congress commissions, however, Dutt also insisted that the definition of fascism associated with Dimitrov could apply to any right-wing dictatorship because the formula ommitted reference to the mass basis of fascism. 'But that's his definition', he was told. 'Whose?', Dutt enquired; 'Stalin's', came the reply.

Dutt's inclination to stress the old oppositionist mentality could be accommodated in the Popular Front formula, because differences in emphasis reflected legitimate national variations affecting the Comintern's primary purpose. But on the the movement's primary purpose there was complete clarity. As Togliatti told the congress:

> For us it is absolutely indisputable that there is complete identity of aim between the peace policy of the Soviet Union and the policy of the working class and the Communist parties of the capitalist countries. There is not, and cannot be, any doubt in our ranks on this score. We not only defend the Soviet Union in general. We defend concretely its whole policy and each of its acts.[23]

In Britain the Communists knew that they were confronted with a National Government intent on appeasing the fascist states and apparently determined to repel the overtures for collective security emanating from Moscow. The policy of the National Government was *ipso facto* the main threat of fascism in Britain and Dutt argued as much in his congress speech. Thus his 'Third Period' theses on the organic growth of fascism out of the bourgeois order did not suddenly become obsolete because of the seventh World congress of the Comintern. Similarly the dim view Dutt took of the Labour Party as a contributing factor in the process of 'fascisation' remained salient, given its consistent animosity towards the CPGB, and its predictable refusal to have anything to do with the Communists and the People's Front. He nevertheless realised that some things had changed since 30 January 1933. For, as he told a special conference of the CPGB on his return, 'socialists all over the world have got a country' and this:

> gives rise to the necessity that we have got to maintain our world base against capitalism, [and recognise] that this is our common concern in all countries and therefore we approach the international situation in a different way from 1914 ... You have not simply got two sets of imperialist powers facing each other; but those imperialist powers which are most concerned with the division of the world, which are most driving to war have developed at the same time to fascist forms and their aim of war expansion, representing therefore the most aggressive forces of world capitalism, is combined with the aim of capitalist aggression against the Soviet Union.[24]

The advent of Hitler made war against the Soviet Union likely; this was the new factor. Dutt had made the point in the German Communist journal *Unsere Zeit* just three months after Hitler's government was formed, dismissing the 'noisy and empty' Nazi propaganda against Versailles as a mere cover for essential continuity with the foreign policy of the German bourgeoisie; the real intent of the Nazis, he insisted, was anti-Soviet and for this purpose 'Hitlerism offers to sell Germany as a subservient pawn to Western imperialism for the war on the Soviet Union'. Given the 'unconditional defence' of the Soviet Republic to which Communists were pledged - it was, remember, one of the twenty-one conditions of membership of the Comintern - He was right to scorn the 'absolutely childish repetition of 1914 formulations'. He advised the CPGB membership that the Communist propaganda onslaught against 'bourgeois democracy' in 1918-1921 had been informed by the knowledge that, in the prevailing circumstances, talk of democracy had been ideologically 'the last stage of the reaction to defeat the revolution'. This was no longer the case; today the capitalists themselves had turned against democracy and were ready to embrace open dictatorship. In these circumstances 'once again these same democratic forms', formally reviled, 'become slogans of the struggle against the capitalist line'. Moreover, there was no doubt that the 'main forces' of capitalism were preparing war on the USSR, and Dutt stressed that it 'was absolutely necessary sooner or later that they must come to this'. The People's Front could delay the conflagration and ensure that when it happened the social revolution would not be far behind:

> Where before the dream of democracy was a counter- revolutionary opiate today the fight for democratic rights against fascism has become a mass fight against the main attack of finance-capital. Where before the hypocritical talk of peace was a main weapon of imperialist enslavement, today the fight for peace against the new world war has become a fight of the masses in unity with the Soviet Union, against the main drive of finance-capital.[25]

This was the new moral to which readers of *Labour Monthly* were treated in the autumn of 1935, as Dutt reiterated the familiar slogans concerning the 'bankruptcy of the old liberal social democratic policies', the fascist offensive, and the drive to war.

COLONIAL POLICY

The Comintern's new enthusiasm for the widest possible alliances extended to the colonial liberation struggle, and Dutt took steps even before he left Moscow at the end of the seventh congress to begin repairing the Party's troubled relationship with the nationalist community in India. For some years now the Communists had done their best to isolate themselves, with the most unrestrained attacks on the Congress. The Party also suffered at the hands of the government of India through the Meerut Trial and the severe sentences which were eventually passed on the organisation's leaders. However, the 'conspiracy' case also publicised the Communists as intransigent freedom-fighters in the eyes of many nationalists. The Party had managed to recruit former terrorists active in the Punjab, and one of their leaders, Yashpal, translated Dutt's *Modern India* into Hindi soon after the Party turned to 'class against class'.[26] Though the Party denounced the mainstream nationalists as collaborators with imperialism almost at the very moment when Congress took steps to fight for complete independence, it looked less out of touch with reality when Gandhi abruptly ended the mass non-co-operation campaign in March 1931, a year after it had started. The Party's contention that Gandhi would sell out now seemed prophetic, especially when he agreed to participate in the Round Table talks in London, which the nationalists rightly perceived as a British government manoeuvre designed to delay, rather than forward, the independence of India.

Nehru was one of the many leftish nationalists who saw this as a betrayal. His evolution to the left was such, according to his biographer, that 'the grounding in Marxism, which he had received at the Brussels conference and after, was followed by a near-conversion to communism by practical testimony'.[27] As early as the Meerut trial, he was initially cited by the prosecution as the 'liaison agent between Moscow and India'. But once the Communists progressed to an unadulterated 'class against class' line Nehru became one of the targets for their scorn and he was forced out of the League Against Imperialism at the end of January 1930. However this did nothing to deflect Nehru's attraction to Marxism, and his increasing impatience with Gandhi's spiritualism - especially after the Mahatma's pact with the Viceroy, Lord Irwin, in March 1931. By 1933 he was distancing himself from 'the accompaniments of a growing nationalism - an idealism, a mysticism, a feeling of exaltation, a belief in the mission of one's country, ... something of the nature of religious revivalism'. These were just 'middle class phenomena' which tended to obscure 'the inherent and fundamental conflict between economic interests within the nation'.[28] He now professed to see an organic crisis of capitalism that 'led to Fascism and, in its milder forms, to the formation of so-called national governments'. His old acquaintance Dutt might have used identical words; the national movement was being transformed, Nehru concluded, into a social struggle for economic freedom that was bound up with 'the problems of the world'.[29]

The ultra-leftism of 1928-35 had not, then, marginalised the Communists of India to the extent suffered by their British comrades - indeed when Nehru's allies on the left of Congress formed the Congress Socialist Party (CSP) in October 1934, the Communists, recently rendered illegal, were not long after admitted to its ranks and thus provided with an avenue of open political activity. Dutt assisted this process through his talks in Moscow with M.R. Masani, one of the CSP leaders with whom he made contact after the Comintern's seventh congress.[30] The distance between the Communists and the left nationalists was not as wide as it might have been, because the latter had moved ground. That being said, it is clear that the tactical turn associated with the People's Front made a more durable rapprochement possible. But it is worth recording that the abandonment of 'class against class' was not received with favour by all the militants concerned with colonial liberation.

It has been pointed out, for example, that 'in a real sense ... the years immediately following 1928 marked a highpoint in the Comintern's concern for colonial Africa'.[31] These were years when the Comintern's anti-imperialist polemics were at their most uncompromising. From the second world congress of the League Against Imperialism, at Frankfurt in July 1929, the Communists concentrated on their work among workers and peasants, while stigmatising the bourgeois nationalists as collaborators with imperialism. By the early 1930s able black Communists had been recruited who devoted most of their energies to anti- colonial activity; George Padmore of Trinidad, Jomo Kenyatta of Kenya, E.F. Small of Gambia, I.T.A. Wallace-Johnson of Sierra Leone and Frank Macauley of Nigeria. All of those mentioned were active in Britain at one time or another during the 1930s and but for a Labour government ban, a conference of 'Negro' workers would have been held there in 1930. Naturally the British branch of the League Against Imperialism worked with these militants and could be relied upon to maintain a continuous campaign for African independence, while exposing the injustices and exploitation associated with colonialism. Dutt's *Labour Monthly* accurately reflected the Communists' work in this field; while it carried thirty-six articles on India during the years 1928-35, Africa was the subject of a further sixteen articles (9 of them written by either Padmore or Kenyatta) while another thirty-seven essays were devoted to other colonies and colonial issues.

Once the Comintern redirected the Communist Parties to the fight against fascism and war, however, Padmore, Kenyatta and their co-thinkers turned to Pan-Africanism, in the belief that the Soviet Union had sacrificed its anti-colonialism in order to curry favour with France and Great Britain. The Communists were henceforward considered fickle friends of subject peoples by this influential group and it is true that the emphasis of Communist propaganda changed substantially. Certainly the Italian invasion of Abyssinia in October 1935 was seen by Dutt as part of the fascist offensive against the USSR as well as an expression of the routine objectives of imperialism. The League Against Imperialism nevertheless worked with organisations like the West African Students Union, the League of Coloured Peoples and the *ad hoc* International African Friends of Ethiopia in the campaign against the invasion of Abyssinia. When the League Against Imperialism was folded in 1937, its work was taken up by a *Colonial Information Bulletin*, a decision which must have reflected new priorities in Communist work as well as the small size of the League. The change in emphasis was evident in Dutt's own journal. In the four years 1936-9 the themes of fascism and war preoccupied no less than sixty articles in *Labour Monthly*.

Nevertheless the journal still found space for over forty articles on various colonies and dependent territories - most of them, as usual, on India, but also including eloquent essays on the practicality and desirability of independence in sub-Saharan Africa.[32]

As for Dutt himself, he was, if anything, even more involved in colonial work upon his return to Britain in 1936. This included a great deal of public speaking as well as the usual round of publishing and behind-the-scenes wire-pulling. It was Dutt, for example, who was president of the Indian Political Conference and gave the opening address to its fifth congress in July 1936. It was Dutt who dominated proceedings when radical nationalists such as Nehru and Subhas Bose visited London - leading the welcoming delegations, conducting the formal interviews for the Party press, giving the opening speeches at the specially prepared rallies. Dutt always represented the Party at the Oxford Union or at debates organised by the Majlis at Oxford or Cambridge. Though an uninspired orator, he often carried the day at these set piece events, as when the Oxford Union voted 187 to 76 in support of the Indian National Congress in November 1937, after a debate with Viscount Goschen, a former Governor of Madras. Even during the first months of the Second World War, when the Party opposed the war as inter-imperialist rivalry (see chapter 6) and was therefore unpopular, Dutt addressed a packed meeting jointly organised by the Oxford Union and the Majlis and managed to obtain the signatures of nearly all present for a petition condemning the BBC's decision to ban actors like Michael Redgrave (because they were associated with the anti-war People's Convention set up by the Party).

The conduct of the Party's colonial work was probably more dependent on Dutt's personal input after 1935 than at any previous time - the Soviet Union having effectively devolved all day-to-day responsibility to metropolitan parties such as the British, French, Dutch and American. Perhaps the importance of this shadowy side of the Party's work is best illustrated by Dutt's meeting with Nehru in Lausanne in February 1936. Just weeks earlier Nehru (known as 'the Professor' within the Comintern) had learned of his election to the presidency of the Indian National Congress. The opportunity was thus provided for a timely intervention from Dutt with the purpose of influencing Nehru's forthcoming presidential address - and perhaps the future direction of Congress. In the official version of events, as retailed by Dutt, the meeting in Lausanne was pure serendipity - Dutt visiting Ben Bradley in the same sanatorium as the one in which Nehru's wife was being treated.[33] The lie is exposed, however, in a letter which Pollitt sent to Victor Gollancz in March, explaining the delay in the completion of Dutt's *World Politics*: 'I had to instruct Dutt to leave all his work and go to Lausanne for some important conversations with Nehru'.[34]

On 19 February Dutt filed his report to the Political Committee of the CPGB on sixteen hours of talks:

> during which we were able to cover the whole ground, situation of the movement, both past and future perspectives, existing forces and groupings, problems of mass organisation, especially the peasantry, particular questions and proposals we wished to put forward, his role as president and future action, also report of his talks with LP [Labour Party] leaders and others.[35]

From all of this he was able to divine Nehru's 'strong interest' in the People's Front and his 'fairly close' (to Communist) attitude towards the Soviet Union which was mercifully 'less affected by ILP notions' than that of other Indian socialists.[36] He was shrewd enough to see, however, that Nehru's commitment to the unity of the nationalist movement would contain his left sympathies and that if Gandhi 'stirs a finger, he will almost certainly respond'. In part his reserve was also that of the dedicated Communist judging a distinguished near-Marxist; Nehru was 'essentially a representative of the centre' and the successor of Gandhi, not a revolutionary:

> Within these limits he may give some help to the left; but it will need considerable change and development if he is to come out as an effective leader; and if he does not come out and fight, he may become a prisoner of the right.

Dutt evidently slipped into his accustomed tutorial mode with ease during the Lausanne meeting. Nehru was shown the necessity of campaigning for the collective affiliation of peasant and workers' organisations to the Congress; he was instructed on the need for complete opposition to any collaboration with the Indian liberals; and for a boycott of the 1935 constitution - the outcome of the Simon Commission - and insistence on complete independence for India. Dutt further enjoined Nehru to raise the economic and social demands of the masses and use his influence to include Left representatives in the panels of Congress candidates:

> On the necessity in principle of a revolutionary workers' party for the whole future of the movement, he would finally agree in principle, when pressed, but with obvious reluctance and hesitancy. An examination of the history of the Kuomintang, the conditions of its success in its revolutionary period, and the reasons for its breakdown into a counter-revolutionary

> instrument, impressed him and had some effect on his outlook in relation to this question. I urged that on the basis of his Marxist understanding he should regard with deepest affection and sympathy those early elements who sought to represent our outlook or were coming near to us, even when they seemed difficult or might make mistakes, in view of the enormous importance of these beginnings for the whole future of the movement. He expressed agreement with this.

In fact, for all his diplomacy, Dutt was as aware as Nehru of the inconsiderable significance of the Indian Communists in 1936 and of the centrality to the nationalist struggle, in spite of its undoubted problems, of the Congress. Nehru only complained that the mass disobedience campaigns of 1920-1922 and 1930-1934 began wonderfully but then progressively dribbled off and weakened. This provided Dutt with an opportunity to forward his own strategic view which remained resolutely anti-British:

> Taking up his statement of the problem, I suggested that mass civil disobedience had proved itself a powerful instrument for launching a movement in the first stage, but that something more was needed to follow it up and carry the whole movement a stage further if it was not to end in breakdown, in impotence. What was that something more? That something more could only be the launching of the agrarian revolution, for which conditions were visibly ripening, with sporadic unrest, already the main concern of the govt. and of which it was actively afraid (he agreed). The agrarian revolution, if developing over the greater part of the country, with the simultaneous struggle of the workers in the towns, was the decisive force which could swamp and overwhem British rule and sweep it away, since their white forces would be inadequate to cope with it. This must therefore be the next stage of the struggle after 1920-22 and 1930-34, which must now be prepared.

In fact Dutt succeeded in extracting promises from Nehru to the effect that he would propose the affiliation of the trade unions to Congress, oppose any co-operation with the liberals while maintaining the unity of the left and centre, and 'take a sympathetic attitude to the role and propaganda of our friends in the Congress'. Dutt was far from rejoicing over this measure of agreement and his report ends on a sceptical note. The new tactics hardly depended on Nehru's agreement in any case. Within days two articles appeared in the international Communist press by Dutt and Bradley, designed to ensure that the Indian Communists were fully apprised of the tactical line adopted by the seventh congress in Moscow. These articles spelled out in detail the necessity for 'a united anti-imperialist People's Front', that would involve the Communists in close collaboration with those nationalists who rejected the 'slave constitution' of 1935. The rallying cry was to be complete independence and the convocation of a Constituent Assembly. The Communists would champion the affiliation of workers' and peasants' organisations to the Congress and campaign for the vigorous promotion of their social and economic demands within the nationalist movement.[37] This naturally required the Communists to renounce the sectarianism of 'class against class', carefully nurtured since 1929, and work for trade union unity - the better to build up a broad Left inside the Congress.[38]

The 'Dutt-Bradley Theses' marked the beginning of the Popular Front reorientation of the CPI. But their impact owed much to the fact that Nehru gave his presidential speech at Lucknow just as they appeared. The address greatly exceeded the guarded hopes expressed by Dutt in February; it was simply the clearest exposition Nehru had yet made of his Marxist sympathies. The demands for a Constituent Assembly, for the affiliation of workers' and peasants' organisations, for the promotion of a left social and economic programme and for the unequivocal rejection of the Government of India Act of 1935 all duly appeared. But Nehru also linked the nationalist struggle with the struggle for socialism, and counterposed these progressive movements to the international forces of imperialism and fascism. He asked his audience to 'join hands with other forces in the world who are working for the new civilisation', in a common struggle against world reaction which was preparing another world war. He said he could detect 'a definite fascist mentality' in the rulers of India - as clear a reference to the National Government in Britain as his talk of the 'new civilisation' was to the Soviet Union. Even within the nationalist movement he professed to see a division between the 'handful' of middle class allies of imperialism and the masses of the dispossessed who inclined to revolution. He thus linked his call for a Constituent Assembly to the creation of 'at least a semi-revolutionary situation in this country' and stressed that socialism was the 'solution' to the problems of India and the world, 'not in a vague humanitarian way', be it noted, 'but in a scientific economic sense'.[39]

Dutt was ecstatic and immediately pronounced Nehru's speech a 'landmark' in the differentiation of factions within Congress.[40] Nehru's realistic appraisal of the constraints on his presidency, as communicated to Dutt in Lausanne, were soon to be vindicated however. Ten of the fourteen members of his new working committee were ideological opponents and with Gandhi's assistance they contrived to water down or shelve all of Nehru's radical proposals. After Lucknow, Nehru was attacked as 'the leader of the Communistic school of thought in India' but was unable to reap any benefits from his new image.[41] As Dutt rightly perceived, Nehru - having no independent mass political base of his own - was forced to compromise. But this did not stop him from championing causes close to the Communists - not only collective security, left unity in Britain and Spain, but also opposition to the National Government as a close ally of the fascist powers. Meanwhile the Communists, in spite of restrictions on Nehru's leadership of Congress, advanced their position within the nationalist movement. The alliance with the socialists helped, as did Communist recognition of the Congress as the 'central mass political organisation of the Indian people ranged against imperialism'.

Dutt accurately expressed the relevant balance in his presidential address to the Indian Political Conference in London in July 1936, organised by the League Against Imperialism, where he poured scorn both on those socialists who opposed 'mere nationalism' as irrelevant to India's real problems, and on those nationalists who neglected the social question. Unless the struggle was directed against both British imperialism and the Indian princes and landlords there would be no real independence for India. It was a message he returned to repeatedly; the immediate aim was national independence and the 'democratic revolution', but this struggle relied on the working masses, and their involvement necessarily developed around the aims of socialism. So as to leave his Indian readership in no doubt on the matter, Dutt used the occasion of MacDonald's death in 1937 to contrast the unlamented leader's social imperialism with the character of Communism - 'the true ally and fellow fighter of the colonial peoples'.[42]

Tactically the Communists were intent on remaining within the Congress fold while extending their independent base. Work among the peasants in Kerala, Andhra, Bengal and the Punjab was an important aspect of this activity, but the People's Front also allowed the Party to project itself as a legitimate component of a broader left. This worked in that anti-imperialism, anti-fascism, anti-landlordism and the promotion of a workers' and peasants' social and economic programme were natural parts of the left's political culture - all the more so in view of the strong Marxist influence within the Congress Socialist Party. But the Communist Party had not renounced its hegemonic aspiration and the practice of polarisation. In 1938 it supported Subhas Chandra Bose's bid for a second term as president of Congress in the knowledge that Gandhi had set his face against it, and despite the Communists' own doubts about Bose's radicalism - Dutt himself having questioned Bose about his fascist leanings earlier in the year.[43] When Bose was forced to stand down, the Party supported a further escalation of the conflict by initially backing his Forward Bloc, formed in February 1939. In short they persisted in opposing the leadership of Congress as inherently pusillanimous and insidious, and sought by organisational manoeuvres to achieve a dominance that they failed to get by their mass work.

But the advice from London urged caution. Bose's short-lived re-election as Congress President prompted Ben Bradley to warn of 'disruptive elements on the Left' who threatened to split the nationalist movement by attempting to seize control of the leadership as represented by the Working Committee.[44] This would reflect Dutt's own appreciation of the authenticity of Congress as representative of Indian nationalism and of the need for the Communists to remain within the fold. Even here, of course, Soviet security interests were relevant, with Communist rhetoric referring to the contribution an independent India would make to the 'democratic', anti-Fascist nations. But this was hardly an appeasement of Britain, since the National Government had no intention of allowing an independent India to come into existence.

In an article for *Pravda*, as late as April 1939, Dutt stressed that fascism was 'the main spearhead of imperialist aggression ... especially against the colonial peoples'. He was able to illustrate this contention with quotations from Nazi theorists such as Dr Hecht and Dr Rohrbach who had reasoned that the fatal error had been to allow European culture to get into the colonies; these would be sealed off by the Nazis and their peoples debarred from education and travel abroad. Hence, concluded Dutt:

> Those ideologists who, willingly or unwillingly, serving the interests of fascism, seek to equate fascism and imperialism in general, are showing a criminal blindness to the realities of the most vital concern to the colonial peoples.[45]

This was to overlook Dutt's own capacity for such error in the years 1929-33 while conveniently targetting the Trotskyists for especial odium now. Within months of this publication Dutt would return to his former stupidity with perfect equilibrium. It was as if, to paraphrase a remark made about another dogmatist, the extravagant credulity with which he accepted the wildest change of line was only another side of his bottomless unbelief.[46] But this would be to overlook his bottomless devotion to the USSR.

WORLD POLITICS

The idea that the Communists suddenly became 'reformists' because of the Popular Front is belied by Dutt's *World Politics, 1918- 1936*, his major book of the period, and one of the most successful publications of Gollancz's Left Book Club. The whole thrust of this book was to demonstrate that '1914 had solved nothing': 'all the issues of our epoch, which have been accumulating for nearly two decades since the ending of the war, are coming to a head in the period that is now opening'. It seemed to Dutt that the world was on 'the eve of a new series of revolutionary struggles ... which may even in the most favourable conditions defeat the menace of a new world war'.[47] But his pessimism on this score is evident. The picture carefully created is of armaments production vaulting forward, diplomatic crises abounding everywhere, extreme economic instability and political polarisation. The period since the war had merely enabled the capitalist monopolies to secure 'a far more preponderant position in world economic life and a far more complete and all-pervading influence on the policies of their respective states'. The upshot consisted in:

> The consequent ever sharpening and ceaselessly renewed conflict for the redivision of the world, by economic weapons, by State legislative weapons, by diplomatic weapons and finally by armed warfare, which is in essence the reflection of the conflict of the enlarged world productive forces against the existing social and political forms'. This is the crux of world politics.[48]

The issue of the new division of the world was thus 'definitely in the forefront'; a new imperialist world war was brewing in which the 'revisionist' imperialist powers could be expected to take the offensive. In a sense, argued Dutt, the war had already begun on a regional scale while the general tension and approach to global conflagration exceeded that of 1914. But it is clear that Dutt saw this war arising out of 'the bankruptcy of the existing economic order' and what he termed the characteristic features of the imperialist epoch, rather than the particular reactionary nature of the fascist states - he could still refer to Anglo-American rivalry, for example, as the dominant inter- imperialist contradiction of the period. The People's Front constituted, in this context, 'the typical expression of the present stage of struggle between the existing capitalist rule and the socialist revolution'. Another axis of conflict was 'the extreme point of contrast' represented by 'the relative retrogression of capitalist production and headlong advance of socialist production' in the USSR, which 'raised sharp questions of the future relationship of the capitalist and socialist worlds'. A third big turning of the ways affected the international labour movement: 'the old reformist illusions having received a shattering blow by the experience of the world economic crisis and of Fascism'. Finally:

> the colonial peoples are in movement, alike in Asia and in Africa: the Chinese struggle for national unity and liberation against the policies of partition goes forward; the Indian struggle for liberation is gathering force; the Middle East is in ferment; Abyssinia fights the foreign invader; all Africa is stirring. This not only opens out a new perspective for the colonial and semi-colonial peoples, constituting the majority of the human race, to advance from the passive to the active instruments of history; but this in its turn reacts upon and undermines the basis of imperialism in the remaining countries and the consequent socio-political structure built upon that basis.[49]

What follows these opening salvos is yet another restatement of Lenin's *Imperialism*, via a survey of the years following Versailles. In the process Dutt steps forward as the Sidney Webb of catastrophe; just as his illustrious Fabian predecessor was able to compile impressive lists in the 1880s to demonstrate the 'inevitability of gradualism', Dutt is now able to marshall the facts of collapse and disintegration to show that such optimism is all rot. To take only the previous six years:

> In rapid succession event followed event, bringing down the pillars of stabilisation and of the post-war settlements. In 1930 an emergency regime was established in Germany, suspending parliamentary forms; this continued until the final transition to Fascism in 1933. In 1931 came the suspension of all payments of reparations and war debts; the formation of the National Government in Britain; the collapse of the gold standard in Britain, followed by most other countries; and Japan's invasion of North China, in violation of the Covenant of the League, the Washington Nine-Power Treaty and the Kellogg Pact, followed by Japan's departure from the League of Nations. In 1932 the Disarmament Conference opened while the Japanese guns were bombarding Shanghai and Chapei, and for three years dragged out its fruitless sessions; the Lausanne Conference registered the end of reparations; the Ottawa Conference of the British Empire marked the end of the last remnants of free trade; while the completion of the first Five Year Plan brought the Soviet Union to the position of the first industrial power in Europe and the second in the world. In 1933 Hitler came to power in Germany and inaugurated the

> regime of Fascist terror, with repercussions throughout Europe; Germany left the League of Nations and resumed freedom of action in the military sphere; Roosevelt inaugurated the emergency regime of the New Deal in the United States; the gold standard crashed in the United States, the only remaining great country where the pre-war gold standard had continued; the World Economic Conference ended in swift fiasco. In 1934 German rearmament went forward, and the leaders of the Nazi storm troops were slaughtered in the June purge; Dollfuss was killed in Austria, and Barthou in France; armed struggles against Fascism and reaction took place in Austria and Spain; in France Fascism was held back by the united working-class front and later the People's Front; the transformation of international political relations was signalised by the entry of the Soviet Union into the League of Nations. In 1935 Germany adopted its conscription law, in defiance of Versailles, followed by the Anglo-German Naval Agreement; the Franco-Soviet Pact revealed the new alignment of forces; Italy launched its war of aggression on Abyssinia, in defiance of the League; and Japan repudiated the Washington Naval Treaty. In the beginning of 1936, while Italy went forward with its war on Abyssinia, unchecked by the League's very weak economic sanctions, and Japan went forward with its extending war on North China, the London Naval Conference was marked by the departure of Japan and registered the end of the Washington naval limitation system, Britain announced its rearmament programme, and the German repudiation of Locarno and re-militarisation of the Rhineland opened a new crisis in European political relations.[50]

Notwithstanding the occasional bright spots in this lugubrious catalogue it is obvious that the only future Dutt could see clearly was the one he remembered - the trail of destruction since 1914. With good reason he could see that the German war aims of 1914-18 were back on the immediate agenda, while 'over the future of the League hangs a question-mark'.[51] The prospects for peace were negligible but this in no way provided a rationale for support of British rearmament. His analysis found the 'deeply rooted characteristics' of the imperialist system to be the fundamental cause of the problem, not this or that state. It was a 'system of extreme disequilibrium and discord, with downward trends of production over long periods ... and with centrifugal tendencies', making for a restricted world trade, 'and intensified warfare of the monopolist blocs'.[52] The 'dissatisfied' imperialisms of Germany and Japan were the most open in their preparations for war, 'but in their own fashion the more complicated mechanisms of British or American capitalism are carrying through a transformation which ultimately leads in the same direction'. Dutt could only think deterministically about the approach of war, its accelerated advance being 'as necessary a working out of the inner forces of imperialism at the present stage as each preceding stage of the post-war development has been'.[53]

No stable international co-operation of the imperialist powers on a world scale was possible, according to Dutt, but the entry of the Soviet Union into the League of Nations and the exit of the Powers planning an immediate war had created 'a completely new situation'. The role and significance of the League could now only be judged in relation to the given situation, which was continually changing. Since the line of collective security was 'dependent on the policies of imperialist Governments', he reasoned that it could not be reduced to 'the abstract preaching of a juridicial principle'. The Soviet Union was the only Power in the existing situation that was 'genuinely interested in the line of collective security as a universal line'. Thus the line actually depended on 'the active organisation and struggle of the mass forces in all countries, in unity with the Soviet Union, against war and for peace, utilising the diplomatic machinery of collective security only as an auxiliary weapon to the basic weapons of mass struggle'.[54] In any case 'collective security is no permanent solution of the problem of war', Dutt concluded, 'but at the best a temporary stopgap against the immediate menace of war'. For Dutt all the imperialist Powers were 'a set of double-crossing gangster kings, engaged in a ceaseless internecine conflict over their respective territories and spoils'. The final alliances of contending Powers could still not be predicted and it would be the worst folly to place any trust in the National Government.

In the Communist view, the National Government had been 'the decisive factor in making possible the success of the Nazi offensive'. Dutt argued that, 'if Britain had taken, or were yet to take, a decisive stand, in unity with France and the Soviet Union and the smaller states desiring peace, for the collective maintenance of peace throughout Europe as a whole, the way would not only be barred to Nazi aggression, but the consequent balance of forces for peace would inevitably draw over the still- hesitating smaller states, and also eventually Poland (where there is a sharp division of policy) to the stronger grouping for peace, and would thus finally compel Germany to enter into a system of collective security'. In fact, he maintained, British policy had consistently tipped the balance the other way during the period 1933-6. Yet there was, according to Dutt, a conflict in British policy. While there were those who feared the German- Japanese offensive as a threat to British imperial interests - in March 1933 he mentioned

Chamberlain, as well as Churchill as belonging to this camp in a letter to Pollitt - there were also those, represented for example by the Rothermere press, who wanted to deflect these expansionist aims into Eastern Europe and the USSR; 'the strategic inference is drawn to set one enemy against the other'. Dutt was in no doubt that 'the so far dominant tendency [is] of support for the Nazi war offensive', but suggested that the ultimate outcome of this conflict in policy could be determined by the strength of the mass struggle for peace in Britain. He also seemed to think that, 'with a few more years' development', the Soviet Union 'would become fully impregnable in a military sense'.[55] Dutt's strictly tactical appreciation of the Popular Front can be understood, then, in terms of its potential to change the policy of the National Government, or to contribute in some other way to the delay of a war that was inevitable, and which, when it came, would help in moving the mass movement built up by the Popular Front towards an insurrectionary policy.

THE POPULAR FRONT IN BRITAIN

There is no doubt that the seventh congress of the Comintern reoriented the Communist Parties in a way which complemented the mood for anti-fascist unity in the European left. Strict limits were placed on this process in Britain, however, by both the small size of the CPGB, which offered no electoral threat to the Labour Party, and the small scale of the fascist movement. The official leadership of the labour movement could therefore afford to ignore the Communist unity pleas on both counts, and make the point in passing that the fascist threat and the Communist revolution were equally repellant and symbiotically related.[56] Nevertheless the activist left was more receptive - not just the membership of the ILP and the Socialist League, but also many thousands of Labour Party members who defied their own leadership policy and worked with the Communists. In London the CP's offers of electoral assistance in 1935 were accepted by fifty-seven of the sixty-two constituencies in the County Council. By July 1936 the CP could boast that 1,121 Labour and trade union organisations had declared in favour of Communist affiliation to the party.[57] Undoubtedly the feeling for positive action which the Communists sought to tap was greatly strengthened by the eruption of civil war in Spain, also in July 1936, when fascist rebels led by General Franco attempted a military coup against the Republican Government. Once again a sharp contrast between the militant response of the Communists and the apparent timidity and impotence of the Parliamentary opposition worked in the Party's favour. In January 1937, together with the ILP and the Socialist League, the Party launched the Unity Campaign on the slogans 'Win victory by unity. Destroy the National Government. Roll Fascism back. End war'. It was a call which at its height, according to one study, involved as many as one-fifth of the 90,000 individual members of the Labour Party in London.[58]

Official Labour was so frightened of extra-parliamentary politics, by contrast, that the party and trade union membership was urged to refrain from setting up 'special organisations for any political or industrial purposes' whatever.[59] Accordingly the list of proscribed organisations lengthened and the leadership boycotted each of the four national Hunger Marches organised by the National Unemployed Workers Committee Movement; even the Jarrow crusade, organised by the whole town council, was given the official cold shoulder. From the activist viewpoint therefore the Labour and trade union leaders had created a vacuum which the CP and its allies would inevitably fill. The international and domestic scenes were not conducive to patient faith in the workings of parliamentary democracy. At home the hated National Government - pursuing appeasement of fascism and persecution of the Means-Tested poor - dominated Westminster. Abroad democracies were being swept aside and another world war prepared.

Communist membership trebled between 1935 and 1939 to 17,539 - still numerically puny but exerting a much bigger influence, as indicated by *Daily Worker* sales reaching 200,000 and Communist pamphlet sales above the million mark.[60] But perhaps the best indication of the Party's recent emergence from the political ghetto was the success of the Left Book Club which Victor Gollancz first advertised in February 1936. The idea originated from conversations between Gollancz, Strachey and Stafford Cripps. Strachey was already hand in glove with Dutt and Pollitt, of course, while Gollancz and Cripps had entered a pro- Soviet, near-Marxist phase. Together they decided that Harold Laski should be invited to join Strachey and Gollancz in the task of choosing books to recommend to the Left Book membership. Within three years of its launch the Club recorded 57,000 members and each of its titles were able to reach an estimated readership of a quarter of a million.[61] It has been described as 'the most active and largest body in Britain working for a Popular Front' but also as a 'propaganda machine for communism'.[62] About one-third of the Left Book Club's publications were actually written by Communists and all of them were selected by the Marxist triumvirate. Laski - a prominent Labour Party member and thus nominally furthest of the three from the Communist Party - said that his journey to Marxism had given him 'an increasing confidence in its will; the paradoxical sense that a fighting philosophy confers an inner peace unobtainable without its possession'. It is a testimony of faith that could also serve for Dutt.[63]

Dutt saw the value in having two 'independents' - Gollancz and Strachey - with Laski in charge of the Left Book Club. For as he told Gollancz, it was 'a brilliant piece of organising work all through'; and its success and scope, so far from being injured, is probably the greater because it is recognised by the public as an independent commercial enterprise on its own feet, and not the propaganda of a particular political organisation'.[64]

Dutt knew better, of course. Gollancz had been in the habit of turning to Dutt's colleague Emile Burns on 'points of higher Communist doctrine' when judging the suitability of books for publication even before the Club was launched. After it was launched Pollitt felt able to write to Gollancz in familiar terms pleading against publication of the Communist heretic, August Thalheimer's book, *Introduction to Dialectical Materialism*: 'Don't publish it. Not when I've got to cope with the old bugger [Stalin], the long bugger [Dutt] and that bloody red arse of a dean [Hewlett Johnson]'.[65] The Communist contribution to the Club's quality control hardly depended, however, on Pollitt's three stooges. By November 1936 the organisation of reader's discussion groups - there were a thousand of these in May 1938 - was entrusted to two Communists - Sheila Lynd and Betty Reid - and a future member, John Lewis. These three read all manuscripts submitted for publication and Gollancz's biographer tells us that while Party members vetted manuscripts for political deviations, almost all Club policy decisions were first discussed with Party officials.[66] It is hardly surprising then that Orwell's *Homage to Catalonia* was rejected, and the Club never touched a work by Trotsky. The pro-Communist bias occasioned much controversy at the time - for example in the pages of the *New Statesman* - and it was useful on such occasions to be able to point to publications such as Attlee's *Labour Party in Perspective* to confound such critics; the triumvirate did not point out, however, that the Labour leader's contribution - one of the Club's less successful titles - was distributed with specific instructions to group conveners to contrast it unfavourably with Marxist works on the same theme.[67]

When Laski joined in the praise which greeted Dutt's *World Politics*, on the other hand, Gollancz wrote to apologise for the 'deplorable' note of criticism that had crept into the Labour man's review. Laski had expressed his doubts that the working class could be roused to force Britain into an anti-fascist Anglo-Soviet pact in the manner prescribed by Dutt. Gollancz quickly explained that Strachey, though undoubtedly a better choice as reviewer, was not asked to cover the book because 'it would have looked too much like a family party'.[68] No such misgivings were expressed in relation to the abjectly worshipful tone with which the Club's monthly journal *Left News* invariably celebrated all things Soviet. This included some persuasive justifications of the Moscow Trials, with Strachey arguing that 'the whole future of humanity was dependent on [the] detention and execution' of the guilty parties.[69]

When Brailsford drew attention to a leaked letter from Stalin to the Czech government explaining that Tukhachevsky and his fellow generals were shot because they opposed the Stalin- Litvinov policy - not because they were traitors as officially maintained - it was Dutt who smacked him down in the pages of *Reynolds News*, the *New Statesman and Nation* and the *News Chronicle* in June and July 1937. Brailsford argued that the letter exposed the phoney nature of the charges brought against the generals and showed the Stalin regime to be 'a bloody tyranny ruled by terror and lies'. Dutt countered by denying the authenticity of the leaked memorandum which he attributed to Fascist sources. He then went on to justify the executions as 'necessary measures of defence against treason allied with Fascism'. This episode is instructive, however, chiefly as an example of how Dutt was able to invoke non-Communist sources to support his argument against Brailsford. A *Reynolds News* editorial, an article in the *Army Quarterly* and a piece by Wickham Steed in the *Spectator* are all cited in support of Stalin's executions. Meanwhile Gollancz explained privately to Brailsford that the book he had written for the Club - *Why Capitalism Means War* - could not be published because of a chapter critical of the Soviet Union; to publish such a thing, said Gollancz, would be like 'committing the sin against the Holy Ghost'.[70]

To understand why socialists like Gollancz felt this way - notice that his words are almost exactly the same as those used by Saklatvala - it is perhaps first of all necessary to appreciate that, after the Wall Street crash and the advent of Hitler, the Soviet Union really could appear - in Dutt's words - 'a world of sanity, peace and construction in the midst of the howling anarchy, destruction and conflict of the capitalist world'. It is a reminder not only of the frightening aspects of the world they lived in, but also that they were all victims - including the Communists - of the Big Lie, a technique but recently perfected. Moreover, though Stalin's government worked hard in the promotion of deception, it was always possible to find non-Communist authorities such as the American journalist Walter Duranty to uphold and elaborate on it.[71] Gollancz's own conversion to the Soviet myth owed much to Duranty's *Russia Reported*, for example. Ostensibly independent legal experts such as D.N. Pritt K. C. and the barrister Dudley Collard came back from the Moscow Trials to testify to their impartial procedure and the justice of the sentences dispensed. Scores of other experts waxed lyrical on every aspect of Soviet society.

Gollancz was certainly not the only socialist impressed, in addition, by Russia's apparent lack of racism at a time when the Nazis had founded a warlike state on the basis of it. Nor was he alone in needing a line 'in which', as he once put it in praise of Dutt's *Daily Worker*, 'events are explained in the light of a consistent theory - instead of the hugger-mugger, rudderless drifting to which one is accustomed'.[72] In short if we have to invoke the need for faith and the capacity for self- deception, we should not forget that in the 1930s the circumstances were such that even critics of Soviet totalitarianism were not immune from it; this applies to leading Labour figures, such as Attlee, whom Dutt publicly congratulated for pro-Soviet remarks.

Needless to say, he also found Attlee's effort for the Left Book Club to be 'of no political significance at the present stage', claiming that it had exorcised the crisis 'by the methods of Dr. Pangloss'. More surprising, perhaps, is Dutt's perception of Attlee as possessing 'a more alert, open-minded and progressive outlook than some of his colleagues'. Worthy of mention here was Attlee's participation alongside Communist leaders at the Hyde Park 'unity' demonstration, and the interview which he gave to the *Daily Worker* (which Dutt edited in the years 1936-8), in which the Labour leader had given 'wholehearted praise to the Soviet Union after his return from that country'.[73] Here Dutt had hit upon an important flaw in the Labour case against the Communists. Though allegedly no better than the fascists, according to the official argument against the Party, Communists were apparently building socialism in the Soviet Union and the Soviet state was one of the best bets internationally in containing the Nazi menace. It was not just the odd Labour maverick or trade union leftist who said these things. The pro-Soviet tone was to be found in the *New Statesman* and in *Tribune* from its launch in 1937; the aged Webbs and Shaw lauded Soviet planning but so too did younger Fabians like Barbara Wooton and H.L. Beales; even early critics of Bolshevism like G. D. H. Cole joined the chorus. Praise for the Russians' economic achievements also came from Bevin, Dalton, and the *Daily Herald*.

At one level, recognition of Soviet economic progress could co-exist with total rejection of the Bolshevik political system, and even an honest estimate of the barbarous means by which the Five Year Plans were realised. But for those who subscribed to the theory that state ownership of the economy and centralised planning represented an historical advance over capitalism, there was a powerful reason for giving the Russians the benefit of any doubts about their methods. And if, moreover, one believed that this economic progress was the *sine qua non* of future social, political and cultural advance - that it was, indeed, the fundamental causal force of a desirable, socialist society - reports of brutality were less likely still to deflect one from 'defence of the Soviet Union'. Thus could socialists arrive at the judgement that infringements on personal liberty and civil rights were merely a temporary, perhaps even a necessary, stage in the construction of what would in time become a proper socialist society. Indeed the true believer like Dutt, on the basis of these beliefs, could dismiss stories of slave labour in the Soviet Union altogether as intrinsically ludicrous; what possible use could socialist planning have for this costly, wasteful, inefficient and pre-capitalist form of labour?

This intellectual climate on the Left reached its highest point in the years between 1929 and 1945 because the real catastrophes of the period which the Left actually experienced could be laid at the door of capitalism, and sharply contrasted with the received images of rational progress and heroic self-sacrifice emanating from the socialist Soviet Union. Even those who took seriously the stories of famine, show trials, and brutality could judge that the Soviet system's progressive features were more significant in the long run and would ultimately predominate; the superiority of centralised planning and the causal priority of the material base would see to that. It helps to explain why even someone like Orwell could argue (in 1945, the year of *Animal Farm*) that the Soviet Union was 'a state definitely describable as Socialist', the 'real dynamo of the Socialist movement in this country and everywhere else' and that 'therefore the USSR must be safeguarded at all costs'.[74] Orwell, of course also wanted criticism of 'purges, liquidations, the dictatorship of a minority, suppression of criticism and so forth', but the obvious retort was that this simply played into the hands of the regime's enemies.

Thus the growth of the Communist Party and a sympathetic milieu for Marxist ideas can be explained not only in terms of the world economic slump, the rise of fascism and the approach of war, but also in terms of the apparent strides to socialism taken in the USSR. Dutt and the minority of hardened veterans in the Party had of course convinced themselves of the need to defend the Bolshevik state well before there was any talk of it achieving socialism. For them the all-important breakthrough had been the seizure of state power by avowed Marxists and this revealed an all-important lesson; only Bolshevik methods would suffice. History was on the side of the socialists, they knew that already, but Lenin showed that it also had to be made by socialists - and not in circumstances chosen by themselves. In Dutt's mind this fusion of teleology and realism was an intoxicating brew which rendered him immune - at least in public - to doubts and misgivings. Quoting Lenin, he wrote in 1938:

> If you are not able to adapt yourself, if you are not inclined to crawl on your belly, you are not a revolutionary, but a chatterbox; and I propose this, not because I like it, but because we have no other road, because history has not turned out to be so pleasant as to make the revolution ripen everywhere simultaneously.[75]

THE APPROACHING CONFLICT

And what was all this crawling and adaptation about? It was about power - 'the central problem of our period'. 'If this issue is not faced', Dutt warned in *The Social and Political Doctrine of Communism* (1938), 'all dreams of socialism or a new and better social order become idle, passive speculations, and even reactionary':

> No one should attempt to paint a revolution or dictatorship couleur de rose. It would be better that readers should turn away from Communism rather than that they should give it a kind of sentimental support which is not ready to face the hard realities of struggle against a barbarous and ruthless ruling class. Only before they turn away, let them be quite sure of

> the world to which they are turning, the world of Fascism, imperialist wars and colonial slavery, whose wholesale massacres and destruction are a thousand times greater than the entire record of the proletarian revolution.[76]

Dutt knew of course that he was addressing an audience with a long memory - constructed from experience and five decades of socialist agitation - in which the history of capitalism figured as a mountain of misery.

In accordance with the current line he was prepared to assert that 'war is not inevitable' - if Britain, France and the Soviet Union reached agreement for a collective 'peace pact' - but his heart was not in the argument. All over the world he found evidence of peoples 'becoming drawn into movement and ranged more and more into two camps'. In this way, he argued, 'world history is preparing the conditions and mobilising forces for the near approaching final struggle for the victory of the world socialist revolution'.[77] So 'if, despite all efforts to organise the struggle of the peoples in time, the imperialist ruling classes nevertheless succeed to unloose the horrors of a new world war, that war will see the downfall of their rule and the victory of the working class in a series of leading countries, preparing the way for the victory of world socialism'.[78] This is what Dutt really believed likely.

Meanwhile, for those caught up in its activity, the People's Front acquired a momentum of its own. Communists became part of a broader political culture than anything they had experienced before. It was possible for Party members, sympathisers and their co-workers among the activists in the labour movement to become utterly absorbed in the anti-fascist, anti-war campaign. Some of the old shibboleths were abandoned, put into deep freeze or greatly watered-down in the process. Talk of Soviets and proletarian dictatorship became muted; the hammer and sickle disappeared from the masthead of the *Daily Worker*, while the inside pages carried much more in the way of 'bourgeois ideology' than the sports coverage reviled by Dutt when the paper was first launched. It now offered betting tips, popular fiction and advertisements for cocoa in the name of reaching a wider audience. Special organisations of every sort now proliferated including many which grouped Party intellectuals together as writers, students, actors, film-makers, and scientists - another dent in the Communist purity preached by Dutt in 1932.

The danger with all of this, of course, was that the Party's Leninist principles would be forgotten in the enthusiasm for current tactics. Nevertheless the Party was still treated as a pariah by official Labour. The Socialist League was disaffiliated before the end of January 1937 because its leaders ignored the ban on contact with the Communists. In March membership of the League was made incompatible with membership of the Labour Party and so Pollitt and Dutt, mindful of the needs of Communist entryist work, urged Cripps and company to disband the League and thus remain inside the Labour Party and effective in the campaign for Communist affiliation. Communist permeation of the London Labour Party affected every divisional organisation by 1938, largely because the Party's many recruits from Labour were instructed to remain at their posts.

Dutt's special contribution to the Party's work consisted of constant reminders of the peculiar noxiousness of the National Government at a time when the Left was preoccupied with Hitler, Franco and Mussolini. When rearmament was stepped up in 1937 Dutt announced, in his best Comintern-speak, that it was 'a stage towards Hitlerisation in Britain'.[79] His hatred for the British ruling class had always been based, first and foremost, on its world imperial role to which he was able to add, after October 1917, its role as the leader of the anti-Bolshevik coalition. And a constant fear, expressed throughout the 1930s up to the Munich agreement, was that Britain would engineer a 'Four Power Pact' with Germany, Italy and France against the USSR. Indeed Dutt said this had been the theme of post-war policy. The only other war he could imagine, variants on this theme apart, was an inter-imperialist war. As Munich approached Dutt stressed the role of 'the inner ruling group of British reaction' as the 'directing centre' of the anti-Soviet, fascist Powers.[80] In September 1938, just four days before the Czech government was forced to cede the Sudetenland to Germany, he prophesied that 'either the Alliance of Chamberlain and Hitler ... will succeed in its plot against democracy and peace ... and drag the whole world into war. Or the Peace Alliance of the democratic peoples, including the British people, can yet bar the way'.[81]

The Party's Fifteenth Congress was taking place as the fateful decision loomed and Britain was gripped by fear of imminent war. Dutt used the occasion to argue that the prevalent war hysteria had been whipped up so that Chamberlain could return in triumph proclaiming peace when his betrayal of Czechoslovakia actually brought war nearer. Many years later he announced that Pollitt and Gallacher had argued for an immediate Party manifesto on the war danger, not realising that the reality was the coming sell-out of the

Czechs.[82] Only Dutt's timely intervention from the conference platform - according to his disputed version of events - settled the matter and rescued the Party from a major blunder. Whatever the truth in this story, the Party persisted with denunciations of the war-scare as a cover for peace at any price, even as the whole country prepared for conflict at the end of September 1938. The Munich settlement was announced in the early hours of 30 September, and the central committee of the Party declared that the peace had been 'betrayed to the custody of Hitler' on the following day.

In November Dutt declared that a new world situation now existed, characterised by the 'open alliance of Chamberlain and Hitler'; in January he concluded that 'the second imperialist war has in fact already begun'.[83] At first he was inclined to believe that Chamberlain had secured progress to the dreaded Four Power anti-Soviet alliance long foretold. But in the course of 1939 it became impossible to ignore the evidence of increasing tension between Germany and Britain, which Dutt interpreted as proof that the initiative had passed to the Nazis, especially after the annexation of Czechoslovakia in March. By July 1939 Dutt was able to write that Hitler was turning the screw on Britain while British policy endeavoured to 'canalise' the Nazis toward the East. In no way could British policy be taken as proof of a genuine search for collective security and, for Dutt at least, the National Government's preparations for war were further evidence of the growth of fascism in Britain.

In November 1938 he accordingly warned the Political Bureau against the tendency in some quarters to look with favour on Chamberlain's rearmament programme. Instead he pointed to 'the rapid advance of Fascism on all fronts' in Britain. More than ever the 'Peace Block' (that is an alliance of Britain, France and the Soviet Union) depended on the removal of Chamberlain and Daladier:

> We need to emphasise anew ... the declaration of the Fifteenth Congress of the Communist Party that the whole course of the Chamberlain Government is directed not only to the support of Fascism abroad, but to the establishment of Fascism in Britain as the prerequisite for his aim of a war of destruction against the Soviet Union.[84]

Rearmament, according to this devious logic, was designed 'to paralyse opposition to [Chamberlain's] policy and conceal his real pro-Fascist aims'. In reality, Dutt reasoned, 'the question of defence cannot be separated from the question of policy ... isolationist rearmament ... could not defend the people of this country. By his policy Chamberlain is giving away allies, armed forces, natural resources and strategic positions on a scale greater than the most intensive rearmament can replace'. The positive alternative, as conjured by Dutt, was to consist of nationalisation of the arms industry, democracy in the armed forces, real ARP, planned agriculture and industrial development, extended social legislation and wealth taxes. But this depended on a People's Front, and there was no sign of that; given the impending emergency, it was thus no policy at all.

Not surprisingly, in these circumstances, some Communists wavered. The *Daily Worker* momentarily succumbed to the mood of relief after Munich and was duly upbraided by Dutt for 'tendencies to capitulate to the war scare'. In the spring of 1939, when the danger of war waxed again, it seems that the entire Party leadership - Pollitt and Dutt included - came out in favour of supporting conscription and into collision with the Communist International. But Dutt was the first to change his mind when the Comintern intervened.[85] None of this is very surprising, much less the enthusiasm for a real anti-Fascist war which Pollitt betrayed in his first draft of a pamphlet and which Dutt felt compelled to 'improve' upon in early 1939.[86] Even some of the Party leaders could not really follow Dutt's ingenious reasoning or approve his facility for abrupt changes of tack. All were agreed, however, that Britain's security depended on an agreement with the USSR. It came as a bitter blow to many militants, therefore, when the Soviet Union entered into a non- aggression pact with the Nazis on 23 August.

But it was still possible for the Party to imagine that this did nothing but inject a sense of urgency into the campaign for the Peace Front. The reality that Stalin had agreed not to join any future combination against the Nazis had not sunk in.

NOTES

1 Dutt to Pollitt, 13.3.33, K4 Vol 1933-4.
2 Dutt to Pollitt, 1.11.33, *ibid*.
3 Clemens Dutt to Palme Dutt, 19.6.30; Dutt to Page Arnot, 12.1.35, K4 Vol 1935-6.
4 Dutt 'To The Communist Students Conference', 27.9.33, K4 Vol 1933-4.
5 Dutt to Pollitt, 2.10.33, *ibid*.
6 Dutt to Pollitt, 20.7.34, *ibid*.

7 Dutt to Pollitt, 5.1.35, K4 Vol 1935-6.
8 Dutt to Pollitt, 20.7.34, K4 Vol 1933-4.
9 Dutt to Secretariat, 22.3.35, K4 Vol 1935-6.
10 Clemens Dutt to Palme Dutt, 27.3.29.
11 *Daily Worker* 12.7.31.
12 Dutt to Clemens Dutt, 7.12.34, K4 Vol 1933-4.
13 Strachey to Dutt, 24.12.31, cited in H. Thomas, *John Strachey*, Eyre Methuen 1973, p113.
14 *Ibid*, p120.
15 *Ibid*, p123.
16 Clemens Dutt to Palme Dutt 17.12.30. With this letter correspondence is broken for one year. See also Clemens' letters of 6.1.34 and 27.1.34. For Salme's relationship with Dutt see the file containing their correspondence in the library of the CPGB.
17 H. Thomas, *John Strachey*, *op cit*, p124 and p134.
18 *Ibid*, p130.
19 Dutt to Varga, 12.3.35, K4 Vol 1935-6.
20 J. Degras (ed), *Documents of the Communist International*, Vol 3 1924-1943, Oxford University Press 1965, pp346-9 and 355-8.
21 Dutt 'Fascism and Anti-Fascism in Relation to the Approaching Revolutionary Crisis', speech to the seventh congress of the Comintern, 5.8.35, K3.
22 Dutt to Secretariat, 14.4.35, K4 Vol 1935-6; Margot Heinemann in a letter to the author identified Dutt as a source of resistance to the broad alliance orientation of the Popular Front; for Dutt's work in the commission see Reminiscences of Palme Dutt, *Our History Journal*, *op cit*.
23 Quoted in F. Claudin, *The Communist Movement*, Penguin Books 1975, p187.
24 Dutt, *Decisive Days Ahead*, CPGB 1935, pp7-8.
25 Dutt, 'Fascism and International Politics', *Unsere Zeit*, 24.4.33, K4 Vol 1933-4; and Dutt, 'The New Emergency'. *Labour Monthly*, 7,10, October 1935, pp590-595.
26 B. Chandra, *Nationalism and Colonialism in Modern India*, Orient Longman, New Delhi 1979, pp223-51.
27 S. Gopal, *Jawaharlal Nehru:A Biography 1889-1947*, Vol 1, Cape 1974, p108.
28 D. Norman (ed), *Nehru: The First Sixty Years*, Bodley Head 1965, pp306-7.
29 *Ibid*, p315.
30 M.R. Masani, 'The Communist Party of India', *Pacific Affairs*, Vol XXIV, March 1951, pp21-2.
31 E.T. Wilson, *Russia and Black Africa Before World War 2*' Holmes and Meier, New York 1974, p159.
32 H. Rathbone, 'The Problem of African Independence', *Labour Monthly*, 18, 3 and 4, March and April 1936.

33 S. Gopal, *Jawaharlal Nehru*, *op cit*, pp200-220.
34 R. Dudley Edwards, *Victor Gollancz: A Biography*, Gollancz 1987, p234.
35 R.P. Dutt, untitled document, 19 February 1936, K4 Vol 1935- 6; the whole document is reprinted in J. Callaghan, 'Jawaharlal Nehru and the Communist Party', *Journal of Communist Studies*, 7,3, September 1991, pp350-366.
36 Nehru is favourably contrasted to 'M' on this point; probably a reference to M.R. Masani of the Congress Socialist Party whom Dutt talked to in Moscow the previous autumn - and not Krishna Menon as I suggested in *ibid*.
37 R.P. Dutt and B. Bradley, 'The Anti-Imperialist People's Front', *Inprecorr*, 16,11,7 March 1936, pp297-300.
38 Dutt and Bradley 'Towards Trade Union Unity in India', *Inprecorr*, 16,12,25 April 1936, pp325-8.
39 Nehru's speech is contained in D. Norman (ed), *Nehru: The First Sixty Years*, *op cit*, pp424-447.
40 R.P. Dutt, 'The Indian National Congress at Lucknow', *Inprecorr*, 16,20, 1936, 559.
41 B. Chandra, 'Jawaharlal Nehru and the Capitalist Class', in B. Chandra, *Nationalism and Colonialism in Modern India*, Orient Longman, New Delhi 1979, p188.
42 R.P. Dutt, Presidential Address to the Fifth Indian Political Conference, July 1963, K3.
43. *Daily Worker*, 21 January 1938; See also Dutt's 'Greeting to the *Sahyadri*, 29 November 1937 and his 'MacDonald and India', *Bombay Chronicle*, 10 November 1937, K4, Volume 1937-8.
44 B. Bradley, 'Indian Nationalism After Tripuri' *Labour Monthly*, 21,3, March 1939, p301.
45 R.P. Dutt, 'The Colonial Peoples Fight For Democracy and Against Fascism', article prepared for *Pravda*, 19.4.1939.
46 It was said about Cardinal Newman. See G. Himmelfarb, *Victorian Minds*, Peter Smith, Massachusetts 1975, p313.
47 R.P. Dutt, *World Politics 1918-36*, Gollancz 1936, p7 and pp9- 10.
48 *Ibid*, p23.
49 *Ibid*, pp33-34.
50 *Ibid*, pp73-74.
51. *Ibid*, pp75-6; see on this issue W.D. Smith, *The Ideological Origins of Nazi Imperialism*, Oxford University Press 1986.
52 Dutt, *World Politics*, *op cit*, p78.
53 *Ibid*, pp108-9 and pp303-310.
54 *Ibid*, p164.
55 *Ibid*, p289 and pp303-310.
56 National Joint Council of Labour, *Democracy versus Dictatorship*, Labour Party, March 1933.
57 J. Wood, 'The Labour Left and the Constituency Labour Parties, 1931-51', unpublished PhD. University of Warwick 1982, p67.

58 J. Jupp 'The Left in Britain 1931-41', Msc dissertation, University of London 1956, p182.
59 National Joint Council of Labour, *Communist and Other Organisations*, Labour Party, June 1933.
60 N. Branson, *History of the Communist Party of Great Britain 1927-1941*, Lawrence and Wishart 1985, p191.
61 D. Caute, *The Fellow-Travellers*, Yale University Press, revised edition 1988, p172.
62 S. Samuels, 'The Left Book Club', *Journal of Contemporary History*, 1,2, p68; J. Symons, *The Thirties: A Dream Revolved*, Faber and Faber 1975, p94.
63 R. Dudley Edwards, *Victor Gollancz*, *op cit*, p229.
64 *Ibid*, p236.
65 *Ibid*, p245.
66 *Ibid*, p237.
67 D. Caute, *The Fellow-Travellers*, *op cit*, p172.
68 R. Dudley Edwards, *Victor Gollancz*, *op cit*, p237.
69 J. Strachey, 'The Soviet Trials', *Left News*, 15, July 1938, p885.
70 R. Dudley Edwards, *op cit*, p267.
71 See, S.J. Taylor, *Walter Duranty*, Oxford University 1990.
72 R. Dudley Edwards, *op cit*, 252.
73 *Daily Worker*, 5 August 1937.
74 G. Orwell, *Collected Essays, Journalism, and Letters*, Volume 3, Penguin Books 1970, p169 footnote; the phrases quoted were used in a review of Laski's *Faith, Reason and Civilisation*.
75 R.P. Dutt, 'Lenin Lives in the World Communist Movement', *Daily Worker*, 19 January 1938.
76 R.P. Dutt, *The Social and Political Doctrine of Communism*, Hogarth Press 1938, reprinted 1942, p15 and p22.
77 *Ibid*, pp30-31.
78 *Ibid*, p31.
79 Notes of the Month, *Labour Monthly*, 19,4, April 1937, pp204- 5.
80 Notes of the Month, *Labour Monthly*, 20,4, April 1938, p216.
81 *Daily Worker*, 17.9.1938.
82 Notes of the Month, *Labour Monthly*, April 1971, pp180-1; Idris Cox and Ted Bramley denied this version of events.
83 Dutt, 'New World Situation', *Labour Monthly*, 20,11, November, 1938, p655; Outlook for 1939, *Labour Monthly*, 31,1, January 1939, p4.
84 Dutt, Political Letter to Political Bureau, 1.11.38, K4 Vol 1937-38.
85 K. Morgan, in *Against Fascism And War*, Manchester University Press 1989, p72 and p78, suggests that Dutt originally opposed conscription in the spring of 1939 but the true position is revealed by Ted Bramley in F. King & G. Matthews *About Turn*, Lawrence & Wishart 1990, pp240-241.
86 K. Morgan, *ibid*, pp80-82.

6
A Succession of Wars

Confusion in the Central Committee

As late as 1 September 1939 the *Daily Worker* was still worried about the possibility of some sort of British accommodation of Hitler. Speculating as to the real motives behind preparations for the evacuation of children from the big cities, it suggested that perhaps it was 'part of a war of nerves directed against the people of Britain preparing them for sweeping concessions to the Fascist aggressors'.[1] Two days later Britain declared war on Nazi Germany. The Party's first response was to argue that the war 'can and must be won' but added that victory was not possible if 'the men of Munich - men who for years have been abandoning democracy's defences to Fascism - remain in power here and in France'.[2] In the days that followed, the Communists maintained their agitation for a war on two fronts, arguing that the removal of the National Government was a prerequisite for success against the Nazis. The war could then become a true people's war continuing the struggle against fascism and militarism begun in China, Abyssinia, and Spain.[3]

On 11 September the *Daily Worker* reported that the Nazis were 'touting' a 'treacherous peace offer', designed to 'split France and Britain', while Pollitt, in a pamphlet called *How To Win the War*, demanded action not 'revolutionary-sounding phrases' from the Left to defeat the 'fascist beasts'. Thus the CPGB, notwithstanding certain reservations, welcomed Britain's declaration of war. Yet by the end of the month the same 'peace' manoeuvre from Hitler, to which by now the Soviet Union had added its support, was hailed as genuine by the Communists. If Britain and France rejected this offer they alone, according to the *Daily Worker*, would be responsible for the war.[4] This dramatic *volte face* - which now characterised the war as 'inter- imperialist' - stunned many socialists and was effected only after a bitter row in the Party leadership and the replacement of Pollitt by Dutt in the top job.

We now know that on 9 September, only a few days after the British war declaration, the Secretariat of the Comintern was instructed by Stalin to characterise the war as imperialist and unjust on both sides. On 14 September - three days before the Soviet annexation of eastern Poland - the first Russian radio broadcast to pronounce on the war communicated this verdict. There is a very strong probability that Dutt, in common with other Communist leaders in other countries, possessed a short wave radio receiver and heard this particular message. On the same day Pollitt received a telegram from Moscow which summarised the new line.[5] Thus on the day that his pamphlet *How To Win the War* appeared, Moscow undermined Pollitt's argument, and the very next day Dutt asked the Political Bureau to reconsider the CPGB's position. Pollitt, meanwhile, instinctively suppressed the telegram from Moscow conveying the new position.

The Party leader initially refused Dutt's request, arguing that the Party should support any resistance to fascism as it had before. Dutt characteristically warned against any line which threatened to bring the Party into collision with the Comintern and suggested that the Hitler-Stalin pact had created 'a completely new situation'. He felt that the Party line did not recognise the 'parallel responsibility of both imperialist camps' in creating the war - an imperialist war in which the working class had to concentrate the struggle against its 'own' government. On 22 September, he accordingly submitted amendments to the Party's original war resolution. The central committee was reminded that Chamberlain had helped Hitler and that the British government was an imperialist government fighting an imperialist war which the Party could not support; only a 'People's Government' could defend the country against Fascism.[6] Dutt was happy to wait, however, until the Party's representative at the Comintern, D.F.Springhall, returned from Moscow and, in Dutt's words, 'established our contact with international comrades'.

Springhall was able to perform this function on 25 September, by reporting to the central committee on what Dimitrov and Andre Marty had told him before he left Moscow. The Party had to unmask the imperialist character of the war and work for the destruction of British capitalism - the British Communists having particular regard for the colonies and rendering them assistance in every way. The Party had to understand the USSR's need to manoeuvre. After some disjointed questioning of Springhall, Pollitt moved an adjournment so that the Political Bureau could meet to consider his report. Here Dutt, William Rust and Springhall came out completely behind the Comintern position while Pollitt, Gallacher, Campbell, Burns and Ted Bramley resisted it. The real balance of forces was revealed by the fact that the Political Bureau went on to appoint a new Secretariat composed exclusively of the pro-Moscow triumvirate led by Dutt. Dutt's elevation was effected specifically to reassure the Comintern that all was well with the British section. Unable to agree on the nature of the war, however, the Political Bureau produced a compromise statement in the name of the *Daily Worker* editorial board, which combined elements of both the old and the new analyses of the war. After the Political Bureau meeting, the Secretariat composed a new statement in secret so that when the central committee meeting resumed on 2 October Dutt began the session intending to erase all traces of compromise from the Party's war line and obtain unqualified support for the Comintern.

Thus it was Dutt who kicked off by referring to 'an impotence of leadership of the Party' and to 'a humiliation, a complete incoherence worse either than the old line or the new'.[7] 'We must and shall reach clearness and effectiveness of the line today':

> We have given time because we don't want a mechanical vote of acceptance on grounds of discipline while all the feelings and all the convictions are elsewhere. We want acceptance of this line by the members of the Central Committee on the basis of conviction. Absolute and complete conviction, because on that basis will this line which is going to make enormous demands on all of us be fought through and be really effectively carried through.[8]

Having issued this warning Dutt then proceeded to teach the central committee the basics of the new position. The war, he pointed out, was different from that of 1914 because 'the Soviet Union is in existence'. But,

> it is not because the Soviet Union has turned its policy that everyone has got to turn, as you will sometimes hear comrades in the Party say. It is an absolutely foul slander that belongs to the *Daily Herald* and the Labour reformists. It is because there is a new world situation, in relation to which the Soviet Union first grasped how to act.

Dutt reminded those present that since 1917 the basic antagonism of the modern world was the antagonism of capitalism and the socialist USSR. 'That basic antagonism covers every other', he asserted, and 'all the particular phases of imperialist conflict, fascism and democracy and the rest of it, are phases in relation to that basic antagonism'. Decoded, this meant that the duty of all present was to defend the Soviet Union and not worry too much about 'fascism, democracy and the rest of it'. Dutt also sought to tempt his colleagues with the prospect that the new line somehow promoted revolution in the West - 'imperialist war means a revolutionary perspective' he cooed. It would also be wrong to deny the appeal which intransigent confrontation always had for him. But Dutt had to mobilise all his powers of sophistry to find revolutionary implications in the new situation - only four days earlier the Russians had issued a joint declaration with the Nazis calling for peace. No doubt this could be read as a manoeuvre, every move of self-preservation on the part of the USSR deserving absolute support. But how did any of this negate the distinction between bellicose fascism and bourgeois democracy or advance the cause of revolution?

Dutt argued that Nazi Germany had been weakened by the Non- Aggression Pact and that British and French imperialism were emerging more and more as the leaders of world reaction.[9] Their world roles had changed, said Dutt, so therefore the significance of the old distinction had gone - which was no more than saying that their relationships with the USSR had changed. This being the case, the war was a matter of inter-imperialist rivalry and it was a nonsense to oppose imperialism and at the same time call for a change in its government as the Party's compromise line now demanded. The Party had to denounce the war as an imperialist conflict but, following the instructions Dimitrov gave Springhall, Dutt warned that there was to be no talk of turning this imperialist war into civil war; the Party had to move by stealth towards the revolution with policy and propaganda focussed on 'simple concrete issues'.

Dutt's address is less interesting for its defence of the new line than for the insights it provides into his own mentality. At intervals he returned to the need for 'absolute certainty and the conviction of every Party member' even if this required a 'merciless, ruthless clearing' of the Party in closed meetings. It was no use saying 'well I don't agree with this line but it is an international decision so I have to vote for it'. Communist discipline, he argued, 'is not a mechanical robot discipline'. And yet he also went on to assert that 'the duty of a Communist is not to disagree but accept', quickly adding that 'those comrades forget that there is the duty of a Communist to think and to understand the line in order to be capable of applying it'. He was tying himself in knots, wanting unanimity, thinking it a Communist duty but demanding conviction - knowing that Pollitt, Campbell and Gallacher could not find it in themselves, knowing that the cracks in 'absolute certainty' had been present for some time. 'The crisis', he concluded, 'has shown dangerous tendencies existing in the Party':

> We know anti-International tendencies, a contemptuous attitude to the International, anti-Soviet tendencies, the kind of thing that began already at the time of the [Moscow] trials, talk of the collapse of the International, talk of the Soviet Union following its interests and the like, talk of our being an independent Party, all kinds of things like that, that are reflections of enemy outlooks, of imperialist and labour reformist outlooks that have no place in the Party.[10]

He finished on a threatening note: 'any member who in such a moment deserts from active work for the Party will be branded for his political life'. He wasn't thinking about the ordinary branch member; it was clear to all present that he meant Pollitt.

Emile Burns thought that Dutt had raised the stakes precisely so that 'as many as possible will vote against it so that he and his colleagues can be represented as the real nucleus of the Comintern'. Gallacher said he had never heard 'a more unscrupulous and opportunist speech'; Dutt had joined the rest of them in congratulating Pollitt for his *How To Win The War*. He had also participated in producing the compromise line published in the *Daily Worker* on 30 September, but now disowned it. Gallacher had never known 'anything so rotten, so mean, so despicable, so dirty as a creature to come along here and say "we three were opposed to it"'. As for the substance of Dutt's address, Gallacher found it so incoherent - 'every conceivable phrase was brought in' - that at one stage in his zeal to bury the old anti- fascist line Dutt appeared to be arguing for the defence of a potential Soviet Germany against rapacious Anglo-French imperialism.[11] Gallacher was not prepared to accept the new line as it stood and reminded his colleagues of what happened when 'mechanical acceptance' of 'social fascism' had weakened the movement.

Dutt's frigid tone had also annoyed Campbell who observed that 'he talks as if he was some schoolmaster sent to correct a class of unruly children, someone arriving from some other planet, and not one of the principal parties in all the mistakes which he enumerated at such length'. More to the point, Campbell observed the absurdity of the position they now found themselves in:

> the war we predicted has come, it has broken out in the place we said it would break out, but we have got to revise completely our fundamental conceptions of the character of that war. We have now got to blame the war on to Poland and France and Britain.[12]

Everybody present knew that Dutt's opening discourse was an appeal to their loyalty to the Soviet Union. But his usual facility for fitting tactical zigzags into the big picture, the Communist *zeitgeist*, was defeated by the sheer inanity of the Soviet line. As Campbell pointed out, after quoting from *Pravda* and *Izvestiya*, 'the danger is no longer a danger of a fascist domination of Europe, the danger is the danger of British and French imperialism miraculously breaking through the Siegfried line, over-running Germany, installing a government in Germany which will fight the Soviet Union and then going on to a war against the Soviet Union, and so on'.[13] A defeat of British and French imperialism, Campbell argued, was also a defeat of the British and French people and the arrival of a fascist-dominated Europe; he could not accept that resistance to this was no longer relevant. Look what happened in Germany when the Communist Party 'pursued a line of isolating itself from the other labour and democratic forces'. Like the KPD, argued Campbell, Dutt's position offers world revolution and will reap the iron heel. To do anything other than to emerge as 'the deadly enemies of fascism, resolved not to allow fascism to conquer another foot of territory' would, in Campbell's opinion, 'be an act of unprecedented political treachery to the people of this country'.

There is no doubt that this was how Campbell, Pollitt, and Gallacher really felt. But there was another set of deep convictions tearing at the members of the Central Committee which was put by Maurice Cornforth (the Party's expert on Marxist philosophy and a former student of Wittgenstein's) in simple, straightforward language:

> I believe that if one loses anything of that faith in the Soviet Union one is done for as a Communist and a Socialist. I remember very distinctly being very impressed by something Comrade Pollitt said at a Party Congress in which he made the statement about the Soviet Union, that they can do no wrong and it seemed to me at the time that this was rather a funny statement to make. But the fact of the matter is that a socialist state, I believe, in that position, can do no wrong, and is doing no wrong, and this is what we have to stick to, so these are the reasons why personally I commenced to turn political somersaults, because that is what it means.[14]

Springhall expressed his own faith in the Soviet Union even more succinctly - by arguing that since 'Comrade Stalin has also read *Mein Kampf*, there was no question of the Russian's mistaking Hitler's long-term strategy. William Rust, another member of Dutt's Secretariat, went one better in observing that the USSR had already greatly increased its power as a direct result of the Non-Aggression Pact 'and is now manoeuvring for a position where it intends to prepare the way for a further extension of that power'.[15]

Some Communists - Kuusinen was one - had long since concluded, in the absence of the European revolution, that the spread of Communism was dependent on Soviet power. In a small Party like the CPGB, the prospect of revolution was so distant that, when not immersed in day to day campaigns, members took considerable psychological strength from the progress of the world movement. The argument that the strength of the Soviet Union was the key to all Communist futures could not be lightly dismissed. It was just so difficult to find any evidence of progress in Stalin's current policy, a policy which went against the grain of everything that they thought they had been saying since 1933. As Burns put it:

> How is it possible to ignore the whole of the history preceding the actual situation in August or September of this year? How can this be ignored? How can it be ignored that the fascist countries were the consistent aggressors branded in every article, every book? In the August issue of the *Communist International*, you will find a whole series of articles in which it is indicated that war against the fascist countries, under any circumstances so to speak, is a holy war.[16]

A closer inspection would have revealed that Dutt, for one, had faithfully stressed the role of Britain in the fascist offensive and had ingeniously found evidence of 'fascisation' in Britain for many years. Burns overlooked this side of the argument, referring only to Dutt's 'persistent underlying sectarian tendencies'.

Pollitt, having been corrected on many occasions since 1933, knew that Dutt had never quite shared his anti-fascist fervour, or rather had expressed this fervour in a very different way. Dutt had always sought, in effect, to minimise the significance of bourgeois democracy in National Government Britain; as he never tired of pointing out, fascism emerged out of bourgeois democracy and the British variant had sought to orchestrate an anti-Soviet fascist offensive since 1933. Pollitt had a much clearer and more honest understanding of the nature of fascism and his instincts were to 'smash the fascist bastards once and for all', as he admitted at the central committee meeting. He also confessed to shame 'at the lack of feeling, the lack of response' aroused in the Party leadership by the fight of the Polish people. But he acknowledged that he had known for some time the drift of the Comintern's line; that, ludicrously, the non-aggression pact had apparently bestowed a progressive role on fascism, that somehow the revolutionary perspective was improved if the British were to lose all the democratic gains of the past. He confessed his disgust at 'the comrades who can so lightly in the space of a week, and sometimes in the space of a day, go from one political conviction to another'. He could see, furthermore, that this derived from Soviet manoeuverings:

> The world situation has compelled it to do many things which none of us expected, to preserve its independence and integrity, to make it increasingly difficult for any aggressor to make war on Soviet territory proper. I say it is a disquieting thing that that policy has been carried out at the price of antagonising very important sections of the working class movement ...
>
> I say this, and I only say what comrades who are sitting over there have themselves said but won't say for a book. That the thing that has disturbed them in recent months has been the disappearance of internationalism in the pronouncements that have been made from Moscow. I believe that is true.[17]

Pollitt predicted that the USSR would very soon require assistance against Fascism. He argued that the Nazis had emerged strengthened by the Soviet-German pact, that Germany was 'the last country' where there would be revolution in Europe. The Comintern was now saying the exact opposite of all of this and had treated the Party representative as a mere 'office boy', whose function was simply to relay its messages. Yet Pollitt recalled that in his last conversation with Dimitrov, the Bulgarian:

> ... explained to Campbell and myself for hours that one of the greatest shortcomings of our Party was that we did not know how to look after the national honour of our country. That phrase 'national honour' occurred time and time again. And I tell you our honour is at stake now. It is at stake as a Party.[18]

To the one man listening for whom the idea of 'national honour' was completely alien, Pollitt finished by saying; 'If you want to have political conviction, Dutt, you have to learn how to present a case in a different manner to what you did this morning'.

Dutt in fact professed himself mystified by the hurt tone of Pollitt's and Campbell's and Gallacher's contributions to the discussion; 'can't you see that we are fighting to save their lives', he asked the others. He meant political lives, of course - he always maintained that he worked to get Pollitt back into the secretaryship of the Party as soon as he could. There was just the matter of inconvenient opinions to be got over - the source of the dissenters' 'truculent attitude':

> That is them insisting on the sanctity of their private opinions. Comrades, a Communist has no private opinions. That is, he has no sanctum of private opinions that he is going to hold apart from the collective thinking and the collective decisions of our movement.[19]

This was calculated to deepen the contempt for Dutt which some of the others had already expressed, not because of the totalitarian note struck here but because, as Gallacher put it, the dissenters could find no conviction whatsoever in anything the triumvirate had said.

How could they forget that only weeks earlier Dutt himself had approved Pollitt's *How To Win The War*, and why should they think that Dutt actually believed some of the more obvious nonsense in the current line? The point applied to all of them, of course, because even the dissidents very quickly rallied to the official position and most of the central committee had already changed their minds. In some respects they all looked like men of straw and embarrassed themselves with their shallow apologetics. But even on this occasion their behaviour was not that of programmed robots as their enemies always maintained, or at least that is not the whole story. Their deepest convictions were involved; especially their belief in international solidarity with the first workers' state, the minimum expression of which was the unity of the Comintern behind the leadership of the CPSU. They did now what they believed should have been done in 1914 and forced themselves against the torrent of public opinion in the name of internationalism. In 1939 it was the wrong thing to do, but this does not mean that it was easy to do it - they knew perfectly well what obloquy would now befall them but they were ready to risk more than just the reproach of their former friends.

There was also the matter of their profound mistrust of the British state - a suspicion which they shared with some of their fellow socialists. Fenner Brockway of the ILP could not oppose the war unresevedly as he had in 1914 but he recalled encountering Dutt on a train the morning the Communist Party became anti-war and found that 'he was overjoyed that it had returned to the classical line'.[20] The memory of 1914 was still vivid and both of them had argued at one time or another against Britain's democratic credentials. Even now Brockway worried about lending support to British imperialism - proving the point that such disquiet was not simply inserted by a foreign power. Dutt had long believed that Britain played a peculiarly reactionary role in world politics. Though the Party had mobilised against the fascist menace in particular since 1933, he had frequently reminded it that the satisfied imperialism of Britain rested on the backs of subject peoples; Britain was only democratic, as Orwell put it, 'Not Counting Niggers'.[21] If Dutt was impervious to the patriotic feelings stirred in Orwell the moment the war broke out, it was because his entire life had taken shape against such sentiment. It was perfectly possible for him to feel comfortable with a political line which set him on a confrontationist course with the British state; this was his purpose in life after all. The new manifesto, which the Party published on 7 October, accordingly stressed the predatory nature of the unfolding conflict:

> This war is a fight between imperialist powers over profits, colonies, and world domination ... The leaders of the Labour Party and Trade Union movement have sided fully with the Government of Chamberlain and Churchill and are attempting to get the working class movement to support their imperialist war aims.[22]

It was a line which the Party could expect to be well received in the colonies. When India, for example, was unceremoniously declared a belligerent, just hours after Britain's declaration of war against Germany, the Congress Working Committee took 'the gravest view' of the Viceroy's action despite Anglo-French professions of support for freedom and democracy. The Congress observed:

> ... the history of the recent past is full of examples showing the constant divergences between the spoken word, the ideals proclaimed, and the real motives and objectives. During the war of 1914-18, the declared war aims were preservation of democracy, self-determination, and the freedom of small nations, and yet the very Governments which solemnly proclaimed these aims entered into secret treaties embodying imperialist designs for the carving up of the Ottoman Empire. While stating that they did not want any acquisition of territory, the victorious Powers added largely to their colonial domains. The present European war itself signifies the abject failure of the Treaty of Versailles and of its makers, who broke their pledged words and imposed an imperialist peace on the defeated nations.

India demanded the right of self-determination. The Congress:

> ... therefore invites the British Government to declare in unequivocal terms what their war aims are in regard to democracy and imperialism and the new order that is envisaged, in particular, how these aims are going to apply to India and to be given effect in the present. Do they include the elimination of imperialism and the treatment of India as a free nation whose policy will be guided in accordance with the wishes of her people? [23]

Dutt sought to answer this question with the argument that the war had only come about because the Nazis had grown strong enough to turn against the British empire - British policy having earlier built them up for an anti-Soviet crusade. Britain had not the least intention of relinquishing its control of India but the interests of all peoples demanded the speediest termination of the war.[24] By February 1940 the *Daily Worker* was able to refer to months during which the French and British Governments had *chosen* to extend the conflict instead of ending it.[25] Dutt took up this theme at an open air meeting in Hyde Park in April when he told his audience that the extension of the war to Scandinavia had been a 'crime' whose responsibility lay with 'Chamberlain, Reynaud, Attlee and Blum'.[26]

NEW FRIENDS FOR OLD

Some Communists revelled in those periods of the Party's history characterised by intransigence and isolation; they saw these episodes as moments of ideological and revolutionary purity.[27] Dutt was one such. At the Central Committee meeting of December 1939, for example, having noted the 'extreme sharpening of the attack' against the Party, he observed that the new 'ferocity' was a sign 'that things are moving' - evidence of conditions that 'should be extremely inspiring to every revolutionary'. In fact the Party had fought a by-election at Stretford just days earlier and polled a little over 1500 votes - all the smaller for the fact that the ILP had amassed three times as many. Dutt preferred to see this as 'a basis of revolutionary opposition', though the truth was that the Party had fought the campaign as if its candidate, Eric Gower, represented the whole Labour movement rather than a Communist 'revolutionary opposition'. The war between Russia and Finland,which had ignited at the end of November, undoubtedly hindered the Party's attempt to disguise its real identity by reminding the Stretford electors of Stalin's brutality and of the Communists' subservience to all things Soviet. Dutt, unmoved as ever by public opinion, tried to persuade his comrades on the Central Committee that 'the Finnish conflict means that within less than three months of the beginning of the imperialist war, direct war on the Soviet Union has begun'. But this was to make no difference to the Communist 'stop the war' campaign, even though a cessation of imperialist hostilities was arguably a precondition for the concerted war against Bolshevism which Dutt kept predicting.

Far from showing signs of strain, then, Dutt kept his sectarian head and during 1940, as the Blitz raged, actually found the presence of mind to run a debate in the pages of *Labour Monthly* on the theoretical pros and cons of Christopher Hill's recently published *The English Revolution 1640* - the debate having begun when an anonymous reviewer (Jurgen Kuczynski) argued that Hill was wrong to describe seventeenth century England as feudal. Dutt was evidently worried that Hill had contradicted Marx's verdict to the effect that English society was already 'definitely bourgeois'. Clearly, if the Party had its back to the wall Dutt felt that this was no reason to get sloppy about theoretical matters. On the contrary, now was the time to test its Bolshevik mettle.

The price to be paid, of course, was the loss of most of its former allies. The Soviet attack on Finland had been the last straw for the *New Statesman*, which compared Stalin's dictatorship with all the other 'totalitarian regimes'.[28] Dutt argued that the war with Finland had to be seen as 'a class issue' involving the Socialist State, 'which defends the interests of the workers all over the world', and 'the Finnish semi-Fascist state [which] is the outer tentacle of an octopus whose vital centres are London and New York'. He reminded his readers of the repression of Communists in Finland in 1930 and traced to the Finnish state the butchery of General Mannerheim during the civil war of 1919. By early December 1939 Dutt was able to boast to a crowd in Hyde Park that the 'establishment of the Finnish People's Government is the beginning of a new epoch in Europe' - but it was one of the shortest epochs on record; Moscow's puppet 'workers' government, headed by Kuusinen, came to nothing and Dutt's sister-in-law Hella actually played a part in negotiating the peace treaty of March 1940.[29]

The 'winter war' was added to the recent list of Soviet outrages that had peeled away the rings of Communist credibility in Britain. But there were still sympathisers who had rationalised the Moscow Trials, the Hitler-Stalin Pact, the partition of Poland and the *volte-face* over the meaning of the war. Strachey, for example, at first supported the change of line over the war. Years later he traced his return to social democracy to the impact of Keynes in the late 1930s - he was working on a critique of Keynes, with the assistance of Dutt and Dobb, in May 1938. But in fact it took the battle for Norway to detach Strachey from the Communist line and even after that he felt the need to write to Dutt in May 1940 apologising for the latter's 'poor return for all the extraordinary trouble you took about my political education'. Strachey said he would 'always be profoundly grateful' but explained that 'I am a different kind of man, with different basic reactions, to yourself'.[30]

Unlike Strachey, Gollancz was unable to call the war imperialist and predatory on both sides. But while refusing to accept that there were no decisive differences between fascism and democracy, he continued to stress the gains of the October Revolution which allegedly made the USSR a progressive phenomenon in the world. Though filled with doubts Gollancz, as Laski admonished, continued to treat the Party as an errant friend that had accidentally gone astray; 'I can't take that kindly view', said Laski, 'Dutt and Co. don't go anywhere accidentally'.[31]

The meaning of the Party's war policy suddenly became frighteningly obvious to Strachey and Gollancz by May 1940 when Dunkirk was evacuated. The fall of France in June only heightened fears of an immediate Nazi invasion. Gollancz and Strachey now claimed that the Communists had weakened the will to resist in France and were guilty of 'the worst betrayal of the working class in modern history'.[32] Even a four hour lecture from Dutt on revolutionary defeatism failed to calm Gollancz's fears. In fact few of the celebrities of the Popular Front were now able to stand alongside the Communists, for whom the change of government - as Churchill became Prime Minister - made no difference. There is no record of any sense of personal loss at this parting of the ways so far as Dutt is concerned, but we know that his close colleague D.N. Pritt 'was consumed with bitterness against all those who had once been his friends'; and Pritt's wife 'was reduced to utter misery, cut off from all social contact with the people she had loved'.[33] No doubt the stoic Dutt would have said that it was better to have no friends in politics in the first place - the Party certainly had none in May-June 1940 and, putting on a brave face, claimed that it was happy to 'leave Mr Kingsley Martin, Mr Strachey and Mr Gollancz to their dungheaps'.[34]

But even the Communists were alarmed that summer. Referring to 'the appalling catastrophe that has befallen the French people', the *Daily Worker* made no reference to its calls for peace with Hitler. Communist propaganda turned to an emphasis on the need for a workers' government that would arm the people; behind the scenes Gallacher lobbied for permission to visit Moscow - presumably to intercede with Stalin for something more tangible.[35]

Dutt meanwhile tried to fill the gap created by the loss of the Left Book Club by encouraging *Labour Monthly* readers' groups and running a series of conferences under the journal's auspices during 1940 and the first half of 1941. *Labour Monthly* claimed a readership of around 10,000 in December 1939 and was up to a print run of 20,000 twelve months later, even though an estimated 1,500 sales were lost because of the export ban of July 1940.[36] By this time the journal was acting as the theoretical organ of the Party rather than the voice of 'international labour' and the increase in circulation must be attributed to a drive to get more Communists to read it, rather than successful penetration of a broader Left.[37]

Steps were certainly taken to cope with the difficult situation the Party now faced. The mounting hostility towards the Communists - one prominent member remembers 'the vast majority of people almost hysterical in their hatred of us' - reinforced the siege mentality.[38] On the brink of illegality, the Party made preparations for an underground existence in the event of a complete ban on its activities. Its activists in the Labour Party were called in - there was no longer any point in entryism. More emphasis was given to 'cadre work' within the Party and Dutt played a leading role in such training with lectures on Leninism. With barely concealed distaste he explained to one 'Group Leaders' Course' in March 1941 that the trajectory taken by the Party after 1935 had represented 'a special line of tactics that involved a very close association with all kinds of bourgeois liberal elements'. The 'big and sweeping changes, of violent destruction, of the collapse of states' which lay ahead called for a very different approach. The international class struggle pitted world imperialism against the working class. When this was understood, Dutt concluded, it was 'impossible' to imagine a conflict of interests between the needs of the Soviet Union and those of the proletariat.[39]

Dimitrov's instructions to Springhall had particularly called attention, however, to the inadvisability of revolutionary rhetoric; the Party was required to limit itself to 'unmasking the imperialist character of the war'. But when Pollitt stood as a by-election candidate for West Ham, Silvertown in February 1940 he hardly mentioned the Party's war line at all. In other by- elections the Communists stressed a pacifist position which seemed to accord with the Party's support for Hitler's 'peace offer'. Another favourite theme in the spring of 1940 was Britain's guilt in the extension of the war to Norway and Denmark. But as we have seen the 'stop the war' line was dropped altogether when an invasion of Britain looked likely in June 1940. The Party then focussed on the danger of a ruling class capitulation. By November, however, Dutt announced that the invasion scare had been a government ploy to divert attention from its domestic problems; only the socialist revolution, he instructed his readers, offered a real alternative to fascism and imperialist conflict.[40] Thus the Party had returned to 'unmasking the imperialist war', but it is clear from the foregoing that there was no consistent agitation for the 'revolutionary defeatism' of 1914.[41]

THE PEOPLE'S CONVENTION

The Party's efforts, though inconsistent, certainly worried the War Cabinet especially when the *Daily Worker* announced its intention in September 1940 to give substance to the call for a 'People's Government' by launching a popular movement for a 'People's Convention'.[42] Dutt was prominent in the conception of this movement which was envisaged as a loose coalition around defensive slogans for the preservation of living standards, for trade union and democratic rights and for a pro-Soviet foreign policy. The Convention was to meet for the first time on 12 January 1941 and in the event 2,234 delegates attended, claiming to represent well over a million people.

Communists were not alone of course in remembering the First World War with horror. Anti-war sentiment had grown as the memory of the Great War took shape in the 1920s. Over one hundred thousand people had signed the Peace Pledge in the 1930s to 'renounce war and never again directly or indirectly to sanction another'. When the war against fascism began, sixty thousand people in Britain stuck to their pacifist views. But though the Party had talked pacifism and allied with pacifists during the months after the declaration of war, the Convention principally attracted the sort of working class activists who belonged to either the Party or its periphery in the unions and the local Labour Parties. *Tribune* denounced the whole affair as 'mischievous, phony, dishonest, a fraud, a swindle, snare and delusion from start to finish' - because the Communists ran the whole show for their own shallow purposes. Nevertheless it also admitted that the Convention:

> ... was a great success as a conference. The hall and overflow meetings were packed. The speeches were able. The audiences were enthusiastic, and mostly composed of good, honest-to-God workers whose attachment to Socialism, democracy and a decent peace and whose loathing of Fascism could not be questioned. Much of what it said was the authentic voice of large and growing bodies of opinion, representing genuine, deeply felt and widespread grievances.[43]

Dutt, Krishna Menon, Pollitt, and Paul Robeson received the warmest applause. Dutt's speech referred to the 'sinister war aims' of the Coalition Government. The British state had 'made this war inevitable', he argued, because it had been 'driven by ... vicious, anti-popular hostility to democracy, socialism, the Soviet Union and the Peace Front'. The People's Convention had to become 'the democratic rallying ground towards which all who seek seriously to fight the present Government and corrupt ruling class and to prevent the catastrophe threatening our country' would adhere. He assured the delegates that 'a People's Peace is possible and can be won by the united endeavours of the peoples in all the warring countries, in the first place, together with the peoples in the countries not yet directly involved in the war, with the people of the Socialist Soviet Union'. Failure, he warned, 'would mean ruin and enslavement' whichever imperialism were to conquer.[44] Pollitt's speech, hailed as 'marvellous', covered similar ground - but it seems appropriate in view of his distaste for the current line that he could remember none of it within minutes of its rousing conclusion.[45] Perhaps his mind had returned to the just war against fascism that he really believed necessary.

The *Daily Worker* and *The Week* were suppressed by the Government on 21 January, the decision to ban them having been taken in December, probably on the assumption that the Communists could become a real nuisance via the People's Convention. The BBC also took a dim view of the new front and promptly banned Michael Redgrave and other actors who became associated with it. Dutt took a personal interest in the Redgrave affair as we have seen. When he addressed a packed meeting of the Oxford Union and Oxford Majlis on 'the British public and the war' in March he finished by exhorting his audience to sign a petition condemning the BBC's action and succeeded in obtaining the signatures of nearly all present. Significantly the Government chose to ignore the Party's factory bulletins and journals, however, which generally avoided anti-war propaganda and focussed on bread-and-butter issues. But Dutt purported to see the ban as part of a 'systematic offensive of the reactionary propertied interests towards their aim to establish fascism, the Hitlerite type of system, in this country; and this was the view upheld by the first full meeting of the National Committee of the People's Convention in February.[46] In his reports to the Political Committee of the Party he emphasised the continuities in the transition from Chamberlain to Churchill as representative of 'the same reactionary monopolist interests'. The character of the People's Convention was to follow from this, the main task being 'to rally the working class movement and develop the broadest front of defence, reaching to all sections prepared to stand against the present totalitarian drive'.[47]

However, Dutt could already see in April 1941 that the extension of the war around the borders of the Soviet Union created a danger 'from both imperialist camps', and the 'inevitable transformation of the imperialist war into an anti- Soviet war'. The word 'inevitable' reminds us that whatever the other disagreements that had divided them over the war there was unanimity among Communists that all the capitalist powers were deadly foes of the Soviet Union. Dutt now enjoined the Party leadership to 'see that by our propaganda we maintain a close popular understanding of successive steps in the Soviet policy' - in other words they were to take steps to prepare the activists for a new line should the USSR come under attack.[48] Dutt's May Day speech in Hyde Park accordingly covered every eventuality - except, of course, the entry of the USSR into the war as an ally of either the fascists or the British near- or crypto-fascists. It is worth examining Dutt's speech if only to show the rag-bag of complaints now masquerading as a coherent policy.

Dutt started on old ground, by asserting that Chamberlain had got Britain into the current mess by trying to isolate the Soviet Union, only to come unstuck when the Nazis turned against the British empire. Now Churchill had replaced Chamberlain:

> He is said to make great speeches and there may be some who care for fly-blown rhetoric without a trace of constructive policy or leadership, but the working class movement of old knows Churchill as the imperialist swashbuckler, the jingoist, the die- hard Tory, the enemy of the workers.

Sidney Street, Gallipoli, the General Strike, India and the Norway fiasco were now paraded for inspection as supporting evidence. Having demonstrated Churchill's reactionary credentials Dutt progressed to 'the whole ruling class' which:

> ... is responsible for the present desperate situation to which they have brought the people ... the responsibility is theirs and the present evils cannot be cured until they are removed from power. Their foreign policy of support for reaction all over the world brought the people to the present perilous pass and they are still handing out £2.5 million of British money to Franco, at the same time as he maintains the bloodiest fascist terror in Spain and prepares to come out openly on the side of the Axis powers. There is a crisis of shipping. Ships are lacking in the present urgent need but it was these ruling gangsters who demobilised the shipguards and set up a special clause under the Bank of England with £10 million of money to destroy the shipyards of this country and today in consequence the ships that are needed cannot be produced or repaired fast enough.

In a similar vein Dutt drew attention to the crisis of food supplies and inadequate numbers of bombproof shelters, as if to indict the Government for an inefficient prosecution of the (imperialist) war, concluding that 'these people, these corrupt, degenerate, parasitic members of the ruling class who hold power ... are incapable of defending the interests, the lives and safety of the people of this country'. Indeed he spoke darkly of the danger of 'an imperialist peace [that] would be no peace, but only an alliance of the oppressors, of the most reactionary fascist and pro-fascist forces all over Europe against the people'. At the same time he asserted that the bulk of the ruling class favoured a prolonged war. Dutt disliked this too. It was a policy which meant increasing dependence on the USA; 'the resources of the labour of the people of this country, the future labour in the years after the war, are now mortgaged to the American millionaires'. This was the price British capitalism was prepared to pay for the survival of its world empire. Finally, he warned that either side in the war might attack the USSR.[49]

It was this increasingly likely attack on the Soviet Union which came to dominate Dutt's thoughts in June as 'every day more news is published of impending hostilities'. The Hess Mission aroused suspicions of an Anglo-German deal. All the talk of a Nazi invasion of Russia was not to be trusted either - it could be designed 'to turn attention from the desperate situation in Britain'. Fortunately, mused Dutt, 'the USSR stands ready for every eventuality ... Stalin has taken the helm of the Soviet Government'. Such thoughts were not contained in random diary entries but put before the Party leadership after careful consideration.[50] It was a sign of the Party's helplessness that Dutt had to list all these guesses for their collective consumption. Right up to the eve of the Nazi invasion he held back from predicting the 'inevitable' though his Notes of the Month - exactly twenty years of practice behind him - saw 'the extreme tension of the present situation [bearing] the character of the lull before the storm'.[51] With one hundred German army divisions now massed on the USSR's frontiers Dutt chose the moment to demonstrate that he had finally mastered the art of understatement.

THE PEOPLE'S WAR

The next day, however, he called for 'rapid and complete victory over Hitlerism ... by joint action', when news of Operation Barbarossa reached London. But the Nazi invasion of the Soviet Union made no difference to the question of a 'People's

Government' - his first reaction was to express 'no confidence in the present Government, dominated by Tory friends of fascism and Coalition Labour leaders'.[52] Churchill's immediate offer of help to Russia made no difference to Dutt, who issued a press statement denouncing the speech for its 'half measures'.[53] He argued for support for the Soviet Union combined with continued struggle against Churchill and British imperialism. Pollitt's instincts, on the other hand, were for complete support for the Government which had reiterated its determination to crush the Nazis. In what was probably the Comintern's last intervention in the affairs of the CPGB Dutt was rebuked and Pollitt's line upheld.[54] Pollitt could now return in July as secretary of the Party, no doubt feeling vindicated in his stance of September 1939, while Dutt was obliged to compose an article expounding the new line.

Some idea of the drama which socialists saw in the war on the Eastern front is conveyed by Isaac Deutscher's essay '22 June 1941', written just eight months after the struggle began, and all the more piquant for being the work of one expelled from the Polish Communist Party for 'exaggerating the threat of Nazism'. Deutscher was already convinced that Russian resistance was 'proof of the vitality of revolutionary society' and that the war in the East represented 'the most profound class conflict of our epoch, a conflict on a gigantic scale ... *a war between socialism and capitalism*'(emphasis in original):

> The destiny of the world now hangs in the balance across the vast spaces of the USSR. Everywhere - in occupied Europe, in the British Empire, in both Americas - people are listening with the same anxiety and hope to the sounds from the distant battlefields. This does not mean, however, that the conflicting class interests have now been replaced by a peaceful class idyll. But in the present war divergent class interests have become temporarily so intertwined that a diehard English conservative, a liberal, a bourgeois democrat, a Polish socialist, a Komsomol youth from a kolkhoz - all link their hopes and fears to the struggle on the Don and the Neva.

If a Trotskyist could reason thus, a Stalinist could be expected to strain every nerve to assist the beleagured citadel. Once the collaboration of the two governments became certain, therefore, Dutt explained that the Party's fight was no longer against Churchill 'but against the pro-fascist forces in the ruling class and in the Government'. The main demand now had to be an immediate 'Pact of Alliance' between Britain and the USSR. When this was actually signed on 12 July (as the British-Soviet Pact of Mutual Aid) Dutt was happy to announce that it had created 'a new world situation and a new political situation in Great Britain'.[55] The same message was cabled to the New York *Daily Worker* with Dutt adding that the new-found allies could 'look with confidence to the ever closer friendship and collaboration of the people of the United States':

> Such a united national front must embrace not only the working class and progressive forces who are friendly to the Soviet Union but also all those who, while opposed to the social and political system of the Soviet Union, recognise the common interest and necessity, from the standpoint of the national interests of the British people, or from their imperialist interests, for common action with the Soviet Union for the military defeat of Hitler.[56]

On 30 July 1941 an article by Dutt in the New York *Daily Worker* was already demanding; 'Open the Western Front'.

Dutt had intended to mark the twentieth anniversary of *Labour Monthly* by drawing on two decades of his Notes of the Month for a new book demonstrating the prolonged crisis of British imperialism and the necessity of a socialist revolution. This *Crisis of the British People* was advertised in *Labour Monthly* as a remarkable vindication of the Marxist method and across its 640 pages Dutt was no doubt able to show the continuous thread of Lenin's *Imperialism* running throughout his own work.[57] But the book never saw the light of day and no manuscript survives (disappointed subscribers had to make do with *Britain and the World Front* [May 1942] - which dwelt on the need for a more efficient war effort). It was not Russia's entry into the war which had rendered the book obsolete, but the Moscow line of alliance with Britain together with Russian insistence on Communist support for Churchill. A 'new world situation' was how Dutt described it, but it was the beginning of the end for the Leninist world-view on which the Comintern had been founded, though it is unlikely that anyone in Britain saw this immediately.

One thing that was certain was that if nothing was to be done to weaken the British war effort the anti-imperialist struggle had to cease for the time being. In India the Communists had wanted to turn the war-crisis into an opportunity for national liberation. Two weeks after the Nazi invasion of Russia Pollitt was compelled to write to the CPI describing the 'fundamentally new situation', warning against 'any sectarian attitude of the Communist Party, any standing aside and not pulling our full weight in the common effort to defeat Hitler, any putting forward impossible demands ... '.[58] But it was not until the middle of 1942 that the CPI was completely won over to the new position, becoming in the process a renegade and traitor in the eyes of the nationalist community. P.C. Joshi, the

Party leader, did his best to reconcile the anti-fascist imperative with the Communists' vanguard pretensions in the national struggle by claiming that a 'people's war' against fascism would transmogrify spontaneously into a war of national liberation.[59]

The argument failed to impress Congress, particularly as the CPI was rewarded with legality just a month before the beginning of Gandhi's Quit India campaign and another fierce round of Government repression. While the nationalists languished in jail the CPI was able to capitalise on its privileged legality, boosting Party membership from 5,000 in 1942 to 30,000 in 1946. To make matters worse, from the perspective of Congress, the Communists almost immediately began to talk of its obstructive rival, the Muslim League, as 'the political organisation of the second largest community in our country'.[60] By 1945 the Party's zeal for the 'people's war' had created a real headache for Dutt who was expected to make sense of its many policy innovations. Not only had it legitimised the Muslim League - an organisation formerly derided as a reactionary, communalist tool of the British - the Party had also come out in favour of Pakistan and had discovered no less than seventeen 'nations' on the subcontinent in total.

Dutt was partially responsible for the policy innovations of the CPI if only because of neglect. In May 1942 in a letter to the CPI he outlined the division of labour which would allow him to ignore politics on the subcontinent until the end of the war:

> In our agitation on this side ... we abstain from handling the internal issues of the Indian movement, and concentrate on the demand for a National Government for India to enable the Indian people to organise their defence in concert with the United Nations.

All he was prepared to say was that the general line in India required:

> maximum mobilisation against Fascism, irrespective of political differences;no action of the present rulers, so long as they stand by the alliance and resist Fascism, should deflect us from this line, which is in the interests, not merely of the world front of the peoples, but of the Indian people whose future cannot be separated from the world front of the peoples.[61]

Thus all of Dutt's public statements on India after June 1941 concentrated on Britain's refusal to take genuine steps of decolonisation. In this work he was as assiduous as he had ever been. Of course during the period when the war had been characterised as 'imperialist,' Dutt's relations with the nationalists had never been closer, as the presence of Indira Gandhi at meetings of the People's Convention symbolised. Relations might have been expected to sour thereafter but Dutt remained useful to the nationalists because of the steady stream of pro-independence propaganda which flowed from his pen. Radicals such as Nehru were well aware of Dutt's scarcity value, especially in the circumstances of war-torn Britain. Some of them also shared many, if not all, of his views.

Krishna Menon, for example, the secretary of the London- based India League - in which pressure group Communist influence was 'considerable' [62] - was so close to the Party that its members treated him as one of their own.[63] The Labour Party leadership also regarded him as a Communist - and he increased his contributions to *Labour Monthly* and speeches at CP- organised meetings when he resigned from the Labour Party in 1941. It certainly looks significant that while Krishna Menon remained on intimate terms with the Communists after June of that year - despite the Party's return to support for the war - the India League was, if anything, much less active in the promotion of nationalist propaganda. If the relationship was as close as it seems, it could explain how Dutt managed to receive inside information on world politics from an Indian source in the 1950s. Krishna Menon was highly regarded by Nehru and exercised a special influence on him after independence, serving at various times as UN delegate, roving ambassador, confidante, Minister without Portfolio and Minister of Defence.[64]

INDIA TO-DAY

Dutt did no harm to his personal prestige among the radical nationalists when his *India To-day* was published in 1940. Forty years later it was still held to be the best Marxist survey of India's economic and political history in the colonial era.[65] While distancing himself from the simplicities of 'conventional national propaganda' Dutt presented the 'spectacle of squalid poverty and misery' of India as inextricably connected to imperial rule. In accordance with Comintern orthodoxy he depicted the arrested economic development of the subcontinent, contrasting 'limitless potential wealth and actual neglect and failure'. On the way he lambasted Malthusian explanations of India's plight as the 'easy lies that comfort cruel men', the favourite philosophy of reaction 'laughed at by scientists and economists of all schools'; 'Cut off his legs - this man is too long for his bed', such was the logic of the over-population theory.

Dutt invited his readers to consider the Central Asian Republics of the Soviet Union by way of an instructive comparison. Twenty years before, he insisted, these republics were even more backward than India. But in just two decades they had marched streets ahead, whether the analyst examined industrial or agricultural production, standards of education, public health or general cultural development; 'the contrast between the Soviet Union and India', he concluded, 'is the contrast between civilisation and barbarism'. Here it is enough to observe that the contrast was widely accepted in these terms on the Left and among colonial nationalists. The lesson, which he did not fail to point out, was that the way forward after independence had to be structured around central economic planning - already another accepted axiom of the radicals like Nehru.

Marx appears in Dutt's text as an analytical pioneer of the Indian situation, revealing both the destructive role of British rule in India and its regenerative impact. But Marx analysed only the first two periods of imperialist rule - the stages of Merchant Capital and Industrial Capital - and much of Dutt's exposition dwells on the third, and last, of its phases - that of Finance Capital. According to Dutt the latest transition had served to intensify the exploitation of India as a source of raw materials and as a market for British goods while doing nothing to develop India as an industrial nation. 'Such industrial development as has taken place', Dutt concluded, 'has in fact had to fight its way against intense opposition from British finance capital alike in the financial and in the political field'.[66] Far from the picture of 'rapid industrialisation' drawn by Dutt and Roy in the early 1920s, the analysis now found only 'deindustrialisation'. The main though not the only culprit, according to Dutt, was imperialism.

But continuity with the Dutt-Roy theses of old reappeared when he turned to the 'basic problem of India', the agrarian problem. As before he stressed the over-pressure of the population on agriculture because of the thwarting of other economic channels. The deleterious impact of this was aggravated by land monopolies, low technique, the sub-division and fragmentation of holdings, the growth of the landless, and the burden of rent and debts. Various Royal Commissions had identified these pernicious structures since the 1840s but British policy had served only to encourage them. Landlordism was an artificial creation of foreign rule and completely functionless. So also was the moneylender and the mountain of debt. Dutt was nevertheless forced to acknowledge the existence of literally millions of petty landlords and moneylenders. He was adamant that only large-scale farming could serve a free India's vital economic needs, however, and trusted that 'the initiative and action of the mass of the peasantry themselves' would effect the necessary redistribution through the thicket of individual vested interests.

This was perhaps the least convincing part of the argument. Yet Dutt devoted at least half of the 540 pages of the book to the rise of Indian nationalism and the political problems associated with it. If he was accorded respect within the Congress it was at least in part because he accepted a great deal of its own version of reality. He paid due homage to the INC, for example, as 'the alternative claimant to power in succession to British rule', dismissing the claims of the Muslim League in the process whilst attributing the main responsibility for communalism to the British. The undoubted vacillations of Congress were explained as the consequence of its conflict with the British bourgeoisie, on the one hand, and the fear of the masses felt by the Indian bourgeoisie when faced with the possible loss of its own privileges. But Dutt argued that the solution of this contradiction depended on mass involvement in the national struggle, certainly not a sectarian refusal to join it. He was adamant that 'the central aim' of the British was to hang on to India but equally certain that the Raj had become a shell 'ready to crumble at a touch':

> The Western romantic intellectuals of the period of imperialist decay, who sought to find solace for their woes over the advance of modern civilisation, by contemplating the filthy pigsty of Holy Russia and finding there the shrine of eternal spiritual values and an imagined docile and devout peasantry, whom the modern currents of democracy and socialism could never reach, were worshipping a carcass and blind to the abounding power of life and awakening of the real masses who were about to shatter their mirage. So, too, to-day the sapient Western traveller, who goes to visit the immemorial East in India, whether to drink at the muddy fountain of Oriental spiritual higher thought, or to expose with patronising scorn the innate backwardness of 'Mother India', is visiting only a museum of mediaeval lumber, and is blind to the living forces of the Indian people.[67]

Perhaps; but since Dutt had never even visited India he was not far removed from such religiosity himself in these flights of rhetoric which were little more than expressions of confidence in the old mole of history. All the more so, we must conclude, in that 'the living forces' were by his own account so effectively stunted in growth by the imperialist parasite. There was also more than a passing resemblance to the 'romantic intellectual' in Dutt's rather simple image of a unified nationalist movement sweeping away the foreign hanger-on and advancing in disciplined formation - not counting the local bourgeoisie - to 'a colossal programme of industrial development' and integrated economic planning for the whole of India. He was not the only one beguiled by this vision, of course, but he certainly did his best to make it persuasive and can thus be held responsible for making light of the many real problems which stood in the way of its realisation. In his defence it has to be said that he was preoccupied with the job of refuting a mountain of arguments, to which most educated opinion in Britain subscribed, 'proving' the impracticality of Indian independence and the 'intractability' of its problems.

It is clear at any rate that Dutt stood for a united India - he even regarded the creation of a separate Burma in 1937 as a regrettable imperialist manoeuvre. He envisaged 'a real Federation based on the natural geographical-economic-cultural divisions and groupings of the people'. In common with most of the nationalists he saw the constitution of 1935 as a meticulous plot to deny this possibility with its disproportionate representation of the princely puppets and promotion of communal constituencies. But he envisaged no genuine centrifugal tendencies among 'the masses'. Communal divisions were virtually conjured away as 'a special product of British rule', an effect of a 'declining imperialist ascendancy'. When the communal organisations were unmasked, moreover, Dutt only found 'small ultra-reactionary groups dominated by large landlord and banker interests playing for the support of the British Government against the popular movement'. This was Nehru's view too and there was a lot to be said for it; but it was hardly sufficient.

THE WORLD FRONT

The Indian nationalist leaders made two offers of co-operation with the British - in September 1939 and in the summer of 1940 - but both were conditional on the treatment of India as an equal and were accordingly rejected. The Communists though enthusiastic supporters of the war effort after 22 June 1941 - talking, indeed, of 'unconditional' support - did not approve of every aspect of the British Government's conduct of the conflict. The obvious example is their immediate advocacy of a second front, but the same critical attitude can be seen in their running critique of British policy in South Asia. The Anglo-American press release known as the

Atlantic Charter referred in August 1941 to the 'right of all peoples to choose the form of government under which they will live'; but Churchill specifically excluded its application from 'India, Burma and other parts of the British Empire'. Dutt took every opportunity to fulminate against these double standards and to argue that the collapse of Burma and Malaya and the disastrous fall of Singapore in February 1942 had to be understood as an indictment of colonialism. Popular support for the *ancien regime* was simply lacking and Britain's unwillingness to reach a settlement in India could thus be likened to one of 'the worst military fiascos of the war' because it prevented the full mobilisation of India's resources behind the Allied campaign.[68]

When Stafford Cripps was despatched to India in March, Gandhi advised him to take the next plane home because his compromise offer refused the nationalist's demand for the formation of a representative National Government. Dutt backed Congress explaining that the deal Cripps had in mind involved a post-war substitute for independence which threatened to prepare the way for partition.[69] In the American Communist journal *New Masses* Dutt asked rhetorically 'what sincere democrat can oppose the demands of the Indian National Congress?'. The Cripps offer had restricted itself to jam - 'highly dubious jam' - tomorrow. The Congress, according to Dutt, 'were told that British power must remain dictatorial and absolute, that Indian Ministers might at the most control canteens and stationery'.[70] But, as Dutt knew perfectly well, the Indian Communists had already urged Congress to reach agreement with Cripps. The CPI's brief, after all, was to fight for 'maximum mobilisation' and not to allow any 'action of the present rulers, so long as they stand by the alliance and resist Fascism, [to] deflect us from this line'. These were Dutt's own instructions.

Dutt therefore had the more congenial task and an Olympian base from which to effect it. He was able to urge the British Government to take full advantage of 'the serious offer of a settlement' which Gandhi made on the eve of the Quit India campaign, while 'deploring' the threat of civil disobedience which accompanied it. Given the close proximity of the Japanese armies such a disruption would be 'suicidal' and Dutt denounced Gandhi for the 'appeasement of Fascism'.[71] Dutt was able, nevertheless, to take the Congress view urging that 'the way must be found to reach a settlement which makes possible the free and honourable co-operation of the great Indian nation', while advising the leadership of the CPGB that 'our Party has the responsibility to lead the most intensive campaign for the immediate reopening of negotiations on the basis of the recognition of Indian independence and the establishment of an Indian National Government as an ally of the United Nations'.[72] Dutt led the way in August 1942 by writing to Churchill demanding the removal of the Secretary of State for India, L.S. Amery, and the resumption of negotiations on the basis of recognition of the 'just national aspirations of the Indian people'.[73]

Meanwhile in India Dutt's conception of the Indian nation was being undermined by the CPI's pursuit of 'maximum mass mobilisation against Fascism, irrespective of political differences'. The Communists came out in favour of Pakistan and, having decided in favour of the 'national' rights of Muslims - influenced no doubt by the Muslim League's collaboration in the war effort - proceeded to discover incipient nations all over the place on the basis of seventeen major language groups. When Congress resumed normal functioning in 1945 Communists were refused membership for the first time - such was the deterioration in relations. Unfortunately for Dutt the CPI's innovators were able to invoke Stalin's authority for the new nationalities policy - the great sage having remarked in 1925 that although 'India is spoken of as a single whole ... there can be hardly any doubt that in the case of a revolutionary upheaval ... many hitherto unknown nationalities, each with its own language and its own distinctive culture, will emerge on the scene'.[74] It may not be a coincidence that Stalin's writings on the national and colonial question were reprinted in English in 1941 - that is shortly before the CPI's discovery of a multinational India.

In fact the Indian Communists first adumbrated the new nationalities policy in the so-called Party Letter of May 1941 and Dutt's *India To-day* (which was, of course, banned in India) was invoked in the ensuing controversy by those who attacked the leadership. Dutt's contempt for Jinnah's Muslim League as a self-serving clique of reactionaries was well known and apparently borne out by its miserable showing in the last round of elections - a mere 4.6 per cent of the 1937 vote despite the fact that the constitution reserved 480 of the 1,581 seats for Muslims on a strictly communalist basis. When Jinnah declared for the creation of Pakistan in March 1940 nobody - least of all Jinnah - knew what it meant. Nevertheless the enlarged plenum of the CPI's central committee resolved in September 1942 that the Dutt orthodoxy was redundant. In the same month Dutt himself referred vaguely to the need for 'far-reaching concessions' by Congress in the interests of national unity, but his hope was that the unspecified concessions would appease the Muslim League and prevent the partition of the subcontinent.[75]

But where Dutt had only seen evidence of cultural backwardness and imperialist manipulation in Muslim support for Jinnah, the CPI saw 'advancing consciousness'. The new line argued that an 'all-India consciousness' could only be realised 'through and in terms of' the plurality of actually existing languages and interests. In championing 'every nationality' as a 'progressive lever', the CPI claimed that the various nationalities would push shoulder to shoulder for Indian independence.[76] Dutt published the full text of the CPI's reasoning in *Labour Monthly* but refrained from comment. The new policy was potentially a public relations disaster in Britain - where the opponents of independence had always played the minorities card - and a source of division and acrimony in India. In the event Dutt would have to address the CPI leadership in person to help sort out the mess, but that would have to wait until 1946.

SPIRIT OF TEHERAN

Well before the Cold War resumed on a more intense basis in 1947 Dutt had plenty of opportunities to identify cracks in the 'world democratic front against fascism'. He talked, for example, of the disquiet in ruling class circles about the advance of the Red Army as early as March 1942, and scorned accompanying fears of the 'supposed menace of a Soviet domination of Europe'. That autumn the Western allies reached an agreement with the Vichy military chief of Algeria, Admiral Darlan, providing Dutt with evidence that all sorts of conservative intrigues were brewing with a reactionary order in post-war Europe in view.[77] Naturally, as the war progressed, the shape of things to come became much clearer and there was more evidence that class and post-war power considerations were becoming uppermost - as suggested by Britain's imposition of Marshall Badoglio in Italy, British intervention in Greece and its apparent *modus vivendi* with Franco's Spain.

Until 1946, however, the main thrust of Soviet propaganda served to minimise suggestions of a conflict of interests between the 'Big Three'. The very idea of a 'non-imperialist coalition of states' involving Britain and America was a nonsense from a

Leninist standpoint, but following the twenty-year 'treaty of alliance and mutual assistance' signed by Churchill and Stalin in May 1942, Dutt enthused about 'the organisation of world peace for a whole generation ahead', and the lasting amity that was now possible between erstwhile irreconcilable enemies.[78] As a Communist Dutt had no trouble reconciling such images of peaceful coexistence with the expectation of a radical redrawing of the map. There was no reason to think that friendship between the Big Three amounted to a new Congress of Vienna. If the USSR was strengthened by the alliance with Britain and America, if it was able to create a sphere of influence in Eastern Europe, if the war - as a Marxist would expect - radicalised the millions and if the alliance held in the face of these developments, the spread of socialism as Dutt understood it was not hindered by Stalin's diplomacy. Britain was finished as a Great Power, the European empires were set to go for good and the Americans seemed happy at the prospect. The Soviet Union, on the other hand, was emerging as an industrial and military colossus.

It was not necessary to be a Communist, however, to believe that the USSR had become a decisive force in the world and to feel that this was a change for the better. The talk everywhere on the British Left was to this effect. Few socialists could imagine the construction of a better Britain without the friendship and co-operation of the Soviet Union. Cole described the USSR as the 'principal rallying point for the forces of Socialism throughout the world' in 1941, and said it was absurd to think of a post-war socialist settlement in the absence of Soviet assistance. Laski, Brockway, Emrys Hughes and Konni Zilliacus took the same view, so did Kingsley Martin's *New Statesman* and the *Tribune* of Nye Bevan and Michael Foot. It was an argument put by the chairman of the Labour Party annual congress in 1942; in the pages of *The Times* just as in *Tribune* and the *New Statesman* some sort of domination of Eastern Europe by the USSR was seen as the price that had to be paid for the recent bitter past.[79] The Americans, on the other hand, were viewed with rising suspicion by all elements on the Left as the war came to a close.[80]

The pro-Soviet sentiment which reached its peak after the battle of Stalingrad had beneficial repercussions for the Party. Up to 1943, 'the strength of pro-Soviet feeling, especially in the press, was such as to inhibit any public expression of doubt about Soviet policies, intentions, or virtues, and any politician who dared to break that taboo found shot and shell flying round his head'.[81] This was the context in which recruitment to the Party increased so fast that it was impossible to keep pace with it administratively. It peaked at something like 50,000 in 1943 and some factory branches were able to measure the membership in hundreds for the first time. Of course other factors played a part in making the Party popular - one could mention the vacuum left by the electoral truce, the Communists' factory work[82], the war-induced radicalism, and the agitation of the 'barrack-room lawyers'. But the real novelty was official connivance in the promotion of Stalin as a hero in a situation where it proved impossible to challenge the widespread belief that the success of the Red Army reflected glory on the system that had created it. By January 1942 a public opinion poll showed 86 per cent of respondents wishing to see Britain and Russia working together after the war.[83]

Stalin did his best to remove the surviving flies in the ointment. The Internationale, for example, was replaced by a new Soviet anthem which Churchill arranged to have broadcast on the BBC shortly after his return from the Teheran conference of November - December 1943. The Comintern had been unceremoniously dissolved four months earlier, thus removing one of the most prominent objections to the CPGB's renewed bid to affiliate to the Labour Party. The hapless Dutt had only recently contrasted the folding of the Labour and Socialist International with the continuity of the Comintern, quoting Stalin to show that 'a party which has set itself the aim of leading the proletariat in struggle must represent, not a chance congregation of individuals, but a monolithic, centralised organisation whose activities can be directed according to a single plan'.[84] A year later Dutt mentioned Shaw's suggestion that the dissolution of the Comintern might be a good tactic in a letter to Beatrice Webb - but only to scoff derisively at the very thought of it.[85] Another year on he reported to the Party's organisation bureau that news from the district branches demonstrated that the decision to dissolve the Comintern had been received 'with full understanding and appreciation of the timeliness of this step'.[86] Once again, the Russians had identified a new world situation moments before everyone else. In the event the decision failed to tip the scales in favour of Communist affiliation, Morrison observing to the 1943 Labour conference that the CPGB was 'a very different and very much less responsible body than the Communist Party of the Soviet Union'.[87]

Communist subservience to the Soviet Union had never been more transparent and yet circumstances, as Dutt correctly anticipated, had never been more propitious for Communist advance. Dutt's first reactions to the news of Russia's entry into the war suggest, as we have seen, that he expected to use these circumstances to build the Party in its accustomed oppositional role and saw no reason to give unqualified support to the Government. He also disapproved of the decision to 'kill' the People's Convention which he saw as the embryo of a 'broad democratic movement' fighting for winnable reforms.[88] In a polemical exchange with H.G. Wells on the twenty-fifth anniversary of the Bolshevik Revolution Dutt was still commending Party organisation and discipline in terms of the rigid factory paradigm enlisted by Lenin in *One Step Forward, Two Steps Back*. Wells had welcomed Dutt's invitation to celebrate October 1917 by saying that it was 'difficult to overestimate the mischief the Communist Party has done to mankind in the past third of a century'. 'I welcome your invitation', Wells continued, 'because I have long desired an opportunity of dealing plainly with you personally, and now your demand for this article has delivered you into my hand'. Dutt had the last word, of course, lambasting Wells for the 'aristocratic anarchism' typical of 'unstable intellectuals' who reflected the 'petty bourgeois mode of life'.[89]

Left to his own devices Dutt would have preferred the Party vanguard to have been just one element inside the People's Convention - obviously setting the agenda and tone but not coextensive with it. He envisaged 'really big, potential mass support for the Convention' around a programme that would include 'driving out the Munichites', the demand for a second front and policies on food, production and wages. The Anglo-Soviet Friendship committees which actually replaced the Convention did not have this campaigning potential and it is at least arguable that the broad democratic front which Dutt wanted surfaced within the CPGB instead by 1944, thus diluting the Party's cadre force.[90] The new type of member was less constant and reliable and membership was already at least ten thousand below its wartime peak by 1945. But the loss of members also underlines the transient nature of the Party's greater popularity, dependent as this was on public sympathy for the beleagured Soviet Union. British circumstances did not allow Dimitrov's advice to Pollitt concerning the Party's role in defending 'national honour' to be translated into mass practice. In France, Italy, Greece and Czechoslovakia mass Communist Parties emerged immediately after the war, to a large extent because the Communists were seen as the true patriots and anti-Fascists. None of the tactical options open to the CPGB could have conjured a similar outcome in Britain.

Instead the Party hoped to ride on the coat-tails of Allied victory and what the Communist press called 'the spirit of Teheran' - the apparent accord struck at the first meeting of the Big Three in November 1943. Thus in January 1944 Dutt was to be found anxiously concerned about the recent defeats of Government candidates in by-elections. Even though the electors were returning leftist critics of the government Dutt could now only see the danger of division. The Teheran agreements, he said, 'have opened out the greatest and most inspiring prospect for united advance to win speedy victory and to win the peace'. Nothing could be allowed to detract from these objectives - not even the election of the odd dissident or two.

When Earl Browder announced the decision to dissolve the American Communist Party, Dutt calmly described it as corresponding 'to the peculiar concrete conditions' of the USA where 'the fight for Teheran ... takes place inevitably within the framework of the two traditional older parties' because of the absence of a mass labour movement. 'The issue of socialism', Dutt observed to the British Party leadership, 'cannot arise as an immediate issue in these conditions and its presentation as such could be equivalent to splitting the progressive Teheran camp'. In Britain, where there was 'no question' of either major party reneging on Teheran, Dutt saw no need to liquidate the CPGB but it is obvious that he would have changed his mind very quickly if the Russians had decided otherwise.[91] And he must have considered this possibility because, as he said himself, Teheran meant the 'lasting partnership' of the Big Three.[92] In the event, however, 'Browderism' was denounced as a 'revision of Marxism' when Jacques Duclos opened a Soviet-inspired attack on the CPUSA's decision in April 1945, and explained his errors as proceeding from a correct appreciation of the significance of Teheran which was then 'distorted into a complete new theory'. Dutt's failure to notice this at the time was not lost on disturbed members of the British Party.[93]

In the context of Stalin's determination to let nothing stand in the way of agreement with Britain and America - as long as he could have certain 'spheres of influence' - Dutt was to be found welcoming the 'international economic collaboration' signalled by the Bretton Woods agreement in August 1944 and reserving his displeasure for 'persistent sniping' by its critics. At the Yalta summit of February 1945, 'the spirit of Teheran', was apparently sealed with Churchill taking the initiative in carving Europe into Russian and Western zones of dominance, much to Stalin's approval. Dutt knew nothing of this, of course, but the general satisfaction emanating from Yalta was unmistakeable even to observers lacking his sensitive antennae. By April he was arguing in favour of a continuation of the coalition Government in Britain into the peace - why upset the applecart now? This enthusiasm proved fleeting and it has to be said that his main theme both before, and especially after, Yalta was on the need for 'a Labour and progressive electoral alliance' that would include the Communists as well as Liberals and Common Wealth. Still the moment was significant; for approximately six months he argued that those who stood for an independent Labour victory were 'dangerously unrealistic' and seemed to believe that the preservation of 'national unity' could mean a Communist niche in a future National Government. Like a great many other wartime ideas - such as a federal Europe - which soon seemed fantastic to the British, Dutt's confidence in the post-war prominence of the Communists had been taken quite seriously in ruling circles and was by no means confined to his own wishful thinking.[94]

Communist support for 'progressive humanity' - or the Soviet Union as it was also known - required great dexterity for the simple reason, which completely eluded Browder, that there was never a perfect fit between the policies of the Big Three. Dutt was thus constantly on the alert for the points of tension. Already in January 1945 he was inclined to blame Churchill - rather than the Cabinet as a whole - for Britain's intervention against the Communists in Greece and 'the menace of reactionary policy cutting across the aims of liberation'; he noted disturbing signs of Allied demobilisation of the Left in Belgium too.[95] By March he was ready to stand as a candidate in the Sparkbrook constituency of Birmingham, specifically to oppose the Secretary of State for India, L.S. Amery. Dutt despised Amery as a former appeaser of Hitler as well as 'the gaoler of India', a man responsible by his 'complacency and indifference' for the ravages of the Bengal famine of 1943-44. In fact the Russians were not much interested in the fate of India - or indeed of Greece - as long as Churchill let them have their own way in Poland. Dutt was thus to a large extent left to his own devices, forced to extemporise in his commentaries on the world situation but experienced enough to find the interstices between an apparently redundant Leninism and the 'spirit of Teheran'. If Stalin had secured agreement on a new balance of power in Europe Dutt was prepared to hail this as a progressive settlement and act according to a prepared text; if the agreement should break down he could claim to have noticed imperialist aggression all along. It was the practical application of his favourite formula - extreme suppleness and flexibility alongside resoluteness of purpose.

NOTES

1 *Daily Worker*, 1.9.1939.
2 *Ibid*, 4.9.39.
3 *Ibid*, 5.9.39.
4 *Ibid*, 30.9.39.
5 See Dutt to Clemens Dutt, 10.4.1930, Clemens Dutt File; M. Johnstone, introduction to F. King and G. Matthews (eds), *About Turn: The Communist Party and the Outbreak of the Second World War; The Verbatim Record of the Central Committee Meetings 1939*, Lawrence and Wishart 1990, p23.
6 Dutt, Amendments to Resolution Endorsing Declaration of 2 September, 22.939, K4 Vol 1939-40.
7 King and Matthews, *op cit*, p67.
8 *Ibid*, p68.
9 *Ibid*, p75.
10 *Ibid*, p86.
11 *Ibid*, p93.
12 *Ibid*, pp103-104.
13 *Ibid*, p104.
14 *Ibid*, p131.
15 *Ibid*, p142.
16 *Ibid*, p161.
17 *Ibid*, pp202-4.
18 *Ibid*, p209.
19 *Ibid*, p285.
20 F. Brockway, *Towards Tomorrow*, Hart-Davis 1977, p143.
21 G. Orwell, *Collected Essays, Journalism and Letters*, Vol 1, Penguin, Harmondsworth 1970, pp434-8.
22 Quoted in D. Childs, 'The British Communist Party and the War 1939-1941', *Journal of Contemporary History*, 12, 2, 1077, p240.
23 Quoted in Dutt, *India To-Day*, Gollancz 1940, pp13-14.
24 Dutt, *Why This War?*, CPGB November 1939, p8, p15, p18.
25 *Daily Worker*, 1 February 1940.
26 Quoted by V. Gollancz, *Russia and Ourselves*, Gollancz 1941, p97.
27 E. Trory, *Imperialist War*, Crabtree Press, Brighton 1977.

28 K. Martin, The Man of Steel, *New Statesman*, 9 December 1939.
29 Dutt, Finland - The Facts, *Daily Worker*, 30.11.39; Dutt, Speech in Hyde Park, 3.12.39, K4 Vol 1939.
30 H. Thomas, *John Strachey, op cit*, pp195-6.
31 R. Dudley Edwards, *Victor Gollancz*, Gollancz 1987, p311.
32 J. Strachey, 'The CP Line Now', *Left News*, July 1940; V. Gollancz, 'The Lessons of France', *Left News*, July 1940, p1495.
33 R. Dudley Edwards, *op cit*, p328.
34 E.M. Winterton, 'Left Intellectuals and the War', *Labour Monthly*, July 1940, p360.
35 J. Attfield and S. Williams (eds), *1939: The Communist Party and the War*, Lawrence and Wishart 1984, p32.
36 *Daily Worker*, 12.12.39; Dutt, Memorandum on the *Labour Monthly*, K4, Vol 1941.
37 See the informed discussion in K. Morgan, *Against Fascism and War, op cit*, pp272-277.
38 D. Hyde, *I Believed: The Autobiography of a Former British Communist*, Reprint Society 1952, p83.
39 Dutt, *Leninism*, Marx Memorial Library, March 1941, pp5-6.
40 Dutt, Notes of the Month, *Labour Monthly*, November 1940.
41 For a detailed survey see K. Morgan, *Against Fascism and War, op cit, passim.*
42 N. Branson, *History of the Communist Party of Great Britain, 1927-1941, op cit*, pp292-301.
43 *Tribune*, 17.1.41.
44 Dutt, Speech to the People's Convention, 5 January 1941, K4 Vol 1941-2.
45 K. Morgan, *Against Fascism and War, op cit*, p205.
46 Dutt, 'An Appeal To All Democrats', *World News and Views*, 31.1.41, p3.
47 Dutt, Draft Political Letter, 30.4.41; see also his Outline of Political Report, 12.2.1941, K4 Vol 1941-2.
48 Dutt, Outline of a Political Report to Enlarged Meeting, 15.4.41, *Ibid.*
49 Dutt, May Day Speech Hyde Park, 1.5.41, *Ibid.*
50 Dutt, Draft Political Statement: The British People and the Soviet Union, 18.6.41, *Ibid.*
51 Dutt, 'After Twenty Years', 21.6.41, *Ibid.*
52 Dutt, Draft Political Statement: A Call To Action, 22.6.41, *Ibid.*
53 Dutt, Press Statement on Churchill's Speech, 24.6.41, *Ibid.*
54 Harry Pollitt's notes, 5 Aug 1959 on 1939-41 pp17-18 (CPGB archive. See *About Turn, op cit*, p42.
55 I. Deutscher, '22 June 1941', reprinted in *New Left Review*, 124, November-December 1980; Dutt, 'The United National Front of the British People', *World News and Views*, 13.7.41, p1.
56 Dutt, Cable to New York *Daily Worker*, 17.7.41, K4 Vol 1941-2.
57 The Book was advertised in *Labour Monthly*, April 1941.

58 S. Roy (ed), *Communism in India: Unpublished Documents 1935- 45*, National Book Agency, Calcutta 1976, pp263-5.
59 P.C. Joshi, *The Indian Communist Party: Its Policy and Work in the War of Liberation*, CPGB 1942, p16.
60 *Ibid*, p16.
61 Dutt, Letter to India (CPI), 10.5.42, K4 Vol 1941-2.
62 F. Brockway, *The Colonial Revolution*, Hart-Davis 1973, p37.
63 Douglas Hyde, interview.
64 K. Vijay, *British Opinion and Indian Independence*, unpublished M. Phil, London University 1970, p285 and p325; H. Tinker, *Men Who Overturned Empires*, Macmillan 1987, pp93-4.
65 Editorial comment, *Seminar: Marxism and India*, Number 178, New Delhi, June 1974, p10.
66 Dutt, *India To-Day*, Gollancz 1940, p150.
67 *Ibid*, p500.
68 Dutt, 'India - What Must Be Done', *Labour Monthly*, September 1942, p259.
69 Dutt, Statement on India, 31.3.42, K4 Vol 1941-2.
70 Dutt, 'India - What Must Be Done', *New Masses*, 14.8.42.
71 Dutt, Political Statement on Indian National Congress, 7.8.42, K4 Vol 1941-2.
72 Dutt, Report on India, 20.8.42, *Ibid*.
73 Dutt, To The Prime Minister, 21.8.42, *Ibid*.
74 J.V. Stalin, 'The Political Tasks of the University of the Peoples of the East', May 1925, in J.V. Stalin, *Marxism and the National and Colonial Question*, Lawrence and Wishart 1936, pp210- 211.
75 Dutt, 'India - What Must Be Done', *Labour Monthly*, September 1942, p266.
76 G. Adhikari, *Pakistan and Indian National Unity*, CPGB 1943, p13.
77 Dutt, Notes of the Month, *Labour Monthly*, March 1942. See also his Notes for April 1942 and February and March 1943 - especially p38 and p70 respectively for the last two.
78 Dutt, Notes of the Month, *Labour Monthly*, July 1942, p194.
79 See G.D.H. Cole, *Europe, Russia, and the Future*, Gollancz 1941, pp27-34; H. Laski, *Faith, Reason and Civilisation*, Gollancz 1944, pp45-62.
80 J. Schneer, *Labour's Conscience*, Unwin Hyman 1988, p44.
81 P.M.H. Bell, *John Bull and The Bear:British Public Opinion, Foreign Policy and the Soviet Union 1941-1945*, Edward Arnold 1990, p7.
82 J. Hinton, 'Coventry Communism: a study of factory politics in the Second World War', *History Workshop Journal*, 10, Autumn 1980.
83 P.M.H. Bell, *op cit*, p 103.
84 Dutt, Lenin and Stalin on the Party, *World News and Views*, 12.6.41.
85 Dutt to B. Webb, 9.6.42, K4 1941-2.
86 Dutt, To the Organisation Bureau, 4.6.43, K4 Vol 1943-4.
87 *Labour Party Annual Conference Report*, 1943, p166.

88 Dutt to Pollitt, 13.11.41, K4 Vol 1943-4.
89 Wells correspondence 3.10.42 to 8.10.42, K4 Vol 1941-2.
90 See J. Hinton, 'Killing the People's Convention', *Bulletin of the Society of Labour History*, Number 39, Autumn 1979.
91 Dutt, Raise the Fighting Spirit, 18.1.44, K4 Vol 1943-4.
92 Dutt, 'Lenin in 1944', *Daily Worker*, 18.1.44, p1.
93 Dutt, 'The Errors of Browder's Revision of Marxism', *World News and Views*, 7.8.45.
94 See D. Carlton, *Anthony Eden*, Allen and Unwin 1986, p185.
95 Dutt, Notes of the Month, *Labour Monthly*, January 1945, p1. and p5.

7
THE COLD WAR

THE ATTLEE GOVERNMENTS

By the summer of 1945 the CPGB wanted a 'popular victory' in the general election with an 'overwhelming majority' of Labour and progressive MPs behind it - including Communists. The Party's domestic programme was very similar to Labour's - emphasising the nationalisation of land, coal, steel, power and inland transport; a national medical service and comprehensive social security; full employment; a massive housing programme; and guaranteed prices in agriculture. In a vague and perfunctory fashion it also talked of planning, but its 'Five Year Plan' was devoid of detail save for references to the need to re-equip industry and to direct capital investment to where it was needed. On this basis it envisaged 'compelling big business and monopoly to work on lines laid down by the Government in the interests of the nation'.[1] Foreign policy hardly figured in the election campaign but the differences between Labour and the Communists in this area were already considerable.

Dutt did his best to accentuate these differences in his own campaign in Sparkbrook and was duly attacked by the Labour candidate - a local worthy, Alderman Percy Shurmer - for being more interested in the people of India than the citizens of Birmingham. There was truth in the accusation, of course, and Dutt tried to marginalise Shurmer by claiming that his fight against Amery was 'nationally and internationally recognised in the world's press as a key fight against Tory reaction'. He was able to quote the good wishes of Gandhi, Nehru and a host of Asian politicians in support of this claim, as well as British celebrities such as Augustus John, J.B.S. Haldane and his old friend Shaw, who referred to Dutt's record of 'scholarship and service and uncompromising devotion to the interests of nine tenths of the nation'.[2] The electors of Sparkbrook remained unimpressed and the Labour nonentity walked home with a landslide.

In Britain the swing to the left was a swing to Labour and the Communists returned only two MPs - Gallacher and Phil Piratin. But it was seen as a defeat for Tory reaction all the same. Dutt expressed the Party verdict on the election as 'a grand clearing-out operation': 'At last the turn of the Labour Party has come, for which generations of the labour movement have worked and waited, to form a Labour Government with a Parliamentary majority. A new political situation opens'.[3] It was nothing less than 'a glorious political leap forward' - 'the counterpart of the sweep to the Left throughout Europe'. The electors were to be congratulated for having rid Britain of the 'Munichites', Tory Diehards and 'irresponsible adventurists' such as Churchill, Beaverbrook and Brendan Bracken. Dutt was also confident that the Labour manifesto, *Let Us Face The Future*, represented 'a positive programme of concrete measures'. Socialists such as Nye Bevan now looked forward to a Labour political dominance for as far as anyone could see ahead, but Dutt warned that 'it is only necessary to survey the field to see that the situation confronting the new Labour Government is crowded with problems which will require all the understanding, the united endeavour and the co-operation of the entire labour movement and the whole nation'.[4]

This was more than a veiled threat. Dutt observed that Labour's Parliamentary majority was not an accurate reflection of its support in the country - one poll in May 1945 showing 55 per cent of electors favouring a Popular Front Government. The exclusion of the minor parties was in large measure the result of the 'fantastically unjust representation' afforded by the electoral system which constricted real choice to the Labour-Tory alternative, and enabled Attlee to obtain three-fifths of the seats on just under half of the votes. This was no basis for 'the permanent ascendancy of the labour movement', according to Dutt. On the contrary, as *The Times* noted with satisfaction, the election had re-established the two-party system, Dutt commented that:

> The grounds for their satisfaction are transparent. They assume with confidence as the necessary concomitant of the two- party system the 'swing of the pendulum' and therefore the automatic future return of Toryism. They assume a long period of peaceful alternation of Toryism and Labour, reproducing the classic Nineteenth century parliamentarism, preventing the execution of any long-term Labour programme and guaranteeing the maintenance of the status quo.[5]

For the sake of his argument he assumed that Labour actually intended to change the *status quo* for the better - but that is not what he had said just two years earlier. Given that he was under orders not to rock the boat, it is interesting that in the summer of 1943 he was already talking of the ideological convergence of the two main parties within 'a planned and organised monopoly capitalism with a wide sphere of State regulation and control'. The political counterpart of such a system, he alleged, was either a 'permanent coalition' or its practical equivalent in a 'thinly veiled ... alternation of barely distinguishable parties agreed on fundamentals'.[6] Dutt even imagined the unions assigned to 'a neutral economic role' as junior partners of corporate power. Shorn of the jargon, it was a passable description of 'Butskellism'. But in the wake of Labour's landslide victory Dutt and his colleagues had decided to give the Government's domestic programme their full backing.

Thus he declared that the policies outlined in the King's Speech had 'won a universal welcome from all sections of the working class movement and from the broadest sections of democratic opinion'.[7] He was even content to call simply for the practical implementation of the promise of self- government for India, Burma, and Ceylon - raising no doubts as to the real content of the proposed self-government much less of its extension to other dependencies. In October 1945 Maurice Dobb surveyed the economic situation with considerable empathy for the government's plight - a financial Dunkirk confronted it, and much rebuilding had to be done before higher living standards were possible. It was already apparent, however - at least to the Communists - that cuts in the military establishment were required to finance priorities like the modernisation of capital equipment in the basic industries.[8] Increasingly they identified the link between foreign and domestic policy as Labour's folly in playing the Great Power game, and thus denying itself the resources for progressive reconstruction at home. As early as the Party's Eighteenth congress in November 1945 it was argued that without a major change in Bevin's foreign policy Labour would not be able to produce the much needed 'over-all economic plan going far beyond anything so far contemplated'. It would be fair to say however that such reservations did not at first detract from the Party's sense that progress was being made; as the editorial in the *Modern Quarterly* put it in December 1945, 'we are living in a revolution'.[9]

In January 1946 Dutt found evidence of the USA's 'increasingly open, aggressive, imperialist world role', in the conditions attached to the loan which Labour was forced to negotiate after the abrupt ending of the Lend-Lease programme. He could see that American hegemony was served by a policy of global 'free markets' - hence the insistence on sterling convertibility and the removal of various restrictions and limitations, such as those on payments and transfers for current transactions, on exchange controls and in respect of import controls and state trading. Like the *Tribune* Left and even certain members of the Cabinet, Dutt thought that American intentions would make socialist planning more difficult. But he also saw positive features in the loan conditions in so far as 'the protagonists of a closed Empire bloc' had been defeated. Labour was thus enjoined to make the best of 'the short breathing space' afforded by the loan for purposes of 'drastic reorganisation of the British economy and especially the reorganisation and modernisation of the basic industries'.[10]

Throughout 1946 the Communists were broadly supportive of the domestic measures by the Attlee administration. Arthur Horner looked forward to a 'new team spirit' emerging in the state-owned mines and argued that, though nationalisation was not socialism, it was 'a progressive and important stage in the march towards greater productive efficiency'. The origins of Communist enthusiasm for production drives can be dated with precision - 22 June 1941 - and the 'patriotic' spirit engendered then survived into the peace. In June 1946, for example, Campbell was still calling for more effort from the unions on this front. The capitalists could not be expected to interest themselves in this question - or so he reasoned, having allowed his concern to see socialism succeed to eclipse the matter of profits - so it was down to the workers now that 'the labour movement is to some extent in the political and economic leadership of the country'. Gallacher reviewed Labour's first year in office in a similar vein:

> What a change for the erstwhile overlords, for those who had come to think of themselves as the divinely appointed rulers of the country ... Now they speak in an atmosphere that is completely beyond their reckoning. Their pretensions are laughed at, their posturing is greeted with derision and scorn.

Even Dutt begrudgingly admitted that progress had been made, observing in January 1947 that events had followed the 'typical character of the whole modern period' with Britain lagging behind more advanced Continental developments - where Communists had entered office - but all the while moving in the right direction.[11]

Unlike some of his colleagues, however, Dutt kept at least one eye on the ball. The trouble, he reminded his readers, was that 'Social Democracy is flesh of the flesh and bone of the bone with Toryism in its basic imperialistic outlook'. If only Britain would realise that its days as a beneficiary of imperialism were 'finished for good and all', it would be possible 'to rebuild Britain, to recall our manpower for the tasks at home, to concentrate our economic resources on imperative needs of reconstruction and technical development and re-equipment in Britain'. But it took the somewhat sterner voice of Moscow, through the medium of Eugene Varga just one month later, to remind the Party of the 'general crisis of capitalism' and the role of Social Democracy in prolonging the system: Writing in *Labour Monthly*, Varga argued that Labour was guilty of having effected a state capitalist adaptation which left the old ruling class undisturbed. More to the point it had been chosen to spearhead an increasingly desperate struggle against the Soviet Union. 'In this respect', he concluded, 'the existence of a Labour Government is more advantageous to the British bourgeoisie than a Conservative Government would be'.[12]

The article obviously reflected the USSR's deteriorating relationship with its former allies, but even now Varga was careful to avoid a blanket condemnation of everything the Labour Government had done. Although state ownership was judged an attempt to solve 'the contradictions between the social character of production and the private character of appropriation within the framework of the bourgeois social system', in a second article, which appeared in August 1947, it was also deemed 'progress in the direction of the new type of democracy'.[13] The 'new type of democracy' was code for current Soviet policy in occupied Eastern Europe. It was thus inexpedient to deny that nationalisation was 'progressive'. But immediately after the appearance of Varga's first article Dutt stressed that nationalisation was 'no more than a legal device' changing 'only the form of capitalist class ownership'.[14] In an excess of zeal he reminded his readers in July that 'the tendency to increase the range of state ownership has been especially characteristic of monopoly capitalism, irrespective of whether under a Conservative, Liberal, Labour, or Fascist Government'.[15]

Such negativity had little purchase and was in any case superfluous to requirements. It was enough that the Party was less complacent in its assessment of Labour's domestic programme. From the spring of 1947 it began to criticise the half- heartedness of Labour's state capitalism - rather than the fact of it - and to bemoan the concessions it made to opponents of planning (such as Hayek), who seemed to think that a growing public sector would stifle democracy. The Party began to demand more nationalisation, stricter price controls, ubiquitous planning targets - in short 'a practical and binding national economic plan'.[16] But Labour's failures on this front were always traced to its foreign policy - and this was the real issue.

APPROACH TO WORLD WAR THREE

The Communists were quicker than the Labour Left to realise that the Coalition's decision to intervene in Greece had been taken with the active support of Attlee, Bevin and Dalton. Pollitt saw at once that external threats to topple left governments in Italy and France could be expected to follow.[17] In 1945 the Communists reckoned, however, that the actual turn of events would depend on the global balance of contending forces. No one could doubt that mass Communist Parties had emerged in Europe and Asia - and few realised that the Soviet Union was prepared to see them neutralised if that was the price of a share in the victors' spoils. On the contrary, there was media talk that 'the next war will be with Russia', on the eve of Labour's electoral success as Allied conflict over the future of Poland and Austria became known. Dutt predicted in September that Bevin's foreign policy would lead to 'the utmost helpless dependence of this country on the United States' if it continued down the established tracks. That same month the London Conference witnessed acrimonious exchanges between Bevin and Molotov, and by November Dutt could see that a 'Western Bloc' excluding the Soviet Union was already emerging.[18] In December he was able to add American support for the Kuomintang in China and British military assistance to the former colonial powers in the repossession of Indochina and Indonesia to his arraignment of Western policy.

During the course of 1946 socialist critics of Bevin's policy were able to fashion a plausible theory of what was going on, and one on which the Communists could agree with the labour left. The moral force of Dutt's analyses was gravely weakened, of course, by his inability to criticise any aspect of Soviet foreign policy. But until Europe was finally divided in the summer of 1947 left critics of Soviet policy in Eastern Europe were able to find commmon ground with the Communists in their critique of British foreign policy - the undoubted servility of the Communists towards the USSR notwithstanding. Indeed the most systematic exposition of this critique was produced by the Labour left-wingers, Richard Crossman, Michael Foot and Ian Mikardo, in *Keep Left*, which appeared in May 1947. Like the Communists they reasoned that

British policy was determined to maintain the country's world role - and therefore its imperial power - despite financial insolvency and shortages of every key resource. To succeed in this project Britain had to enlist the financial and military support of the USA and had manipulated American fears of Soviet expansionism with this end in view. There was a threat to the *status quo* - no one could doubt it - but if Communism was strong in Italy, France, Greece, Yugoslavia, Czechoslovakia, Indonesia, China and Vietnam, and an emerging force in Malaya and Burma, and if militant nationalism threatened European colonialism elsewhere, this was not to be attributed to the miraculous work of Stalin's policy, nor was it proof of Soviet expansionism. *Keep Left* argued that these genuine movements by the people had to be made to look like part of a Soviet conspiracy to persuade small-town America to tolerate a continuation of the war into the indefinite future.[19]

Dutt read Churchill's Fulton Speech in just this way, claiming that it was at least 'semi-official' and proof of Britain's preparedness to play second fiddle to the Americans in an attempt to hang on to global possessions which it could not otherwise afford.[20] But it was not until the enunciation of the Truman Doctrine in March 1947 that the Russians publicly abandoned hope of peaceful coexistence, based on the deal they thought they had made at Yalta. The American commitment to contain Communism was rapidly followed by concerted efforts to restore the health of capitalism in Europe, with the June announcement of Marshall Aid. Russia's response - the terms of the European Recovery Programme were designed to exclude it - was to intensify its direct control in eastern Europe with the creation of command economies and one-party dictatorships on the Soviet model. In September the Communist Information Bureau (Cominform) was created by Stalin at a meeting in Poland representing the East European Communists plus the French and Italians; this was simply a device for the maintenance of a monolithic front in the propaganda war with Britain and America. Thus the brief period of harmony between the Big Three came to an end. On the one hand the US and Britain openly returned to their view of the Soviet Union as exporter of evil revolution. And on the other, the Soviet Union retaliated with a return to sectarianism. Zhdanov set the tone at the meeting in Poland with his picture of a world divided into two camps, and the Yugoslav delegates gave a foretaste of what was to come with a broadside against the Italians for having failed to prepare for insurrection.[21]

DUTT'S COUNSEL IN INDIA

As always on these occasions the abrupt hardening of Soviet policy was quickly generalised without the slightest regard for what the Communist movement might have been saying in particular areas of policy. Dutt was left with a major problem in India, an area of policy he had only just begun to sort out since the CPI began to go its own way in 1942. In August 1945 - emerging from 34 months imprisonment - Nehru wrote to Dutt complaining about the Communists' flirtation with the Muslim League:

> You must realise that it pains me to see the gulf that has arisen between the Congress and Communists in India ... Politically the fact that has gone most against them and aroused the greatest resentment is their attitude on the communal question. They have become full-blooded supporters of Jinnah's demands (unspecified and vague as they are) and in the name of Congress-League unity they demand a complete surrender by Congress to Jinnah. I have no doubt that they have worsened the communal problem by their attitude. Communists who have joined the Muslim League appear to be more rabid Leaguers than others. All this has been greatly resented. I hope that changed circumstances will gradually tone down these differences.[22]

Dutt's written response is not known but it is clear that he had been critical of the CPI's policy in his correspondence with its leader P.C. Joshi. Indeed Joshi retaliated by accusing Dutt of 'shameful lethargy' in relation to India since 1941. At the end of November 1945 Dutt reminded him of the wartime division of labour between the two parties arguing that 'it is entirely due to our work [that is, the CPGB's] that both the Labour Party and the TUC within this period have passed resolutions on India in terms of our campaign'. This boast could hardly be supported, but he was on firmer ground in stressing that the Communists would have been playing into the hands of opponents of independence had they stressed the new found divisions of the Indian people. A 'Memorandum' which Dutt received from the CPI argued that 'the central question' - persistently ignored by the British Communists - concerned 'the Muslim League, the character of the League, its demand for Pakistan, and the attitude of the Congress to this demand'. Dutt refused to accept any of this, insisting that such questions were the province of a democratically elected Constituent Assembly. Like Nehru, he insisted that questions concerning the distribution and exercise of power in an independent India could only be dealt with by such a free parliament.

He had formally applauded Adhikari's original report on the

nationalities question as 'a valuable theoretical insight' but on all the substantive issues remained unconvinced by it. Indeed Dutt recalled that even Adhikari had stipulated the need for a Communist campaign to 'disillusion' the Muslim masses 'against Pakistan'. Joshi himself had said that the 'dreamland of Pakistan leads nowhere except to stalemate'. But by 1944 the CPI had revised these judgements and Dutt was appalled to see that its propaganda equated Congress with the Hindus and the League with the Muslims. To make matters worse the Party had drawn closer to the League, placing itself, in Dutt's words, 'in opposition to the body of national sentiment following the Congress'.[23] Dutt's position in November 1945 was the same as that expressed in *India To-Day* in 1940; he was, in other words, not yet cognisant of the League's mass support - acquired in the interim - nor of its power to block independence until the demand for Pakistan was conceded. The first flicker of a change was visible, however, on the eve of his departure for India in March 1946, when he acknowledged the 'genuine national content behind the Pakistan demand' which he explained - much as Adhikari had in 1942 - in terms of the extension of the national struggle to new mass elements whose sense of national identity had previously lain dormant.[24]

He still denied, however, that there was any evidence of a popular desire for secession in the six British-demarcated provinces mentioned by Jinnah as the basis for Pakistan - namely Sind, Baluchistan, Punjab, North West Frontier, Bengal and Assam. The majority of people in these areas were not even Muslims - not that Dutt accepted religious affiliation as any basis for national identity. Dutt publicly criticised the CPI for stressing the justice in the demand for Pakistan and for forgetting its own past condemnations of the League for encouraging a reactionary Pan-Islamic sentiment. The Indian Party, he said, was also guilty of approving the recent exodus of Muslims from the Congress and ignored the fact that support for the League was 'a sign of political backwardness'. In Dutt's view the CPI had fallen into an obscurantist trap in identifying religion with nationality and had allowed Jinnah's communalist manoeuvre to promote the retrograde step of partition with its acquiesence and support.[25]

At the end of the war the ban on Dutt's entry into India was unexpectedly lifted. Thus when Attlee despatched Stafford Cripps' Cabinet Mission to negotiate a settlement in February 1946 - soon after the mutiny of the Indian navy at Bombay - Dutt was able to follow it in March. Over the next four months he addressed thirty-five public meetings, and held talks with Nehru, Gandhi, Cripps and Jinnah. But it is clear that his main purpose was to combat the CPI's nationalities line. In his interview with Jinnah Dutt wanted to know why the Muslim League refused to support a plebiscite on the question of partition and what would happen to the Hindus in the six affected provinces. He questioned whether religion could be the basis of nationality, and enquired whether the League would abolish landlordism - and on every question Jinnah was studiously vague save on the certainty of partition; there was 'no unity between the two major nations in India', he insisted. 'Our whole way of life is totally different, distinct and even antagonistic'.[26] Three days later Dutt issued a press statement on the Communists and Congress, reminding the latter that his connection with Indian politics predated the formation of the CPI and that 'in all those years I have always stood for the greatest possible unity of the national movement in India'. He made it clear that he wanted a rapprochement of the CPI and Congress and said he had 'reason to believe that this view is shared by many representatives in the Congress'. His opposition to the CPI line was even the subject of comment in the press. The *Bombay Chronicle Weekly* reported that the humourless, 'hatchet-faced' emissary had 'caused quite a severe headache to the Party leaders' and gloated that he had disagreed with P.C. Joshi at public meetings.[27]

Dutt's 'travel notes' show that he enjoyed his Indian sojourn and the unaccustomed celebrity that went with it. The banning of his books had perhaps only served to increase his notoriety, though it angered his comrades that *Mein Kampf* was freely available at a time when *India To-Day* was proscribed.[28] Dutt was nevertheless famous as the eminence grise 'RPD' of Meerut fame, praised as the man who had fought Amery, and as the guru whose Notes of the Month were required reading in the India Office, let alone the Party. He addressed mass meetings in Delhi, Bombay, Calcutta, Madras and Simla. The CPI was now big enough to provide a selected Communist audience of 8000 militants for one of his Calcutta speeches. In Bombay he received cabled greetings on his fiftieth birthday from Pollitt, whom he jokingly described as 'a once trusted colleague'. Eight hundred people attended the birthday party including 'grizzled old veterans of the Bombay workers who remembered the days of Ben Bradley and were full of fire and animation'. The twenty-fifth anniversary of *Labour Monthly* fell in July and 'the evangelist of inter-racial cooperation', as he was called in one testimonial, was showered with greetings from all around the world, but especially from the colonies.[29]

In July Dutt attended the CPI's central committee where he concluded his main business in India. Recently published CPI documents show that Dutt shepherded the Party away from the 'communal poison' into which it had degenerated. He persuaded it to reject the Party's 'unqualified recognition of the right of Muslim nationalities to establish independent sovereign states' and debunked the idea that Jinnah's League could be regarded as the national organisation of the Muslims in India. While recognising that the League had acquired a mass base, he insisted that the Party had to stand for Congress-League unity. The problem of national minorities was to be dealt with by advocacy of 'voluntary Indian union'. In short the Communists were to repeat the slogans of 1917 - self-determination and even the right of secession yes, but within a single, federal state. Dutt's determination to win a united independent India blinded him to the fact that its devotees lacked the central apparatus of power - unlike the Bolsheviks - to prevent the disintegration of the projected Union. Upon his return to London Dutt presented a report to the CP leadership which reproduced this advice, only adding that the preferred strategy was faced with 'the intolerant sectarianism of the Congress policy ... which leads nowhere'.[30]

It goes without saying that Dutt rejected the Cabinet Mission Plan which Cripps produced on 16 May 1946, as did Congress. This unsuccessful compromise solution rejected partition but provided - chiefly in deference to the Muslim League - for a weak central government and relatively strong provincial assemblies able to freely form groups among themselves for particular purposes; they would also be able to insist on a complete reconsideration of the Union after a decade. For Dutt the Plan simply accentuated sectarian divisions, creating four broad zones - one Hindu, two Muslim, and a group of some twenty autonomous principalities.[31] It was clear that this would fall apart at the first touch and was pregnant with all sorts of possibilities of war and foreign manipulation. The central planning which the Communists and the Congress radicals envisaged as necessary for modernisation and social progress in India would be impossible. Dutt in particular had always warned against a Philippine-type formal independence in which the reality of imperialist control and exploitation continued unchanged.[32] And with the descent towards Cold War steepening at the end of 1946 it seemed particularly apt to stress that danger again. The Labour government in London was searching for a phoney independence, according to Dutt - one that would prolong Britain's military presence in South Asia and protect its economic interests in the region.[33]

In 1947 Dutt was forced to write to the Secretary of State for India complaining of the pre-emptive arrests of CPI militants, which followed the publication of documents disclosing official preparations for the military suppression of an Indian revolt. Dutt appealed to Nehru for a personal intervention against the repression and received his assurance that the police raids were made 'without the authority or knowledge of the Ministers' in the interim Government.[34] The authorities in Britain must have feared further trouble from the Communists, however, when the first ' Communist Empire Conference' was convened in London at the end of February involving the Parties of Canada, Australia, South Africa, India, Ceylon, Burma, Malaya, Palestine and Cyprus. Dutt gave the keynote address, which predicted an attempt by the leading colonial powers to experiment with new constitutional forms in order to prolong colonialism. It was an old trick, he suggested, exemplified by the pseudo- independent states of Egypt, Iraq, and Transjordan. His message, therefore, was that the colonial Parties had to gear themselves for a struggle for real social and economic independence. But there was as yet no mention of insurrection - indeed Dutt stressed that imperialism on a world scale was weakened; and he invoked UN opinion, the world influence of the USSR and the advance of the working class movement in Europe to make the point. This was very far from from a strategy of reliance on the armed struggle in the colonies themselves.[35]

But Dutt was lagging dangerously behind Soviet policy. Just a month after the Empire conference of the Communist Parties, Mountbatten was made the last Viceroy of India amid mounting communal violence. The danger of complete disintegration and chaos forced the negotiating parties to accept the inevitability of partition and the creation of an independent India and Pakistan. The Communists immediately entered their objections to 'dismemberment' and Soviet writers talked of a 'nominal false freedom', much as Dutt had warned of in the past. But Dutt was now ready to strike a balance over the Mountbatten Plan, which he described as an 'enforced retreat of imperialism accompanied by complex manoeuvres ... [which] qualify in practice the formal transfer of power and protect the essential political, economic, and strategic interests of British capital in India'.[36] Dutt continued to see a 'great evil' in partition and 'the seeds of future conflicts', if only because 'the delimitation of frontiers holds possibilities of endless discords', which provide 'a fertile ground for the disruptive intrigues of rival imperialist powers'. Nevertheless he also saw possibilities for 'far-reaching democratic advance' under the proposed arrangements, and perceptively observed that Nehru's 'courageous and progressive' stand in the UN over racist South Africa was a portent of the independent and progressive role in world affairs that could be expected from his future governments.[37]

Dutt's advice to the CPI continued to stress the need to overcome the recent estrangement from Congress. But Soviet writers were already calling Congress 'reactionary' and were unable to find anything positive to say about the forthcoming independence. It was just weeks after the end of the Raj that the Cominform was set up, and the tone of belligerence intensified. The danger was said by Zhdanov to consist in overestimating the enemy; the Italians, as we have seen, were upbraided for their failure to seize power. And by February 1948 a warlike disposition had spread to the colonial parties, which contrasted sharply with the constitutionalist orientation of the immediate post-war period. Even the Chinese, embroiled as they were in a civil war, had earlier counselled caution and insisted on the CPGB's leadership of the Parties within the British Empire. But at the 1948 congresses of the CPI, and the World Federation of Democratic Youth and the International Union of Students - both held in Calcutta - a new agenda took shape, personified at the youth congress by the Vietnamese delegates in military uniform.

At the CPI congress Joshi was removed from the leadership and replaced by B.T. Ranadive. Dutt and Joshi were both denounced as 'utterly reformist' in the Politbureau.[38] The Party was moving towards insurrection as advised by the foreign delegates attending the congress - significantly they represented Yugoslavia, currently the favoured conduit of Stalin's policy, and China and Mongolia. There was also present the President of the Australian CP, Lawrence Sharkey, who talked of the 'coming war' in the Indian political situation and lost few opportunities to profess 'his utter contempt for the CPGB'.[39] Sharkey is the likely courier of the new intransigence to the Malayan CP, which decided on armed struggle in May, at the fourth Plenary Session of its central committee. They proclaimed the Labour government in Britain as 'irredeemably imperialist'. Before the end of the year the Communists were waging war in India, Malaya, Burma, and Indonesia, as well as China and Vietnam. But though the line was insurrectionary, the Communists were only able to proceed because all the areas concerned were afflicted by seemingly endemic disorders. Even in India, where the new policy was perhaps at its most reckless, it was possible for the Party to promote and latch on to peasant struggles for land - especially in Telengana (in the principality of Hyderabad) where they reached revolutionary proportions.[40] All that the discredited Dutt could do in protest was preserve a discreet public silence on the insurrectionary course, while maintaining clandestine contact with Joshi despite his expulsion from the Party.

Of course he publicly fulminated against the 'offensive' which he accused the Indian authorities of letting loose against the CPI, and stressed the shortcomings of the partitioned subcontinent. But he showed no enthusiasm for the CPI's military adventure. When Gandhi was assassinated on 30 January 1948, Dutt responded in his March 'Notes of the Month' with a tribute that dwelt on his 'greatness of spirit, his honesty, courage and love of humanity', arguing that these qualities 'shine through and transcend the many inconsistencies and contradictions, even failures, of leadership which were the expression of the social conditions of his era'. His encomium honoured Gandhi's 'burning hatred of the shackles of a false civilisation,' and his unique ability to bridge the gap, during the transitional era of Indian nationalism, between 'the actual bourgeois direction of the national movement and the awakening but not yet conscious masses'. Dutt wrote with a real feeling for the man who 'gave his life and blood to save India from the hideous orgy of communal carnage and reaction that had followed on the ill-omened August settlement'.

COLD WARRIOR

In Terence Rattigan's play *Love in Idleness*, performed at the Lyric theatre in 1945, one of the characters was a man of ideas who walked around with *Labour Monthly* under his arm dropping names like Dutt. It was a sort of respectability born of a war in which he could appear - sandwiched between Lord Derby and Anthony Eden - on an enemy blacklist. During the conflict even the BBC had been keen to enlist Dutt's talents, asking him to give a talk on 'the press in wartime'; in the end he actually spoke to an American audience on the theme of 'words as bullets', in a programme featuring Paul Robeson and Leo Huberman, which linked up with a New York discussion organised by *New Masses*.[41] But this brief celebrity could not last. Dutt was in any case more familiar with his sinister public image, which sometimes assumed an Orwellian dimension as in the devious 'Eurasian' intellectual invoked by Kingsley Martin.[42] He may even have played up the part of public enemy number one. Maurice Dobb was both amused and surprised that Dutt actually preferred the photograph of himself which showed a grim-faced fanatic staring unswervingly into space; this seemed to Dobb to be intended to alarm the readers of his pamphlets and articles rather than to win them over.[43]

After the summer of 1947 it was the image of the messianic sectarian which entered the popular press. Dutt seemed the prototype of the Communist robots inhabiting Cold War propaganda. He was discovered to be 'the real power in the Communist Party': when the passionate Pollitt 'goes off the Party line', one article began, 'it is the quietly spoken Mr Dutt who gently puts the Communist leader back in place again'.[44] He was the friendless 'lone wolf' of the Party, 'one of the most formidable enemies of the Western world', the man who 'laid down the line for the colonial peoples', whose 'cold rasping voice' always had the last word inside the CPGB, a man who gave 'the odd impression of a doctor who is working himself to death'.[45] Much of the damage was done by defectors from the Party such as Douglas Hyde and Charles Darke. Hyde's revelations in particular portrayed Dutt as 'utterly unhuman', devoid of emotions and idealism, but cynical in his dictatorial application of the latest orders from Moscow. Dutt was stung enough to describe Hyde in turn as 'a dim, damp, Uriah Heep type of figure, regarded by all as a weak vessel'.[46]

But even his enemies could not entirely agree about Dutt. He could be observed by all 'oscillating like some bony dragon-fly' between the Party headquarters at King Street and his flat in Muswell Hill, but that was the extent of the consensus. Some thought him 'a brilliant and passionate speaker', notably the socialist journalist Alien Brien, who said the real Communist orator was 'the dark, hooded eagle Mr R. Palme Dutt'.[47] G.D.H. Cole thought that Dutt belonged to 'the amoralist wing of the Party', but other, generally hostile, commentators could still refer to his integrity and marvel at how 'a man of intellectual brilliance amounting to genius, who could have won the highest academic honours ... preferred to devote himself to his chosen cause, the cause of international Communism'.[48] This was the way Gollancz, writing in 1968, preferred to remember Dutt. A man of 'austere dedication', whom he 'admired', 'revered' and 'loved ... for the undemonstrative kindness you habitually felt in him'.[49] By 1971, the journalist from the London *Evening News* found that Dutt had a 'great wit and a genuine feeling for humanity', that he was a 'most likeable and persuasive Marxist'. By then, of course, he was seventy-five years old.

In his prime as the Cold War began to dominate world politics, Dutt was revered in Communist circles wherever the *Labour Monthly* with his regular-as-clockwork analyses of global issues, and their whiff of prophetic insight, could be smuggled into the country. One comrade, who accompanied Dutt to the thirteenth congress of the Israeli Communist Party, remembered the 'tremendous affection and acclaim' with which he was greeted and the tributes to *Labour Monthly's* for the role that it had played in Party education groups during the years of illegality when the British mandate prevailed in Palestine. He also recalled the panic of officialdom when the eleven hour plane journey was interrupted with stops in Athens and Cyprus (the latter under military control), and Dutt endangered security by leaving the aircraft to walk around the tarmac. But there was also the memory of 'the messianic certainty with which he stated his views' and the knowledge -now - that 'it didn't help ... to get a balanced view ... to question and to doubt'. For Dutt, in speech or in print, 'capitalism was always on the edge of disaster and the working people at the threshold of victory'.[50]

The question of the extent to which Dutt actually believed what he said, as opposed to repeating what was deemed to be tactically expedient by Moscow, has been answered with reference to particular episodes in the Party's history, as I have indicated throughout this book. But on some of the big questions we can be sure that Dutt, in common with many others, was a believing sort of person. He was obviously especially prone to self-delusion on the matter of Soviet socialism. In his mind morality and revolutionary politics were intertwined; he was fond of quoting Lenin to the effect that the revolution's success was the highest law - *salus revolutionis suprema lex* - not just a useful Latin tag for the justification of terror and the denial of individual rights, but something to which, like Lenin, he subscribed philosophically. Morality outside of the class struggle and the struggle for socialism was a nonsense for both of them. The end justified the means of violence; and some level of violence was held to be endemic in revolutionary change.

And it is perhaps easier for someone utterly convinced of ultimate ends, and prepared to sacrifice their own life in their cause, to sacrifice the lives of others. But, perhaps more to the point, it was also evidently very difficult to imagine the regime of cruelty and unreason which Stalin had actually constructed. Shootings, repression - yes, these had been justified since 1917; but systematic, irrational terror, millions in slave labour or done to death? This was beyond the reckoning of men like Dutt. In puzzling over Dutt's transition from revolutionary to apologist, moreover, we have to remember that at the beginning, in October 1917, the roles were happily fused. Converts had been blinded by the light and had voluntarily made 'unconditional' commitments. Perhaps when it became clear that the new gospel was making little real progress in Britain Dutt - with his cosmopolitan perspective - was especially inclined to find consolation in the apparent consolidation of the Bolshevik regime, together with the ebb and flow of the Communist and anti-colonial cause beyond these shores. If this was the case, it was a powerful source of rationalisation to be always able to find forward movement, proof either of the profound material mainsprings of progress - of the inevitability of final victory (Marx) - or of the triumph of will, tactics, and organisation (Lenin).

The world in 1948 must have looked replete with evidence of both. By a combination of armed might and popular upheaval Communism had spread through Europe and Asia. But it was also subject to a ferocious attack. In some countries it was a war of bullets; for Dutt it was a war of words in which he excelled. He was determined to prove, for example, that Josef Goebbels had invented the phrase 'iron curtain' - which Churchill adopted in his Fulton speech - with the object of proving the Nazi provenance of Western Cold War objectives. After prolonged controversy in the pages of *The Times*, *The Times Literary Supplement* and other journals, he finally succeeded in demonstrating that the phrase appeared in *Das Reich* on 25 February 1945, and was prominently displayed in *The Times* the same month, where Churchill, no doubt subconsciously, picked it up. His dubious triumph was sealed when the *Oxford Dictionary of Quotations* accepted Dutt's case. In fact the phrase has more recently been traced back to Lady Snowden's *Through Bolshevik Russia* (1920).[51] It was a trivial episode, but indicative of the way Dutt was becoming a mere controversialist.

In early November 1947 he ran rings round Lord Vansittart, the former diplomat and Germanophobe, in a BBC debate chaired by

Dingle Foot on the subject of the Cominform, which Vansittart took to be a resuscitated Comintern. Dutt argued that the Comintern was 'as dead as the First International which scared Lord Vansittart's grandparents'. The argument turned to the prospects of Soviet military intervention in the affairs of countries outside Europe with Dutt insisting that they were nil; the real danger came from the USA.[52] Occasionally Dutt was still able to put the Communist case in debates of this sort - for example arguing with Arnold Toynbee and Christopher Hollis MP in another radio set-piece on 'the Soviet idea' or at the annual dinner of the London Majlis in July 1948, with Mountbatten, Lord Pethick Lawrence and Krishna Menon sharing the limelight.[53] But circumstances were changing fast.

In September 1947 he was banned from attending the congress of the Socialist Unity Party in Berlin. The two-camp polarisation predicted by *Keep Left* was rapidly becoming a reality. Former critics of British foreign policy, such as the *Tribune* Left in the Labour Party, became increasingly anti-Communist as the Soviet Union tightened its grip in Eastern Europe and the USA baled out the British economy with Marshall Aid. After the Prague coup in February 1948, and the beginning of the Soviet blockade of Berlin in April, the Communists were subject to tremendous psychological pressure. The world communist movement had never before appeared so menacing. It was bigger, more obviously militaristic, and better understood than previously as a totalitarian regime. Even in Britain virtually every industrial dispute became the work of 'Communist wreckers'. In 1949 Communists were driven from office in certain unions and the TUC withdrew from the Soviet-supported World Federation of Trade Unions. Legislative steps were taken to prevent Communists working in the civil service. The number of countries where *Labour Monthly* was banned was extended to include Kenya, Zanzibar, Tanganyika, Singapore and British Guiana. A condition of siege gripped the Party. A less dramatic but telling sign of the times was delivered when Dutt debated with A.J.P. Taylor at the Oxford University Labour Club in June 1949. The audience greeted him with loud, derisive laughter after he told them that Communists were not afraid to admit mistakes.

COLONIAL ECONOMIC POLICY

While Communist credibility rapidly waned in Britain, the outlook was significantly better in the colonies. The war had played a disruptive and radicalising part in Africa and the Middle East, as well as in Asia. Apart from the troops and carriers it raised - something like one million of them - Africa's contribution to the British war effort was considerable. This took the form of increased production drives in food and raw materials, while produce prices were kept artificially below market prices by the colonial authorities. Imported manufactured goods, on the other hand, were scarce and accordingly expensive; farmers had to produce and sell more to have any chance of affording them. Where such incentives failed to operate - as in the mines and plantations of Nigeria - labour was sometimes directly coerced. As consumers the Africans were affected by shortages, restrictions and inflation. If a given country earned dollars - such as the Gold Coast - they were spent by Britain and exchanged for sterling balances that could not be spent on sterling goods. To these economic pressures must be added the disturbing influences of the demobilised troops in 1945, and the memory of an anti-Fascist war fought in the name of principles of democracy and national self-determination, as laid down in the Atlantic Charter.[54] As yet the Foreign Office was still complacent, but it was soon to discover that even an unprecedented pace of constitutional reform in Africa lagged behind local aspirations.

In the Middle East, where there was oil to be thought about, officials saw the threat of Communism in the most unlikely places - such as Palestine, Iraq, and Iran - and it became the received wisdom that Britain's future in the region depended on its contribution to local economic development.[55] Bevin set the tone in September 1945, with his argument that the Russians wanted a port in Tripolitania (modern Libya) in order to get their hands on the mineral resources of tropical Africa - especially the uranium.[56] Bevin was also convinced that the British standard of living depended on these colonial resources and said so publicly. In fact the whole government was convinced that the restoration of the West European economy depended on a more systematic exploitation of such resources, and by the summer of 1947 the American Government began to take the same view. This explains why the Labour government was as zealous in its promotion of colonial 'development' as it was in denying the existence of British imperialism. Modern research has shown that the Empire-Commonwealth had never been so exploited as it was between 1945 and 1951.[57]

Dutt was virtually the only informed socialist critic of what was going on - certainly in Britain. Labour's own colonial experts, such as Arthur Creech Jones and Rita Hinden, were too closely associated with the policy to be able to judge it objectively; significantly, there was no economic critique of 'development' to be found in the pages of Hinden's journal *Socialist Commentary* at any time during the life of the Attlee governments. *Tribune* also became an enthusiastic supporter of British policy in Africa and all - except doughty opponents of Empire such as Fenner Brockway - seem to have given the government the benefit of the doubt for the time being. By contrast African nationalists in Britain - such as Kenyatta, Nkrumah and Dr Azikiwe - soon felt betrayed by the government and had reason to be grateful for Communist assistance.[58] Labour's colonial experts drew attention to the Party's work in this regard, contrasting it with Labour's neglect. In 1948 Hinden warned Denis Healey, Labour's International Secretary, that:

> There are now over 3000 colonial students in this country, and there is a constant stream of visitors from the colonies - very often delegations of a political nature ... While the Labour Party does nothing to meet and greet these people, the Communist Party does everything. The Communists bring out a regular African News Sheet which is distributed free to everyone who asks for it, always - I understand - accompanied by a letter inviting visits to their Colonial Department and expressing readiness to take up any grievances or problems ... I need hardly add that these offers are often taken advantage of. I know, from the very considerable contact with the students here that few of them have any real respect or affection for the Labour Party; they feel that the Party takes no interest in them, even though its spokesmen are ready enough to say that Africa is the solution of all Britain's economic problems ...[59]

Hinden was not exaggerating. During the course of 1948 the cry of colonial development was taken up by Attlee, Cripps, Strachey, Harold Wilson, Creech Jones, Bevin - virtually the whole of the government at one time or another. Typically the message, as Cripps told an African Governor's Conference, was that 'the whole future of the sterling group and its ability to survive depends ... upon a quick and extensive development of our African resources'.[60] Strachey's abortive groundnuts scheme was a product of this thinking. Less well known but more effective forms of exploitation were also put in place as the development drive came to resemble what has been called 'a second colonial occupation'.[61] Bulk buying arrangements, price fixing, monopolistic trading conditions, the maintenance of the forced lending system represented by the sterling credits system described above; in these and other ways 'development' was used to pay for British reconstruction. Thus, while eight million pounds flowed from Britain each year between 1946 and 1951 under the terms of the Colonial Development and Welfare Act, the sterling balances held in Britain rose by £150 million, while the West African marketing boards alone held a further £93 million on deposit in London by 1951.

Dutt noted that in all the schemes for African development, 'the most conspicuous feature is the complete exclusion of Africans from any role save to provide the labour-power to be exploited'.[62] His biggest single literary effort of the late 1940s attempted to draw all the strands of past and present colonial policy together, to mount a massive attack on imperialism, giving due regard to policy in Africa - the new Eldorado. He exposed the monopoly profits, the system of unequal exchange, the expropriation of dollar surpulses from the sale of commodities such as Malayan tin - all the methods and consequences - including war - of the Labour 'development' strategy.[63] Even hostile reviewers conceded that he had written 'a voluminous and well-documented indictment' of Labour's record.[64] But this critique of British colonialism was more ambitious than a mere exposé of policy; it also attempted to demonstrate that Britain's domestic economic problems were rooted in a crisis of Empire.

The Communists made many cogent observations on the domestic ramifications of Britain's world role. They rightly contrasted the increasingly onerous expenditures on defence with the austerity at home - an expenditure planned to rise to 14 per cent of national income after the outbreak of the Korean War in June 1950. They talked of the relationship between this global role and the manpower shortage, the Balance of Payments deficit, rationing, under-investment in British industry, subordination to the goals of American policy, entanglement in an increasing number of regional wars and diplomatic support for reactionary (but anti-Communist) states such as South Africa. But Dutt was not content with these specifics. He wanted to insist that the recent dollar crisis, the balance of payments crisis, the devaluation crisis and the raw materials crisis, were all expressions of a deeper crisis that had been endemic since the first world war. On the broadest canvas, the crisis of Britain, he argued, was part of the general crisis of capitalism and imperialism identified by Lenin. He invoked Lenin's judgement on the 'decaying', 'putrefying', 'moribund' nature of monopoly capitalism. He was determined, as Lenin had been in 1916, to regard the entire socio-economic and political structure of

Britain as resting on imperialist foundations. In other words, he was still convinced that Labour reformism and parliamentary democracy rested on the super-profits of Empire and that Britain's crisis - to which neither Marshall nor Keynes could provide an answer - was the crisis of '*the parasitic metropolis of a world empire*.[65]

This was to ignore any evidence of dynamism in the British economy since the first world war, and to suppose, erroneously, that such prosperity as indirectly underpinned parliamentary democracy had only extraneous sources. Dutt naturally assumed that the Russian and Chinese revolutions, and future colonial revolts to come, were among the deepest underlying causes, as well as symptoms, of the general crisis. He sought evidence of 'increasing parasitism' in the British economy in its relative industrial and trading decline, its 'relative technological backwardness', and its inability to find a capital surplus for export. But he was on much safer ground when dealing with the 1945-51 conjuncture. In this analysis he was able to show that 'the main immediate cause of Britain's post-war deficit was the [government's] gigantic foreign military expenditure'. In pursuit of its traditional world role Britain had accepted 'the heaviest arms burden in the world in proportion to population' by 1951.[66]

The biggest weakness in Dutt's attempted synthesis, then, was his continued dependence on theoretical schema drawn from Lenin, which could not explain, and so chose to ignore, all the evidence of capitalist vigour. Dutt's reader is invited to believe that the possibilities of progressive capitalist development in Britain 'reached exhaustion' with the loss of its 'industrial world monopoly'. The economic boom, already underway when the final version of Dutt's thesis was published, could not be explained in terms of his argument. While maintaining that the entire structure of Britain rested on imperialist foundations, moreover, Dutt chose to ignore this argument when he came to discuss the economic consequences of foreign policy; when he wanted his readers to believe that Empire was a burden and a drag on British productive effort, he reasoned that the 'tribute' of Empire was simply spirited away in non-productive activities. He never satisfactorily explained the alchemy by which the profits from imperial raw materials, markets, cheap labour, and foodstuffs could only benefit a powerful parasitic minority while the burden of foreign economic policy was borne by the rest and actually 'retarded' Britain's economic development.

COLONIAL BRITAIN

The Communists were in fact stuck with a tangle of contradictions derived from the recent abrupt changes in Soviet foreign policy. While Dutt was reasoning à la Lenin that the whole superstructure built on the foundations of imperialism was soon destined to collapse, the CPGB was being hustled into a programme of parliamentary reformism. This change can be traced to the immediate post-war appearance of Popular Front governments in France, Italy, Austria, Belgium, Norway, and Denmark, not to mention the so-called 'People's Democracies' in Eastern Europe. In this context, and Stalin's diplomacy of peaceful coexistence with his wartime allies, the prospect of many different national roads to socialism began to emerge. The Comintern was gone, its sections now allegedly mature enough to chart their own way through the complexities which had rendered it redundant. Stalin talked of socialism 'even under the English monarchy', and in March 1946 Dimitrov announced that every nation 'will effect its transition to socialism ... by its own road, dependent on its historical, national, social and cultural circumstances'. In France Maurice Thorez said there was a French road to socialism, and in 1947 Pollitt referred to a 'British road to socialism' distinct from the Soviet experience, and without having to resort either to revolution or the dictatorship of the proletariat.[67] It was long assumed that Stalin was behind this change in British Party policy - the suspicion has only recently been confirmed.[68]

The Cold War and the creation of the Cominform produced a large volume of militant rhetoric from the CPGB, but there was no turning back to *Soviet Britain*. In 1951 the CPGB adopted a new programme - the *British Road to Socialism* - which asserted that the People's Democracies had demonstrated the possibility of a parliamentary transformation of Britain. 'The enemies of Communism accuse the Communist Party', it said, 'of aiming to introduce Soviet Power in Britain and abolish Parliament. This is a slanderous misrepresentation of our policy'.[69] It was not simply a question of removing the 'bogey of revolution'. With the exception of the 'imperialist war' phase, the Communists had since 1935 followed a popular front orientation that made them relatively open to broad alliances and in sympathy with the national culture. This policy had enabled the Communist Parties to grow quite dramatically in certain European countries, especially where the war provided an opportunity for the Communists to emerge as the patriots. The calculation was that the patriotic card was still playable.

Dutt argued, for example, that 'the first essential necessity for the recovery of Britain is the restoration of Britain's national independence from American domination. Without such national independence all other programmes and measures of policy for rehabilitation would be illusory castles in the air'.[70] The argument that Britain was in danger of falling under the sway of US policy had been common currency on the Left even before Marshall Aid. But it was the Labour Left which dwelt on these fears before June 1947, and the Communists who virtually monopolised them afterwards. Once the Cold War began in earnest, Dutt traced the 'enveloping process' by which Britain succumbed to the USA to the Anglo-American Loan Agreement of December 1945. But Communist propaganda focused on the Marshall Plan's 'permanent organs of American economic supervision in Britain', and, of course, the Atlantic Pact of 1949 which had reduced Britain to 'an armed satellite under effective American control'.

Not content with this, the Party launched a fierce polemic against American cultural imports - film, books, comics, dance music, social science, the lot. Since imperialism was decadent, its culture could only be debased. The Party's Cultural Conference of 1951 was structured around this theme, crudely juxtaposing 'the American threat to British culture, to all that is good and vital in our national tradition'. An entire edition of the Party journal *Arena* was devoted to 'national pride' in British culture, while American culture was depicted as an arm of 'the American trusts'.[71] Britain, it was said, had already become an American colony.

Dutt was given the task of explaining this colonial status to the CPI, which had latterly taken up arms to free India from British imperialism. He explained that the CPGB's new programme 'places in the forefront the aim of the national independence of Britain from American domination', and suggested that this complemented the Party's demand for colonial liberation because the ruling class in Britain had sold out to the USA precisely in order to retain an imperial role. He listed - in bizarre fashion, given his audience - evidence of the gravity of the British situation as illustrated by the 'importation of repulsive Hollywood films and the strangling of the British film industry, and the use of Marshall Aid to import obscene trash which has to be destroyed by the magistrates'.[72] Perhaps the Indian Party would be more impressed by Britain's loss of real sovereignty owing to US control of Britain's armed forces. Dutt said that those who had connived to bring this about were 'traitors' akin to Petain, creating a Vichy-like vassalage of Britain. Needless to say, 'the principal agency of American ideological penetration and propaganda in Europe', according to Dutt, was 'Social Democracy'.

Britain was now 'a dependent satellite country' playing an imperialist role as junior partner to the hegemonic USA. All this makes sense in terms of Cold War logic and the calculation that the Party would be able to tap anti-American sentiment in Britain. But Dutt introduced another policy departure in his communication to the CPI. The British, he said, wanted a 'durable friendship' with the Empire peoples 'upon the basis of equal rights' and amounting to 'a new, close, fraternal association'. This sounded suspiciously like a Commonwealth - the sort of thing which Dutt had habitually denounced since 1920 as a mask for social imperialism. That this was raised in 1951 made no sense at all, although Dutt did his best to argue that the proposed arrangement was 'in the concrete interests of the British people and the peoples of the present Empire'. The British needed food and raw materials, the colonies required equal exchange and circumstances propitious for the transition to industrialisation. These interests would be satisfied by the close association and co-operation which Dutt now envisaged.[73] Perhaps they could but it was not obvious why it was necessary to say this now - at a time when Labour was almost fanatical in its promotion of the Commonwealth. Unaccustomed as Dutt was to make such departures, one would have to assume that this was another brain- child of Stalin's. Again the suspicion has only recently been confirmed and Dutt himself alluded to the truth much later when writing in the *Daily Worker* (8.3.53), immediately after the dictator's death - he praised Stalin's direct help in preparing the section in the *British Road to Socialism* which pointed 'the way to a new close, voluntary, and fraternal association of the British people and the liberated peoples of the present Empire'.[73] But as we shall see in the next chapter, Dutt repudiated the idea altogether when Stalin was safely dead and buried.

Dutt's own draft outlines 'for a long-term programme', which he composed in October and November 1950, show a man preoccupied with the Soviet Union's Cold War agenda and accordingly concerned to a disproportionate extent with the Party's role in the international conflict between the USSR and the USA.[74] Thus what was to develop as the *British Road to Socialism* - the Party programme, in one form or another for the next forty years -

began with Dutt puzzling over how Britain was to be extracted from the American embrace, emancipated from its colonial economic status and brought into close co-operation with the 'socialist bloc'. With Stalin's instructions no doubt still ringing in his ears, Dutt argued that Attlee had been guilty of conducting 'criminal colonial wars' and of 'forming a War Bloc with American capitalism' which the Party had to undo by withdrawing Britain from NATO and bringing about nuclear disarmament. The Party itself was to remain based on Marxism-Leninism, democratic centralism and working class internationalism. On this basis, Dutt wrote, the organisation could grow to represent the 'overwhelming majority' against a 'handful' of monopolists. A 'great People's Front', excluding right-wing Labour, could be established, leading to a Parliamentary majority and extra-Parliamentary struggles to break the power of the rich. Such a government could establish a 'People's Democracy' by means of nationalisation (without compensation) of the commanding heights of the economy and measures to abolish the monarchy and House of Lords and to clear out the bureaucracy, judiciary and armed forces. It was Stalin and stealth rather than Lenin and revolution.

RETURN TO CRISIS

D.N. Pritt claimed that he 'did not grasp the full tragedy of the story' of the Attlee Governments until a decade later when he had marshalled all the facts.[75] The accumulated evidence made no difference to the basic plot, however, which the Communists had adumbrated as early as November 1945; an opportunity for socialist reconstruction was sabotaged by an imperialist foreign policy. Nearly twenty years later - all thoughts of 'state capitalism' forgotten - *Let Us Face The Future* still looked 'a remarkable manifesto' just as the Communists had judged it in 1945 - a genuine response to popular aspirations.[76] Indeed the Party had no real quarrel with Attlee's domestic reforms, no more than Labour's supporters had. After Marshall Aid was announced, however, the Party began to stress the inevitability of slump and economic crisis.[77] Though Europe was suffering from a crisis of under-production and the USA displayed classic symptoms of over-heating, Dutt refused to admit that a massive transfer of funds across the Atlantic would help both economies. Already in October 1947 he could only see the chronic dollar shortage in Europe, an impending crash in the USA, and a self-defeating greed in American policy.[78]

By early 1948 Dutt's verdict was revised to the extent that he now saw the European Recovery Programme as an attempt to cushion the shock of the gathering American slump, as well as a means of exercising political and economic control over Europe. But the Communists continued to insist on the inadequacy of Marshall Aid as a solution to the global dollar shortage - a position they shared, incidentally, with British policy-makers and which events served to reinforce when the American recession actually came in 1949.[79] No tangible benefit could be derived from Marshall Aid, according to Dutt, because the funds would be swallowed up by the inflated war machine - the obstinate policy of excessive military expenditure now having been transformed into a precondition of American aid. Stafford Cripps' austerity programme was simply a sealing of 'the alliance of a Right Wing Labour Government and Big Business to seek to solve the crisis along orthodox capitalist lines at the expense of the workers'. All over Europe, it was maintained, the 'Marshall Standard of Life' was the same - higher prices and profits, higher indirect taxes, lower real wages, and increased productivity on the basis of intensified work regimes.[80]

The Government was guilty of nothing less than the 'betrayal of Britain'. Dutt pointed out in January 1949 that British imperialism still involved direct territorial domination of one- quarter of the globe, while the new American empire was based on financial and economic hegemony over the entire capitalist 'camp'. The enfeebled European colonial powers had been graciously allowed to keep their possessions and pay the costs of regional wars such as those in Indonesia, Malaya and Indochina while the Americans creamed-off the profits.[81] Britain's peculiarly large burden included the maintenance of garrisons and military establishments in Hong Kong, Malaya, Burma, Ceylon, Aden, Transjordan, Iraq, Sudan, Egypt, Eritrea, Somaliland, Gibraltar, Malta, Cyrenaica, Cyprus, Kenya, Tanganyika, Nigeria, Gold Coast, Sierra Leone, Greece, Germany and Austria.

The Party predictably demanded a reduction of 700,000 in the armed forces in 1948 - which would have brought the total down to half a million. It also wanted equal pay for women, steel nationalisation, compulsory planning targets, modernisation of the basic industries and increased taxes on profits and capital. By its twenty-first congress in November 1949, however, Pollitt, predicted that the actual policy of cuts in social expenditures announced in October, when Hugh Gaitskell replaced Cripps as Chancellor, would lead 'to the development of mass unemployment on a colossal scale' - aided and abetted as this would be by 'the beginning of the greatest crisis of overproduction the world has ever seen' emanating from the USA.[82] Judged against the Communists' own proposals and their prophecies of impending collapse Labour's general election programme in 1950 was seen as 'an insult to the intelligence of the working class' - a case, according to Gallacher, of 'back to Gladstone' which made the contest 'fraudulent' even by the Liberal-Tory contests of old. On all outstanding issues, it was alleged, there was no difference between the two big parties.[83] Dutt stood against Bevin in the campaign that February and was trounced - even Gallacher and Piratin lost their seats; but Labour's majority was cut to just five and the international situation, Dutt's abiding preoccupation, was as grim as anyone could remember.

As the McCarthy anti-Communist campaign got off the ground in the USA, Russia and China concluded a mutual defence treaty which was seen as a united front against the capitalist world. In June the Korean War began and a world conflagration looked likely. As far as the Communists were concerned it had already begun; local wars against Communism were raging throughout Asia with Britain itself embroiled in Malaya and in conflict with nationalist sentiment in Iran, Cyprus and Egypt. Convinced as they were that another economic slump was just around the corner the embattled British Communists, more isolated than at any time since June 1941, were in no condition - mentally or organisationally - to take their new-found parliamentary reformism seriously. In the 1951 election they fielded just ten candidates and performed even worse than they had done in 1950. Dutt and the privileged few who knew that Stalin had prodded the Party to adopt the *British Road to Socialism* would have only regarded it as a strategem of war. It is most unlikely, in other words, that the Party leadership had been converted to democracy - Dutt and company had simply been directed to give the appearance of democrats.

NOTES

1 CPGB, *Communist Election Policy*, CPGB 1945, p6.
2 Sparkbrook Election File.
3 Dutt, Notes of the Month, *Labour Monthly*, August 1945, p225.
4 *Ibid*, p230.
5 *Ibid*, p228.

6 Dutt, Notes of the Month, *Labour Monthly*, June 1943, p165.
7 Dutt, Notes of the Month, *Labour Monthly*, September 1945, p267.
8 M. Dobb, 'The Economic Situation and the Labour Party', *Labour Monthly*, October 1945, p300 and p302.
9 Editorial, *Modern Quarterly*, new series, 1,1, December 1945, p1.
10 Dutt, Notes of the Month, *Labour Monthly*, January 1946, pp8-9 and p11.
11 A. Horner, 'Nationalisation of the Coal Industry', *Labour Monthly*, February 1946, pp 44-5; J.R. Campbell, 'Where Is The Production Drive?', *Labour Monthly*, June 1946, p171-2; W. Gallacher, 'A Year of Labour Government', *Labour Monthly*, August 1946, p235; Dutt, Notes of the Month, *Labour Monthly*, January 1947, p5 and pp7-8.
12 E. Varga, 'The General Crisis of Capitalism', *Labour Monthly*, February 1947, p57 and p60.
13 E. Varga, 'Democracy of a New Type', *Labour Monthly*, August 1947, p237.
14 Dutt, 'Lessons of the Crisis', *Labour Monthly*, March 1947, p72.
15 Dutt, Notes of the Month, *Labour Monthly*, July 1948, p196-7.
16 See for example, J.R. Campbell, 'More Planning and More Democracy', *Labour Monthly*, May 1947, pp142-6; and M. Heinemann and N.J. Klugmann, 'Britain's Economic Strategy', *Modern Quarterly*, Spring 1947, pp148-51.
17 H. Pollitt, 'Lessons of the Labour Conference', *Labour Monthly*, January 1945, p24.
18 Dutt, Notes of the Month, *Labour Monthly*, September and November 1945, pp265-6 and 326-8 respectively.
19 R. Crossman, M. Foot and I. Mikardo, *Keep Left*, New Statesman pamphlet, May 1947, p32.
20 Dutt, Weekly Letter: Churchill's Speech, 8.3.46, K4 Vol 1946.
21 'Declaration of the Cominform', *For A Lasting Peace, For a People's Democracy*, 1,1, November, p1: the same issue also contains A. Zhdanov's, 'The International Situation'.
22 Quoted in S. Gopal, *Jawaharlal Nehru*, *op cit*, p305.
23 Dutt to Joshi, 30.11.45, K4 Vol 1945.
24 Dutt, India and Pakistan, *Labour Monthly*, March 1946, pp86-7.
25 *Ibid*, p89.
26 Interview with Jinnah, 13.4.46, K4 Vol 1946.
27 Dutt, Press Statement: Communists and the Congress, 17.4.46, K4 Vol 1946; *Bombay Chronicle Weekly*, 9.6.46, K6 Vol 2.
28 C. Branson, *British Soldier in India*, CPGB 1944, p24.
29 Dutt, 'Travel Notes', *Labour Monthly*, May-August 1946.
30 M.B. Rao (ed), *Documents of the History of the Communist Party of India Volume 7, 1948-1950*, People's Publishing House, New Delhi 1976, pp16-17; Dutt, *Report on India*, July 1946, K6, Vol 1946-50.
31 Dutt, *Freedom For India: The Truth About The Cabinet Mission's Visit*, CPGB, July 1946, p4.

32 See for example, Dutt 'The Indian Awakening', *Labour Monthly*, June 1928, p337.
33 Dutt, The Crisis in India, *Communist Review*, 18.12.1946.
34 Dutt's letters to Pethwick Lawrence, 16.1.1947 and 28.1.1947, and a letter to Nehru, n.d., can be found in K4 Volume 1947; Nehru's reply can be found in Press Reports and Comments, Volume 2, 1946-50, K6.
35 See Dutt, 'Britain and Empire', *Labour Monthly*, February 1947, pp37-42; and his 'The British Empire and the Fight For Democracy and Peace', prepared for *Democratie Nouvelle*, 15.3.47, K4 Volume 1947.
36 Dutt, 'The Mountbatten Plan For India', *Labour Monthly*, July 1947, p213.
37 *Ibid*, p215.
38 M.B. Rao (ed), *Documents of the History of the Communist Party of India* Volume 7, *op cit*, pp696-7.
39 A. Short, *Communist Insurrection in Malaya*, Muller 1975, p47 and p53.
40 See S.S. Sanghatana, *We Were Making History: Life Stories of Women in the Telengana People's Struggle*, Zed 1990.
41 The broadcast was on 28 November 1942; see Broadcasting File 53.
42 Kingsley Martin in *New Statesman and Nation*, 30.3.1940.
43 As related to me by Brian Pollitt.
44 *Observer*, 17.10, 1948; *People*, 8.2.1948.
45 *John Bull*, 28.4.49; *Evening Dispatch*, 30.9.50; *Public Opinion*, 22.6.51; *Sunday Express*, 3.6.51; *Saturday Evening Post* (Philadelphia), 1.1.55; *Sunday Express*, 3.6.51; *Saturday Evening Post* (Philadelphia), 1.1.55; *Sunday Times of Malta*, 11.7.54.
46 D.Hyde, *I Believed*, *op cit*; Dutt, Press Reports Volume 3, K6.
47 Charles Darke, *Sunday Express*, 3.6.51; Alan Brien, *Truth*, 4.3.55.
48 G.D.H. Cole, *New Statesman and Nation*, 4.8.56; Frederick Marks, *Public Opinion*, 22.6.51.
49 V. Gollancz, *Reminiscences of Affection*, Gollancz 1968.
50 *Evening News*, 16.6.71; Solley Kaye to author.
51 See H.B. Ryan, 'A New Look At Churchill's Iron Curtain Speech', *Historical Journal*, 22, 1979.
52 Broadcasting File 53.
53 Dutt, Press Reports and Comments Volume 2, K6.
54 See D.A. Low and A. Smith (eds), *History of East Africa*, Volume 3, Clarendon Oxford 1976; M. Crowder (ed), *Cambridge History of Africa*, Volume 8, 1940-1975, Cambridge University Press 1984, especially chapter one.
55 See W.R. Louis, *The British Empire in the Middle East 1945- 1951*, Clarendon Oxford 1984, pp214-215, p307, p632, p640.
56 *Ibid*, p29.
57 For example, D.K. Fieldhouse, 'The Labour Governments and the Empire Commonwealth 1945-1951', in R. Ovendale (ed), *The Foreign Policy of the British Labour Governments 1945-1951*, Leicester University Press 1984, p95.

58 Azikwe is quoted to this effect in *Daily Worker*, 29.10.49; See also N. Nkrumah, *Autobiography*, Panaf Books 1973, p43.
59 D. Goldsworthy, *Colonial Issues in British Politics 1945-1951*, Oxford, Clarendon 1971, p146.
60 D.A. Low and J.M. Lonsdale, Introduction: Towards the New Order 1945-1963, in Low and Smith (eds), *History of East Africa*, *op cit*, pp8-9.
61 *Ibid*, p13.
62 Dutt *Britain's Crisis of Empire*, Lawrence and Wishart 1949, p90.
63 Dutt, *The Crisis of Britain and the British Empire*, Lawrence and Wishart 1953, especially chapters 9,10,12 and 14.
64 R.H.S. Crossman, in *New Statesman*, 1.7.53.
65 Dutt, *Crisis of Britain and the British Empire*, *op cit*, pp381-2.
66 *Ibid*, p401 and p404.
67 M. Djilas, *Conversations with Stalin*, Pelican 1969, p90; H. Pollitt, *Looking Ahead*, CPGB 1947, pp87-90.
68 See G. Matthews, 'Stalin's British Road?', *Changes*, 14-17 September 1991.
69 *British Road to Socialism*, CPGB 1951, p14.
70 Dutt, *The Crisis of Britain and the British Empire*, *op cit*, p409.
71 See M. Barker, *A Haunt of Fears*, Pluto 1984, pp21-5; see also Dutt, 'The Fight For British Independence', *Communist Review*, February 1951, pp43-44.
72 Dutt, 'The Fight For British Independence', in *British Road to Socialism*, Adhunik Prakashan, Allahabad 1951, p31.
73 G. Matthews, 'Stalin's British Road?', *op cit*; Dutt, The Communist Programme and the Empire, *op cit*, pp36-48.
74 Dutt, Draft Outline For a Long-Term Programme, 1.10.50; Dutt, Revised Draft, 9.11.50 in *Memorandum and Reports* K3.
75 D.N. Pritt, *The Labour Government 1945-51*, Lawrence and Wishart 1963, preface.
76 *Ibid*, p16.
77 H. Pollitt, *For Britain Free and Independent*, CPGB February 1948, p4.
78 Dutt, Britain's Crisis and World Crisis, *Labour Monthly*, October 1947, pp295-6.
79 Dutt, Notes of the Month, *Labour Monthly*, February 1948, p38: For British policy see S. Newton, 'Britain, the Sterling Area, and European Integration 1945-1950', in *Journal of Imperial and Commonwealth History*, 13,3, May 1985, p163 and p173.
80. M. Hudson, 'The Marshall Standard of Life', *Labour Monthly*, October 1948, pp380-383.
81 Dutt, 'The Betrayal of Britain', *Labour Monthly*, January 1949, p6.
82 See *Report of the Twenty- First Congress of the CPGB: Communist Policy to Meet the Crisis*, CPGB, November 1949, p8 and p10.
83 W. Gallacher, 'What a Programme!', *Labour Monthly*, April 1949, p170; W. Gallacher, 'Next Year's Election', *ibid* June 1949, p334.

8
Disintegration of the War Party

Things Fall Apart

In August 1950 Dutt informed the Party leadership that the CPI was 'virtually inoperative as a political leadership, with its former strong mass connections in part destroyed' - and this at a time, reportedly, of huge sympathy among Indians for North Korea as well as hatred of Anglo-American aggression. Instead of capitalising on this situation, however, the CPI was passing through 'a sharp crisis of policy' and Dutt realised that 'the situation [was] still critical'. Nevertheless the root of the problem had been identified:

> It is now officially admitted by the present Party leadership that enemy influences of a Trotskyist-Titoite character controlling the leadership ... have been responsible for sabotaging, disrupting and paralysing the Party.[1]

Dutt traced the problem back to the CPI's second congress of February 1948 where, he said, two of three fraternal delegates 'were Yugoslavs who participated for several weeks beforehand in close association with a factional section of the leadership in the preparation of the Congress'.

Together these elements had conspired to put the CPI on a path of 'suicidal insurrectionism' and authoritarianism which threatened to liquidate the Party. They had denied, according to Dutt, the colonial status of India, choosing instead to regard the national revolution as accomplished, the better to depict the Indian ruling class 'as a single counter-revolutionary bloc' and 'leading partner' in alliance with imperialism. This ultra-leftist leadership had proceeded to slander Mao and the Chinese Communists, had denied Stalin's theory of the colonial revolution, had seen Party membership fall from 90,000 to 20,000, the AITUC decimated and the Kisan Sabhas (peasants organisations) virtually destroyed. Ranadive, Dutt reported, had been sacked but the apparatus was still controlled by his supporters who were now calling for the 'Chinese path' and civil war.

Dutt blamed his faithful disciple P.C. Joshi for starting the descent into error when the former general secretary hailed the Mountbatten award as a victory for Indian liberation. Joshi may indeed have derived the idea from Dutt's own equivocal response to the settlement but without adding the accompanying reservations and disclaimers of his guileful mentor.[2] But this was mere bagatelle compared to the monstrous deceptions uncovered by the Trotskyist-Titoite conspiracy theory. The truth, of course, was rather different - the CPI had been used, and was still being used, as a tool in the Cold War. Ranadive's insurrectionary policy had indeed been prompted by the Yugoslavs but they had only acted according to Soviet policy.

But that was in February 1948. By July 1948 Tito's refusal to permit the integration of the Yugoslav state into a Russian-dominated bloc had led to his Party's excommunication from the Cominform. Tito was then publicly anathematised as a Trotskyist, fascist and spy. Until 1950 these 'revelations' concerning the profound corruption of the Yugoslav Communists were not allowed to disturb the CPI's insurrectionary posture; the Party continued to pursue the armed struggle begun in February 1948, on Yugoslav-Soviet advice because during these years Moscow's attitude to the new Indian state veered between indifference and hostility. Only when India's policy of non-alignment in the Cold War showed signs of success did the Russian stance change. It then became convenient to brand the CPI policy as the work of the evil Titoites. The medium for the new instructions was the Cominform journal *For A Lasting Peace, For A People's Democracy* in which articles by Dutt appeared designed to effect the desired changes.

Joshi, who was expelled from the CPI in 1949 for 'Right Reformism', contacted Dutt in August 1950 to apprise him of the situation after Ranadive's removal from the leadership. According to this communication the 'spirit and ways' of Ranadive's ultra-leftism continued to dominate the CPI and Joshi referred to the 'corruption that inevitably follows acceptance of the Trotskyite outlook and organisational practice'.[3] Joshi explained that by 'a series of palace revolutions at the Party centre and in the provinces', following the expression of Soviet disapproval of Ranadive, a new leadership had emerged around Rajeshwar Rao. In Joshi's view this new leadership was 'acting and thinking in the tone and style of war-lords and sub-war-lords'. He added:

> Of course they cannot last even so much as B.T. Ranadive-Bhowani did, but if they have their normal run and the Party is left by you and other foreign comrades to find its feet, I am warning you in time in all seriousness, that the CPI will not be left with more than 100 active cadres

> and an active membership of about one to two thousand to be the basis to restart all over again'.[4]

Unbeknown to Joshi, Dutt had already taken 'emergency and normally impermissible steps in 1949 to endeavour to establish contact' with the Soviet Communist leaders, 'begging' for intervention to stop the madness that was wrecking the CPI. Dutt had on this occasion suggested an article in *For A Lasting Peace For A People's democracy* and was rewarded with permission to compose an appropriate essay in January 1950 which 'released the battle against the sectarian tendencies' in the Indian Party.[5] (Joshi, incidentally, was readmitted to the CPI in May 1951 - the same month in which he launched a new journal - *India To-Day* - in order, as the reverential editorial of the first issue observed, to propagate 'the principles of Marxism-Leninism which R.P. Dutt has brilliantly formulated for our whole modern epoch')

There is no suggestion in the surviving correpondence that the problems in the CPI were anything other than the Trotskyist-Titoite corruption, as officially proclaimed. This does not mean, of course, that either Dutt or Joshi actually believed the official code. They may have been simply 'doing their duty', convinced that the official lies were 'objectively' necessary for the purpose of maintaining Communist unity, which Tito certainly damaged by his refusal to submit to Stalin. This interpretation can explain why an intelligent man like James Klugmann of the CPGB, who rose to the rank of Major during the war in the service of the Special Operations Executive, could produce *From Trotsky to Tito* in November 1951 purporting to show that Tito had always been a fascist-Trotskyist-spy. Yet Klugmann had first hand knowledge of wartime Yugoslavia [6] and Tito's Partisans and had taken a special interest in the revolution thereafter. It is difficult to believe that Klugmann swallowed Soviet propaganda in good faith when he wrote his mendacious polemic; it is much more likely that he too was simply doing his duty.

By 1948 leading Communists were practised in the art of rationalisation over such matters. Over ten years earlier Dutt had impatiently asked why anyone should be sceptical about the charges levelled against 'the bankrupt plotters of Trotskyism', who were accused of attempting 'to ride the Fascist whirlwind ... to win power and rule over a truncated Russia':

> The history of the working class movement is littered with examples of individual degeneration and transition to the capitalist camp ... the camp of the most reactionary sections of capitalism and to the persecutors of Socialism.[7]

One had only to think of MacDonald, Doriot, and Mussolini. Indeed Dutt might have raised this type of sophistry to a much higher level in 1948 because it was now possible to cite the fact that the whole Central Committee of one Communist Party had been lured into a fatal trap by its own General Secretary, a man who was already a secret police agent when he entered the Party, many years earlier, with 'a dazzling reputation' for Communist rectitude. The fabulous idea that a veteran organiser, student of the Lenin School, and Comintern representative - a man who rose from the ranks to the highest position in the Party - was all along an enemy agent who succeeded in having the entire Central Committee murdered - this was actually true.[8] On such grains of truth the pearls of paranoia, self-delusion and deceit could grow.

The Communist who believed in the necessity for unity and 'iron discipline' could not tolerate division within the Party or the movement; the one who did was not a Communist - certainly not in the opinion of Dutt's generation. Lenin himself had habitually treated dissenting opinion as proof of alien class influences. The movement he established was designed to wage war; it expected repression in return, let alone spies and ideological contamination. If Tito defied Stalin, and thus threatened to split the ranks, it was as well to anathematise him. Such logic [9] sprang from a whole web of assumptions central to the Communist project of 1919; Dutt was not necessarily aware of doing anything special when he applied it. In the present circumstances, moreover, he could write to the CPI knowing that once the 'Titoite-Trotskyists' were firmly dealt with, the Party would be returned to the tactics for which he himself had been denounced in 1948.

He accordingly contacted the Party on 6 December 1950 denying the short-term prospects for armed struggle and demanding that the CPI utilise all opportunities for legal activity, including the coming general election. He also stressed the positive contributions to world politics of the Nehru government. He pointed to its peace propaganda, its refusal to support the West in the second phase of the Korean War (the crossing of the Yalu river), and its support for Mao's claim on the Chinese seat at the UN. The CPI was advised to give qualified support to Nehru, even though his domestic programme was said to contain little that could be called progressive.[10]

Normally this would have been the end of the matter. However, Dutt reckoned without knowledge of the disintegrating forces of regionalism which acted on the CPI - forced, as it was, to compass the whole subcontinent. An early warning sign had been the nationalities policy of 1942. Sub-nationalisms did not go away after Dutt's intervention of 1946, in fact the clamour for separate states intensified and even Nehru reluctantly adapted to the pressure.[11] Regional patriotisms grew, as independent India made the major languages media for mass education. The CPI soon discovered that it was strongest where it became the custodian of local nationalist sentiment. In the years immediately after independence, when the Soviet Union clearly did not expect Indian unity to survive, the CPI established itself in regional struggles such as the Telengana peasants' uprising. By the time Dutt was called upon to end the insurrectionary line the situation was further complicated by the Chinese revolution which some Indian Communists were quick to invoke as an appropriate object of imitation. In certain regions the Maoist route to power seemed tailor-made for local conditions and thus exacerbated the centrifugal tendencies with which the CPI was beset. As early as January 1951 Dutt was forced to specifically warn 'against drawing a mechanical parallel with China'.[12]

He conceded, in the same interview with CPI leaders, that armed struggle was ultimately inevitable, but dwelt on the need for the CPI to support Nehru's foreign policy and build a 'broad democratic front' from below involving the mass of Congress in an (anti-American) peace campaign. Dutt's determination to quash the armed struggle faction is revealed by his claim that the Andhra CPI had been enfeebled by its support of peasant war; in fact this proved to be wishful thinking - the CPI recorded spectacular successes in the 1952 general election in Andhra and Telengana. It must have been a surprise for him to discover that a certain tactical stickiness was in evidence. Dutt seems never to have stopped to consider if 'the masses' had any memory; as he chopped and changed his arguments over the years in response to abrupt changes in Soviet policy, 'the class' was simply supposed to follow orders. In a small organisation like the CPGB, where the membership was more easily controlled from the centre, these zig-zags exacted a cost that was measurable in hundreds of lost activists. But in India Dutt was beginning to find that what he and the Soviet Union had said in 1947, and what the CPI had been doing by way of armed struggle since 1948, had left permanent marks on the organisation and would not go away.

Between them the CPI's foreign gurus had managed to botch the whole question of Indian independence. The Russians had encouraged insurrection on the grounds that independence was entirely phoney, while Dutt talked of an enforced retreat of imperialism. Elements within the CPI further confused the picture by treating independence as an accomplished fact. By the time the Russians began to realise that Nehru's government might be useful to them Moscow was forced to accept, in effect, Dutt's original appreciation of the 'progressive' possibilities of a politically free India; they insisted, however, on the notion of the continuing economic colonialism of Britain, the junior partner of American imperialism. Thus in 1953 Dutt referred to the continuation of the 'struggle for the achievement of real national independence' because 'British capital still in fact dominates the Indian economy'.[13] Later that year he gave the fraternal delegates' address at the third CPI conference where he described India as a 'semi-colony'. It boiled down to a disapproval of Nehru's economic programme - which had apparently abandoned nationalisation and industrialisation - alongside cautious support for Indian foreign policy. Britain, Dutt hastened to add, was caught in an American 'economic stranglehold' but remained imperialist for all that.[14] But Britain's alleged colonial status was already becoming superfluous to polemical requirements and the main Communist propaganda drive in Europe had turned to the question of peace - Russian policy being for peaceful coexistence, with the USA cast in the role of imperialist aggressor.

The conclusion of an arms pact between the USA and Pakistan in February 1954 pushed Nehru even closer to the Soviet Union's position in foreign affairs. The CPI, however, no doubt mindful of the marginality of all of this in the lives of its constituents, still stood for the removal of the Congress Government. Dutt tried to convince it that there could 'be no separation of the fight for national independence from the fightfor peace' because 'the interests of the struggle of the colonial people for national independence are inseparably linked with the democratic and anti-imperialist peace camp and with all moves which serve the cause of world peace'.[15] This was the old story that what was good for Russia was good for everybody else. It was considered by the CPI Central Committee in October 1954 but the Party continued to regard Congress as a creature of British imperialism. When Nehru visited Russia the following year it signalled the beginning of economic co-operation between the two countries and such warm relations that Soviet commentators began to find progressive features even in the Indian leader's domestic policy. The divided CPI meanwhile belatedly agreed to support Nehru's world role but remained split on his economic programme.

At every stage in this unedifying spectacle the pragmatic Russian policy was dressed-up in a spurious appeal to 'theory'. This dogmatic verbiage was real enough, of course, to the participants but hardly as an aid to analysis. A grotesque example of its consequences is provided by the occasion of one of Dutt's attempts to justify Soviet policy, this time in October 1954. The words of his article in the Cominform Journal were changed by its Bucharest-based editors. Dutt had written:

> The struggle for national independence in the countries in the sphere of British imperialism is no longer against British imperialism, but against British and American imperialism.

But the last six words were mysteriously deleted and replaced by:

> but first of all against the direct rule of Britain and the growing penetration of American imperialism.[16]

The instant this appeared a row broke out in the Political Bureau of the CPI over its meaning. Unable to agree, it then wrote to Dutt demanding an explanation. As Dutt bitterly complained, this placed him in 'an impossible position' - unable to defend the argument and unable to expose its provenance; the truth is that he was also unable even to account for the change - was it an error or did it mean something to somebody? He did not know.

Even more revealing of Dutt's helplessness in the absence of a firm central co-ordination of Communist policy is a letter he composed on the eve of his departure from the Soviet Union in March 1956. Following a conversation with 'K' (probably Kuusinen) Dutt submitted a confidential report on the CPI to the Soviet Party. After Khruschev's triumphant visit to India in the previous year, and Nehru's prominent role in the Bandung conference of 'non-aligned' countries, it was obvious to even the most casual observer that Russia's hostility to independent India was dead and buried. But the CPI had not been brought into line. Dutt said that it would be 'undesirable' for the CPGB to intervene in its affairs, but the real problem was that despite his best efforts - which included a new book, *India Today and Tomorrow* (1955) - his own authority in the Indian Party had waned since independence. Factionalism did not help the smooth transmission of changes in the line, of course, and Dutt knew that the CPI contained 'sharp differences' of opinion at the leadership level on the issue of the Nehru government. In fact he predicted that the central committee would publicly divide two-thirds/one-third at its coming congress in April unless something was done immediately to stop it:[17]

> It seems to me urgently desirable that discussion should take place (even, if necessary, postponing the Congress) to ... ensure that an agreed and united political line should be presented and adopted at the coming Congress'.[18]

Noteworthy here is the casual assumption that such a postponement was within the gift of the Russians. To assist his superiors Dutt proceeded to name names.

Dutt's analysis of the Indian factions maintained that twenty members of the Central Committee supported Nehru's foreign policy and a second Five Year Plan, but this group stressed a perspective of increasing conflict with Congress because it found domestic policy to be essentially reactionary and anti-democratic. A faction of six, a 'right opposition' with the support of P.C. Joshi, advocated co-operation with Nehru and aimed at the formation of a coalition government of National Unity which would include the CPI. But to these had to be added a further five members of the Committee - significantly from Andhra and Telengana - who denied the reality of Indian independence, regarded Nehru's foreign policy as a manoeuvre and denounced the second Five Year Plan as part of a programme of monopoly capitalism. Of the eight provincial party conferences, according to Dutt, six supported the majority and two were for the 'right opposition'. The situation was grave because a split could not be discounted at a time when the Party had become an electoral force to be reckoned with; in fact, as Dutt penned his report, the CPI was just twelve months away from forming its first government - in the southerly state of Kerala. None of this prevented the CPI from splitting in April 1964 when the CPI (Marxist) was born, and it is significant that the splitters included the Andhra Communists - those who had first invoked Mao's teachings back in 1948.

It was not until August 1956 that any attempt was made to explain the debacle of CPI policy since independence without recourse to the Yugoslav conspiracy theory. Dutt was then able to announce to the CPGB leadership that 'mistakes' had been made because 'the achievement of national independence was conceived as a step which could only be won with the working class (that is, the Communist Party - JC) in the leadership of the national movement'. It was now belatedly recognised that political independence could be won by the bourgeoisie and Dutt was even prepared to extend this insight to cases where the path to independence involved constitution-making by the colonial authorities themselves, as in Africa.[19]

LACK OF AUTHORITY AT THE CENTRE

Dutt's 'normally impermissible' steps to establish direct contact with the CPSU leadership demonstrate that no satisfactory arrangement existed to facilitate a two-way flow of information on the issues which preoccupied him. What he wanted was 'some normal practice of contact', as he put it, between the CPGB's International Department, over which he presided, 'with a corresponding section of your [that is, the Soviet] apparatus' - such as the French Party apparently enjoyed.[20] The problem specifically concerned the British Party's colonial work, especially in relation to certain countries where there was as yet no developed Communist Party. Dutt observed that though there was 'much coming and going' in London, there was no regular channel to the CPSU 'by which we can share this information'. He also pointed out that the CPGB was frequently approached for advice on matters on which it lacked the necessary authority or expertise. The Iraqi Party, for example, had made numerous appeals to the CPGB to help resolve its internal disputes. This problem was compounded in the case of Egypt where no less than nine organisations had contended for the title of authoritative Communist Party. Dutt's assistance here had helped to reduce the groups to three. But it had been more difficult to help the Party in Burma, and in the case of Nigeria, according to Dutt, the British Communists had not been well served by contradictory analyses in the world Communist press. All this spoke of the CPGB's urgent need for Soviet support and co-ordination.

Dutt was hardly exaggerating. The Communists in the British colonies and semi-colonies had acquired the habit of looking to London for guidance in the days of the Comintern. In the absence of direct links with Moscow the CPGB remained the nearest authoritative resource for many of them. The insurrectionary Parties in the late 1940s may have scorned Dutt as a 'reformist' but his *Labour Monthly* continued to champion their cause. And of course there were many more nationalists who saw Dutt as their friend, including a growing number of Africans. *Labour Monthly* obviously had much to say about China, Korea, India, Burma, Malaya, Vietnam, Indonesia and Greece - countries where the Communists were at war - but it also championed the nationalist and anti-racist case throughout Africa. The range and detail of its colonial concerns are simply too extensive to do justice to here but if we take the years between 1950 and 1954, prominent coverage was given to issues such as apartheid in South Africa, constitutional reform in the Gold Coast, opposition to a Central African Federation, the Seretse Khama affair in Bechuanaland, the Mau Mau uprising in Kenya, police repression in Nigeria, and the armed coup in British Guiana. It is not surprising that by the late 1950s *Labour Monthly* was being delivered to the head of state of more than one newly independent country.[21]

Dutt even managed to keep in touch with Nehru and met with him as late as June 1956.[22] Indeed someone in a position of authority in the Indian Government was close enough to Dutt to give him inside information on Indian and international affairs. In 1955 his informant - another 'K' - (Krishna Menon perhaps?) told Dutt how his own and Nehru's positions had been strengthened in the Government since Khruschev's visit, though there were 'many enemies active against both'. The project to nationalise steel had been pressed through 'by personal role of N(ehru) and K against attempted sabotage and is not yet secure'. Their present task in India, Dutt was informed, was not yet socialism more an 'elementary building up'. Dutt's interlocutor was also able to shed light on the leading protagonists in the Cold War and to warn of the 'immediate danger of conflict' in the Formosa straits - 'within weeks', he was assured. Eisenhower was said to possess a 'very sharp understanding' of the menace of the H-bomb but John Foster Dulles was described as a 'sectarian doctrinaire; stupid but not likely to be shifted'.[23] All this was essentially tittle-tattle, but then Dutt was unlikely to submit more sensitive information to paper.

The authorities in London knew that the Communists' work among colonial students resident in Britain could establish lasting allegiances of this sort. Unhindered by the indifference, condescension and racism of the labour movement, the Communists put effort into their colonial contacts, with results that reached far into the future. As recently as 1992, for example, the Chief Minister in the Left Front Government of West Bengal - where there were well over 200,000 Communists - was Jyoti Basu who was recruited by the CPGB in the late 1930s while at the Middle Temple qualifying for the Bar.[24] The Cold War alerted officialdom to dangers of this sort but, despite the concern expressed by people such as Rita Hinden, the main alternative voice to the CPGB in the expression of dissent in colonial matters - the Labour Party - did not act as a magnet for the embryonic nationalist movements even in the 1940s.

The seriousness with which the CPGB cultivated colonial contacts is revealed by a report compiled by Dutt in January 1954 which refers to its work among Nigerians resident in Britain since the end of the war. The Party arranged the first general meeting of Nigerians in London in 1948, though Emile Burns had apparently been running classes in Marxism for them 'over a series of years' before. Dutt records that 'a very considerable growth of Party influence and recruitment took place after the General Election in 1950'.[25] Then something like 150 Nigerians were recruited into the CPGB in London:

> since most of these had come into the Party through contact with groups of Nigerians and without previous political experience, and would have had difficulty in finding their bearings if scattered in the ordinary Party branches, they were organised in 'Robeson Branches'.[26]

Further recruitment followed.

Strictly speaking, of course, special branches of any sort had no place in a Communist organisation and the arrangement Dutt refers to was contrary to Party rules. When the London District discovered the 'Robeson branches' it ordered their disbandment against Dutt's advice. Dutt saw that the dispersal of the Nigerians would make them vulnerable to 'disruptive tendencies from alien influences' - specifically the Foreign Office and the Colonial Office. In 1948 they had created, so he alleged, special groups for this purpose masquerading as Yoruba cultural organisations - the Egbe Omo Odudwa and its offshoot the Action Group. Dutt believed that their function was to retard the growth of the National Council of Nigeria and the Cameroons (NCNC), set up in 1944. Against this 'imperialist' influence Dutt evidently saw the 'Robeson branches' acting as a Red wedge inside the NCNC; there were grounds for optimism on this score - its leader Dr. Nnamdi Azikwe, later to become the first Prime Minister of independent Nigeria, openly commended Communist policy and admired Dutt's *Labour Monthly*.[27]

But while Dutt's International Department took 'a strongly critical' view of Egbe Omo Odudwa, Emile Burns seems to have approved of the now-dispersed Nigerians' joining it. The combined effect of these decisions was to scupper the ideological development of the group. According to Dutt, order was only restored when the 'Robeson branches' were re-established in April 1953. Further progress was hampered, however, by the absence of a unified Communist Party in Nigeria itself. Dutt's International

Department was instead faced with a multiplicity of small, fractious groups and - as his plea to the Russian Communists in March 1956 revealed - was unable to invoke the authoritative voice of the CPSU in resolving differences between them. The Party's appetite for colonial work, however, was as big as ever. Press reports noted that its Colonial Department called a private conference on colonial issues in December 1953 with two hundred delegates in attendance. This was probably preparatory of the Conference of Communist and Workers Parties scheduled for March-April 1954. But as was observed at the time, it was also a reminder of the complex web of connections which allowed the CPGB to recruit and train - as well as co-ordinate - overseas Communists. It had links with (among others) the London branch of the Caribbean Labour Congress (CLC), the Federation of Indian Students, the West African Students Union (WASU), the London Majlis, the Union of Mauritian Students, the African National Congress, the West African Youth League (Sierra Leone), the Civil Liberties Union, the Democratic Liberation Movement of the Sudan, and the Progressive Workers' Party of Cyprus (AKEL). The Secretary General of AKEL, Pappaioannou, and the number two in the Malayan CP, H.B. Lim, were both said to have been trained in London - as were leading members of the Indian, Pakistani and Ceylonese Parties - while Communists such as Billy Strachan (CLC) and Amendola Thomas (WASU) held leading positions in the London-based colonial pressure groups.[28]

The progress of Communist colonial politics in Britain continued to look good, then (or dangerous, depending on one's viewpoint), by comparison with that of the Labour Party. Even the *Manchester Guardian* could see Labour's shortcomings - noting that its most recent statement, prepared for the Scarborough Conference of 1954 - was 'a string of amiable platitudes'. Dutt, by contrast, focussed on the many signs of revolt and decay within the Commonwealth when he gave the political report, in April, to the second conference of Communist Parties 'in the sphere of British imperialism'. The Parties of Malaya and Burma were absent on this occasion because of the armed struggle in their countries, and of the twelve who sent delegates none represented sub-Saharan Africa. But African affairs featured prominently in the congress deliberations. Dutt argued that 'all the lying talk of voluntary granting of self-government' stood exposed by the repression in Kenya and Malaya, by the forced removal of Cheddi Jagan's government in British Guiana and by the plans for a Central African

Federation - opposed by all the leaders of black Africa. But for all the fighting talk, Dutt's speech was remarkable only for its assertion that the 'fight for peace' was central to the progress of the national liberation movements, for this was current Soviet policy. He accordingly argued that reduced international tension would transform the UN 'from its present distortion [as] a rubber-stamp for imperialist aggression into its proper role as a machinery for peace and the rights of nations'.

METAL FATIGUE AFFLICTS THE MONOLITH

Just seven years after the Yugoslav Communist Party was anathematised as a nest of fascists, the Russians patched up their quarrel with Tito and conceded that there were 'different roads to socialism'. That was in May 1955, but a great deal had happened in the meantime, and the monolithic unity of old was suffering from something akin to metal fatigue; superficially it looked much as before, but in reality was ready to break. Some of the West European Parties - notably the French - had invested considerable effort in the denunciation of the Yugoslav state. It was said to rest on the super-exploitation of workers; bloody repression was held to be the norm; the prison camps were over-flowing; the complete restoration of capitalism was on the cards. The British Party was relatively slow to take up the cudgels but Klugmann's *From Tito to Trotsky* was all the more embarrassing for that - it was still in print when all the charges against Tito were dropped without sensible explanation.

Tito's rehabilitation now cast an extremely sinister shadow over the trials and executions of alleged 'Titoites' which had begun in June 1949. Laszlo Rajk, Foreign Minister in the Hungarian Government, and three of his fellow defendants, were hung as spies in the pay of imperialism after a public show trial which followed the model established in Moscow in the 1930s. Less than three months later the spotlight fell on Traicho Kostov, a leading member of the Bulgarian Communist Party. After thirty years of underground work on behalf of the Party, armed insurrection and finally a Government post, Kostov was revealed to be another Titoite conspirator and police agent. Unlike Rajk, however, Kostov refused to 'confess' before he was executed. Throughout Eastern Europe the purge cost the lives of many Communists whom Stalin suspected of nationalism, toleration of intellectuals, and failure to appreciate the 'leading role' of the CPSU. In all, as many as 2.5

million Party members were purged between 1948 and 1952, of whom as many as 250,000 were imprisoned and an unknown number executed.[29]

The truth is that these events did not lead to a mass disaffection inside the world Communist movement. The trial of Rudolf Slansky, Secretary General of the Czechoslovak Party, which opened on 22 November 1952 provides a measure of the self-delusion which British Party members shared. Slansky's indictment - which provided compelling evidence of Stalin's anti-Semitism - did not lead to any public expression of concern at the highest levels of the CPGB even though the leadership of the Party had close personal contacts with the Czech leadership. Eleven of the fourteen defendants in the case were Jews and the prosecutor dwelt on this fact to demonstrate their predisposition to treachery. But once again the charges of espionage, Trotskyism, and nationalism - with the added twist of Zionism - were swallowed whole. Even the Jewish head of the Anglo-Soviet Friendship Society - one of whose jobs was to arrange trips to Russia - never suspected that his own inability to secure a visa for the Soviet Union in these years had anything to do with anti-Semitism; it was simply unthinkable that the socialist workers' state, the real victor in the war against Nazism, could be motivated by anti-Semitism, much less that the polemics against 'rootless cosmopolitans' during the Slansky trial had anything to do with it.[30]

But though they kept their peace for the moment, many members of the Party must have been troubled by the campaign against the 'Titoites'. Their misgivings could only have been strengthened by the exposures of Stalinism emanating from socialists and former Communist insiders. To the work of Anton Ciliga, Walter Krivitsky and Koestler - published in English in 1940 - was added the post-war testimonies of Alexander Barmine, Dallin and Nicolaevsky, Victor Serge, Margareta Buber-Neumann, Freda Utley and, in a different way of course, Orwell.[31] The Cold War brought many other accounts of the 'god that failed' and it was no doubt this Cold War context which caused many Communists to publicly decry the evidence amassing against the Stalin regime; the Cold War was a time to stick with one of the two sides in the real world, an effective 'third road' being considered more illusory than ever.

Dutt hardened himself and his readers against the blast by trying to pretend that it was the anti-Bolshevik black propaganda of old. He reminded his audience, just weeks after Churchill's Fulton speech, that it had been Churchill in 1919 who said that 'it were better to smash the Bolshevik egg before it hatched than to be compelled to chase Bolshevik chickens all over the world'. But now that the chickens were everywhere, Dutt scoffed, 'the attempt [is made] to treat Communism as if it were some kind of sinister plot':

> It is time to end the conspiracy mania in dealing with Communism ... the myths and rubbish about police and talk of Fifth Columns, it is time to end this claptrap and seek seriously to understand why millions place their confidence in Communism today.[32]

When however, after 1948, it was Stalin who was finding all the plots and conspiracies and executing Communists, the bad news about Russia was not so easily dismissed. There is no record of Dutt seeking to expose as lies the horrendous story of persecution revealed in Margarete Buber-Neumann's *Under Two Dictatorships* (1949), for example, which told how exiled members of the German Communist Party were imprisoned in Stalin's gulag and then handed over to the Nazis during the the period of the Hitler-Stalin Pact.

But it is difficult to believe that Dutt and other leading Communists did not read the book or that its story - and that of equally chilling testimonies of other former Communists - left them unaffected. That some massive turning of a blind eye was involved is obvious, especially in view of Dutt's later admission that he and other Party leaders had raised questions 'concerning the conduct of the [Soviet] security organs' at a meeting with Comintern leaders in the late 1930s. When their enquiries about the disappearance of Rose Cohen - a close friend of both Dutt and Pollitt - were met with an angry refusal to discuss the matter - so angry, according to Dutt, 'that soundings were made to find support among us for the replacement of the General Secretary [Pollitt]' - there it was allowed to rest; it was never brought before the Central Committee of the Party.[33] Dutt's moral confusion may be gauged from the fact that he offered this evidence in the 1960s as if it exonerated him of complicity in the cover-up. In his inflexible mind, no doubt, the scales of justice were loaded down not with the dead bodies of Stalin's victims but with those of imperialism - in Dutt's view the cause of both world wars. In any case all judgement on the Stalin regime within the Communist movement was heavily informed by the supposed progressive economic changes inaugurated in the late 1920s - the material basis of the golden age to come. This argument survived well into the 1960s - and not just among

Communists - until the facts of Soviet economic sclerosis became known.It goes without saying that Dutt's amoralism was rooted in the crude economic determinism and materialist teleology of his Bolshevised Marxism.

Dutt naturally used all his ingenuity to show that Stalin's critics 'objectively' supported or drew succour from the decadent imperialist camp. In a polemic which was prompted by the BBC's dramatisation of *Nineteen Eighty-Four*, for example, in December 1954, he began by invoking Orwell's background as 'an ex-Etonian former colonial policeman'. He then moved on to 'the philosophy of Orwell' as revealed in the offending dystopia - allegedly that 'violence, lies, and torture can enslave humanity'. These were reflections of the ideas:

> not of Communism, of which he knew very little but of present-day Western monoploy capitalism, whose outward manifestations he [Orwell] experienced with horror and loathing, but without understanding either the cause or the cure. This can be very simply demonstrated. The central 'heresy' of his 'rebel' hero, for which he is tortured, is that 'reality is something external, objective, existing in its own "right"'. This is the standpoint of materialism, of Communism. The central axiom of the tyranny which he describes is that 'reality is not external; reality exists in the human mind and nowhere else'. This is the characteristic standpoint of all current Western idealist philosophy, favoured by the ruling class.[34]

By such methods as these Dutt scored his debating points and rationalised the Soviet police regime away.

Dutt had always professed his detestation of intellectuals as inclined to chase after any hare that happened to come along. This was Comintern orthodoxy in the early days and certainly not something of his own invention - but he upheld it vigorously both by keeping the intellectuals in check within the CPGB and by maintaining his own rigid submission to 'proletarian internationalism' or - what was the same thing - 'defence of the Soviet Union'. In this way he succeeded in erasing his own original identity - the Oxbridge radical - and was always hard on others of this stamp who failed to make the transition to proper Communist rectitude. But after nearly twenty years of Popular Frontism, the CPGB was an organisation grown accustomed to a disproportionately large number of professional intellectuals within its ranks, and one that was more tolerant than in former times of their separate groups, special interests and initiatives. In such an organisation the deference which Dutt had been familiar with in the inter-war years was not so secure, and the handful of Party leaders no longer completely monopolised the interpretation of theory.

Indeed the Party emerged from the Second World War with a thriving intellectual life. Whereas Maurice Dobb had once been conspicuous as the Party's lone academic, he was one of many by 1945. The revived *Modern Quarterly*, for example, was able to draw on the services of an array of sympathetic thinkers (party and non-party) including J.B.S. Haldane, J.D. Bernal, V. Gordon Childe, Hyman Levy, Rutland Boughton, Howard Fast, Derek Kartun, Norman MacKenzie, Peter Medawar, Douglas Garman, Sam Aaronovitch, Ronald Meek, Max Morris and many others. All manner of potentially wild things were discussed in its pages - intellectual liberty, belief and action, Picasso, Andrew Marvell, absolutism and ethics, science and the art of music, Keynes, education, and so on. It was evidence of a sort of pluralism, and certainly of critical thought, that most subversive of things.

The Party was also groping towards some permanent, programmatic form of Popular Frontism, which basically pitched a broad coalition of forces against a 'handful of monopolists' and therefore had to be more tolerant of diversity than was ever envisaged in the 1920s. But the old mechanisms of democratic centralism were still in place and when the Party flexed its muscles the line was expected to be binding. For no apparent reason the leadership took a public stand, for example, to end months of controversy to back Stalin's endorsement of the Russian agronomist Lysenko, whose theories contradicted orthodox Mendelian genetics. J.B.S. Haldane resigned from the Party in consequence of his inability to support this move. The intensity with which Party intellectuals debated aesthetics in 1950-51, by contrast, was indication that this was manifestly not the Party of 1920-1935. Needless to say a few objected to the 'Rightward drift' signalled by the abrupt 'conversion' to parliamentary reformism - notably Eric Heffer, a future Labour MP and near-Trotskyist, who objected to the idea of a peaceful transition to socialism and insisted that the Party 'must never forget that social democracy is not the opposite of fascism but its twin';the Party was also treated to the scorn of the Australian Communists which accused them in 1948 of 'Browderism applied to British conditions'.[35] But even the Cold War could not obliterate the changes which the Popular Front began and which the spirit of the 'People's War' kept alive. The Party had been given a licence - and to some extent a language - to think in terms of a national and popular road to socialism.

Although Dutt was prodded by the Russians to find an appropriate programme in which to express some of this as we saw in the last chapter, he was in many ways the least suitable person for the job; nobody in the British Party had worse credentials as a 'national Communist'.

He nevertheless made an unwitting contribution to the development of such an orientation at a much earlier point in the Party's evolution when he presided over the *Labour Monthly* debate on Christopher Hill's *The English Revolution* in 1940, which I mentioned in chapter six. This was an important step in the emergence of a substantial Marxist historiography in Britain, though at the time Dutt was probably more concerned with the rebuttal of Hill's departures from 'orthodoxy'.[36] Nevertheless a process of intellectual discovery had begun to which other gifted Party intellectuals could contribute.In 1946 a Party historians group came into existence which functioned as a centre for the discussion of research concerned with the national, popular radical tradition in England, giving due weight to the 'battle of ideas' and thus removing Marxism from the reductionist logic in which Dutt excelled. This was not incompatible with short-term Party objectives, of course, and members of the group were prominent in the campaign to defend British culture against the 'threat' posed by America in the early 1950s. But at least on paper there was a glaring contradiction between the quest for critical, open, Marxist histories and a slavish mentality on all things Soviet coupled with blind obedience to Party norms. The point is underlined when we consider that, apart from Christopher Hill, the historians group contained academics of the calibre of Eric Hobsbawm, E.P. Thompson, John Saville, Victor Kiernan, Rodney Hilton, Dorothy Thompson, Royden Harrison, George Thompson and George Rudé.[37]

DEATH OF STALIN

Four days after Stalin's death on 5 March 1953 Dutt addressed a commemoration meeting at Shoreditch Town Hall where he referred to:

> ... the radiance of the immortal creative genius whose lifework over half a century has led the way in liberating one-third of humanity from the grip of the exploiters, brought socialism from a dream to joyful reality, smashed the monster of fascist barbarism and slavery, and to the very last was opening new vistas of uncharted advance to Communism.[38]

This was the hackneyed eulogy which appeared with only slight variations throughout the Communist world. When compared with Dutt's tribute to Gandhi, his scripted genuflexion can seem all the more obviously a work of bad faith - like that of a cynical priest who must maintain the power of the fetish. When Dutt gave the graveside speech to mark the seventieth anniversary of Marx's death on 14 March the religious aspect was even more prominent; Stalin and Marx were said to be henceforward united in memory and Lenin was invoked to show that 'the teachings of Marxism are all-powerful because they are true'.[39] Nevertheless if Dutt is to be judged by his later statements about Stalin - well after the twentieth congress of the CPSU - he seems to have genuinely believed in Stalin's supreme role in the building of socialism and it is unwarranted to dismiss his attitude as purely cynical.

In fact the paranoid superman of the Kremlin had been on the brink of another massive purge at the time of his death and his lamentable legacy included an Eastern Europe badly shaken by the years of terror between 1948 and 1952. In East Germany the economic 'Bolshevization' course taken with Stalin's approval in 1952 had produced severe food shortages by the spring of 1953 and a flood of refugees crossed over into West Berlin. The regime's policy of increased production drives and reductions in real wages provoked spontaneous strikes in June which spread very quickly into a general uprising against the government. Severe repression followed reminiscent of Kronstadt, with scores shot and some 25,000 arrested; as Brecht witheringly put it 'the people had forfeited the confidence of the government'. Would it not be easier he asked 'for the government to dissolve the people and elect another?'. Could this be what was meant by 'democracy of a new type'?

Only a few days after the uprising Beria, Stalin's chief of secret police, was arrested - a loser in the power struggle among Stalin's lieutenants; by December he had been shot. Was this how they changed governments under socialism? It was beginning to look like it in view of the barbarity involved in the earlier downfall of Trotsky, Zinoviev, Kamenev and Bukharin. But the comrades had even more reason for disquiet with the rehabilitation of Tito in May-June 1955. This now pointed the finger at the Communist leaders who had conspired in the execution of Slansky, Rajk, Kostov and the rest. And what of the story that the Indian Communists had been led astray by 'Trotskyite-Titoists', how did this look now? The trouble was that though all the pieces of the jigsaw were in the process of being assembled, no-one in the CPGB - or at least no-one with an interest in the truth - was yet able to fit them together. The intellectuals in the Party had so far looked the other way; judged by their public pronouncements they knew more about the history of seventeenth century England than of the history of the Communist movement. Of course this is not to deny that many Party members had been genuinely troubled since the Moscow Trials - Dutt himself referred to it when he lambasted the doubters in the Central Committee in September 1939. But in the end they kept their peace, judging that the merits of socialist construction and international solidarity outweighed the signs of cruelty and irrationality. The Soviet defeat of the Nazis seemed to vindicate this judgement and produced new moral capital for Stalin to exploit. But then the creeping doubts returned, the difficult decisions had to be taken again, perhaps with a heavier heart.

When Khruschev read his famous secret report on Stalin's crimes to the twentieth congress of the CPSU in February 1956 the cracks in the Communist monolith were rent asunder. The delegates were told of a tyranny which executed thousands of innocent people without trial or explanation, at Stalin's whim, deported whole peoples and violated 'every norm of revolutionary legality', as Khruschev put it, 'against anyone who disagreed with him in any way whatsoever'. Dutt was in Moscow for the congress - and wrote an article for *Trud* eulogising the city as the 'heart of the world' - but like all the other fraternal delegates was excluded from the closed session where Khruschev made these revelations. A summary of the speech nevertheless appeared in the *New York Times* on 16 March, and on 4 June the whole text was available in the West. In non-Communist eyes it was recognised immediately as a crude attempt to find a scapegoat for a history of terror which damned the whole system; but the speech also broke the spell in which the Communist movement had been caught.

Dutt and the Party hierarchy reacted differently. After all it had only been three years since Stalin's death. Dutt had then insisted that any criticism of the former General Secretary consisted only of a 'turbid torrent of filth and lies, compounded in equal parts of barbaric ignorance and malice'. Stalin had 'steered the ship of human hope' with consummate skill, leaving the future course 'plain ahead'. Indeed Dutt waxed lyrical about Stalin's 'genius and will' to such an extent that he felt obliged to explain to his readers how his focus on the last in a 'succession of four figures of incomparable genius' was related in any measure to

Marxism, the putative materialist theory which eschewed 'great man' explanations of anything:

> Marxism is a science alike in the field of theory and action; and precisely because it is a science ... it requires mastery; and mastery implies a master. For this reason living Marxism finds expression in the 'greatest head', the 'central figure' and the 'genius and perfect understanding' whose theoretical and practical leadership most effectively carries forward the fulfillment of Marxism.[40]

But it was not just the prospect of all these words coming back to haunt him which conditioned Dutt's response. Clearly the danger now was that the leadership would stand condemned as either conscious participants in the cover up or guilty of culpable ignorance and neglect. Given that the likes of Pollitt had visited the Soviet Union over fifty times how could it be that they did not know what was going on? This was the obvious question and the leaders were necessarily on the defensive. Some of them would have seen the twentieth congress in terms of power struggle in the CPSU and hoped that Khruschev's days were numbered. The whole thing might just blow over.[41] For decades past these men had grown used to secrecy and the telling of lies in the interests of the cause. They had persuaded themselves that they knew best, that in spite of everything great 'objective' advances had been made that were worth defending. Their very longevity in the leadership had knit them into a coterie dominated by Moscow. They had worked for years in circumstances that could not have been better designed for the fostering of double-standards - not least the powerful sense of mission that bound them together, the shared hardships, the inevitable secrecy and deceit. They must have been shocked by Khruschev's revelations, but they were also bitter to think that he had blundered so badly in the narrow interests of a power feud.

A Pandora's Box had been opened and almost immediately the questioning letters arrived at the offices of the Party journals. Most of the membership remained preoccupied with domestic issues, however, and by early March the *Daily Worker* declared the discussion closed. When the Party congress convened later in the month the debate was contained in closed session. The international ramifications of Khruschev's speech were a different matter - in Eastern Europe in particular the critique of Stalin could not be so easily contained. Victims of various show trials were rehabilitated, further attacks on Stalin appeared in the Soviet and East European press and less slavish Communists than those in the CPGB leadership openly discussed the issue. The first public (though very partial) summary of Khruschev's speech in the CPGB was provided by Pollitt in April and then Dutt added his own contemptuous comments to the 'Great Debate' in May.

The 'Great Debate' opened by the twentieth congress, according to Dutt, was concerned with the future of mankind in the nuclear age, the future of the labour movement and 'the future of the transition to socialism, for the completion of national and social liberation throughout the world'. It was certainly *not* concerned with criticisms of Stalin:

> That there should be spots on the sun would only startle an inveterate Mithras-worshipper ... To imagine that a great revolution can develop without a million cross-currents, hardships, injustices and excesses would be a delusion fit only for ivory-tower dwellers in fairyland who have still to learn that the thorny path of human advance moves forward, not only through unexampled heroism, but also with accompanying baseness, with tears and blood.[42]

These comments set off a howl of rage against Dutt which severely shook him. For a moment the 'amoral wing of the Party', as Cole called him, was confronted by its heart.

Dutt had composed the offending lines on 16 April. There is nothing to suggest that he saw the full text of Khruschev's speech until early June, when it was published in the *New York Times* and the *Observer*. At the end of March he had written of Stalin's 'violation of collective leadership' and 'abuse of the security organs' during 'the later years of emergency' but quickly concluded that these abuses had been corrected leaving 'socialist democracy' fundamentally unaffected.[43] Like Pollitt he made no reference to the most disturbing facts concerning the wholesale destruction of the CPSU at Stalin's hands, which of course was more difficult to square with such complacency. An untitled document dated 19 June reveals that 'the Political Committee [had] had under consideration the full unofficial published version of Comrade Khruschev's Report'. But it made no difference to Dutt's evaluation, which continued to stress that the 'outrages and crimes' had arisen 'only during a specified period of abnormal strain between 1934 and 1953'. He added that it was not yet clear how much of the mischief had been caused by 'enemy agents' but observed that the period in question consisted of the years during which socialism had been constructed and this was the essential fact.[44]

Dutt's correspondents did not see it this way. Since March he had parried the attack with weasle words about 'very incomplete information'; now he was told in private correspondence 'that every

Party member is shaken to the core by these revelations' and that 'the prestige in which you were held in many circles hardly exists any more'.[45] Derek Kartun resigned immediately from the advertising work he had done for *Labour Monthly* and one of its editors, Noreen Branson, wrote to register her distress before the editorial board could convene. Alick West, whom Dutt had recruited into the Party twenty-one years earlier, complained bitterly of Dutt's callous words and his implication that only political innocents had moral feelings. He told Dutt of the suicide of one of Dutt's Mithras-worshippers.[46]

His replies were full of regret, self-criticism and proposals for face-to-face talks to clear the air. He was soon in print acknowledging his blunder. But when a fuller discussion was published in June nothing substantial had changed. He now talked of 'the increasing peaceful strength, manifest invincibility, success of economic construction and scientific advance of the socialist world' - and this in a piece that was supposed to be coming to terms with Stalinism! Khruschev's speech was useful only as whitewash, Dutt finding evidence that a:

> gigantic process of review, correction and renewal, extending to every field of political and legal structure and administration, of party organisation and methods of leadership, of ideology and research and also of policy, both economic and in the field of international relations, has been developing over the past three years in the Soviet Union since the death of Stalin and reached a high culminating point at the Twentieth Congress in February.[47]

Here Dutt paused to apologise for the 'unfortunately worded' lines which had given rise to 'justifiable criticism' in May. He had been concerned with the 'larger questions' of the hour and had not noticed that it was 'unsatisfactory to treat [the Stalin issue] in this fashion'. But the opportunity having been forced upon him Dutt was now prepared to admit that 'criminal misdeeds' had 'stained an era of heroic achievement'. Ignoring the recent allegations of Stalin's military incompetence made by Walter Ulbricht Dutt situated the blemishes as follows:

> Future history will assuredly not fail to pay tribute to the epic accomplishment of this period, the completion of the construction of socialism, the withstanding of the onslaught of the Nazi blitzkrieg before which every other army had fallen, the joint victory over fascism, and the speed of reconstruction from the heaviest devastation ever known, under the conditions of the perpetual menace and harassment of the cold war from the war-enriched and unscathed United States. Future history will not

> fail to pay tribute to the heroism, unity and heaven-storming achievement of the Soviet people through these ordeals, the policy and leadership of the party, and the genius, unyielding courage, steadfastness and devotion to the revolution of Stalin, also in this later period when some of his very virtues turned to defects, his steel-hardness to harshness, his unwavering shouldering of responsibility to methods of personal leadership, and his vigilance and suspicion, indispensable in every true revolutionary, to an increasingly violent frenzy which caused executions, not only of the counter-revolutionary enemies and agents, but also of friends and comrades.[48]

Stalin was clearly deserving of our gratitude and sympathy, the pure gold only turning to base metal by a sort of dialectic in which he figured as a victim. Dutt was keen to deny that the Twentieth Congress could anticipate 'the final verdict of history'. Yet everything he said left no doubt that he was confident - why should he not be? - that when history judged, the 'crimes' would be as relevant in assessing Stalin as the slavery of Athens in weighing the contribution to world progress of the ancient Greeks - in other words not at all. As long as people believed that the Bolshevik state had laid the foundations of a superior economy he had reason to think that this judgement could be accepted even now, within months of the twentieth congress. The will to power may, as Nietzsche once maintained, account for intellectual deception but, as Dutt's case shows, self-deception also feeds on idealism and ideology.

After all Khruschev was claiming that the unique and peculiar character of the situation that arose was that in spite of the 'cult of personality' and the 'crimes', nothing had changed in the reality of 'class power'. All the while society was advancing to Communism. Stalin's rule did not represent another Fuehrerprinzip, simply a malformation of the apparatus. And so as Dutt pointed out 'despite all the evils, the masses of the people were continuing to enjoy and exercise self-rule in running their affairs to a degree unknown in any capitalist democracy' - just as the Webbs had said back in the 1930s. The trouble was that the fascist danger created congenial circumstances for the abuse of the 'security organs', increased espionage and suspicion and Stalin's regrettable 'ideological deviation' concerning the intensification of the class struggle as final victory drew nearer. Furthermore, Dutt gravely admonished, there was 'our own responsibility' for Stalin's errors. But the reader who expected a confession of guilt was soon disappointed; Dutt was merely referring to the argument 'that with all the objective conditions ripe for socialist revolution in Western and Central Europe, such as would have solved all the problems alike of the Russian and all the peoples of Europe to march forward together in happy and peaceful construction, we were not successful to mobilise our peoples and left them [the Russians] to struggle alone'.[49]

Whatever limited use Khruschev had intended by de-Stalinization, the situation - despite the efforts of people like Dutt - had got beyond the Party managers' control. The minority within the CPGB who strongly objected to the leadership's successful stifling of discussion were given a voice in mid-July when two members of the Historians' Group - Edward Thompson and John Saville - took the risk of publishing their own journal for Party members, *The Reasoner*. In the same month the leadership bowed to pressure by announcing its intention to appoint a commission on inner-Party democracy, that is democratic centralism, and to call a special conference to debate all the issues. It also says something about the uncertainties created by Khruschev, and perhaps also about the effects of twenty years of Popular Frontism, that Saville and Thompson were not instantly expelled.

Of course such a publication as *The Reasoner* had no place in the Party's conception of democratic centralism, but two other things stand out today when considéring this initiative. In the first place the editors acknowledged that 'religious faith' had governed Communist perceptions of the Soviet Union because 'of our general failure to apply a Marxist analysis to Socialist countries'.[50] This was to announce in effect a project that could not be satisfied with Khruschev's dubious analysis of the 'cult of personality'. The second observation worth making is that by October the editors were ready to suspend publication in the interests of Party unity - which reminds us that the Party would not have been ripped apart, rather it would have been slowly eroded, by the process of critical thought but modestly begun, had not the Hungarian revolution entered the picture. Most of the third and final issue of *The Reasoner* was typed and duplicated before the dual crisis of Hungary and Suez erupted but the editorial and an article by Thompson were composed as the fighting in Budapest raged on. It was clear to the dissidents now, even if not before, that the Party must condemn the Stalinism of the erstwhile de-Stalinizers.

For at the end of the previous July the first sign that Kruschev had misjudged the degree of Soviet bureaucratic control over de-Stalinization was signalled by rioting in the western Polish town of Poznan where a strike became a spontaneous rebellion against the Soviet occupation and was put down by army tanks. By October the country was on the brink of a revolution - and Soviet intervention - and was only channelled to safety by the arrival of a new Party leadership under the apparently 'national' Communist Gomulka. In Hungary a similar adaptation of the apparatus merely fuelled popular aspirations and discontent, resulting in an armed uprising which was finally crushed in November by overwhelming Soviet forces. Even though these events coincided with the beginning of an Anglo-French attempt to topple the Egyptian government - an intervention which under other circumstances would have reminded Party members why they were Communists - the crisis of Stalinism had reached a more intense stage because it was suddenly obvious that the problem was not simply a problem of the past.

Suffice to say that the Executive Committee of the Party, meeting in emergency session as the Soviet intervention began, came out in support of the Russians. Inevitably it was Dutt, on 4 November, who 'proved' that Hungary was being 'saved from the menace of counter-revolution' and that its Communist leader Imre Nagy 'had capitulated to the forces of reaction'. A month later it was once again Dutt who prepared a 'draft statement' for the Executive Committee explaining why the eleven-year old regime was so weak that it required outside 'help' to save it from 'fascism'. With some artistry Dutt found the answer in Hungarian history and the 'international context'.[51]

But while the old Party leadership was in no doubt that the Hungarian tragedy was all the work of fascists and the CIA, the organisation lost some 7,000 members by the end of 1956 and the decline continued into 1959, making the deficit 10,900 in total, or 32 per cent of the Party's original strength. The exodus included ordinary members, trade union leaders, *Daily Worker* personnel, Party intellectuals and Young Communist Leaguers; but none from the Dutt-Pollitt generation of leaders. By their control over the agenda and composition of the commission on inner-party democracy, moreover, the old guard ensured that the centralism which perpetuated their rule remained intact. In addition the attempt by dissidents such as Christopher Hill to obtain an investigation into the Party's anti-Titoism during the period 1948-1955 was thrown out.

AFTER 1956

Dutt never accepted the truth about Stalin. At the time of the second wave of de-Stalinization, begun by the twenty-second congress of the CPSU in October 1961, all Dutt's literary energies were consumed in making light of the incipient split in the Communist movement between Russia and China which was signalled by Khruschev's open attack on the anti-Soviet attitude of Albania (China's ally); Maurice Dobb pointed out in *Labour Monthly* that Dutt's summing-up of the twenty-second Congress was 'inadequate to the point of being misleading', so craftily had he omitted all reference to Stalin's 'major political errors', and the fact that it was the ordinary Soviet judicial system - not 'special procedures' as he alleged - which Khruschev had condemned in reference to the faked trials of the Trotskyists, Zinovievists and Bukharinites.[52] There was as yet, however, no sense in which Dutt was conspicuously out of step with the rest of the Party. 1961 was also the year when the *Observer* reported Dutt's performance at the CPGB's twenty-seventh conference - this 'mystical figure ... the real power in the Party' - 'rising to heights of near majestic prose', according to the TUC publication *Labour*, in his expression of satisfaction with the 'rout of imperialism' in Hungary and confidence in the Communist future.[53]

Dutt scoffed at any suggestion of an approaching fissure, downfall and disruption of international Communism. The Party in Britain had recovered its position since the split in 1956 and though he acknowledged that 'all the enemies of Communism are having a jubilant laugh' because of what he called the 'Albanian question', he dismissed reports of a Sino-Soviet rift as bogus. Dutt had put tremendous energy and emotional investment in the maintenance of Communist unity and - perhaps as his hopes for Britain receded - now increasingly looked to the national liberation movements of the 'Third World' as the main weapon of Communist advance and solidarity. He was sixty years old in the year when Stalin was knocked off his pedestal, a man with a past which he could not help but use as a guide to the future. Just as Lenin had written of his hopes for the East shortly before his death, Dutt increasingly invoked the combined might of China, India and the colonial world in the 1950s and, like Roy in 1920, talked as if the prospects for socialism in Britain depended on the efforts of the subject peoples and former subject peoples of Africa and Asia.[54]

His Marx Memorial lecture of 1957 predicted that in freeing

themselves of colonialism these peoples were 'undermining the basis of imperialism in the West and thereby creating the conditions for the emancipation of the working class in these countries from their former illusions and subjection to capitalism to enter the path of advance to socialism, the path of Marxism'.[55] Exactly the same argument was put before the leadership in closed discussions where he talked of the Party's 'neglect' of colonial work and its failure to seize the opportunity for advance in this area provided by the launch of Fenner Brockway's Movement For Colonial Freedom. Dutt argued that reformism in Britain would be undermined by the disintegration of the colonial system and stressed that the colonial peoples were the Communists' best allies. He also warned of the danger that 'the increasing flow of coloured workers into Britain' would be used as 'a reserve for reaction' once the economic downturn made a policy of divide and rule expedient.[56]

His prestige within the Party as an expert on colonialism was responsible for the rare spectacle, produced at the organisation's Special Congress in 1957, of a defeat for the Executive. The Party had created a Commission to redraft the *British Road to Socialism* in the summer of 1956. This Commission invoked the idea which Dutt himself had championed five years earlier to the effect that a socialist Britain would propose to all Commonwealth countries 'voluntary participation in a close fraternal association', based on national independence, equal rights and non-intervention in each other's internal affairs. The purpose of the 'association' would be the promotion of the member nation's mutual economic, political, and cultural interests and mutual defence against imperialist attempts to undermine their independence. As I observed in the last chapter, it was all very reminiscent of the 'empire socialism' which Dutt had derided in his attacks on the ILP in the late 1920s. Under Stalin's directions Dutt chose to forget these objections in 1951 when the 'fraternal association' was first given a public airing. Now that Stalin was safely dead and buried he changed his mind again and opposed the idea within the Commission. He was not to be impressed by the argument (put by George Matthews) that 'a Socialist Government in Britain should not, and will not be able to, wash its hands of the problems arising from the existence of the British Empire' - the line taken by Lansbury and Wheatley thirty years earlier and espoused by himself just five years ago. But the Commission wanted to take the parallel with 'empire socialism' even further and - dutifully following the superior wisdom of the dead dictator - disclaim the Party's interest in the destruction of the

British Commonwealth. Dutt now boldly insisted on the deletion of this loose talk but failed (29 votes to 5) to persuade the Commission to remove the reference to a 'fraternal association'. His success came, however, at the Party's twenty-fifth congress when a majority of delegates (298 against 210) supported his contention that 'close voluntary fraternal relations' would suffice while the more formal relationship smacked of imperialism.[57]

George Matthews waited until 1991 before confessing Stalin's direct authorship of some of the ideas in the *British Road to Socialism* and showing that the 'fraternal association' of Commonwealth countries was one of them.[58] Of course the delegates at the Party congress were not to know any of this though they might have been expected to remember Dutt's defence of the 'fraternal association' when it was first mentioned five years before. The episode is instructive, therefore, in showing both the genuine anti-imperialist sentiment of the Party membership and the apparent ease with which it could forget the past pronouncements of leaders like Dutt whose career was littered with adamant expositions of mutually contradictory arguments. Of course it also shows how easy it was for the tightly-knit leadership to keep secrets from the membership. But more than anything it shows us two different specimens within the leadership - Dutt, who deferred to Stalin even when he knew better, and Matthews whose devotion was based on a more honest, though less incisive, intellect.

Ironically imperialism was already a practical problem in relations between Stalin's successors in Russia and China when Dutt was busy excising it from the Party programme in Britain. As long as the dispute between these states could be denied Dutt denied it but he had every reason for dismay when it finally boiled over in 1962; it was a year when he received an Honorary Doctorate of History from Moscow University and was pictured in *Pravda* with Khruschev and Brezhnev. It was also the year when a simmering border dispute between China and Nehru's India flared into war. By 1963 the Chinese Communists were encouraging sympathetic factions in other Communist Parties. In 1964 Nehru died - 'a dear and honoured friend, one of the great figures of our age', as Dutt called him at a memorial meeting in St. Pancras organised by the Indian Workers' Association. (Attlee was also present, Dutt remarking on 'how satisfactory it was that we could at last speak on the same platform without his needing to be in terror of Morrison chasing him'). The story of shattered illusions and personal gloom which this succession of unexpected events created for Dutt seems complete with the death of his wife, Salme, just four months later.

She had maintained such a low profile in Party life that it is doubtful if more than a few beyond the leadership circle were even aware of her existence. It is true that she contributed articles to *Labour Monthly* in 1955 and 1956, using the pseudonym 'Sancho Panza', but this was little enough from one who had helped to create the Party and it is difficult not to notice the irony in her choice of pen name with its suggestion that Dutt was her Don Quixote; perhaps she had begun to see him as an extravagant idealist forever tilting at windmills? As for Salme's own state of mind as she neared death there is nothing to record except some lines from her poem 'Last Will':

> I am old now. Marooned on an island
> Where the tide had taken its refuse.
> I have sold my land for a crust of bread
> And have nothing to leave you but care.
> I could have swam and saved you some joy
> But had gazed too hard at the stars.
> The weeds took advantage and entangled
> My rudder. I was kept as their prisoner.

The year of Dutt's personal loss was also the year the CPI finally split and the CPI (Marxist) was born demanding a pro-Chinese line and taking most of the Party membership in the Communist strongholds of Maharashtra, Madhya Pradesh, Andhra Pradesh, West Bengal and the Punjab. But as the divisions and contradictions which assailed Dutt's vision of things mounted, he simply wrote them out of his script. In 1963 he wrote:

> the successive critics have always fallen by the wayside and passed into oblivion; the caravan moves on. Marxism-Leninism has again and again been proved, and continues to be proved, by the event, by practice.[59]

It was the same story when he came to write his history of *The Internationale* two years later - papering over the cracks, reinterpreting embarrassing moments in the Party's history, lying by omission so that a picture of ever-gathering strength was conveyed of the sort that he used to ridicule in the writings of Ramsay MacDonald.[60] His silence on the Sino-Soviet conflict was at first so complete that when he commented on the war between China and India in October 1962 - dutifully describing India as a cat's paw of imperialism - the mainstream press speculated that he might be a crypto-Maoist. There seemed every reason to think, for example, that he would warm to China's lauding of Stalin.[61] But this was a profound misjudgement of the depth of his devotion to the Soviet state and it was not long before the Maoists were denouncing him as a revisionist. His eulogy to Nehru was mocked for its silence on the anti-Communist repression in Telengana, while his demand for a plebiscite to determine the future of Kashmir when India and Pakistan went to war in September 1965 offended the Maoist depiction of India as an aggressor which had to be forcibly resisted.[62]

When, finally, he did comment on the Sino-Soviet controversy - his early hopes concerning 'the deep underlying unity' of all socialist countries presumably shattered - he found all sorts of objective weaknesses in the Chinese revolution to explain the Maoist aberration away. There was the lack of a pre-1917 Marxist tradition, for example, the weakness of the working class in a largely peasant nation, the strong petty bourgeois influences on the predominantly 'national' revolutionary movement and the personality cult of Mao - itself only a symptom of an increasingly voluntaristic politics evident since the 'Great Leap Forward'.[63] Naturally Dutt forgot to mention the many contributions of Soviet policy to this greatest of all schisms in the Communist world.

Dutt soldiered on to retirement from Party office in 1965 explaining in suitably militaristic metaphor to his friend D.N. Pritt that:

> All the penalty of our prolonged legality prevented the fulfillment of the old army toast of 'bloody war and quick promotion'. The authorities having failed to shoot us ... there was nothing to do but to step down and give a chance for others.[64]

The war party which he had played such a prominent part in creating in the years immediately after 1920 was by now redundant. His old comrade Harry Pollitt had died five years earlier, returning from a trip to Australia. All the obituaries, even those composed by his political enemies, testified to Pollitt's human qualities, not least to his sense of humour which was allegedly otherwise absent among his colleagues. (A bemused Dutt rather proved their point when he commented in self-defence; 'if you tell me a joke, I laugh'.) Indeed one Indian journal dwelt on the contrast between Dutt and Pollitt to make the general observation that 'the typical Communists' in the CPGB were, like 'the rasping hatchet-faced Dutt ... not typically British. The typical Britishers in it are not too emphatically Communist'.[65] Certainly Dutt's capacity for detachment from national politics was unusual, if not unique, in the British Party as was its corollary - his unswerving 'internationalism'. But the project of 'national roads to socialism', the dissolution of the Comintern and the splits between Communist regimes gradually undermined the iron discipline and revolutionary opportunism which Dutt revered. In different hands the Party would drift so very far that when the Soviet Union crushed Dubcek's Prague Spring in 1968 it condemned the intervention as did the vast majority of European Communists - all of them searching for a new identity and miles away from the combat organisation preparing for civil war which Dutt had wanted to fashion in the 1920s. Dutt, of course, could only see the 1968 decision as 'a stain on the honour' of the Party and led the pro-Soviet minority within the CPGB which sought to overturn the Executive's decision; as in 1929 *Labour Monthly* promoted Dutt's factional views, showing that it remained his private fiefdom in its fifth decade of existence. Fifty years of iron discipline in the cause of the Soviet myth and Dutt was nevertheless confronted with sabotage at every quarter. In 1970 he was still convinced that 'Khruschev put his foot right in it at the closed session':

> He treated Stalin as though he had been an absolute idiot, an incompetent. This kind of treatment by a little fellow like Khruschev simply gave an impression of spitefulness.[66]

It was a bizarre judgement from any angle, but now 74 years old, Dutt was too far gone to know any better. In his mind he had managed to diminish even the 'crimes' - poor substitute for a real appraisal that they were - to minor misdemeanours and he persisted with his argument that 'the building of socialism and the defeat of Nazism were incomparably greater achievements than the most enormous of Stalin's faults'. He had remembered something of Lenin's Testament - the passage where Lenin condemned Stalin's rude manner - and still imagined that he could fob off his critics with it. He had never liked Stalin personally, he now volunteered, 'but that had nothing to do with the political line which was always extremely good'.[67] And yet in the making of a film to celebrate the fiftieth anniversary of *Labour Monthly* in 1972 the old man was heard to mutter 'I put my money on Germany, the terrible mistake was that it was only Russia'.[68] Perhaps, in the end, something of the tragedy got through, could no longer be denied.

But if so it was a rare lapse of concentration which allowed it to show and the evidence points overwhelmingly to Dutt's satisfaction with the Communist record. In preparing his book on *The Internationale*, for example, he had considered the inclusion of an anecdote to illustrate the 'basic guilt of the accused'. Fortunately, although Dutt changed his mind about publication, this curious fragment survives and acquires an especially sinister light today in view of the fact that the Soviet state itself eventually admitted the falsity of the charges brought against the leading Bolsheviks in question. Dutt's 'evidence' concerns 'a lengthy day's visit to the village at some distance from Moscow' where Bukharin and Radek were at work in the summer of 1935. Here 'under the seal of absolute secrecy' they apparently 'gave him a serious and alarming account ... of the net in which they had become involved and of the dilemmas with which they were faced'. Dutt was told in very general terms, with no names mentioned, of how 'opposition to the party, however much it might be felt to be justified at a given moment, can lead by its own logic step by step into the camp of counter-revolution'. He was accordingly advised to never enter this 'fatal path of conflict with the party' and retired with 'the memory of this talk ... like a nightmare' weighing on his mind during the ensuing period. At first Dutt tried to convince himself that these old 'friends and comrades' had presented 'an allegory to test him' but he had 'a lurking suspicion' that their confessions of guilt were true and only failed to report them to the party by taking refuge in the 'cowardly evasion' that he had no grounds for certainty concerning their sins. Thus 'when the trials followed, of Radek, and subsequently of Bukharin, it was as if a weight were lifted from the writer's [Dutt's] consciousness that, however terrible, the facts at last were out'. Dutt now read the trial statements of both men and as he did so 'he felt as if he were reading the same story a second time, since their narrative corresponded so closely with what they had told him on that summer's day and evening in 1935, even with many of the same phrases'[69]. Was Dutt a pathological liar or a witness to the sort of 'confession' Arthur Koestler made famous in *Darkness at Noon* - the trapped men still wanting to be useful to the Party by insisting on the sin of opposing it? One would not bet against the first option.

The *Great Soviet Encyclopedia* describes Dutt as, among other things, the great unmasker of the theory of the 'peaceful transformation' of the British Empire into a 'Commonwealth of independent and equal states'.[70] On the face of it this looks like another case of self-delusion shattered by the actual course of events; by the time Dutt retired from Party office in 1965 there was overwhelming evidence that decolonisation did not depend on an armed struggle - nor did the British economy depend on the possession of colonies. The collapse of the 'labour aristocracy' and consequent radicalisation of Britain which Dutt predicted in the 1950s simply did not happen. Decolonisation took place without even causing the sort of disturbances which afflicted France as it stumbled down the same road.

When Lenin wrote his theses on the national and colonial question in 1920, the colonies, dependent territories, Dominions, and semi-colonies totalled over 77 per cent of the world's territory and contained something like 69 per cent of its population; by 1963, as Dutt acknowledged, these figures had shrunk to 7.7 and 1.7 per cent respectively.[71] Though he occasionally invoked the idea, Dutt never did develop a theory of neo-imperialism to explain why colonies had become superfluous to metropolitan requirements. But when he reported in 1963 on the fact that fifty countries had achieved independence since the Second World War, almost entirely under the leadership of a national bourgeoisie, he was quite sure that this had only been possible because of the existence of the 'world socialist camp'. There was never any suggestion then that Dutt was disappointed by the way things had worked out. On the contrary, he recalled the impotent rounds of anti-imperialist protests from his youth against the 'atrocities of imperialism and colonial wars' and of how before 1917 there had been no victories to celebrate. But since the defeat of fascism and the creation of a socialist bloc, he steadfastly contended, all kinds of small countries had been able to defy imperialism. If there was any doubt about this, he advised the sceptical, one had only to listen to what the likes of Castro, Nkrumah and Patrice Lumumba said about their debt of gratitude to the Soviet Union. These were the same people who praised Dutt himself and the *Labour Monthly*[72] and there is every reason to believe that his perception of the advance of the colonial world and of the forward march of socialism remained strong up to his death in 1974, the year of the Portuguese revolution and a further accession of Marxist power in Africa.

FINAL YEARS

Although our sense of what is right and fitting might demand otherwise, 'the caravan', as Dutt put it, did go on both for himself and for world Communism in the years between 1956 and his death. Up to his retirement from Party office in 1965 his published work was as voluminous and persuasive as it ever had been - much of it concerned with the cause of disarmament and peace in accordance with Soviet foreign policy pronouncements. In the summer of 1963 John Berger called Dutt 'the most brilliant political commentator writing today in English'.[73] And much of this brilliance was to be found in his writings on what was now called the 'Third World'. Current events ensured that Africa occupied a bigger place than previously in Dutt's own work as well as in the pages of *Labour Monthly*. Although the pace of decolonization had quickened on the continent, there was much left to be resolved and many obstacles to be overcome. The British Prime Minister Harold Macmillan might talk of 'the wind of change' but the Sharpeville and Langa massacre in South Africa and the civil wars in Algeria and Congo suggested revolutionary rather than constitutional routes to independence.

For Dutt the crisis which erupted in the Congo in 1960, provoked by the secession of the copper-rich province of Katanga, was another opportunity to recount the historical record of imperialism and expose its baleful legacy and current machinations. No-one could do this better than Dutt and within weeks of the start of the crisis the readers of *Labour Monthly* had learned of the brutal history of colonial exploitation in the Belgian-controlled heart of Africa since King Leopold's day, of the eye-witness accounts of murder and mayhem reported earlier in the century by the likes of E.D. Morel and Roger Casement, and of the continuation of this rapacity by Belgian monopolies such as the Societé Generale and Union Minière du Haut Katanga and British interests like the Tanganyika Concessions.[74] The Congo was of course part of a bigger tragedy for Dutt though he insisted that even taken by itself it was comparable in proportion to population to the genocidal record of Nazism; a population estimated at twenty million in 1900 stood at just thirteen million sixty years later.[75] Reflecting on Africa as a whole Dutt wrote:

> No continent has been so ravaged by imperialism as Africa ... plundered and devastated for close on five centuries by the European marauders and robbed of human and material wealth to provide the foundations of the American capitalist 'miracle' and British family fortunes. This is not merely the ancient record of the horrors of the slave traders, but has continued to our day with the butchers of the Congo, the Nazi torturers in Algeria or the Apartheid Legrees of South Africa. The resultant wreckage of life and society has been termed by the disdainful bandits a region of natural darkness and backwardness.

Africa was carved up, Dutt observed:

> without regard to history, tradition, popular sentiment or ethnological or

> national groupings of the people. But the national independence struggle has necessarily had to be conducted first within the existing state boundaries against the imperialist power ruling a particular segment. Hence the newly independent states have necessarily arisen in the first place on the basis of the divisions originally imposed by imperialism. The new rulers have in consequence inherited a terryfying complex of frontier and regional problems, all the more acute as popular consciousness grows in strength. With unconcealed satisfaction the imperialist experts have counted on these complications to disrupt the new Africa, paralyse the new states with internal regional discords, set them at loggerheads with one another, and thus create a happy hunting ground for renewed imperialist influence.[76]

Under these circumstances Dutt was an advocate of Pan-Africanism - something he had ignored altogether at the time of the momentous Fifth Pan-African Congress at Manchester in 1945. He had a long record, however, of work with many of the movements' leaders - such as Nkrumah and Kenyatta - and spoke in its support at the first All-African Students Conference in London in October 1960 when the idea was still gaining ground among the twenty-seven participating organisations. He was thus ready to hail the Organization of African Unity, immediately after its creation at Addis Ababa in May 1963, as 'an event of historic importance in the advance of African and world liberation'.[77] Nkrumah's message to *Labour Monthly* in July 1961 was now recalled as a prophecy; 'soon the artificial boundaries which divide Africa', Ghana's President had written, 'will be completely obliterated'.[78] Dutt also believed that 'the fight for All-African Unity [was] a specific form of the national liberation struggle against imperialism'; he paid homage to 'the wisest leaders of the African freedom struggle from the great DuBois onwards' who 'had already insisted that the aim must be an All-African struggle against imperialism' and eventually the union of all African states.[79] In this continuing anti-colonial work Dutt not only remained in touch with the African radicals but spoke also to a broader British Left concerned with the multiple emergencies and conflicts of decaying colonialism. Otherwise divergent strands of socialist thought - including the post-1956 New Left and many who looked to *Tribune* for leadership - made common cause on the many issues arising from the depredations of colonialism, not least in opposition to the institutionalised racism of countries such as South Africa and Rhodesia.

Dutt was naturally a bitter and eloquent opponent of apartheid at a time when few outside of the Left, at least in Britain, were moved to act against it. Indeed when the UN Political Committee voted 68 to 5 in condemnation of apartheid in December 1958, Britain's vote - like those of France and Portugal - was with the minority.[80] In 1960 Harold Macmillan signed a declaration against racial discrimination at the Commonwealth conference - but so too did the Prime Ministers of Australia and Southern Rhodesia, both racist states. Immmediately afterwards, Dutt pointed out, Britain refused to ratify the ILO convention condemning 'colour' discrimination in employment practices. With such an equivocal record how could Britain be expected to stand up to South Africa? The Communists had no such expectation and so maintained their own unceasing opposition to apartheid which brought them into frequent contact with exiled South Africans in the African National Congress (ANC). Dutt was involved for example in the 72-hour 'black sash' vigil outside the Commonwealth Premiers Conference in March 1961 to mark the anniversary of the Sharpeville killings, and joined forces with ANC leaders such as Oliver Tambo at many a political rally in London. At one such gathering on May Day in 1964 he addressed the theme of 'Africa's Forward March' and - at a time when racist violence against black peoples had become conspicuous again in the USA as well as in Africa - pointedly paid special honour to W.E.B. DuBois, for his opposition to 'all false theories of African or Afro-Asian racialist separation from the international working class movement'. But he was also quick to see the danger of racism becoming a major divisive issue in Britain itself.

The opposing fear - that the Communists would exploit tensions created by immigration - had been voiced by the Conservative Front Bench as early as July 1948 when the House of Commons was told that 'so many of the West Indians who had come over on the "Empire Windrush" were already happily placed in Communist homes'.[81] No doubt this was exaggerated but the Party's work among minorities was real enough and Dutt had alerted it to the problem of racism at a time when the official fiction obstinately maintained that there was no such thing in Britain - well before the Notting Hill racist attacks of 1958. In fact a *Labour Monthly* conference on 'Britain's Colonies and the Colour Bar' was scheduled for October 1958 before these disturbances erupted and Dutt referred to 'the ugly danger signals of colour bar violence' in his opening speech.

He observed that the Left had agitated for legislation against discrimination for many years and cited Fenner Brockway's 'excellent Bill on this matter' which the Labour Front Bench had chosen to ignore. The main problem, he argued, was in the private sphere affecting clubs, restaurants, landlords, dance halls, advertisements and the like; 'therefore we cannot rest', he told his audience, 'until we achieve the same level of civilised legislation in this country as already exists in Socialist countries, which makes every form of practice or preaching of racial hatred, colour discrimination or the like a penal offence to be wiped out with all the resources of the state and the law'.[82]

The Communists denied any objective existence to 'race', of course, and regarded racism as a malevolent ideology that was all the more likely to be fostered in times of economic and social crisis. Dutt naturally detected it in proposals for the legislative restriction of immigration, biased as these invariably were against black-and brown-skinned people. But he was especially concerned to make the connection between the racism which openly operated in places like Kenya, Bermuda, Rhodesia and South Africa and the prejudices which came to the surface in Notting Hill. 'The myth of the superior ruling race with the right to conquer and oppress "lesser breeds without the law"', he had occasion to observe, 'is the familiar myth of all empires and tyrannies'. The habit was hard to quit when huge profits were dependent on the oppression of native peoples: 'we have to recognise', he concluded, 'that the question goes a little deeper than just racial prejudice'.[83] So-called 'race issues' were in fact invariably connected to structures of power and dominance and it was within relations of class and imperialism that racist prejudices were reproduced. It was an argument which possessed the merit of denying the 'natural' or 'instinctive' nature of racism and one that rejected the fatalism of those who said that racist prejudices had somehow taken on a life of their own. But it also contained a reductionist thrust which could subsume the issue of racism altogether under the 'bread and butter' struggles of socialists. But then the same logic had led many socialists to pay little attention to British imperialism and Dutt had spent all his life reminding them of its existence. As he approached his seventieth birthday he was just as keen to argue that 'colour prejudice ... can be finally eradicated only by changing social-political institutions, and meanwhile actively combatting the poisonous growth'.[84]

There was no shortage, then, of good causes to absorb Dutt's energies. Conscious though he was of the continued economic and strategic hold of the imperialist powers, by 1960 Dutt was happy to record Britain's failure to forge the Commonwealth into an instrument of anti-Communism; the advance of the independence struggles and of the 'non-aligned' states since Bandung had seen to that. Though the Commonwealth Premiers' Conference of 1960 was the first in which representatives of the Afro-Asian states equalled those of Britain and the white Dominions, Dutt already saw that the continuation of the trend to independence would bring hitherto suppressed conflicts - such as the North-South distribution of resources and the survival of the racist regimes - on to the agenda, as the African and Asian states came to predominate.[85] He viewed the Common Market, in this context, very much as a 'White Man's Club' designed to serve about five per cent of the world's population by discriminating against the rest. He saw, however, that Britain was caught in a dilemma:

> For Britain to enter the Common Market, with its avowed aim of eventual complete economic-political integration would mean to say a final farewell to its dreams of world power as the centre of the Commonwealth, and to become no more than a constituent State in a West European combination dominated by West Germany. On the other hand, to fail to enter could mean to reduce Britain to increasing economic inferiority and failure in face of the two giants of the capitalist world, the United States and the Common Market.[86]

Dutt predictably opposed the Common Market option as being a restrictive military-economic bloc and went on believing that the peoples of the Third World would 'refuse to accept the present halfway stage and continue their revolt and advance to complete economic and political independence from imperialism, or ... as the imperialists define it ... to Communism':

> Here is the spectre which haunts them, which drives them to make concessions, to acclaim the national aspirations which formerly they crushed, or to repudiate the colour bar and racial discrimination of which they were most zealous upholders ...
>
> Truly the fear of Communism is the beginning of wisdom even for the most hard-boiled imperialists.[87]

To the end Dutt admitted only 'vindication' in the record of Marxism and died on 20 December 1974 only a few days after completing his last triumphalist survey of world politics which appeared in *Labour Monthly* the following January. As if from the grave he told his readers that the 'era of detente' then in prospect was 'the reflection of the new balance in the world today', the most decisive factor of which was 'the accelerating advance in the relative strength and constructive role of socialism represented by the Soviet Union ... immune from the crisis of the capitalist world'. On this foundation the advance of the peoples everywhere depended.[88] Many tributes to Dutt followed - Fenner Brockway's referred to Dutt's 'intellectual integrity and his passion for human progress', but was unable to say in what this intellectual integrity consisted. In India his passing was marked by naming the CPI centre in New Delhi 'R. Palme Dutt Bhawan'.

When Dutt first met representatives of the Comintern in December 1919 at a conference of the International Socialist Student Youth organisation it was their seriousness and clarity on the question of power that impressed him; that here was a movement that would fight imperialism and be as organised and disciplined as the enemy.[89] This rings true both as an assessment of the essence of Bolshevism and as an implicit expression of Dutt's hatred of 'the enemy'. The conviction that socialism had all the answers, that it could make everything anew, that its coming was inevitable - none of this was peculiar to the Communists. Lenin answered the needs of those who shared his sense of the apocalypse and believed that the hour demanded a fighting organisation capable of seizing power. The first was rationalised in his compelling theory of the imperialist epoch with its vision of wars, civil wars and revolutions. The second requirement was met by his New Model Party. Here the emphasis was on ideological purity, the strictest internal discipline, and a ruthless opportunism in the interests of the revolution; civil war conditions would tolerate no less. But a sustained commitment to all of this was not likely in the absence of the revolutionary's essential quality; hatred of the oppressor and a profound belief in the futility of constitutional reform.

The Communists' second great merit in Dutt's eyes was their belief that a sufficient degree of homogeneity pertained in the international workers' movement to admit of its central direction. The logical corollary of this - which outsiders could never understand - was the conviction that the right tactic to adopt locally was determined by international considerations. This was internationalism - so grievously lacking in August 1914 - and its organisational expression was subordination of the national sections to the centre. Dutt's national nihilism suited him better than anyone else in the CPGB for stern adherence to these principles. The Comintern was conceived as the union of different divisions in a single army; this was its strength (and fatal weakness). Dutt's generation of Communists had the memory of the First World War to remind them of the price that could be paid for national autonomy in the socialist movement. Dutt also grew up with a knowledge of and feeling for other countries which became a passionate anti-imperialism. Close association with the generality of leaders in the British labour movement - such as he certainly experienced in the years 1919-1922 - would just as assuredly convince him that this was utterly foreign to their nature.

There was, then, the Party and the International to distinguish the Communists, wrapped up, as it were, in Lenin's persuasive rationale for revolutionary intransigence. At least until the end of the Second World War there was plenty of evidence in global politics to sustain the belief that capitalism had entered a volatile, destructive and authoritarian phase. But the third distinguishing mark of the Communist movement - without which the rest would have meant little - was the Soviet Republic, fruit of the revolution which Dutt had anticipated and then rallied to defend. From the beginning of the Communist movement there was no clear distinction between loyalty to the Party, loyalty to the International and 'unconditional defence' of the Soviet Republic. If it was acceptable to allow international considerations to determine the local line, the position and needs of the Soviet Republic were inevitably part of the arithmetic, and even in the early days this could be the largest part. The massive authority of the Bolsheviks could only assist this conflation of Party, State and International because they dominated all three. The foreign Communists were accustomed to follow the Bolshevik lead within the Comintern and utterly dependent on Bolshevik precept and practice in the job of creating and consolidating a workers' state.

The Communists certainly felt an allegiance to the principles of Leninism as a revolutionary doctrine but they were also committed to the idea of the Soviet state as a bridgehead in the global war against capitalism. Lenin himself often talked as if the preservation of the Bolshevik state and the interests of world revolution were indistinguishable; equally the distinction between the Bolshevik dictatorship and the dictatorship of the proletariat sometimes eluded him. Dutt and his colleagues were conscious that their own frail Party would never have arisen in the first place without the Bolsheviks and could achieve little outside the Comintern. Dutt was of course privileged, as a professional revolutionary and Party leader, to see the inner workings of this relationship for himself; to have some idea of the money, the human talent, the organisational resources put at the disposal of the socialist revolution by the Soviet state. It was relatively easy to conclude that unity was essential when you knew some of this; we can guess that because organisational splits were rare and led nowhere even for the biggest of the dissidents - Trotsky.

If you detested the Labour Party, were conscious of the precarious toe-hold enjoyed by the militant alternative, and committed to a global effort against colonialism, the attractions of the political wilderness outside the Party were not strong. The evidence suggests that for those who rose to prominence in the Bolshevised CPGB and later resigned from it the Labour Party held no attractions. For men and women of this temper it was easy to feel that there was no viable alternative to the Communist movement. When, perhaps, the original revolutionary hopes were near exhaustion the Cold War took over as a cause for steel and discipline. Dutt may have seen that the prospects for Communism in Britain were forlorn, but there was always the dispossessed millions of Asia and Africa to carry the torch. And there was always the Soviet Union. 'Might and right govern everything in this world', Dutt wrote, quoting Joubert; 'might till right is ready'. In his life Dutt was called a liar for saying the Soviet Union was right; just as many of his mistakes derived from the myth that it embodied the might of the historical process.

NOTES

1 Dutt, 'Notes on the Situation in the CPI', August 1950, *Memorandum and Reports* K3.
2 Dutt, 'Provisional Report on the Strategy and Tactics of the CPI 1948-1950', *ibid*, 29 July 1950.
3 Joshi to Dutt, 7.8.1950, India Box 3, Files A-F.
4 *Ibid*.
5 Dutt recalls this episode in another appeal to the CPSU dated 1.3.56, K4 Vol 1956-7.
6 See B. Davidson, *Special Operations Europe*, Gollancz 1980; and R. Kisch, *The Days of the Good Soldiers: Communists in the Armed Forces*, Journeyman 1985.
7 Dutt, 'Fascism, Trotskyism and World Labour', in H.Pollitt and R. Palme Dutt, *The Truth About Trotskyism: Moscow Trial January 1937*, CPGB February 1937, pp13-14.
8 The man in question is Loi Tak, General Secretary of the Malayan CP, who arranged the 'Batu caves massacre' of 1942. See A. Short, *Communist Insurrection in Malaya*, Muller 1975, pp39-40.

9 Koestler showed that this logic could assist the process of extracting false confessions - such was the desire on the part of the accused to be objectively useful to the revolution. See his novel *Darkness At Noon*.

10 M. Ram, *Indian Communism*, Vikas Publications, New Delhi 1969, p45; B.S. Gupta, *Communism in Indian Politics*, Columbia University Press, New York 1972, pp32-3.

11 S. Harrison, 'The Challenge to Indian Nationalism', *Foreign Affairs*, 34, 4, 1956, pp620-36.

12 B.S. Gupta, *Communism in Indian Politics*, *op cit*, pp363-4.

13 Dutt, 'The Development of the Colonial Liberation Movements', *Pravda* 10.2.53, K4 Vol 1953-4.

14 Dutt, fraternal delegates address to the third CPI congress, 2.11.53, K4 Vol 1953-4.

15 Dutt, 'New Features in the National Liberation Struggle of Colonial and Dependent People', *For A Lasting Peace, For A People's Democracy* (FLPFPD), 8 October 1954.

16 Dutt, letter to the editors of FLPFPD, 29.11.54, K4 Vol 1953-4.

17 Dutt, untitled document, 1.3.56, K4 Vol 1955-7.

18 *Ibid*, pp6-7.

19 Dutt, draft report on the disintegration of the colonial system, 27.8.56, K4 Vol 1955-7.

20 See note 17, p9.

21 Nkrumah, Azikwe and Cheddi Jagan were all supporters of *Labour Monthly*. See Press Reports 1960-1965, K6 and the anniversary greetings published in the journal itself.

22 The last visit to Nehru on record is 29.6.56. See *Daily Worker* and Press Reports 1951-9, K6.

23 Dutt, Notes on Conversation with K, 11.7.55, K4 Vol 1955-7. Krishna Menon was accused of crypto-Communism and collusion with Dutt in *India Wins Freedom* by Malauna Azad, which Dutt reviewed for *Flame*, Delhi, 17.2.62.

24 A. Whitehead, 'Calcutta Compromise', *New Statesman and Society*, 20 November 1992, p19.

25 Dutt, Nigerian Commission: Revised Draft Final Report, January 1954, K4 Vol 1953-4, p6.

26 *Ibid*, p7. The reference to Paul Robeson suggests that the term has an American origin but I can find no support for this inference.

27 *Daily Worker*, 29.10.49.

28 See Dutt, Press Reports 1951-6, K6.

29 See F. Fejto, *A History of the People's Democracies*, Penguin 1974, pp246-7 and F.Claudin, *The Communist Movement*, Peregrine 1975, p527.

30 Stanley Foreman in interview with the author. The name on his passport was Israel Stanley Foreman.

31 See J. Callaghan, *Socialism in Britain Since 1884*, Blackwell 1990, p141.

32 Dutt, 'The Power of Marxism', (Marx Memorial Lecture) *Modern Quarterly*, new series, 1, 3, summer 1946, p5.
33 Dutt, letter to *Times Literary Supplement*, 5 May 1966. In this letter Dutt also revealed for the first time in public that he had 'broken off all relations' with Michael Borodin before his arrest in August 1922 and that he first proposed Pollitt as Party leader in 1923. See also M. Johnstone's review of J. Mahon's *Harry Pollitt* in the *Bulletin of the Society for the Study of Labour History*, Volume 33, autumn 1976.
34 See *Manchester Guardian*, 18.12.54 and 1.1.55 in Press Reports 1951-6, K6.
35 Eric Heffer's letter is in *World News and Views*, 1.2.47. Edward Upward refers to this disquiet in his novel *The Rotten Elements*; The Australian CP wrote damning the CPGB in *World News and Views*, 7.8.48.
36 As represented in the debate by Jurgen Kuczynski or 'PF'. See *Labour Monthly*, October 1940-February 1941.
37 See B. Schwarz, 'The People in History: the Communist Party Historians Group 1946-56', in R.Johnson (ed), *Making Histories*, Hutchinson 1982, pp44-96.
38 Dutt, Speech to Stalin Commemoration Meeting, 9.353, K4 Vol1953-4.
39 Dutt, Graveside Speech on the 70th Anniversary of Marx's Death, 14.3.53, K4 Vol 1953-4.
40 Dutt, Notes of the Month, *Labour Monthly*, March 1953.
41 This was certainly the view of Maurice Thorez. See 'The Khruschev Speech, the PCF and the PCI', in R. Miliband and J. Saville (eds), *The Socialist Register*, Merlin 1976, pp58-67.
42 Dutt, The Great Debate, *Labour Monthly*, May 1956, p194.
43 *Daily Worker*, 26.3.56.
44 Untitled document, 19.6.56, K4 Vol 1955-7.
45 Jose Solley to Dutt, 16.5.56; Dutt Correspondence 1956.
46 Alick West to Dutt, 11.5.56, *ibid*.
47 Dutt, Notes of the Month, *Labour Monthly*, June 1956, pp247-8.
48 *Ibid*, pp250-251.
49 *Ibid*, p256.
50 *The Reasoner*, number 1, July 1956, p4.
51 Dutt, For the Political Bureau, 4.11.56; Draft Statement, 11.12.56, K4 Vol 1955-7.
52 Dutt, 'After the Twenty-Second Congress', *Labour Monthly*, December 1961; Dobb's letter is in *Labour Monthly*, January 1962, p46.
53 *Observer*, 9.4.61; *Labour*, May 1961, p105.
54. See for example his Notes of the Month, *Labour Monthly*, January 1956 where *Better Fewer, But Better* is discussed.
55 Dutt, Marxism and Socialism in Britain, Marx Memorial Lecture 14.3.57, K4 Vol 1955-57.
56 Dutt, Draft Report on the Disintegration of the Colonial System, 27.8.56, *ibid*.

57 Dutt, Memorandum on "Fraternal Association" to Programme Commission, 20.10.56, K4 Vol 1955-7.
58 See *Changes*, 14 September 1991.
59 Dutt, Problems of the International Communist Movement, *Marxism Today*, September 1963, p262.
60 Dutt, *The Internationale*, Lawrence and Wishart 1965. This provoked a controversy in *Tribune*, 15.1.65 to 19.2.65. It was also reviewed in *Labour Monthly*, April 1965, by an extremely diplomatic Eric Hobsbawm who implied that the surprising thing was not that it was done badly but that it had been done at all.
61 *Sunday Telegraph*, 3.2.63.
62 H.B. Lim in *Malayan Monitor*, London, 29.2.64, pp5-10; on Kashmir see the *Daily Worker* 10.9.65; on Nehru see the *Daily Worker* 1.6.64 and the *Newsletter*, 7.6.64.
63 Dutt, 'Whither China?', *New Times*, numbers 20-24, May-June 1967.
64 Dutt to Pritt, 14.12.65.
65 Brian Pollitt told me the anecdote about Dutt's response to the obituaries; the contrast between Dutt and Pollitt appeared in *Link*, New Delhi 3.7.60.
66 Interview, *Sunday Times* magazine, 30.8.70.
67 *Ibid*.
68 Stanley Foreman told me this.
69 Dutt, 'Radek-Bukharin conversations ommitted from *The Internationale*', 11 March 1964, CPGB archive.
70. *Great Soviet Encyclopedia*, Macmillan, third edition, 1975, pp163-4.
71 Dutt, 'National Liberation Today', *Marxism Today*, January 1964, p10.
72 Letters survive in Dutt's correspondence files from Nkrumah, Cheddi Jagan, Shirley DuBois and others concerned with anti-colonial issues. External Correspondence, Files 40-42.
73 John Berger in *Twentieth Century*, summer 1963, p135; see K6, Volume 4, Press Reports 1960-1965.
74 Dutt, Notes of the Month, *Labour Monthly* September 1960 and the pamphlet by him *Stand By Congo*, CPGB 1960.
75 Dutt, *Stand By Congo*, *op cit*, p3.
76 Dutt, Hail African Unity, *Labour Monthly*, July 1963, pp301-2.
77 *Ibid*, p300.
78 P. Nkrumah, message in *Labour Monthly*, July 1961 p320.
79 Dutt, 'Hail African Unity', *op cit*, p303.
80 Dutt, 'Britain's Colonies and the Colour Bar', *Labour Monthly*, December 1958, pp530-532.
81 Quoted in D. Goldsworthy, *Colonial Issues in British Politics 1945-1961*, Clarendon, Oxford 1971, p146.
82 Dutt, 'The Commonwealth Today', *Marxism Today*, September 1960, p269 and p272.
83 Dutt, 'Britain's Colonies and the Colour Bar', *Labour Monthly*, December 1958, p530.

84 *Ibid*, p532.

85 *Daily Worker*, 28.12.65; quoted in P. Nazir, *The Life and Work of Rajani Palme Dutt (1896-1974)*, GLC Race Equality Unit, pamphlet nd, pp18-19.

86 Dutt, 'White Man's Club', *Labour Monthly*, October 1962 and The Commonwealth Today, *op cit*, p275.

87 Dutt, The Commonwealth Today, *op cit*, pp276-277.

88 Dutt, Notes of the Month, *Labour Monthly*, January 1975, pp1-3 89. See Dutt's talk prepared for GDR radio, n.d., Broadcasting File. See also Reminiscence of Palme Dutt, *Our History Journal*, number 11, January 1987, p5.

INDEX